Land and society in Britain, 1700–1914

F. M. L. Thompson

LAND AND SOCIETY IN BRITAIN, 1700–1914

ESSAYS IN HONOUR OF F. M. L. THOMPSON

EDITED BY NEGLEY HARTE
AND ROLAND QUINAULT

Manchester University Press
Manchester and New York

distributed exclusively in the USA and Canada by St. Martin's Press

Published by Manchester University Press
Oxford Road, Manchester M13 9NR, UK
and Room 400, 175 Fifth Avenue,
New York, NY 10010, USA

Distributed exclusively in the USA and Canada
by St. Martin's Press, Inc.,
175 Fifth Avenue, New York, NY 10010, USA

British Library Cataloguing-in-Publication Data
A catalogue record is available from the British Library

Library of Congress Cataloging-in-Publication Data
Land and society in Britain, 1700–1914:
essays in honour of F.M.L. Thompson
/edited by Negley Harte and Roland Quinault.
p. cm.
ISBN 0-7190-3413-2
1. Landowners—Great Britain—History.
2. Gentry—Great Britain—History.
3. Great Britain—Economic conditions.
4. Great Britain—Social conditions.
5. Great Britain—Politics and government.
I. Thompson, F. M. L. (Francis Michael Longstretch)
II. Harte, N. B.
III. Quinault, Roland E.
HD593.L36 1996
305.5'232'0941–dc20 95-47915

ISBN 0 7190 3413 2 *hardback*

Typeset in Baskerville 10/12pt
by Action Typesetting Ltd, Gloucester

Printed in Great Britain
by Bookcraft (Bath) Ltd

Contents

List of figures and tables

Figures

Tables

Preface

This book has been produced to honour Professor F. M. L. Thompson by scholars who have been influenced by his writings and encouraged by his help and example. The wide range of subjects chosen reflects the breadth of Michael Thompson's interest in landed society, especially in Britain since the early eighteenth century. These essays throw new light on the social, economic and political history of Britain during the last three centuries.

As editors, we wish to express our gratitude to all the contributors, especially those who have tolerated the tardiness of others. The first versions of these essays were presented to a chosen audience at the Institute of Historical Research in London on 28 September 1990, to mark Michael Thompson's retirement as Director. This agreeable gathering – dubbed by one participant the 'Thompsoniad' – was facilitated by a grant from the Nuffield Foundation, to whom we record our appreciation. Unfortunately, one of the contributions delivered with brio on that occasion, Professor J. Mordaunt Crook's on millionaire's architecture, has outgrown this volume, but will be published separately in due course.

The frontispiece is a photograph taken by Professor Barry Supple (now Director of the Leverhulme Trust) when he and Michael Thompson were fellow editors of the *Economic History Review.* We are grateful to Professor Supple for permission to reproduce it. We would also like to record our gratitude for help, sometimes surreptitious, to Mrs Anne Thompson, Dr Alice Prochaska, Cynthia Hawker, Bridget Taylor, Nazneen Razwi and Joy McCarthy.

We hope that Michael Thompson's reaction to this collection will echo what he wrote about a similar exercise twenty years ago: 'It is a relief to this reviewer to be able to record that the recipient of this volume is indeed honoured by the deed as well as by the thought'.

NEGLEY HARTE
ROLAND QUINAULT

F. M. L. Thompson: an appreciation

As friend and colleague PENELOPE J. CORFIELD

The distinctive initials of F. M. L. Thompson ensure that his name is memorable to a wide readership of all those interested in modern British history. But Francis Michael Longstreth Thompson does not hide behind this formal frontage. He is known throughout the professional historical world as Michael (and to a few as Mike). In terms of personality, he has the capacity to wield power without making enemies, while throughout remaining sociable, informal, relaxed and jovial. As a result, he has many friends around the world, who enjoy his combination of sharp intelligence and irrepressible sense of humour. Meanwhile, in appearance, he remains perennially youthful. For many years his visual sign was the pipe and significant puff of smoke, while his signature tune continues to be a long, infectious, whooping and rumbling laugh that often abides as a *basso profondo* even when the conversation moves on to other topics.

His capacity for hard work is legendary. For nearly forty years, he occupied distinguished posts at three different institutions of the University of London: as Lecturer and Reader at University College, as Professor at the former Bedford College, and as Director of the Institute of Historical Research – one of the veritable pinnacles of the historical profession in Britain. Remarkably, he has served as President of three national historical societies, representing the three major levels of his own research interests – the British Agricultural History Society, the Economic History Society and the Royal Historical Society. He is also a regular attender at national and international conferences, and has worked for the European Science Foundation and for the British National Committee of the International Congress of Historical Sciences. In addition, he has been editor of two major journals, the *Economic History Review* and *Historical Research*. Furthermore, throughout all this, he published extensively – and remained calm, good-humoured, and helpful to others.

As Head of Department at Bedford College (as it then was) between 1968 and 1977, he gave a decisive lead but without apparently doing so. Staff meetings were informal and friendly. Michael often seemed to sit and puff his pipe phlegmatically, while the discussion ebbed and flowed around him. But somehow or other he usually got the decisions he wanted. Relations with the students were notably convivial, punctuated by the regular Christmas parties (where staff and students devised and acted in satirical revues) and the cricket match which was played annually in Regent's Park.

Michael's commonsensical approach was especially successful in calming excess emotions. One summer afternoon a troubled student was having a tantrum in the student common room, where she was throwing the furniture around and creating havoc. A distressed onlooker brought the news to Michael. His response was instant and typical. Without fuss, he went to find the student and challenged her to a game of tennis. No doubt very surprised, she accepted. History does not record who won; but the therapy worked. She ceased to throw furniture (on campus at least) and became one of Michael's regular tennis partners. When he left Bedford College in 1977, it marked the end of a particularly happy and successful period in the life of the Department. As testament to Michael's popularity, all the History students who had graduated during his regime were invited back for a huge farewell party – and they came, literally in their hundreds.

At Bedford College, Michael was a quiet reformer. Yet the solution to some problems lay outside his jurisdiction. In the early 1970s, he produced a prescient discussion paper. It set out the long-term problems faced by a small and financially impoverished institution such as Bedford College. He proposed a radical solution. Bedford should merge with Westfield College on a timetable and to a programme of their joint choosing. This was enough to produce a startled debate, but no action followed. At that time, the institutional framework of academic life seemed immune to change. Ten years later, when Bedford College faced the financial crisis that terminated its independent existence, the validity of Michael's original diagnosis became manifest, although Bedford's hurriedly-arranged rescuing merger turned out to be with Royal Holloway, while Westfield was eventually paired with Queen Mary College.

By that time, Michael himself was facing another set of problems. As the Director of the Institute of Historical Research (1977–90), he had launched a characteristic programme of quiet reform. His approach was ecumenical and modernising. Above all, as the first economic historian to lead an institution that had originally been associated most notably with political history, Michael encouraged historians of all stripes and specialisms to meet at the Institute's famous seminars. The number and range of meetings held there accordingly multiplied.

Yet the climate was not auspicious. In the 1980s the financial problems within the university world in general and within London University in particular had a dramatically adverse impact upon the Institute. Its very existence was repeatedly challenged. The gradual devolution of powers and funds to the constituent London Colleges threatened to leave all the University's central institutions high and dry, without sufficient funding or allies. The full story of the gory battles that ensued – most of them behind the scenes – will await a full elucidation from some future historian. But all Michael's political skills and his knowledge of 'the system' were required to save the Institute, as he successfully did. His calm exterior concealed the intensity of the repeated pressures he was under at that time. He bequeathed, however, a modernising Institute that has survived to fight another day. The vision of a central London meeting-place for research historians from around Britain and the wider world, that had been first promoted by A. F. Pollard in 1921, was successfully sustained more than sixty years later, in the name of that elusive but nonetheless crucial body, an ecumenical and international 'community of scholars'.

No-one has lived that ideal more convincingly than Michael Thompson. No ideologue, he has not felt it necessary to write public manifestos of his belief in scholarship and research. He has, however, shown this in the clearest way by his deeds. As an academic leader, he has been a moderniser but his quietly Whiggish reformism (carefully divested of *quondam* Whig triumphalism) is worlds away from the anti-intellectualism of Thatcherite managerialism.

Thus Michael Thompson has been a consistent standard-bearer throughout his lifetime. He has always resisted the instant fashions of the day. He was not a 'trendy' figure in the 1960s; he did not admire punk in the 1970s; he was not an advocate of 'cuts' in the 1980s; and in the 1990s he does not talk in the latest argot of postmodernism. People can sometimes underestimate him on first meeting; and he can indeed sit apparently dormant throughout a seminar, lulling the speaker into false security, before offering a searching critique of the paper in the debate that follows. But no-one should be deceived. Here is a friend and colleague who has not only lived a life of scholarship but has fought hard to defend its central values too.

As a historian of landed society ROLAND QUINAULT

Although Michael Thompson is one of the foremost social historians of modern Britain, he has described himself, with typical modesty, as 'a historian of landownership and agriculture'. Michael's interest in landed society was not the obvious product of his background and upbringing. He was educated, not at landed and aristocratic Eton, but at the Quaker school, Bootham, at York. Amongst his predecessors at Bootham were John Bright and A. J. P. Taylor: both products of the 'cottonocracy' who displayed little love for the landed interest, although they both liked the countryside and the hospitality of lords.

It was at Oxford that Michael Thompson developed an interest in the history of landed society, inspired by the work and supervision of Professor Sir John Habakkuk. Michael's initial research, on the great agricultural estates in the Victorian period, led to his first article, *The End of a Great Estate*, published in 1955 and his doctoral thesis on 'The Economic and Social Background of the English Landed Interest 1840–70'. Further studies on this subject led up to his major work *English Landed Society in the Nineteenth Century*, published in 1963. In the same year, the 'other Thompson' – E. P. Thompson – published *The Making of the English Working Class* which reflected a then fashionable pre-occupation with the lower rather than the upper ranks of British society.

In the Preface to *English Landed Society in the Nineteenth Century*, Michael recorded his debt to John Habakkuk, 'who originated modern work in this field, supervised my post-graduate work and who read and made valuable comments on a part of my final draft.' He also acknowledged the help of his wife Anne: 'She has not only spurred a naturally reluctant author to work, but has developed an enthusiasm for a subject she found naturally dull.' Since then, Anne has frequently helped Michael in his research and has always been both his most candid critic and his most fervent fan.

English Landed Society in the Nineteenth Century elegantly and insightfully distils a large amount of information culled from a wide sample of landed archives. The book still remains the standard text on the subject and an inspiration for all those working in the field. A few of its assessments seem unduly pessimistic today since recent research (in which Michael has participated) has led historians to question whether the power of the landed interest declined in the Victorian period. I doubt whether he would now entitle his chapter on 1830–80: 'The decline of the landed interest' or his chapter on the period 1914–39: 'Eclipse'. But Michael wrote at a time when landowners were still suffering from the punitive burden of post-war taxation and when the great rise in real property values – encouraged by Britain's membership of the European Community – had not yet occurred. Nevertheless many of the assessments in *English landed society in the nineteenth century* are still sound. For example, he perceptively predicted, a quarter of a century before Mrs Thatcher preached the gospel of occupying ownership, that 'England is about to become a predominantly peasant country – but not in the sense the 19th century reformers had in mind.'

Michael has always been keenly interested in the evolution of agricultural practices. He wrote a survey of 'Agriculture in Wiltshire since 1870' for the *Victoria County History* in 1959 and later wrote several articles on agricultural change. Michael has always had a particular interest in horses, live as well as historical. *English landed society in the nineteenth century* begins with the symbol of the horse and carriage. His equine interests were wittily and perceptively displayed in *Victorian England: the horse drawn society* – his inaugural lecture as Professor of Modern History at Bedford College.

In the late 1960s, Michael augmented his knowledge of estate matters by writing *Chartered surveyors: the growth of a profession.* Then, in his own words, he 'dusted off the hay seeds and entered the unfamiliar world of city streets' to write a commissioned history of the recently defunct borough of Hampstead. In this book he skilfully applied his understanding of estate development to the evolution of one of London's most select suburbs. He again revealed an understanding of political pressures and an interest in recreation. *Hampstead: building a borough* ranks with Dyos's *Victorian suburb: A study of the growth of Camberwell* as one of the best histories of a London suburb. Michael then edited a most useful general volume on *The rise of suburbia.*

Michael's interest in landed society has never been snobbish or exclusive. He has personally experienced as well as written about cottage life in a Hertfordshire village. He was interested in the environment long before it became a fashionable topic, but his conclusions have not always been 'Green'. He has contributed to a book on *The English Landscape* and lectured on most aspects of the English countryside. His interest in the lives of the urban middle and working classes has been well displayed in his social survey of Victorian Britain, *The rise of respectable society* and his editorship of the three-volume *Cambridge social history of Britain 1750–1950.*

Michael is primarily an economic and social historian, but he has not excluded politics from his scrutiny where relevant. He once observed that the interest of historians in analysing the economic or social backgrounds of MPs had obscured 'the obvious facts that sometimes constituents mattered and that public opinion was a great and growing force.' The truth of this observation about Victorian society is apparent to anyone familiar with contemporary newspapers or novels. Michael's studies of *Whigs and Liberals in the West Riding* and *Land and politics in the nineteenth century* exhibited an assured understanding of political issues. More recently, he has illuminated the links between the private and public policy of the third Marquess of Salisbury.

Like all good historians, Michael has been interested in what happens in the long term. He has pointed out that if the wealthy did not succumb to the lure of landownership in one generation, then they often did in the next. In his presidential addresses to the Royal Historical Society, he analysed English landed society in the twentieth century. But he has been careful not to stray too far from his own particular expertise and once observed that 'a continuous history of wealth over nine centuries probably could not be written and if written, would not command a wide market.' Michael has played a prominent role in the ongoing debate about wealth and landownership in modern Britain. He has cast a critical eye over the classifications of Lawrence Stone and the statistics of W. D. Rubinstein. Nevertheless Professor Rubinstein has paid a warm tribute to his academic adversary:

> Michael Thompson stands out as perhaps the kindest and most honourable man I have met in over twenty years of academic life. One of his greatest virtues is that of combining traditional scholarship at its best with genuinely fruitful innovations in research ... he has an uncanny ability to absorb what is valuable in the new while discarding, or passing by, what is not.

Michael has always been suspicious of theories which are too far removed from primary evidence or contrary to common sense. One of the hall-marks of his historical method has been to ask simple, but fundamental questions. He has asked agricultural historians 'What is farming about?' He asked Gordon Mingay 'Who are the gentry?' and Lawrence Stone 'What is a country house?' On one occasion, he even had the temerity to ask Asa Briggs 'What is a Victorian thing?'

Michael's sense of humour has always been exceptional by the standards (admittedly low) of academic historians. His humour has been revealed in his titles, such as *Horses in modern European history: a preliminary canter* and the chapter headings for his book on Hampstead, where 'Character formation' is followed by 'Character assassination'. In Michael's numerous book reviews, his humour has been insightful, as well as funny. He commented about one book that the information provided on beef breeds, milk yields and porkers was 'a useful counter-weight to the high carbohydrate content usual in general agricultural histories.' He observed about another agricultural history: '*C'est magnifique, mais ce n'est pas l'agraire.*'

Michael's literary facility makes his writings a pleasure to read. He conveys to the reader not only his enthusiasm for the subject, but also his enjoyment of the art of composition. The wit and fluency of his writing contrasts strongly with the economy of his conversation. At times he is a masterly exponent of non-verbal communication. He often expresses approval or disapproval merely by the tone of his murmur while he puffs on his pipe. He presides over seminars and committees with a shrewd and genial, but unloquacious manner – very reminiscent of the squires he writes about.

Michael's studies of landed society are not, of course, above criticism. He may, at times, have exaggerated the gulf between the landed rich and the merely rich. He has written little on the role of the monarchy, the church, or the universities either as landowners or in their relations with the landed élite. He has neglected the ways in which the old élite have sometimes aped the recreations and the manners of their social interiors. It might also be argued that he has generally shown little interest in the individual character and ability of particular landowners. But Michael is a true social historian, who is more concerned with the action of groups, than with individuals.

Michael's interest in landed society was originally rather Anglo-centric and he has not carried out research on non-British landowners. But he has given encouragement and help to younger scholars who have studied landed society outside England such as Avner Offer and David Howell. His work for the European Science Foundation and the British National Committee of the International Congress of Historical Sciences, together with his attendance at countless international conferences, has ensured that he has played a prominent part in the comparative study of European landed society.

Michael is one of those rare intellectuals who is prepared to defend landowners when they are attacked as a group. He once enquired why it was worse to rear game birds for slaughter than farm animals. He has also pointed out that David Ricardo, after classifying the landowners as parasitic, at once proceeded to join their ranks. Nevertheless Michael's attitude towards landed society has always been Whiggish, rather than romantic or reactionary. I suspect that he shares the outlook of Trollope's character, the aristocratic Whig, Plantagenet Palliser, who believed in greater equality providing it didn't touch his country house in his own day, or take away her ladyship's ponies.

Michael has always assisted other historians of landed society by commenting on their work in a helpful and constructive way. Many younger historians have benefited from his criticisms and his kindness when he was supervising or examining their theses. The debt of many established historians to him is acknowledged by their contribution to this volume. For forty years, Michael Thompson has illuminated and expanded the study of modern British landed society and made the field his own particular historical property. Let us hope that he retains the title deeds for a long time to come.

Notes on contributors

PENELOPE J. CORFIELD is Professor of History at Royal Holloway, University of London, and has been a visiting professor in Hungary, Japan and the United States. She is the author of *The impact of English towns, 1700–1800* (Oxford University Press, 1982), editor of *Language, history and class* (Blackwell, 1991), and her study of *Power and the professions in early modern Britain 1700–1850* was published by Routledge in 1995.

JOHN CHARTRES is Chairman of the School and Professor of Business and Economic Studies at the University of Leeds. Until recently he was the Editor of the *Agricultural History Review*, and he has contributed chapters to the *Cambridge Agrarian History of England and Wales*. With David Hey, he edited *English rural society, 1500–1800: essays in honour of Joan Thirsk* (Cambridge University Press, 1990).

E. J. T. COLLINS is Director of the Rural History Centre at the University of Reading, and the Editor of volume VII of the *Cambridge Agrarian History of England and Wales, 1850–1914*.

AVNER OFFER is Reader in Recent Social and Economic History at the University of Oxford and Fellow of Nuffield College. He is author of *Property and politics, 1870–1914* (Cambridge University Press, 1981) and of *The First World War: an agrarian interpretation* (Oxford University Press, 1989), as well as of articles on land tenure, agriculture, war, the British empire and modern consumerism.

W. D. RUBINSTEIN is Professor of History at the University of Wales at Aberystwyth, after holding a chair at Deakin University in Australia. He is the author of such works as *Men of property: the very wealthy in Britain since the Industrial Revolution* (1981) and *Capitalism, culture, and decline in Britain* (1993). He is a Fellow of the Australian Academies of Humanities and of the Social Sciences, and of the Royal Historical Society.

PETER CLARKE is Professor of Modern British History at the University of Cambridge, and Fellow of St John's College. His first book, *Lancashire and the New Liberalism* (Cambridge, 1971) was a study in electoral politics. His most recent books are *A question of leadership: Gladstone to Thatcher* (Penguin edn, 1992) and the volume on the twentieth century in the new Penguin History of Britain (to be published in 1996). He is a Fellow of the British Academy and writes frequently for the *Times Literary Supplement* and the *London Review of Books*.

KEVIN LANGFORD read History at St John's College, Cambridge, 1982–5, and is now pursuing a career in financial services.

M. J. DAUNTON is Astor Professor of British History at University College London. His most recent publicatons include *Poverty and progress: an economic and social history of Britain, 1700–1850* (Oxford University Press, 1995) and 'Payment and participation: welfare and state formation in Britain, 1900–51' in *Past and Present* no. 150 (1996). His current research is on the next volume of the Oxford economic history (*Wealth and welfare: an economic and social history of Britain, 1850–1939*) and a history of taxation in Britain since 1842.

DAVID SPRING is Professor Emeritus of History at Johns Hopkins University in Baltimore, Maryland, USA. He is author of *The English landed estate in the nineteenth century* (Johns Hopkins Press, Baltimore, 1963), and editor of *European landed élites in the nineteenth century* (Johns Hopkins Press, Baltimore 1977) and (with E. Spring) of *Ecology and religion in history* (New York, 1974).

NOTES ON CONTRIBUTORS

ROLAND QUINAULT is Reader in History at the University of North London and Honorary Secretary of the Royal Historical Society. He has published numerous studies on modern British political and social history. He co-edited, with Dr John Stevenson; *Popular Protest and Public Order* (1976) and with Professor P. K. O'Brien, *The Industrial Revolution and British Society* (Cambridge University Press, 1993).

DAVID CANNADINE is Moore Collegiate Professor of History at Columbia University in New York, where he has been since 1988, having previously been a Lecturer in History at Cambridge and a fellow of Christ's College. Among his many publications are *Lords and landlords:the aristocracy and the towns, 1774–1967* (Leicester University Press, 1980); *The decline and fall of the British aristocracy* (Yale, 1990) and *G. M. Trevelyan: a life in history* (Harper Collins, 1992); *Aspects of aristocracy: grandeur and decline in modern Britain* (Yale, 1994).

NEGLEY HARTE is Senior Lecturer in Economic History at University College London. He has been Assistant Editor of the *Economic History Review* and Editor of the *London Journal.* He is author of *The University of London, 1836–1986* (Athlone Press, 1986) and (with John North) of *The world of UCL, 1828–1990* (UCL, 1991). With the late K. G. Ponting, he edited *Textile history and economic history: essays in honour of Miss Julia Mann* (Manchester University Press, 1973) and *Cloth and clothing in medieval Europe: essays in memory of Professor E. M. Carus-Wilson* (Heinemann, 1983).

JENNY WEST worked for her Ph.D. as a graduate student of Professor F. M. L. Thompson at the Institute of Historical Research, 1981–85. She was a Research Assistant at the Wellcome Institute for the History of Medicine, 1986–88 and a Research Fellow there, 1988–90. She is author of *Gunpowder, Government and war in the mid-eighteenth century* (Boydell & Brewer: RHS Monograph Series). She worked recently for the Transport History Research Trust and is currently undertaking research for the United Bristol Healthcare NHS Trust.

1

THE RIVALS: LANDED AND OTHER GENTLEMEN

PENELOPE J. CORFIELD

> When Adam delved and Eve span,
> Who was then the gentleman?[1]

Although a choice between Adam and Eve for gentlemanly qualities might appear straightforward, the answer to this ancient riddle has proved historically far from simple. Much social heartache and printer's ink has been expended over the problem of social definition. Who indeed was the gentleman? The question was asked by many in anxious personal enquiry; and by others with an undertone of sardonic protest. If all men were created equals, how did one get status and another not? In particular, how did one become something as desirable and as nebulous as a gentleman and another face rejection as not 'quite quite'?

Such was the lure of this unofficial title – in English social mythology trailing connotations of stalwart landownership – that history was retrospectively amended to bring some illustrious but unlikely candidates into the ambit of gentility. Was Noah a gentleman? Yes, said the anonymous *Boke of St Albans* (1486).[2] Was Christ the carpenter a gentleman? Emphatically so, wrote Sir John Ferne in *The Blazon of Gentrie* (1586): 'Christ was a Gentleman, as to his flesh, by the part of his mother: . . . and might if he had esteemed . . . the vain glory of this world . . . have borne coat-armour.' What about the apostles? Again Ferne was not in doubt. 'The Apostles also . . . were Gentlemen of blood', although he admitted that they had gone down in the world as far as outward occupation was concerned.[3] The gentility of Christ was often attested. But the attribution was not usually dependent upon ancient lineage. For example, Thomas Dekker based the claim upon moral worth rather than armorial bearings. His reference to Christ in 1604 was much repeated:

> The best of men
> That ere wore earth about him, was a sufferer,
> A soft, meeke, patient, humble, tranquill spirit,
> The first true Gentleman that ever breath'd.[4]

These diverse attributions between them indicate the rival strands of external status and personal merit within the concept of gentility.

Social revaluation was certainly contagious. Was Shakespeare a gentleman? His career as an actor and playwright might give cause for doubt, although he did in fact purchase a grant of arms in 1599.[5] But, with time, he had achieved not only theatrical immortality but also personal beatification. The anonymous *Laughing Philosopher* explained in 1777 that a gentleman was made by nature. Title, rank, birth, dress, education, manners, and even foreign travel could not in themselves work the trick. Hence 'Kings are often not *Gentlemen,*' he warned 'while Peasants are so.'[6] He then supplied some famous examples. Henry VIII, although a king, was not a gentleman, on the evidence of his behaviour with his wives. Yet the 'divine' William Shakespeare, son of a Stratford butcher-cum-dealer, was one, and not because of his armorial grant. Similarly, the duplicitous Charles I did not qualify for the title, while the matchless John Milton – son of a London scrivener – did. This made good reading for literary men from modest commercial backgrounds, but it indicated scope for a wider confusion, when landed status and blue blood were still eagerly admired by many, including not a few pedigreed landowners themselves.

'What a Gentleman is, 'tis hard with us to define', as lawyer John Selden observed.[7] Daniel Defoe assented that the problem was sufficiently complex that it might 'serve in the schools for a good *Thesis* and long learned Dissertations may be made upon it.'[8] This essay does not attempt so much. Instead, it analyses the rival interpretations of gentility; and identifies the 'social flotation' of the concept, as it moved away from a strict definition by external status towards a more personalised qualification. The argument does not deny the high standing of the landowner with a distinguished lineage and an independent 'stake in the country'. But it shows that there was more than one source of élite status in English society between the sixteenth and the nineteenth centuries. Hence it is wrong to assume that all 'gentlemen' came from landed stock and owned a landed estate. That was the myth but not the actuality.

I

From its earliest usage in English, the term 'gentle' carried both social and moral connotations, as did 'noble'. It was always a complimentary term. A man described as 'gentil' in Chaucer's time was gentle by 'birth or character', additionally glossed as 'noble', 'excellent', 'worthy', 'well-bred', 'charming', 'mild' or 'tender'.[9] The combination of qualities reflected a chivalric ideal, whereby men of high rank justified their elevation by their gracious and courteous bearing. They were not expected to be proud, haughty, rude or aggressive, but modest, magnanimous, well-mannered and valorous.[10] In theory at least, social and personal qualities were dovetailed, as in Chaucer's 'verray parfit gentil knyght'.[11] This ideal was not cold-bloodedly planned to deflect the potential envy and wrath of the excluded plebeians. Yet the gentle code could be invoked to that effect. John Ball's critique of terrestrial inequality, as a contravention of the primitive equality of Eden, could be theoretically disarmed by appealing to a match between social and personal worth. A 'moralised' hierarchy was easier to defend than a crudely and overtly exploitative one.[12] 'Gentilesse' brought with it obligations as well as status, very much as did 'noblesse oblige'.

Nonetheless, the most common early use of 'gentleman' and of its collective noun the 'gentry' was simply in reference to high-ranking individuals. The linked terms seem to have come into use fairly rapidly in the fifteenth century to describe men of some distinction, often entitled to bear a coat of arms, whether with or – significantly – without the formal title of nobility.[13] There was, however, no strict legal definition of a 'gentleman', either then or later. As land was the chief source of status and power, the term certainly referred to many freehold landowners.[14] At the upper end of the scale, the gentry included the younger branches of the nobility, who by English social convention were not themselves designated as noble. Meanwhile, at the lower end of the scale, the status of the lesser gentlemen tailed away into the ranks of the substantial freeholders or yeomanry. But even the minor gentry – historians sometimes term them mere 'parish gentry' – were powerful figures within their own localities.

By the sixteenth century, a rich if imprecise social terminology was well-established. Beneath the monarchy, a numerically-restricted peerage of dukes, earls, marquesses and other lords held the highest rank. They were often termed 'gentlemen' by courtesy but they were also noble, the '*nobilitas maior*'. The rest of the population constituted the 'Commons' of England, but among their capacious numbers there were many further distinctions of status. They were led by the 'gentry', who included hereditary baronets (a new title created in 1611), knights, esquires and plain gentlemen. Although if elected to Parliament such men sat in the House of Commons, they were frequently differentiated from the ordinary 'commonalty'.[15] Indeed, some social commentators referred to them as the '*nobilitas minor*', although they did not have noble ranking, and this term was still to be found in the eighteenth century. It became, however, increasingly archaic.[16] The status of a 'gentleman' did not need the prop of noble claims. His social lustre embraced the titled aristocracy. Thus, as Chamberlayne noted, 'All Noblemen are Gentlemen, though all Gentlemen are not Noblemen.'[17]

Through these qualifications, there were two overlapping sorts of social division. One was the legal distinction between the very few who were titled nobility and the very many who were commoners. The other was a social distinction that was less well defined but in practice even more important. It differentiated between the élite few (some with titles, some without), who were accepted as the 'gentry' or the 'quality', and the non-élite many, known as the 'common people' or the 'masses' (but not – alas for verbal symmetry – as the 'quantity').

But who constituted this eminent, if non-noble, gentleman, with his family of 'gentlefolks' and his even more grandly-titled consort or 'lady'?[18] Definitional difficulties blurred the picture from the start. A 'gentleman' in chivalric theory was intended to be a man not only of status and independent wealth, but also of sterling personal qualities in intellect, manners and morals. Landed property was held to be the best guarantee of that. It produced men 'whose lands are answerable to their virtues, and whose rents can maintaine the greatnesse of their mind', as Deloney explained optimistically in 1597.[19] There were, however, many problems in practice. There were men of landed estates who lacked ancient lineage; there were men of wealth who lacked either estates and/or lineage; and there were men of personal distinction who lacked all the trappings of land, ancestry and affluence. As a result, there were many diverse claimants to the right to be styled 'Master' or 'Mr'. The title was used contentiously: as when one Hugh Venables of London was indicted before the law courts in 1430 as a gentleman *alias* 'common cutpurse'.[20] It was also used with irony: in the eighteenth century, the fair-spoken and well-mounted highwaymen were known as 'gentlemen of the road'.[21]

Throughout the period from the sixteenth to the nineteenth centuries, the term gained both in popularity and in elasticity. Not only did non-landowners buy into land and acquire the dignity that way;[22] but many non-landowners who did not buy into land were also accorded the status. As a result, there was an undoubted 'rise of the gentleman' in English history, as the title was increasingly coveted, increasingly emphasised and increasingly used. Only very gradually, by the nineteenth century, did the insistent pressures of its social success begin to dilute its appeal.

Established families were frequently resistant to newcomers claiming the status. Sticklers for punctilio therefore maintained that the only true gentlemen were landowners with family pedigrees ('good blood') and with armorial bearings that had been accepted by the heralds of the College of Arms[23] or, in the event of dispute, had been upheld before the controversial Court of Chivalry.[24] This view was repeated over the centuries with great earnestness: most recently in 1900.[25] Yet it was both disputed and circumvented. Eager aspirants were not afraid to gild their own family trees. Hence, although in Tudor and Stuart times the College of Arms toured the counties to adjudicate heraldic claims and to 'disgrade' impostors, there were subtle and not-so-subtle pressures upon them to give recognition to plausible newcomers. These visitations were relatively infrequent – every 20 or 25 years – and imperfectly administered, which allowed ample leeway for social invention.[26] Moreover, both institutions were drastically cut down to size at the end of the seventeenth century. After 1689, the English monarchs ceased to issue writs for the visitations and the social inquisition at once halted, although the College of Arms still survived – indeed survives – as the heraldic registry.[27] Meanwhile, the last years of the civil-law Court of Chivalry were very chequered. It ceased to meet in 1640, with the ending of prerogative monarchy; was ruled illegal by the Grand Remonstrance in 1641; was briefly delegated to a Commission in 1646; was revived in full by James II in 1687 but lapsed again in 1708. Then, despite a last flurry of business in the early 1730s, it simply ceased to meet after March 1737.[28]

More crucially, others simply disagreed that pedigrees and traditional armorial bearings were the sole prerequisites for gentility. Plenty of gentlemen were accepted by the world without these accoutrements. Instead, the potential breadth of the concept had rapidly made gentlemen in England 'good cheape'. That came from a famous interpretation, first penned by William Harrison in 1577 but best-known in its revised form by Sir Thomas Smith in 1583:

> For whosoever studieth the lawes of the realme, who studieth in the universities, who professeth the liberall sciences, and to be shorte, can live idly and without manuall labour, and will beare the port, charge and countenaunce of a gentleman, he shall be called master, for that is the title which men give to esquires and other gentlemen, and shall be taken for a gentleman.[29]

As that made clear, the criteria included the acquisition of certain specialist skills plus the absence of heavy, grinding, sapping, manual labour. It did not preclude all work, for a gentleman might well undertake certain tasks – activity in local government, for example, or the supervision of financial matters – but he was not condemned to incessant physical toil. He had to have sufficient income and sufficient leisure to be able to 'live idly' and to cultivate the social graces. But, other than that, the ideal was not determined by the size of a man's landed estates or by the blueness of his blood. It was a question of public reputation. The boundaries between esquires and gentlemen were often blurred – the esquires ranking above gentlemen as sons of knightly families or as Justices of the Peace – but all had achieved social esteem. For those who had won such recognition, the Heralds would then, if requested, supply a coat of arms 'for money', as Smith noted. But that was an optional consequence and not a necessary cause of gentle status.

Flexibility was thus enshrined within England's honour system. Formal titles – from peerages through to the relatively humbler knighthoods – were allocated by royal prerogative, exercised directly by the monarch or occasionally delegated to a military commander in the field. That allowed some regulation of supply. The early Stuarts were unusual in their prodigality in selling titles, but subsequent monarchs and their advisers were thereafter careful not to devalue the honour by an excess of grants. Only a minority of the gentry were hereditary baronets, or knights of the shire, just as only a minority of all large landowners were peers of the realm.[30] However, these formalities were offset by the latitude of the unofficial title of 'gentleman', which blurred any sharp distinctions between nobles and non-nobles.[31] Nor was that honour under royal control. The monarch could create knights and baronets but could not regulate the wider accolade. As a result, royal policy was perforce non-interventionist. The dictum was often quoted that 'a king may make a nobleman, but he cannot make a gentleman'.[32] Moreover,. there was no sign that the crown objected to this *de facto* limitation. And, in practical terms, successive governments had no need to repine, as the gentry in England – however defined – were not exempt from taxation.[33]

Among non-landowners who claimed gentle status, fifteenth-century office-holders under the crown were the first to gain success.[34] Within the next hundred years, it had become accepted, even by the traditionalist Sir John Ferne, that the informal title was also allowable to the senior professions, all University graduates, practitioners of the liberal (but not the mechanic) sciences, leading municipal office-holders for the duration of the Mayoralty, and England's army commanders,[35] although the rank-and-file soldiery, who did the brutal work of bloodshed, were excluded. The concept kept an aura of knightly chivalry and valour; but it had clearly lost any exclusive association with military prowess. Instead, the criteria were civilian and humanist. And, while 'idleness' was desirable, in the sense of not having to struggle daily for a living, it was not construed as mere frivolity. Thus a gentleman was defined by having the required bearing ('port'), responsibility ('charge'),[36] and personal demeanour ('countenaunce') for the role.

Merchants and dealers posed the greatest difficulty under these criteria. Sir John Ferne, for example, was certain that following the 'mechanicall sciences' as a tradesman or craftsman was a serious barrier to gentility, although it might be waived for an exceptional individual.[37] Much Tudor and Stuart literature endorsed that view,[38] although there was a brief literary flirtation in the 1590s with shoemaking as the 'gentle craft'.[39] Few real-life social pioneers were as bold as Sir Baptist Hicks, a London mercer and silk merchant, whose decision to keep his shop open even after he had been knighted in 1604 scandalised conservative opinion.[40] A snobbish prejudice against trade long continued. For example, when the gawky social-climber Mr Dubster in Burney's *Camilla* (1796) was challenged as to how he had become a gentleman, he replied that it was by 'leaving off business'.[41] That was written during the heightened tensions of the 1790s, but it neatly encapsulated the anti-trade ethos, an attitude that still persists in some circles today.

Even the purists, however, conceded some points. A merchant was redeemed by holding a honorific civic office, at least while in post. But advocates of gentlemanly commerce went further. They pointed out that wholesale trade did not involve brutish or dirty physical labour. And they disputed that indentured apprenticeship entailed a personal bondage that forever marked a man as 'ungentle'. It was obviously a matter of concern, especially to the great London dealers and financiers whose wealth and commercial importance entitled them to claim status. The question was canvassed in a tract of 1629, entitled *The Cities' Advocate in this Case or Question of Honor and Armes: Whether Apprenticeship extinguisheth Gentry?*[42] It concluded very confidently that it did not. An amplified text was reprinted in 1674,[43] suggesting both that the message was still disputed and that its conclusion was still welcome to a City readership. In practice, however, the matter was gradually being decided in favour of commerce. Some of the evidence comes from cases that were disputed, such as those of the clothier, the linen draper, the soap-boiler and the goldsmith, whose claims were argued before the Court of Chivalry in the early seventeenth century.[44] But the system of surveillance was far too haphazard to prevent others from slipping through the net.

Practice, in other words, was pragmatic, even if theory was slower to catch up with the trend. No doubt the non-landed gentlemen long remained in a minority. Yet they were there from the start.[45] *De facto* the English gentleman was always a latitudinarian. Historians have too often ignored – or mentioned only to dismiss – his bourgeois component. But the 1,172 'gentlemen' of London, who were presented to the heralds in 1633–35, were not primarily landowners, even if some may have owned land. Indeed, the recorded occupations for 845 of them consisted of 696 merchants, 67 lawyers, 35 courtiers, 29 medical men, 14 City officials and

4 churchmen.[46] Furthermore, those were minimum figures, since an unknown number refused to respond to the heraldic summons at all. It was enough to provoke Robert Burton to dry satire in his *Anatomy of Melancholy* (1621), averring that: 'Cookery is become an art, a noble science; Cooks are Gentlemen.'[47]

II

Thereafter, both theory and practice complicated matters yet further. The continuing debates in the later seventeenth and eighteenth century showed that the 'social flotation' of the concept was in full spate. Attempts that were made in 1661–64 and again in 1678 to legislate for a compulsory state registration of all coat armour and gentle pedigrees were unsuccessful,[48] and matters were thereafter left to the unofficial social negotiation between claimants and conservatives. In vain, did the Court of Chivalry (before its demise in 1737) strive to restrict new armorial bearings and to prevent painters from depicting them on carriages.[49] The College of Arms after 1689 made no campaign for the revival of the heraldic tours and confined itself to devising, registering and adjudicating heraldic insignia. Little wonder that spasmodic attempts in the seventeenth century to revive the ancient sumptuary laws (repealed in 1604) in order to specify appropriate garb for the different ranks of society did not gain Parliamentary support; and that the Game Laws, which from 1670 to 1831 regulated hunting in the English countryside, prudently did not mention the rights of 'gentlemen', confining hunting permits to the sons and heirs of esquires and above, to freeholders worth £100 per annum, and to major leaseholders.[50]

Two distinct developments continued to broaden the definition of a 'gentleman'. The first of these was the continuing pressure from successful merchants and businessmen to assert their gentility and to join the 'quality'. There was a continuing torrent of writings, attempting to systematise the unsystematic. John Brydall, for example, argued in 1676 that there were four sources of gentility: birth; office; creation; and reputation,[51] the latter leaving plenty of latitude. Significantly, he did not mention owning land as a qualification in itself. But the classification remained imprecise. The Tory traditionalist Edward Chamberlayne noted mournfully in his annual handbook, *Angliae Notitia* (1669), that the younger sons of the gentry went not only into the professions, court and army 'but of late too many of them to Shop-keeping'.[52] However, even he accepted that a non-apprenticed gentleman did not lose rank by engaging in foreign trade; and in the twentieth edition (1702) the publication added, on the authority of the seventeenth-century herald Guillim, that nobles and gentlemen were not degraded by apprenticeship.[53]

Furthermore, in the rival Whig account of *The State of England* (1691), Guy Miège stated baldly that the term stretched upwards to include the nobility and downwards to 'any one that, without a Coat of Arms, has either a liberal, or genteel Education, that looks Gentleman-like (whether he be so, or not) and has wherewithall to live freely and handsomely.' The virtues no longer included 'idleness'. Instead, Miège praised the beneficent effects of commerce as a means to wealth and status, adding: 'The truth is, Gentility with competent Means is an excellent Compound; but without it, 'tis but a wretched Condition, as the world goes now.' It was thus better to be an honest, substantial tradesman than a poor gentleman by birth, 'in this Age especially, where Poverty is ... grown so contemptible.'[54]

The flexibility of usage was noticeable enough to impress a Swiss visitor in 1719. He claimed with fine hyperbole: 'This State of Things has given place to the Abuse of every Man's calling himself *Gentleman in England*.'[55] That was not literally true but there were very many aspirants for the accolade, especially since formal titles were handed out only sparingly. As the ranks of 'the quality' were insidiously broadened, so new sub-classifications were introduced, although these were not used systematically. By the later seventeenth century, people referred not only to the 'landed gentry' or the 'country gentry' but also to the 'city gentry' and 'town gentry'.[56] That indicated a response to the diversity within the concept, even if the divisions were not at all clearly demarcated. To assist the process of identification, a modern historian has also suggested that the urban variety be termed the 'pseudo-gentry'.[57] However, that seems unfairly to imply that the town gentry were fraudulent or pretentious or both; and the suggestion has not generally found favour.

No one social group in eighteenth-century England achieved a monopoly of the unofficial title. Clearly, however, the new power of the 'monied interest' was disturbing to the peace of mind of the landed traditionalists. Evidence of that occurred in 1710, when a Tory-dominated Parliament passed the Property Qualifications Act for England and Wales (but not Scotland), which remained on the statute book until 1838. This restrictive legislation decreed that an income of at least £600 p.a. from land was the prerequisite to stand as MP for a county seat, and at least £300 p.a. for a borough seat. Exception was made only for the eldest sons of peers and the sons of men qualified to be MPs for shires.[58] The Act did not risk a general definition of social worth; nor did it insist upon any form of commoner's title (knight or baronet); but it sought to create a landowning monopoly of Parliamentary power. In practice, however, its impact was limited, partly because 'monied' men set up inventive schemes to gain bogus qualifications[59] and partly because the division between trade and agriculture was not a rigid one. Hence a modern analysis of the 'Honourable Gentlemen' elected as MPs between 1734 and 1832 finds that those with commercial and professional interests amounted to just over half the total (2,555 MPs out of 5,034 studied, or 50.75 per cent) but also points out that many of these commercial MPs were simultaneously landowners.[60]

Participation in parliamentary politics was thus not confined exclusively to men in possession of high birth or rolling acres of freehold land. Blackstone, for example, referred loosely to 'our gentlemen of independent estate and fortune', stressing the importance of independence rather than any particular sort of fortune.[61] As England in the eighteenth century was regularly acknowledged as a 'trading nation',[62] successful commercial and professional men found their way into the élite if they were able to demonstrate sufficient affluence and live in a suitable style.

Gentlemanly status was a matter not for law, but for social negotiation. There was nothing to prevent ambitious individuals from claiming the role. It did, however, demand a sufficiently confident display to gain public acceptance. That helps to explain the success of the many 'courtesy' manuals, which offered to teach the requisite manners and polish.[63] Certainly, the style demanded some attention. A gentleman had to know how to carry his sword, if not how to fight with it, and how to spend his money, if not how to earn it. Daniel Defoe's *Moll Flanders* (1722) explained her matrimonial ambitions in the following terms:

> I was not averse to a Tradesman, but then I would have a Tradesman forsooth, that was something of a Gentleman too; that when my husband had a mind to carry me to the Court, or to the Play, he might become a Sword, and look as like a Gentleman, as another Man; and not be one that had the mark of his Apron strings on his Coat, or the mark of his Hat upon his Perriwig.[64]

This stress on outward appearances produced a very competitive and fashion-conscious society. It also left ample scope for deception, as Moll Flanders found to her cost. She married her 'amphibious Creature, this *Land-water-thing* call'd, a *Gentleman Tradesman*', only to be left deeply in debt, discovering that he was 'a Tradesman that was Rake, Gentleman, Shop keeper, and Beggar all together'.

Real-life examples of 'town gentry' did not, however, always end badly. On the contrary, the title of gentleman was often the outward badge of success in a professional or commercial career, particularly but not solely upon retirement from active business. In Norwich, for example, there were 22 practising attorneys who voted in the 1734 election, all defining themselves not as lawyers but as 'Gentlemen'. Moreover, it was not a matter of exceptional comment, by the eighteenth century, to find bankers, dealers, and other more modest tradesmen also styling themselves as 'Mr' or, more powerfully, as 'Gent.' or 'Esquire'.[65] For example, there were individual vintners, brewers, tanners, theatre-managers and dancing-masters who used the title. Indeed, a survey of 16 British commercial town directories in the 1770s and 1780s[66] has found at least 1,375 townsmen who were then styled as gentlemen or esquires, of whom 601 (43.7 per cent) were listed without an accompanying occupation (although they may nonetheless have had one) while another 774 (56.3 per cent) did record one: of those, 582 were in the professions, 180 in commerce or banking, 7 in manufacturing, plus 5 others. And these figures were far from comprehensive, since the Directories did not set out to provide the total coverage later demanded of the censuses.

Men who prospered even in unglamorous trades were able to redefine themselves as they rose in the world. One Samuel Collins of Tothill Fields voted in the 1784 Westminster election, stating his occupation as a 'rubbish carter'. Someone of the same name and address voted in 1788 and 1796, identifying himself as a 'scavenger'. Finally, Samuel Collins 'gentleman', also of Tothill Fields, went to the polls in 1802.[67] If all these records relate to the same individual, they suggest a process of upward social mobility over a period of 18 years; if to father and son, they suggest inter-generational change; and if to more than one person from more than one family, they at least suggest a measure of residential propinquity between gentlemen and rubbish-carters. Furthermore, in addition to many urban tradesmen, both army officers and senior professional men were allowed the status without controversy, even by the traditionalist heraldic office.[68] Thus, for example, the attorneys routinely and non-controversially named their new association, founded *c.* 1739, as the 'Society of Gentlemen Practisers in the Courts of Law and Equity'.[69]

Between them, these people not only formed the leadership of the growing towns of eighteenth-century England but they also intermingled with the landed gentry of the countryside.[70] There were continuing tensions and snobberies between the rival sources of power and prestige, and much anguish – expressed both privately by individuals and publicly by social commentators – as successive generations faced the competing clashes of old and new claims to status. Traditionalist laments also confirmed the very processes of change that they deplored so strongly. For example, in 1756 John Brown, a literary vicar, poet and playwright, wrote vehemently to express his fear that England's social leadership had been overcome by '*vain, luxurious,* and *selfish* EFFEMINACY'. He agreed that there had been a welcome reduction in aristocratic coarseness, but called also for a full return to ancient chivalry and feudal loyalty.[71] Diatribes such as this were frequent, and as often contradicted by rival experts. That indicates in itself that there was no simple fusion of 'interests' to lay the disputes finally to rest. Yet, just as significantly, it also suggests that the social order was continuously experienced as under stress and adaptation, for without that there would be no cause for debate.

This relative social flexibility can be variously interpreted. It can be argued that England's elastic honours system seduced the commercial world into coveting the style and status of a traditional rural hierarchy. A modern and far-from-conventional Earl has recorded his belief that 'the concept of the gentleman was invented by the aristocrats to keep the middle classes in order'.[72] There are, furthermore, some apparent grounds for supporting this spritely dictum by Bertrand Russell. The imaginative hold that the chivalric ideal and the lure of decorative 'idleness' exercised over England's socially-ambitious bourgeoisie discouraged a direct onslaught upon the concept of honours and titles. It may also have promoted an undue reverence for gentlemanly 'breeding' rather than for ability, have diluted the social glory of the commercial and industrial interests, and inculcated a disdain for mere money-grubbing. Thus capitalism (itself a concept in need of precise definition) found itself in England adopting an amateurish and unbusinesslike ethos – to its own ultimate detriment, in the opinion of a number of historians.[73]

Yet the developing ethos of the gentleman was by no means a simple seduction of non-landed society by the landed interest. It should be viewed instead as a successful business and professional intrusion into the informal honours system, whereby landowners were deprived of a monopoly, and recognition was accorded to wealth and commercial success as well as to birth and land.

III

That was enhanced by the second distinctive development within the concept of the 'gentleman', which occurred as a number of writers promoted the case for a personal gentility that had little or nothing to do with outward circumstances and everything to do with individual morality and merit. The claim had been made long before 1700, but thereafter was given new emphasis. There was not anything as organised as a formal campaign, and meritorious individuals did not all adopt the title of gentleman. But the growing corpus of writing upon moral gentility generated a literary and cultural pressure that made itself felt gradually and often insidiously within the general climate of opinion.

So was launched 'nature's gentleman'. Such arguments drew strength from the old requirement for the 'parfit gentil knyght' to have a fine mind as well as a fine family: the combination of the two made the 'only perfect Gentrie', as Ferne had agreed.[74] By these means, the liberal intelligentsia were able to cut the titled aristocracy and landowning society down to size. It was better 'to boast of Virtue than Birth', wrote a 'Person of Quality' in 1672, perhaps not quite heeding his own lesson.[75] Richard Steele in *The Tatler* in 1710 was one of the first to publicise the case unequivocally. He argued that a courtier, a tradesman, a scholar, all had equal claims to be a gentleman: 'The Appellation of Gentleman is never to be affixed to a Man's Circumstances, but to his Behaviour in them.'[76] He later satirised the idleness of landowners and praised the achievements of commerce. But external role was not the ultimate test: genuine qualities came naturally from within. 'There is an innate virtuous spirit of manners about a real *Gentleman*, which no education can give', the *Laughing Philosopher* agreed in 1777.[77] A journalist in *The World* (1755) joined the attack upon excessive pride in rank and family: later generations would find it odd, he predicted correctly, that the English population was held to be divided into people of 'birth' and those of 'no birth', implying that there were two sorts of people 'some BORN, but the much greater number UNBORN'.[78]

Steele had also chastised in 1713 those empty-headed noblemen who thought of nothing but 'Rank and Precedency' and who sneered at the '*new* Man' of lowlier birth. He accepted that illustrious families had just claims to social respect; but argued that it was illogical for them to condemn successful newcomers, as they had the very talents and drive that characterised the founding father of the high-born family, 'upon whose Reputation they value themselves.'[79] The meritocratic case was also put into verse: John Gay in 1738 quizzed the idle gentleman as a fluttering fly, who did no public service but fed on delicacies produced by others.[80] And in 1733/4, Alexander Pope produced some ringing couplets:

> Worth makes the man, and want of it, the fellow;
> The rest is all but leather or prunella.
> ...
> What can ennoble sots, or slaves, or cowards?
> Alas! not all the blood of all the HOWARDS.[81]

Eloquence from literary men such as these did not, of course, overthrow traditional reverence for rank and birth. There were plenty of people who agreed with Edmund Burke's sonorous pronouncement that 'We fear God; we look up with awe to kings; with affection to parliaments; with duty to magistrates; with reverence to priests; and with respect to nobility.'[82] But such attitudes were not universal. For example, in 1735 one 'Crito', a Lincoln's Inn lawyer, acknowledged the deplorable tendency of some men in the middling ranks of society to look up to their social 'superiors'. However, he riposted that '*Personal Merit* is the only true *Nobility*, and the *Lord* who inherits the *Dignities* without the *Virtues* of his Ancestors, is but a despicable Creature.'[83] Similarly, an anonymous poem to a young nobleman in 1736 repeated that greatness did not lie in externals:

> Who rise to *Glory*, must by *Virtue* rise,
> 'Tis in the Mind all genuine Greatness lies.[84]

Such writings put a cumulative pressure upon the titled aristocracy to justify their pre-eminence by an ethos of service, a case that gained emphasis in the course of the century.[85]

'Nature's gentleman' was thus a meritocrat, but in the name of character and morals rather than intelligence or business skills. Education came to be stressed more strongly as the debates progressed;[86] but schooling was expected to build upon innate qualities of virtue. At the same time, 'nature's gentleman' was not a social leveller. He did not attack titles and honours. But he did expect men of high birth to behave with a restrained dignity and to treat other 'gentlemen', of whatever origin, as their equals. Addison and Steele, the promoters of an urbane and moderate Whiggery, who were themselves sons of professional men, argued thus in their journalistic campaigns devised to tame aristocratic pride, rowdiness and debauchery. The rake was to be urbanised and civilised. High spirits and fine dress were acceptable but only when accompanied by refinement in mind, manners, and morals. Steele provided the classsic pen-portrait in 1713:

> When I consider the Frame of Mind peculiar to a Gentleman, I suppose it graced with all the Dignity and Elevation of Spirit that Human Nature is capable of: To this I would have joined a clear Understanding, a Reason free from Prejudice, a steady Judgment, and an extensive Knowledge. When I think of the Heart of a Gentleman, I imagine it firm and intrepid, void of all inordinate Passions, and full of Tenderness, Compassion and Benevolence. When I view the Fine Gentleman with regard to his Manners, methinks I see him modest without Bashfulness, frank and affable without Impertinence, obliging and complaisant without Servility, cheerful and in good Humour without Noise.[87]

Perhaps redundantly, he added that 'these amiable Qualities are not easily obtained'.

There was in this teaching both a strongly Aristotelian emphasis upon moderation and a religious undertone, with a quasi-Puritan contempt for mere outward show and a stress upon individual morality. But the message was a secular as well as religious one. Samuel Richardson, who came from a nonconformist background, provided a noted literary exemplar in *Sir Charles Grandison* (1753/4). This novelistic paragon was intended to outshine Lovelace, the dashing but debauched nobleman who had proved too attractive as the antihero in *Clarissa* (1748). Admittedly, Richardson allowed Grandison a knighthood and a country estate; but Grandison's merit as a forbearing Christian gentleman was contrasted favourably with the dissolute and thoughtless behaviour of his noble rivals. Variations on this teaching long remained popular with English novelists.[88] It allowed for undue aristocratic pride to be satirised, even while 'gentle' values were inculcated. 'Norman' names constituted a literary indicator of false and empty grandeur. Thus Trollope in the mid-nineteenth century savaged the de Courcys,[89] just as Jane Austen had earlier satirised Lady Catherine de Bourgh, whose proud nephew, Fitzwilliam Darcy, memorably found that his first proposal to Elizabeth Bennet, socially his inferior, was rejected as deficient in 'gentleman-like manner'.[90]

Part of the campaign to 'moralise' and civilise the social hierarchy included opposition to aristocratic duelling. Honour entailed not swagger and fighting, but courtesy and dignity. Again, that was a subject on which Sir Charles Grandison held strongly anti-militaristic views. A readiness to avenge imagined slights with bloodshed was far too impetuous and lawless to suit either Aristotelian moderation or Christian meekness. Many writers and preachers joined the attack on duelling. Sheridan (1775) satirised male braggadocio amusingly when his country bumpkin squire, Bob Acres, found his courage 'oozing out as it were' at the moment of crisis.[91] Of course, literary and clerical campaigning did not immediately transform the behaviour of the young bloods, but it put pro-duellists on the defensive. Hence the custom became gradually outlawed in fact as well as in law.[92]

One sign of that was the decline of sword-wearing, except on ceremonial occasions. The right to bear arms was a legacy of the military role of the medieval knights. Hence, in the early eighteenth century, wearing a sword was still the mark of a gentleman. But, once military necessity had well and truly waned, fashions were gradually adapted. By the 1780s the sword was fast disappearing from daily wear.[93] Richard 'Beau' Nash, the arbiter of manners in early eighteenth-century Bath, had been one of the first to discourage the awkward appendage. A century later, George 'Beau' Brummell, the next undisputed master of gentlemanly elegance, ventured outdoors with nothing more lethal than a cane or brown silk umbrella. Men of fashion followed this lead, taking their style not from princes but from the 'Beaux', both of whom were (from an aristocratic point of view) utter parvenus.[94]

All this indicates that the code of the 'gentleman' was not a straightforward celebration of either 'good blood', landownership, idleness or militarism. It was an urbane and cultivated ideal, that was becoming detached from any very precise social position. As a result, it could be invoked to satirise defaulters from all rungs of the hierarchy. Hence, while some mocked parvenu tradesmen, others mocked the boorish minor squires, who had status in their own locality but lacked city style and polish. William Pitt the Younger allegedly complained at the ignorance and obstinacy of the country gentlemen backbenchers, even while eulogising them in Parliament when he wanted to tax them.[95]

Fielding had already provided the literary prototype of the backwoodsman in Squire Western (1749). Sheridan's Bob Acres of Clod Hall (1775) was another. And George Colman provided a third in Sir Harry Beagle (1761), teased for his inelegant conversational cry of 'Yoicks' and for his habit of evaluating the human physique in terms more suitable for horseflesh.[96] These were the men devoted to 'hunting, shooting and fishing', who were satirised as lacking both brains and conversation. A writer in 1809, who believed that 'Education . . . makes us Gentlemen', lamented: 'How many of the Nobility are far from being truly *Gentlemen* in every respect.'[97] And in similar vein, a satirical poem of 1818 argued that landowners should talk of more elevated topics than turnips and manure, more intellectual matters than stables and food. Otherwise – shades of *The Anatomy of Melancholy* – they merely competed with their own menials:

> Is this a time for senators to vie
> With those who clean a horse, or make a pie?[98]

Meanwhile, the idealised concept was used not only to train the great but also to assimilate the social climber. The old debates about trade and gentility were no longer so heated, since many merchants had assumed the title of gentleman *de facto.* The Stock Exchange's famous motto 'my word is my bond' was a direct parallel with the gentlemanly code of honour. Snobbish jibes against tradesmen (rather than against the nation's commerce) still continued; but others rejected the prejudice. For example, *The Spectator* depicted in 1711 the sagacious merchant Sir Andrew Freeport in contrast with the old-fashioned backwoods squire Sir Roger de Coverley.[99] Daniel Defoe also strongly promoted the commercial interest, noting (1727) that many landed families were founded upon trade. Thus 'to say a Gentleman-tradesman is not so much nonsense, as some people would persuade us to reckon it.'[100] George Lillo – a jeweller turned dramatist – promptly had a great popular success with his play *George Barnwell* (1731), which featured a handsome young apprentice merchant. This gave a sympathetic rendering of commercial life and was apparently well liked in the City, even though Barnwell himself was led into crime and came to a sad end.[101]

Collectively, these writers argued against an undue reverence for ancient family. They did not advocate a cult of discovering plebeian or mercantile ancestors; but they helped to assuage the sensitivities of those who had them anyway. Edward Gibbon thus did 'not blush to descend' from a trading branch of the Kentish Gibbons, explaining that 'Our most respectable families have not disdained the counting-house, or even the shop'.[102] However, newcomers were expected to adopt the gentlemanly style. Gawky ex-shopkeepers, like Fanny Burney's Mr Dubster (1796) were satirised, to encourage them to acquire social polish;[103] and the ultra-rich India 'nabobs' and overseas merchants were satirised, to tone down their vulgar display of wealth. The selfish creed that '*Gold* is *God*' did not accord with 'pure Morals and true Virtue', as a satire of the nabobs declared in 1773.[104] Indeed, friction over the claims of 'new money' tended to heighten over time, because society's power structures were under continuing pressure to accommodate new business and industrial fortunes. There was a further poetic protest in 1818:

> All praise to Commerce and the swelling sail
> Yet may its influence too much prevail.[105]

Amongst such complexities, the gentlemanly ideal was pushed and pulled in rival directions by the overlapping claims of land, wealth and virtue.

For those who wished to honour personal merit, it became a testing social art to distinguish the man of honour from the fop or hypocrite. It was not enough to rely solely upon family background, although adventurers who could not name their parentage were at a disadvantage. The art instead required a careful process of discrimination and assessment. But as it was impossible to give each newcomer a thorough moral audit, the world often fell back upon externals, this time in the form of dress and, above all, manners. An urbane courtesy to all, without servility or fussy ceremoniousness, was the desideratum. Chesterfield's controversial *Letters ... to his Son,* which were published in 1774,[106] endeavoured to teach the gentlemanly style – with the famous if unheeded advice 'often be seen to smile, but never heard to laugh.' But his calculative good breeding risked degenerating into mere hypocrisy. There was continuing concern that externals might prove deceptive. Women were allegedly the most prone to be misled, but all were vulnerable to clever impostors. As a character in Shillito's drama about *The Man of Enterprise* (1789) commented: 'The world is grown to such a pass, that it requires some judgement to distinguish real gentility from the herd of its servile imitators.'[107]

Familiarity began to dilute respect in practice, even while the ideal remained undimmed. A letter in *The Connoisseur* (1755) joked about the multitude of self-styled gentry: all the 'women' had become 'ladies', and 'Every priggish fellow, who can clap a queue to his peruke and hang a sword awkwardly dangling by his side, thence assumes the importance as well as the name of a Gentleman.' Citizens, actors and authors used the title, the writer continued; and no doubt a search through garrets and cellars would find many more.[108] The *Laughing Philosopher* (1777) was similarly worried that society's heroes might prove fops or frauds: 'It is Virtue joined to the most refined Manners which constitutes the Gentleman. The young Men of this Age entirely mistake the character: they emptily think, that it consists in flutter, dress, and grimace, or riding a horse full gallop through the streets to pay morning visits. . . . [But] It is Honour, godlike Honour, that stamps alone the heavenly character.'[109] Encouraged by such arguments, the young Vicesimus Knox in 1778/9 ventured the radical thought that: 'There is many a nobleman, according to the genuine idea of nobility, at the loom, at the plough, and in the shop.'[110]

IV

Rival concepts of gentility carry with them major analytical implications for interpreting the economic history, the language and the culture of the gentleman. In the first place, the definitional complexities make it difficult to classify and to count the gentry – as it was for contemporaries. It is certainly very misleading for historians to assume that everyone styled as a 'gentleman' was *ipso facto* a landowner. That takes as an axiom what was really a matter for debate. Hence historians who classify all 'gentlemen' as 'landowners' merely build a systematic bias into their analysis, falsely inflating the category of 'landowners' by inserting many professional and commercial 'gentlemen' into their ranks. Such results give but a spurious confirmation to the mythology that England's ruling élite was always an agrarian one.

Equally, historians of urban society who doubt the bona fides of townsmen using the label of gentleman compound the same error. The term was used very freely by successful urban businessmen, office-holders and professionals, as well as by *rentiers*, living off private incomes without occupation. 'The word gentleman re-echoes from one end of the kingdom to the other', declared in 1824 an anguished traditionalist – the self-styled 'Chevalier' Lawrence – arguing that the armorial gentry should resume the name of nobility and stand on equal terms with their continental peers.[111] That might have helped historians but English practice had long decreed otherwise.

It follows that estimates of gentry numbers need to specify the definition employed. For example, in *c.* 1500 there were perhaps 500 knights, 800 esquires and 5,000 other gentlemen entitled to bear arms, making a 'lesser nobility' of 6,300 heads of household; but these were minimum figures as they excluded the non-armorial gentry.[112] Between 1500 and 1688, both the numbers and the percentage of England's cultivated land owned by the 'middle and lesser gentry' rose significantly from about 25 per cent (1436) to 45–50 per cent (1688), a huge shift achieved at the long-term expense, not of the great magnates, but of the crown and church.[113] Such data obviously referred to landownership; with non-landed assets, the position was yet stronger.

Gregory King's computations of English society in 1688 provided further estimates, valued for their scope rather than for their absolute accuracy. His best-known estimate gave 800 baronets, 600 knights, 3,000 esquires and 12,000 gentlemen, totalling 16,400 'gentry' heads of household. But he was thinking essentially of landowners, for in this version of his calculations he listed merchants, professions and office-holders under other headings.[114] Thus King's estimates were very cautious, in contrast to the many inflated figures in circulation. A debate in Parliament illustrated that. When discussing taxation in 1692, Paul Foley, a Herefordshire Whig, spoke of some 100,000 gentlemen, while Edward Seymour, a West Country Tory, doubled the figure to 200,000.[115] Both spoke vaguely and no doubt hyperbolically – Seymour certainly so. But a wider definition and less caution would certainly surpass King's total. Indeed, a modern historian notes that there were in 1702 'roughly' 32,000 county Commissioners for the Land Tax, few of whom were not gentlemen.[116]

Precise figures were never sought, still less obtained, by eighteenth-century governments. Contemporaries took the absence of official control or intervention as a matter of course. Only one man conducted heraldic visitations to check upon gentry coats of arms in the eighteenth century; and he turned out to be an impostor who was fined, pilloried and imprisoned in 1727 for levying money under false pretences.[117] Even without official records, however, some long-term trends are apparent. Thus it is known that, as a result of continuing restraint in granting knighthoods, the eighteenth-century gentry comprised more than ever a non-titled group of esquires and gentlemen commoners, as the number of knights and baronets did not keep pace with population growth but actually fell from 1,150 in 1700 to 859 in 1800.[118] This trend put 'gentility' still further beyond the control of kings and governments. Meanwhile, the eighteenth-century complaints about the extension of the unofficial title manifestly implied that the number of gentlemen of all sorts grew considerably; and that the non-landowners increased as a proportion among them.

In aggregate, it is therefore reasonable to conclude that the incomes of all those with plausible claims to gentility were becoming increasingly diversified and less restricted, to include non-agrarian as well as agrarian resources. The turnover of personnel was no doubt greatest among those with speculative businesses, but it was also found among landed families.[119] After 1690, the percentage of England's cultivated acreage owned by the 'gentry' grew slightly from a high figure of 45–50 per cent to about 55 per cent of the total in 1873.[120] That has been taken to imply a conservative case for a protracted social continuity between the seventeenth and nineteenth centuries. Yet the information by definition relates only to one form of property, and to one sort of gentleman. It also says nothing about the scale of turnover, as families moved into and out of landownership. Hence the appearance of landed continuity concealed a wider diversification.

Another speculative set of social estimates, by Patrick Colquhoun in 1814, confirmed the complexities.[121] He found that Great Britain and Ireland together had 46,861 household heads who were baronets, knights, country gentlemen, and 'others having large incomes'. These ranked below the titled aristocracy as a 'second class' (out of seven). It was a group substantially based upon land, but also including the wealthiest commoners. Next came a further 12,200 household heads, comprising senior state officials, leading clergymen, eminent lawyers and physicians, substantial merchants and manufacturers, and bankers of the first order. They formed the 'third class'. Both groups were likely to have been styled 'gentlemen', making a total of 59,061,[122] of whom 12,200 (20.66 per cent) were not designated as landowners or as very rich. These were also no more than minimum estimates, because a sizeable but unknown number of the large 'fourth class' – comprising middling professionals, merchants, manufacturers and men on moderate incomes – also claimed the coveted status. That suggests that by 1814 there were well over 60,000 'gentlemen' and that at very least 20 per cent of these were not primarily landowners. In practice moreover, in a larger total, the non-landed urban percentage must have been much higher than that. Nineteenth-century directories indeed listed numerous town residents explicitly under the collective name of 'gentry'; and those urban residents were certainly not landowners, since many of them were additionally recorded under the 'trades and professions'.[123]

If these socio-economic boundaries lacked precision – and Colquhoun did not suggest that his seven-class model was used by his contemporaries – the language of social description equally lacked clarity.[124] The rival definitions of 'gentility' contributed to the ambiguities. That raises a second set of implications for historians. The differing interpretations show that there is not an invariate one-to-one correlation between key words and the social structures to which they allude: some concepts are at once powerful but imprecise in usage. There are many examples of such malleability in the language of social description. Thus the 'gentleman' was, like the Church of England, latitudinarian in practice, even if numerous exasperated devotees wished otherwise. That does not make the concept of gentility any less 'real' or less culturally important. Indeed, it was the social flexibility of usage around a constant moral ideal that launched the gentleman on his long career. But this complexity highlights the need for historians to interpret past linguistic evidence with care. In these matters, a learned quotation of one contemporary dictum does not suffice to delineate a social structure, and still less does it suffice to prove or disprove a social trend.

Indeed, the 'English gentleman' was already by the eighteenth century almost too popular. He figured in plays, poems, novels, magazines: the successful monthly periodical was entitled *The Gentleman's Magazine* (1731–1907). There were tracts by him[125] and about his interests, from accountancy to bawdy-ballads.[126] The breadth of the term was notable: in eighteenth-century legal testimony, it was not unusual for witnesses to refer to a man who 'looked like a gentleman' or 'behaved like a gentleman', without imputing any very great social elevation to him.[127] Yet the high-ranking Prince Regent, Beau Brummell's 'fat friend', was lauded not as the supreme aristocrat but as the 'first gentleman of Europe'.

Moreover, in the nineteenth century, a 'gentleman' was the legal designation for a person living off private income without an occupation. At the same time courtiers were 'gentlemen-in-waiting'; Members of Parliament were 'Honourable Gentlemen'; jurors were 'gentlemen of the jury'; soldiers were 'gentlemen in red'; highwaymen were 'gentleman of the road'; priates were 'gentlemen of fortune'; doubly genteel valets were 'gentlemen's gentlemen' (1725); commercial salesmen were 'gentlemen travellers' (1822); and the Devil himself had long been the 'old gentleman' or 'the gentleman in black'. After all that, it seems otiose to record that a stranger could also be referred to as 'a fine gentleman'. It was 'a term of complaisance', which could be used ironically. Dr Johnson included that in 1755 as one of the five central meanings of the word.[128] A less magisterial dictionary (1721) had already expressed its alarm at the number of upstart 'gentlemen', warning sternly that '*you cannot make a silken Purse out of a Sow's Ear.*'[129]

Ultimately, the vocabulary itself began to diversify under the strain of multiple meanings. Originally, 'gentry' was the collective noun for many gentlemen. But the two terms began imperceptibly to diverge. By the later eighteenth century, the predominant emphasis within the term 'gentry' was shifting up the social scale, although it was still used in the Victorian era to refer colloquially to any group of men.[130] One famous tome helped to consolidate the high status of the collective noun. That was the regular publication from 1846 onwards of Burke's *Dictionary of the Landed Gentry*,[131] which singled out the landowning variety and strengthened the mental associations between gentry and landownership. But the meaning of 'genteel' travelled in the other direction. Initially, it was a laudatory term, as the adjectival reference for good gentlemanly behaviour. By the early nineteenth century, however, it was increasingly used to sneer at people of modest social origins, who were trying too hard to ape good manners in order not to be 'common'.[132] Their anxious parade of status was held to lack the inner ease and outward *savoir faire* of true gentility.

'Gentleman', meanwhile, did not follow either of these routes to specialisation. Instead, the concept became extended, retaining its respectability but shedding coherence and prestige as it did so.[133] Tennyson in 1850 thought the 'grand old name of gentleman' was by then 'defamed' and 'soiled'.[134] Later, when 657 prostitutes in 1890 reported that they had been first seduced by a 'gentleman', they meant clerks, commercial travellers, shop assistants, and men dressed more smartly than ordinary workmen.[135] The diffusion of the term was thus a linguistic index to wider social changes. That was what de Tocqueville (himself a nobleman spouse of an English middle-class wife) meant when he wrote in 1856: 'Its history is the history of democracy itself.'[136] Indeed, modern societies retain a diluted but universal version of the gentlemanly address. All men, irrespective of rank, are now styled 'Mr.', may be written to as 'Esq.', and colloquially hailed as 'Squire'. As a result, Mervyn Bunter's comment in 1937 that 'Gentleman ... is what I should designate as an elastic term' was by then a masterly understatement.[137]

Thirdly and finally, these rival conceptions have significance for debates about gentlemanly culture. Too often it is assumed that the gentleman stood proxy for the values of a traditionalist aristocracy. He is taken to be the heir to feudal values, landed, glorying in his estates, contemptuous of business routines, proud of his hereditary rights, hostile to wealth creation, uninterested in city life, and devoted to ornamental idleness and sports.[138] Indeed, the challenge cricket matches between 11 amateur 'Gentlemen' and 11 paid 'Players' – played intermittently between 1806 and 1829 and then regularly until 1962 – are often taken to symbolise an endemic anti-commercialism among England's élite.[139] No doubt, some landowners had all those characteristics, and a greater number had some of them. However, recent research has emphasised aristocratic enterprise rather than torpor;[140] and it is far from proven that such a 'package' of views typified a major of landowners, let alone of England's multifarious gentlemen. Certainly, these individuals did not halt the long centuries of economic and imperial expansion before 1914.

Instead, the definition of gentility remained disputed.[141] There were shifts in emphasis, from the fourteenth-century knight of chivalry to the eighteenth-century man of manners to the Victorian product of a good public school. Yet such latitudinarianism served not to embalm a caste but to blur divisions among England's élite, divisions that might otherwise have been more rigid: between titled and untitled society; between business and land; between professionals and non-professionals; between town and country; and between the upper class and bourgeoisie. It signified not stasis but flexibility. For example, one tract in 1720 addressed itself to 'Gentlemen of All Ranks and Orders'. Yet Beckford in 1761 named the country gentlemen as part of the 'Middling People of England',[142] while the Burkes in 1846 saw the landed gentry as the lower tier of the aristocracy.[143] All these variants indicated the opacity of class definitions, which continues to puzzle historians.[144] While formal titles were highly restricted, informal honours were unregulated. That was especially characteristic of the Anglo-American tradition where the diversities of custom and practice rather than the formalities of legal privilege held sway.[145] Other nations had their own complexities; but visitors to England remarked upon the hybrid English gentlemen.[146]

Viewed from outside, the ideal had limitations. It came to be depicted as lacksadaisical, snobbish, effete. Its ethos was not necessarily anti-wealth or anti-work (other than hard physical labour) but it could be so represented, as it sought to civilise rather than to celebrate production. Ultimately, in a mass society, the gentleman could not stretch to accommodate all citizens. The ideal was partly appropriated by other interests such as the professions,[147] partly ignored. Yet it was rarely attacked directly. Denunciations of inherited titles or wealth did not obliterate the merits of personal honour. Even Laski's sharp modern polemic on *The Danger of Being a Gentleman* (1939) ended with nostalgic regrets for a code of probity and service.[148]

Who was then the gentleman? In practise, he was eclectic. His numbers were legion, although not infinite. In principle, his word was his bond; while, culturally, he strove to blend and civilise the rival claims of the landowner, the businessman, the courtier, the man of letters, the army officer, the respectable leaders of the 'middling' citizenry, even the Prince Regent, and the secular saint.

Notes

The author wishes to thank Tony Belton, Peter Clark, Tony Claydon, Chris Evans, Edmund Green, Tony Henderson, David Reader, Paul Slack, Amanda Vickery, as well as colleagues at numerous research seminars, and the editors for discussion and references. An early version of this paper, presented at the Conference for Michael Thompson, began with a tribute to him as benevolent Head of the History Department at Bedford College (as it then was) 1968–77 and then as the admirable 'first gentleman' of the Institute of Historical Research 1977–90.

1 From John Ball's radical sermon (1381), itself an adaptation of an old religious ballad: R. Hilton, *Bond men made free: medieval peasant movements and the English*

Rising of 1381 (New York, 1973), pp. 211–12, 222; and J. E. Mason, *Gentlefolk in the making: studies in the history of English courtesy literature ... from 1531–1774* (Philadelphia, 1935), pp. 7, 303–4.

2 W. Blades (ed.), *The Boke of St Albans by Dame Juliana Berners* (facsimile edn, London, 1881), *sub* 'How gentlemen shall be known from churls'. In this version, gentlemen were descended from Noah's son Japheth and 'churls' from Japheth's brother Ham, whose son Canaan was cursed by Noah to be a 'servant of servants': *Holy Bible*, Genesis: X, 25. An alternative made Abel the first gentleman, Cain the first churl.

3 J. Ferne, *The blazon of gentrie* (London, 1586), pp. 97–8. Ferne, knighted in 1604, was a small landowner, common lawyer and minor office-holder under the crown. His study became a standard authority: L.C. Stevenson, *Praise and paradox: merchants and craftsmen in Elizabethan popular literature* (Cambridge, 1984), p. 87, n. 28.

4 T. Dekker, *The Honest Whore*, pt. I (London, 1604), p. 78.

5 Anon., *The laughing philosopher*, also cited as *Momus: or the laughing philosopher* (Dublin, 1777), pp. 80–1.

6 Shakespeare's father had applied in 1596 for a grant of arms but did not pursue the claim, whereas in 1599 Shakespeare himself did so successfully, his arms being subsequently displayed on his tomb at Stratford: *Dictionary of national biography.*

7 J. Selden, *Table talk* (London, 1659), p. 21.

8 D. Defoe, *The compleat English gentleman*, ed. K. D. Bülbring (London, 1890), p. 12.

9 F. N. Robinson (ed.), *The works of Geoffrey Chaucer* (London, 1957), p. 953.

10 See R. Kelso, *The doctrine of the English gentleman in the sixteenth century* (Urbana, I11., 1929), esp. pp. 70–110.

11 G. Chaucer, *The Canterbury Tales*, Prologue, l. 72, in Robinson, *Works of Chaucer*, p. 18.

12 See C. Wright Mills, *Elites and society* (Penguin, 1966), pp. 7–23, 145–8; G. L. Field and J. Higley, *Elitism* (London, 1980), pp. 18–47, 117–30.

13 See variously G. R. Sitwell, 'The English gentleman', *The Ancestor*, I (1902), pp. 58–88; N. E. Saul, *Knights and esquires: the Gloucestershire gentry in the fourteenth century* (Oxford, 1981), pp. 6–29, esp. 26–9; and D. A. L. Morgan, 'The individual style of the English gentleman', in M. Jones (ed.), *Gentry and lesser nobility in late medieval Europe* (Gloucester, 1986), esp. pp. 16–19. For gentry wealth *vis-à-vis* the fifteenth-century baronage, see also S. Payling, *Political society in Lancastrian England: the greater gentry of Nottinghamshire* (Oxford, 1991), pp. 1–3.

14 It has been estimated that a gentleman in 1640 might have an average annual income of under £100, whereas a baronet had £1,000–£1,500. By 1815, the respective figures were £600 and £4,000, with many regional variations: G. E. Mingay, *The gentry: the rise and fall of a ruling class* (London, 1976), pp. 11–13.

15 D. M. Palliser, *The age of Elizabeth: England under the later Tudors, 1547–1603* (London, 1983), pp. 68–71. For an excellent discussion of evolving concepts, see K. Wrightson, 'Estates, degrees, and sorts: changing perceptions of society in Tudor and Stuart England', in P. J. Corfield (ed.), *Language, history and class* (Oxford, 1991), pp. 30–52, including pp. 37–40 for the complexity of the 'gentleman'.

16 For a determined reference to the major and minor nobility, see, e.g., J. Brydall, *Ius imaginis apud Anglos: the law of England relating to the nobility and gentry* (London, 1675), p. 38. By the nineteenth century, the resurrection of the 'minor nobility' was a nostalgic campaign of a few traditionalists [see n. 111 below].

17 J. Chamberlayne (ed.), *Angliae Notitia: or the present state of England* (21st edn; London, 1704), pt. III, p. 298.

18 A 'lady' originally partnered a 'lord' but by the 1600s the term was also adopted, in lieu of the cumbersome 'gentlewoman', for the partner of the 'gentleman'. The *Oxford English Dictionary* [subsequently *OED*] (*sub*: lady, 4) notes that 'lady' retains a residual social superiority over the gentleman, adding 'Hence, and not directly as the result of the sentiment of gallantry, the customary order of words in "Ladies and Gentlemen".'

19 T. Deloney, *The Gentle Craft*, pt. I (London, 1597; in 1637 edn), p. 44 [pagination added].
20 R. L. Storey, 'Gentlemen-bureaucrats', in C. H. Clough (ed.), *Profession, vocation and culture in later medieval England* (Liverpool, 1982), p. 95.
21 An alternative was 'gentlemen of the shade', quoting from Shakespeare's *Henry IV Part 1*, Act 1, Scene 2.
22 Historians have yet to devise a satisfactory way of measuring the scale and pattern of movement into and out of landed society. In 1941, R. H. Tawney proposed the counting of manors to gauge the respective landholdings of the peerage and landed gentry: R. H. Tawney, 'The rise of the gentry, 1540–1640', *Economic History Review*, vol. XI (1941), pp. 1–38. But the manor as a unit of accountancy was successfully disparaged by J. P. Cooper, 'The counting of manors'. *Economic History Review*, 2nd ser., vol. VIII (1956), pp. 377–89, repr. in Cooper, *Land, men and beliefs*, ed. G. E. Aylmer and J. S. Morrill (London, 1983), 17–42; and J. H. Hexter, 'Storm over the gentry', in Hexter, *Reappraisals in history* (London, 1961), pp. 124–9. For the extent of social fluidity, see also L. Stone, 'Social mobility in England, 1500–1700', *Past and Present*, no. 33 (1966), pp. 18–19. It must not be assumed, however, that success was measured only by landholding; nor that the social movement was only from town into countryside.
23 The College was empowered to accept persons ('not vile born') owning at least £10 a year in land or £300 in moveable goods – both relatively low totals by the standards of seventeenth-century landowning wealth [see n. 14 above]. Between 1560 and 1640, the College granted the right to bear arms to nearly 4,000 applicants (including William Shakespeare): see Mingay, *The gentry*, p. 5; and L. Stone, 'The inflation of honours, 1558–1641', *Past and Present*, no. 14 (1958), p. 47.
24 See G. D. Squibb, *The High Court of Chivalry: a study of the civil law in England* (Oxford, 1959); G. D. Squibb, *The law of arms in England* (Wilts., 1953), pp. 1–14; and P. H. Hardacre, 'The Earl Marshal, the Heralds, and the House of Commons, 1604–41', *International Review of Social History*, vol. 2 (1957), pp. 106–25. Interestingly, parliamentary opposition to the Court of Chivalry in 1640 was led by the young Edward Hyde, later leader of a moderate royalism: E. Hyde, *The life of Edward Earl of Clarendon, written by himself* (Oxford, 1857 edn), vol. 1, pp. 67–8.
25 See 'X' [A. C. Fox-Davies], *The right to bear arms* (London, 1900), and overview in Sitwell, 'English Gentleman', pp. 77–88.
26 For a fascinating account of one of the last heraldic tours, in which the young Gregory King studied heraldry and social investigation, see P. Styles, 'The Heralds' visitation of Warwickshire, 1682–3', *Transactions and Proceedings of the Birmingham Archaeological Society*, vol. 71 (1953), pp. 96–134.
27 M. Noble, *A history of the College of Arms, and the lives of all the Kings, Heralds, and Pursuivants from the reign of Richard III . . . until the present time* (London, 1804), pp. 315–16.
28 Squibb, *High Court of Chivalry*, pp. 68–72, 86–9, 92–3, 105, 117. Since the Court was dormant not abolished, it was (briefly) revived in May 1954 to adjudicate between Manchester Corporation and the Manchester Palace of Varieties Ltd: *ibid.*, pp. 123–7.
29 T. Smith, *De republica Anglorum* (1583), ed. M. Dewar (Cambridge, 1982), pp. 71–2. For the complicated authorship, see M. Dewar, 'A question of plagiarism: the "Harrison chapters" in Sir Thomas Smith's *De republica Anglorum*', *Historical Journal*, vol. 22 (1979), pp. 921–9.
30 Mingay, *The gentry*, pp. 17, 53. The Tudors were sparing with titles. Elizabeth I was annoyed when the Earl of Essex knighted 81 men in Ireland in 1599. James I was more prodigal, creating the new hereditary title of baronet in 1611; but the later Stuarts returned to the policy of circumspection: *ibid.*, pp. 4–5; Stone, 'Inflation of honours', pp. 49, 50–1, 52–4, 59–62.
31 As critics often note, historians find it difficult to write about the aristocracy and the gentry without substantial overlap, because the cadet branches of titled families were, under English law, gentle and not noble; and because titled noblemen

were also courtesy 'gentlemen'. See Mingay, *The gentry*, pp. 1–17; J. V. Beckett, *The aristocracy in England, 1660–1914* (Oxford, 1986), pp. 16–42; and D. Cannadine, *The decline and fall of the British aristocracy* (New Haven, 1990), pp. 8–15.

32 Often attribued to James I, the saying became a commonplace. Thus Edmund Burke reported it with the introduction 'Somebody has said . . .': R. B. McDowell (ed.), *The correspondence of Edmund Burke, vol.* VIII: *Sept. 1794–April 1796* (Cambridge and Chicago, 1969), p. 130: Burke to William Smith, 29 January 1795. John Selden's version of this was: 'The King cannot make a Gentleman of Blood . . . nor God Almighty, but he can make a Gentleman by Creation': Selden, *Table talk*, p. 21.

33 That was pointed out by Smith, *De republica*, p. 72.

34 Storey, 'Gentlemen–bureaucrats', pp. 90–7.

35 Ferne, *Blazon of gentrie*, pp. 33–60, 72–3.

36 *OED* defines a common meaning of 'charge' (no. 12) as task, duty, responsibility, trust, which is probably the sense intended here. But possibly it invokes a rarer usage of 'charge' (no. 6), meaning a heraldic device upon an escutcheon; but the context suggests a reference to duty rather than to heraldry.

37 Ferne, *Blazon of gentrie*, pp. 68–9.

38 See variously Stevenson, *Praise and paradox*, pp. 83–7; Kelso, *Doctrine of the English gentleman*, pp. 60–7; J. P. Cooper, 'Ideas of gentility in early modern England', in Cooper, *Land, men and beliefs*, pp. 46–77; and L. Manley, *Literature and culture in early modern London* (Cambridge, 1995).

39 Stevenson, *Praise and paradox*, pp. 183–5, 202–4, 209, 211: citing popular works by Rowley, Dekker, and Deloney. However, the cult quickly ran thin, being parodied, e.g. by Beaumont and Fletcher's play, *The Knight of the Burning Pestle* (1611): *ibid.*, pp. 209–10.

40 *Dictionary of national biography* [subsequently *DNB*], *sub*: Hicks, Baptist, (1551–1629), later 1st Viscount Campden and ancestor of the Earls of Gainsborough. His promotion owed much to the eminence of his brother, Sir Michael Hicks, chief secretary to Lord Burghley.

41 F. Burney, *Camilla: or a picture of youth* (1796), eds. E. A. and L. D. Bloom (Oxford, 1983), p. 431.

42 [E. Bolton], *The Cities Advocate, in this case or question of honor and armes: whether apprenticeship extinguisheth gentry? containing a clear refutation of the pernicious common errour affirming it, swallowed by Erasmus of Rotterdam, Sir Thomas Smith in his Common-Weale, Sir John Ferne in his Blazon, Ralph Broke, York Herald, and Others* (London, 1629), pp. 13–14.

43 Re-entitled [E. Bolton], *The Cities Great Concern* (London, 1674).

44 Squibb, *High Court of Chivalry*, pp. 176–7.

45 This crucial point is also stressed by Morgan, 'Individual style of the English gentleman', pp. 21–6. With reference to Tudor and Stuart England, there is scope for fresh research to discover who actually styled themselves 'gentlemen' – without assuming that all who did so were automatically landowners. Studies have tended hitherto to focus upon rural society, but there are some references to expansion in the numbers of 'urban gentry'. For changes in south Wales, contrast: H. Lloyd, *The gentry of south-west Wales, 1540–1640* (Cardiff, 1968), pp. 15–21, 205–12; and P. Jenkins, *The making of a ruling class: the Glamorgan gentry, 1640–1790* (Cambridge, 1983), pp. 20–42.

46 J. H. Grant, 'The gentry of London in the reign of Charles I', *University of Birmingham Historical Journal*, vol. 8 (1962), pp. 197–202: returns for City of London and adjacent parishes. Of these 1,172 gentlemen, 309 were sons of Londoners, 863 sons of non-Londoners; and of that latter group, 785 (91 per cent) were sons of country gentlemen: *ibid.*, p. 199.

47 'Democritus Junior' [R. Burton], *The anatomy of melancholy* (1621; Oxford, 1652), pt. 1, sect. 2, memb. 2, subsect. 2.

48 Styles, 'Heralds' visitation of Warwickshire', p. 117.

49 Squibb, *High Court of Chivalry*, pp. 92–3.

50 See N. B. Harte, 'State control of dress and social change in pre-industrial England', in D. C. Coleman and A. H. John (eds), *Trade, government and economy in pre-industrial England* (London, 1976), pp. 148–51; and P. B. Munsche, *Gentlemen and poachers: the English game laws, 1671–1831* (Cambridge, 1981), pp. 12–13.
51 Brydall, *Ius imaginis*, pp. 57–8. For other Restoration surveys, see, e.g., R. Allestree, *The gentleman's calling* (London, 1660); E. Waterhouse, *The gentleman's monitor; or, a sober inspection into the ... rise and decay of families* (London, 1665); and Anon. [W. R. Ramesey], *The gentleman's companion: or a character of true nobility and gentility ... by a person of quality* (London, 1672).
52 E. Chamberlayne (ed.), *Angliae notitia: or, the present state of England* (London, 1669; in 5th edn, 1671), pt. 1, pp. 311, 313.
53 *Ibid.* (20th edn, London, 1702), p. 301: the assertion was then repeated annually. In 1704, Chamberlayne's son, John, inherited and from 1708 published the guide as *Magnae Britanniae notitia: or, the present state of Great-Britain* (London, 1708–55).
54 G. Miège, *The new state of England* (London, 1691), pt. II, pp. 226, 230.
55 M. Misson, *Memoirs and observations in his travels over England*, transl. J. Ozell (London, 1719), p. 200.
56 'Country' and 'landed gentleman' were so termed from at least 1647: see *OED*, *sub* 'landed'. For 'city gentry' and 'country gentry', see Waterhouse, *Gentleman's monitor*, p. 71; and G. Jacob, *The country gentleman's vade mecum* (London, 1717).
57 A. Everitt, 'Social mobility in early modern England', *Past and Present*, no. 33 (1966), p. 70.
58 See *Statutes at large*, 9 Anne cap. 5 (1710/11). Legislation along these lines was first mooted in 1696 but was several times defeated in the Lords: see E. and A. G. Porritt, *The unreformed House of Commons: parliamentary representation before 1832* (Cambridge, 1903), vol. I, pp. 166–70.
59 For fictitious qualifications available to men of wealth both before and after an amending Act of 1760, see *ibid.*, vol. I, pp. 170–8. Very few candidates were excluded under this legislation, which was replaced by a general property qualification in 1838.
60 G. P. Jubb, *Members of Parliament, 1734–1832* (New Haven, 1955; reprinted 1972), pp. 54–73.
61 W. Blackstone, *Commentaries on the laws of England* (Oxford, 1765–9), vol. 1, p. 7: the independent gentlemen for him were 'the most useful as well as considerable body of men in the nation.'
62 'Trade/commerce' was gradually enlarged into 'trading/commerical empire'. See, e.g., Miège, *New state of England*, pt. II, p. 229, for England as 'one of the most trading Countries in Europe' (1691); R. W. Chapman (ed.), *Boswell: life of Johnson* (Oxford, 1976), p. 347, for Boswell on 'this great commercial country' (1765); and J. Hanway, *The defects of police the cause of immorality* (London, 1775), p. 247, for the '*British commercial* empire'.
63 See Mason, *Gentlefolk in the making*; G. C. Brauer, *The education of a gentleman: theories of gentlemanly education in England, 1660–1775* (New York, 1959); and, from a large contemporary literature, two popular exemplars: J. Gailhard, *The compleat gentleman: or, directions for the education of youth* (London, 1678); and W. Darrell, *A gentleman instructed in the conduct of a virtuous and happy life* (London, 1704).
64 D. Defoe, *The fortunes and misfortunes of the famous Moll Flanders* (1722), ed. D. Blewett (London, 1989), p. 104.
65 In eighteenth-century records – such as poll books, directories, legal transcripts and parish registers – a suffix or prefix to the personal name was taken to indicate some degree of social status in contrast to the masses, who were still termed only by first name and surname. For the Norwich attorneys, see P. J. Corfield, *Power and the professions in Britain, 1700–1850* (London, 1995), p. 80.
66 Directories Database: for further information, contact the author at Royal Holloway.
67 Westminster Historical Database, 1784–1820: for further information, contact the author at Royal Holloway. I am grateful to Edmund Green for access to the

Westminster Database and for drawing the voting saga of Samuel Collins to my attention.

68 For heraldic acceptance of the gentility of the professions and of other learned men, including poets and historiographers, see R. Holme, *The academy of armory* (Chester, 1688), bk. III, p. 67.

69 R. Robson, *The attorney in eighteenth-century England* (Cambridge, 1959), p. 20.

70 Again, there is scope for much more work on the relationship between urban and landed society in eighteenth-century England, particularly from the urban end, which has been relatively under-researched. But see R. G. Wilson, *Gentlemen merchants: the merchant community in Leeds, 1700–1830* (Manchester, 1971); N. Rogers, 'Money, land and lineage: the big bourgeoisie of Hanoverian London', *Social History*, vol. 4 (1979), pp. 437–54; debate between D. T. Andrew and N. Rogers, *Social History*, vol. 6 (1981), pp. 359–69; and H. Horvitz, '"The mess of the middle class" revisited: the case of the "big bourgeoisie" of Augustan London', *Continuity and change*, vol. 2 (1987), pp. 263–96.

71 J. Brown, *An estimate of the manners and principles of the times* (London, 1757 edn), pp. 44–5, 67. This work ran to many editions and prompted heated debate. See also M. Akenside's 'Ode XI: to the country gentlemen of England' (1758) in Akenside, *The poems of Mark Akenside, M.D.* (London, 1772), p. 326: commencing 'Whither is Europe's ancient spirit fled?'

72 Bertrand Russell (1971) as quoted by W. L. Arnstein, 'The survival of the Victorian aristocracy', in F. C. Jaher (ed.), *The rich, the well-born and the powerful: élites and upper classes in history* (Urbana, Ill., 1973), p. 236.

73 This argument has been applied to modern England, as in M. J. Wiener's much-disputed *English culture and the decline of the industrial spirit, 1850–1980* (Cambridge, 1981) and evoked, in a somewhat different guise, by P. J. Cain and A. G. Hopkins, *British imperialism: innovation and expansion, 1688–1914* (Cambridge, 1993), esp. pp. 22–37; and Cain and Hopkins, *British imperialism: crisis and deconstruction, 1914–90* (Cambridge, 1993). For an overview, see also M. J. Daunton, 'Gentlemanly capitalism and British industry, 1820–1914', *Past and Present*, no. 122 (1989), pp. 119–58.

74 Ferne, *Blazon of gentrie*, p. 23.

75 [Ramesey], *Gentleman's companion*, p. 4. This work also pioneered a call for women's equal rights to education: *ibid.*, pp. 9–13.

76 R. Steele in 'I. Bickerstaff' (ed.), *The Tatler*, no. 207, 5 August 1710. For Sealand's speech praising merchants as an honourable and useful 'Species of Gentry', see also R. Steele, *The Conscious Lovers* (1722), in S. S. Kenny (ed.), *The plays of Richard Steele* (Oxford, 1971), p. 359.

77 Anon., *Laughing philosopher*, p. 79.

78 'Adam Fitz-Adam' in *The World*, no. 114, 6 March 1755.

79 R. Steele in *The Guardian*, no. 137, 18 August 1713.

80 J. Gay, 'Fable VIII: The man, the cat, the dog, and the fly' (1738), in V. A. Dearing (ed.), *John Gay: poetry and prose* (Oxford, 1974), vol. 2, pp. 409–10: finally, the man swats the fly as a 'spunger on the public'.

81 A. Pope, *Essay on man* (1733/4), Epistle IV, II, lines 203–4, 215–16, in J. Butt (ed.), *The poems of Alexander Pope* (London, 1975 edn.), p. 542. A reference to this quotation is found in A. Trollope's *Doctor Thorne* (1858; in Oxford, 1980 edn), p. 395.

82 E. Burke, *Reflections on the Revolution in France* (1790), ed. C. C. O'Brien (Harmondsworth, 1979 edn), p. 182.

83 'Crito' of Lincoln's Inn, in H. Stonecastle (ed.), *The Universal Spectator: or weekly journal* (London, 1735–6), 4 January 1735; an abbreviated version was promptly reprinted in *The Gentleman's Magazine*, vol. 5 (January 1735), p. 9.

84 Anon., *An epistle to a young nobleman from his praeceptor* (London, 1736), p. 4.

85 For vivid documentation of this argument, see P. Langford, *Public life and propertied Englishmen, 1689–1796* (Oxford, 1991), pp. 510–81, esp. pp. 569–81. Langford shows that a sober 'new-model' aristocracy of service was cultivated by the later eighteenth century, but understates the extent of the earlier campaigns from the

efforts of Addison and Steele onwards. See e.g., G. J. Barker-Benfield, *The culture of sensibility: sex and society in eighteenth-century Britain* (Chicago, 1992), pp. 37–104.

86 The stress upon learning, including a classical education from a 'good' school, was notable by the later nineteenth century; but the importance of schooling was argued earlier. See e.g., a children's tract by J. Carey, *Learning better than house and land, as exemplified in the history of Harry Johnson and Dick Hobson* (London, 1808; 1813): Harry Johnson, a landowner's son, refused to study and after many vicissitudes became a barber in the United States ('What a fall for poor Harry': p. 125). Dick, the son of a cow-herd on the Johnson estate, was an apt scholar and eventually became a rich merchant and US Congressman. Dick was then shaved by Harry but did not recognise him in his poverty. The moral was clear (p. 140): 'Whene'er a dislike to your learning you harbour,/ Remember the fate of the gentleman barber.'

87 Richard Steele in *The Guardian*, no. 34, 20 April 1713.

88 See variously H. J. Shroff, *The eighteenth-century novel: the idea of the gentleman* (New Delhi, 1978); M. Shinagel, *Daniel Defoe and middle-class gentility* (Cambridge, Mass., 1968); R. Gilmour, *The idea of the gentleman in the Victorian novel* (London, 1981); S. Letwin, *The gentleman in Trollope: individuality and moral conduct* (London, 1982), esp. pp. 3–21; and N. McKendrick, '"Gentlemen and Players" revisited: the gentlemanly ideal, the business ideal and the professional ideal in English literary culture', in N. McKendrick and B. Outhwaite (eds), *Business life and public policy* (Cambridge, 1986), esp. pp. 98–118.

89 Earl De Courcy and his family were pilloried, e.g. in A. Trollope, *Doctor Thorne* (1858) and *The small house at Allington* (1864).

90 J. Austen, *Pride and prejudice: a novel* (London, 1813), vol. 2, p. 132.

91 R. B. Sheridan, *The Rivals* (1775), ed. E. Duthie (London, 1979), p. 112.

92 For the fluctuating decline in duelling, see V. G. Kiernan, *The duel in European history: honour and the reign of aristocracy* (Oxford, 1988), esp. pp. 185–222; and F. Billacois, *The duel: its rise and fall in early modern France*, ed. T. Selous (New Haven, Conn., 1990). For gentry opinion turning against duelling in later eighteenth-century Wales, see also Jenkins, *Making of a ruling class*, pp. 212–13.

93 A. Buck, *Dress in eighteenth-century England* (London, 1979), pp. 55, 58, 88; C. W. and P. Cunnington, *Handbook of English costume in the eighteenth century* (London, 1957), pp. 100–2, 263.

94 Nash was the son of a minor Welsh gentleman, who was a partner in a Swansea glass-manufactory: see *DNB, sub* 'Nash'. Brummell was the son of a middle-ranking civil servant and protege of Lord North, although Brummell himself implied that he had come from 'nowhere': W. Jesse, *The life of George Brummell, Esq., commonly called Beau Brummell* (London, 1844), vol. 1, pp. 17–30. For Brummell's umbrella, see *ibid.*, vol. 1, pp. 80–1.

95 Anecdote from one Colonel Dillion, as reported in *ibid.*, vol. 1, p. 73.

96 See H. Fielding, *The history of Tom Jones: a foundling* (London, 1749); Sheridan, *The Rivals*; and G. Colman, *The Jealous Wife* (1761) in E. R. Wood (ed.), *Plays by David Garrick and George Colman the Elder* (Cambridge, 1982), e.g., pp. 65–9.

97 S. Pegge, *Anonymiana: or, ten centuries of observations on various authors and subjects* (London, 1809), p. 446.

98 Anon., *The Gentleman: a satire* (London, 1818), p. 5. The comparison with cooks was made earlier in S. Jenyns's satire of *The modern fine gentleman* (London, 1746), p. 3: where this hero was quizzed as 'Half Atheist, Papist, Gamester, Bubble, Rook,/ Half Fiddler, Coachman, Dancer, Groom, and Cook.'

99 *The Spectator*, no. 2, 2 March 1710/11.

100 D. Defoe, *The complete English tradesman, in familiar letters* (London, 1726/7), vol. 1, pp. 368–87, esp. p. 380. He also quoted approvingly a quip, attributed to Charles II, '*That the Tradesmen were the only Gentry in England*': *ibid.*, vol. 1, p. 369. In his final years, Defoe also worked on *The compleat English gentleman*, published posthumously in 1890 [see n. 8 above] but he did not manage to reconcile happily the two sections on the 'Gentleman BORN' and the 'Gentleman BRED'.

101 G. Lillo, *The London merchant: or the history of George Barnwell* (London, 1731); this ran into many editions and was also translated into French (1751), German (1772) and Dutch (1775). For its reception in London, see also *DNB, sub* 'Lillo'.

102 J. B. Bury (ed.), *Autobiography of Edward Gibbon: as originally edited by Lord Sheffield* (Oxford, 1959 reprint), p. 6.

103 Mr. Dubster is first depicted at an Assembly, standing awkwardly 'with the air of a poker': Burney, *Camilla*, p. 69.

104 Anon., *The Nabob: or, Asiatic plunderers – a satyrical poem* (London, 1773), p. 41. But a rival poem defended the East India nabobs from accusations of corruption: see Anon., *The saddle put on the right horse: or, an enquiry into the reason why certain persons have been denominated nabobs – with an arrangement of those gentlemen into their proper classes of real, spurious, reputed, or mushroom nabobs* (London, 1783).

105 Anon., *The gentleman*, p. 15. For the growing intensity of attacks upon businessmen in the later eighteenth century, see J. McVeagh, *Tradefull merchants: the portrayal of the capitalist in literature* (London, 1981), pp. 83–100; and J. R. Raven, 'English popular literature and the image of business, 1760–90' (unpublished University of Cambridge Ph.D. thesis, 1985).

106 P. D. Stanhope, 4th Earl of Chesterfield, *Letters . . . to his son* (Dublin, 1774), vol. 1, p. 268 and *passim*. This work was much reprinted and satirised, e.g., in the amusing Anon., *Chesterfield travestie: or, school for modern manners* (London, 1808).

107 C. Shillito, *The man of enterprise: a farce* (Colchester, 1789), p. 11. This was not a new complaint: e.g., it was Steele's fear that women were led astray by dress and imposing manners that led to his depiction of the 'Fine Gentleman' in 1713 [see n. 87 above]; and the theme recurs in plays and novels of the era.

108 Letter from 'unknown correspondent' to *The connoisseur: by Mr. Town, critic and censor-general* (London, 1755), vol. 1, pp. 419–20.

109 Anon., *Laughing philosopher*, pp. 81–2.

110 V. Knox, *Essays moral and literary* (London, 1778–9), vol. 2, p. 231.

111 Sir James Lawrence, *On the nobility of the British gentry: or the political ranks and dignities of the British Empire compared with those on the continent* (London, 1824), pp. 45, 50. Lawrence, who claimed to be a Knight of Malta, styled himself 'Chevalier' on the continent, where he travelled frequently, but the warrant for both that and his knighthood seems uncertain: see *DNB*. Fittingly enough, he provides the only example so far found of a historic user of the term 'pseudo-gentleman': *ibid.*, p. 24.

112 Mingay, *The gentry*, p. 4.

113 For tabulation, see C. Clay, *Economic expansion and social change: England, 1500–1700* (vol. 1: *People, land and towns*) (Cambridge, 1984), p. 143; and discussion pp. 157–64.

114 See G. Holmes, 'Gregory King and the social structure of pre-industrial England', *Transactions of the Royal Historical Society*, 5th ser. vol. 27 (1977), pp. 66–7. For King's notebook variations, with estimates ranging from 12,000 to 20,000 gentlemen, see J. P. Cooper, 'Social distribution of land and men', in Cooper, *Land, men and beliefs*, pp. 38–9. Here King may well have been experimenting with differing permutations of social categories.

115 H. Horwitz (ed.), *The parliamentary diary of Narcissus Luttrell, 1691–3* (Oxford, 1972), pp. 144, 160.

116 Holmes, 'Gregory King', p. 57.

117 He was Robert Harman, an Irish dancing-master, who had 'visited' Suffolk and 14 other counties: *London Journal*, 22 April 1727.

118 Tabulated in J. Cannon, *Aristocratic century: the peerage of eighteenth-century England* (Cambridge, 1984), p. 32 – but these figures excluded baronetcies that were held by titled noblemen, as they were classified with the peerage: p. 33, n. 101.

119 J. V. Beckett, 'The pattern of landownership in England and Wales, 1660–1880', *Economic History Review*, 2nd ser., XXXVII (1984), pp. 13–14. For a critique of recent studies that have played down movement into landed society, see D. and E. Spring, 'Social mobility and the English landed élite', *Canadian Journal of History*,

21 (1986), pp. 333–51. In addition, mobility from the land has been little studied; but see J. Thirsk, 'Younger sons in the seventeenth century', *History*, 54 (1969), pp. 358–77.

120 The landed gentry's share rose from an estimated 45–50 per cent in 1690 to 50 per cent in 1790 (England and Wales) and to *c.* 55 per cent in 1873 (England only): tabulated in Beckett, 'Pattern of landownership', p. 5. Pioneering estimates were presented by F. M. L. Thompson, 'The social distribution of land and property in England since the sixteenth century', *Economic History Review*, 2nd ser., XIX (1966), pp. 505–17; and augmented by Cooper, 'Social distribution of land and men', in Cooper, *Land, men and beliefs*, pp. 17–42. Reviewing subsequent research, Beckett concludes that, while all figures are subject to a margin of error, the overall picture has stood the test of time well. That meant that between 1690 and 1873, the great landowners and the landed gentry made territorial gains collectively at the expense of the small owners: Beckett, 'Landownership', p. 5.

121 P. Colquhoun, *A treatise of the wealth, power and resources of the British Empire in every quarter of the world* (London, 1814), pp. 106–7.

122 Classes 2 and 3 together constituted under 2 per cent of Colquhoun's total of 3,501,781 adult male householders in Great Britain and Ireland: see *ibid.*

123 E.g., in Preston, three members of the Horrocks manufacturing dynasty were listed as 'gent.' or 'Esq', while their cotton-spinning business Horrockses, Miller and Co. was simultaneously entered under 'trades': Mannex and Co., *History, topography and directory of . . . Preston* (Beverley, 1851), pp. 64, 81. In Maidstone, the Scudamore brothers were listed twice, both as 'gentry' and as 'attorneys': J. Phippen (ed.), *New and enlarged directory for Maidstone . . .* (Maidstone, 1850), pp. 38, 40. I am grateful to David Reader for reference to this source.

124 See P. J. Corfield, 'Class, by name and number in eighteenth-century Britain' and G. Crossick, 'From gentlemen to the residuum: languages of social description in Victorian Britain', in Corfield (ed.), *Language, history and class*, pp. 101–30, 150–78.

125 Including Anon., *The historian's vade mecum: . . . by a gentleman of the Inner Temple* (London, 1741). The anonymous gentleman's output greatly outnumbered works by rivals such as 'A Nobleman', 'A Citizen', 'A Plebeian', or even 'A Lady', although she considerably increased her literary tally in the nineteenth century.

126 Writings about the gentleman included numerous guides to rank and precedence, with minute details about fine gradations of status: see, e.g., Anon., *Of the several degrees of gentry and their precedency* (London, 1719). Other works were variegated, including R. North, *The gentleman's accomptant* (London, 1714); [T. Richards], *The gentleman's auditor* (London, 1707); W. Bradford et al., *The gentleman and traders guide* (Nottingham, *c.* 1770); or Anon., *The gentleman angler* (London, 1726); [A. S., Gent.], *The gentleman's complete jockey* (London, 1697); Anon., *The gentleman farrier* (London, 1732); R. North, *The gentleman farmer* (London, 1726); and [J. H.], *The compleat gentleman soldier* (London, 1702); Anon., *The gentleman and lady's key to polite literature* (London, 1761?); E. Synge, *A gentleman's religion* (London, 1693); and Anon., *The gentleman's bottle-companion: a collection of eighteenth-century bawdy ballads* (London, 1768; repr. Edinburgh, 1979). The *genre* was most popular in the later seventeenth/early eighteenth centuries but continued well into the nineteenth: e.g. Anon., *The gentleman's art of dressing with economy* (London, 1876).

127 E.g., one Thomas Bew, described as 'very much of a gentleman' and 'always behaved like a gentleman', was the keeper of 'a tavern, like all other taverns, where a man might have a woman when he had an occasion': *Proceedings on the King's Commissions of the Peace . . . in the Old-Bailey* (London, 1753), no. 4, pp. 131–2: 2–7 May 1753. I am grateful to Tony Henderson for this reference.

128 S. Johnson (ed.), *A dictionary of the English language* (England, 1755), vol. 1, *sub* 'Gentleman'. The other four meanings were (1) a man of birth, though not noble: (2) a man raised above the vulgar by character or post; (3) the servant that waits about the person of the man of rank; and (4) a term used of any man, however high (i.e., including kings and noblemen).

129 N. Bailey, *An universal etymological English dictionary* (London, 1721; and many later edns), *sub* 'Gentleman'.

130 See *OED sub* 'gentry 3'.

131 J. and J. B. Burke (eds), *A genealogical and heraldic dictionary of the landed gentry of Great Britain and Ireland* (London, 1846–9), 3 vols. By then, the cumbersome title of the first Burke survey had been discarded: compare J. Burke (ed.), *A genealogical and heraldic history of the commoners of Great Britain and Ireland, enjoying territorial possessions or high official rank but uninvested with heritable honours* (London, 1833–8), 4 vols, listing 1,146 families (many with cadet and collateral branches).

132 See *OED sub* 'genteel' for the overlap between the older commendatory meaning and the new sarcastic usage. The compound 'shabby-genteel', however, retained the older sense of the term.

133 K. B. Phillipps, *Language and class in Victorian England* (Oxford, 1984), pp. 5–14; also Crossick, 'From gentlemen to the residuum', pp. 163–5.

134 A. Tennyson, 'In memoriam, A. H. H. – CXI' (1850), in C. Ricks (ed.), *The poems of Tennyson* (London, 1969), p. 964.

135 G. P. Merrick, *Work among the fallen: as seen in the prison cell* (London, 1890), p. 40: but the upper classes were distinguished as 'real gentlemen'.

136 A. de Tocqueville, *L'Ancien régime et la révolution* (Paris, 1856), in Eng. transl. by S. Gilbert (New York, 1955), p. 83.

137 D. L. Sayers, *Busman's honeymoon* (London, 1937), p. 307.

138 See the pen-portrait given in Cain and Hopkins, *British imperialism: innovation and expansion*, p. 24, which in turn quotes from J. Powis, *Aristocracy* (Oxford, 1984), pp. 87–9.

139 By 1900, the Players had won 69 games, the Gentlemen 53 (with 24 draws and 1 tie), the predominance of the Players being dented only when W. G. Grace joined the Gentlemen: scores recorded in F. S. Ashley-Cooper, *Gentlemen v. Players* (London, 1900). For the analogy applied to modern Britain's industrial culture, see D. C. Coleman, 'Gentlemen and Players', *Economic History Review*, 2nd ser., XXVI (1973), pp. 92–116; and refs. in n. 73 above. Further evidence is needed however, to prove whether, and if so when, the gentlemanly code inhibited enterprise and among which social groups; especially as Coleman notes that gentlemanly financiers, for example, were often very successful: *ibid.*, pp. 110–11. Meanwhile, W. Vamplew, *Pay up and play the game: professional sport in Britain, 1875–1914* (Cambridge, 1988), pp. 17, 183–203, notes the extent of commercialism in sport, often disguised by 'shamateurism'.

140 Cannon, *Aristocratic century*, pp. 126–47; Beckett, *Aristocracy in England*, pp. 133–321. Cain and Hopkins agree that the aristocracy combined commercialism with traditionalism; but they saw that formidable mix as essentially safeguarding rather than as adapting the landed élite of *rentiers*: see Cain and Hopkins, *British imperialism: innovation and expansion*, pp. 23–4.

141 The nineteenth-century discussions by (*inter alia*) Trollope, Ruskin, Craik, Gaskell, Arnold, Cardinal Newman, Smiles, Thackeray and the 'silver fork' novelists are much better known than those of the previous century, but both debates covered remarkably similar ground: see M. W. Rosa, *The silver fork school: novels of fashion preceding Vanity Fair* (New York, 1936); M. Girouard, *The return to Camelot: chivalry and the English gentleman* (New Haven, 1981); and P. Mason, *The English gentleman: the rise and fall of an ideal* (New York, 1982), pp. 106–87.

142 See variously Anon., *Most honourable, learned and worthy gentlemen, of all ranks and orders* (London, ?1720), a semi-ironic address in praise of sloth; plus BL Add. MSS 38, 334, Liverpool Papers vol. CXLIV, f. 29 r and v: transcript of William Beckford's speech in Parliament (November 1761), disparaging both the aristocracy and the mob ('the scum and the dregs') but lauding the 'middling people of England – the Manufacturer, the Yeoman, the Merchant, the Country Gentleman, they who bear all the heat of the day and who pay all Taxes to supply all the Expenses of Court and Government.'

143 J. and J. B. Burke (eds), *Landed gentry*, preface [unpaginated].
144 Thus the 'gentry' may be viewed as the middle class in relation to an upper class of great landowners or as an upper class in relation to a middle class of businessmen. Whether classes in England were defined by levels of wealth or by sources of income remains debated; and ambiguities in the status of landed and other 'gentleman' add to the problems. One much-quoted study by W. Rubinstein, 'The Victorian middle classes: wealth, occupation and geography', *Economic History Review*, 2nd ser., XXX (1977), pp. 602–23, displays such respect for upper class landed purity that it classifies even millionaire plutocrats, merchants, bankers, etc. as middle class.
145 In republican America, without formal titles, the gentleman was a cultural ideal rather than a separate status: E. H. Cady. *The gentleman in America: a literary study in American culture* (Syracuse, 1949), esp. pp. 24–7. Thus by the early nineteenth century the social graces had spread well beyond the élite: see R. L. Bushman, *The refinement of America: persons, houses, cities* (New York, 1992), pp. xvii–xviii, 404–5, and *passim.*
146 The English gentleman was not, for example, a direct counterpart of the French 'gentilhomme', as the latter was by no means so pervasive either as an ideal or as an actual title. For foreign visitors' comments on the originality of the English gentleman, see, e.g., de Tocqueville [n. 135 above] or T. Fontane, *Ein Sommer in London* (Dessau, 1854), p. 264: '*Du brauchst kein Gentleman zu sein, du musst nur die Mittel haben, als solcher zu erscheinen und du bist es.*' [You need not be a gentleman, you must only have the means to appear one, and you are one.]
147 McKendrick, '"Gentleman and Players" revisited', pp. 119–36.
148 See H. Laski, 'The danger of being a gentleman: reflections on the ruling class in England', in Laski, *The danger of being a gentleman and other essays* (London, 1939), pp. 13–31.

20 pp

2

ENGLISH LANDED SOCIETY AND THE SERVANTS TAX OF 1777[1]

JOHN CHARTRES

The elegant conveniences of life . . . the true objects of taxation in every well regulated state.[1]

(*Charles Jenkinson, 1777*)

In a commercial and manufacturing country, customs, excises, or taxes, which fall on or eventually affect the merchant or manufacturer, ought to be avoided; so ought any taxes of any kind, which are felt by the lower part of the community . . . A tax upon servants was often strongly recommended, as those that kept them were always presumed to be opulent, and proper objects of taxation: that the operation of the tax would have a double effect; respecting those in the high classes of life, it would be taxing a luxury, and one too of the first magnitude; and as to the middling people of all descriptions, it could not be very severely felt. It was designed to be a tax upon male servants.[2]

(*Lord North, 1777*)

In my view it would be wrong to intensify the rates of taxation in existing fields without making an effort to ensure that services make a proper contribution. What is needed is to broaden the tax base by creating another source of revenue in a field that has so far contributed a comparatively small amount.[3]

(*James Callaghan, 1966*)

Twice at least in times of hardship, British governments have turned to the taxation of services as potentially uncontroversial means of broadening the fiscal base. Neither was very effective, though the subject of this present study, the Servants Tax of 1777, far outlived its twentieth-century successor, Selective Employment Tax. However the swift failure of SET, as a mis-specified compromise between a tax upon services and a simple universal payroll tax, illustrated the tantalising nature of the conflict between a form of taxation liable initially to secure widespread approval and the mechanical problems of its delivery.[4]

The earlier tax sustained the case: Lord North's Servants Tax of 1777 did in fact endure to 1791, surviving his fall to be incorporated into the raft of taxation levied by Pitt, its persistence in the face of consistently disappointing yields proving its attractiveness as a concept. This eighteenth-century tax offers the opportunity to explore some of the many themes visited by Michael Thompson in his work on landed society and, through the surviving records of the tax from 1780, to see what can be observed of eighteenth-century society through its lens. The present chapter will therefore attempt to conduct this preliminary exploration, first setting the tax into context before looking more closely at the tax as record of where and how manservants were clustered in the early 1780s; at their city and country distribution, and what we can adduce from it; and at the inferences that can be drawn from such analysis as to the distributional impact of the tax.[5] Was it so benign as suggested by North in his proposition speech in 1777?

I

A recurrent theme of Michael Thompson's work on eighteenth- and more particularly nineteenth-century landed society was that of the fundamental responsibility shown by the aristocratic and landed élite that ruled Britain between the Restoration and the second Reform Act. Far from sustaining the trenchant criticisms and conspiracy theories of government by a landed élite to be found among the works of the Webbs or the Hammonds, Michael Thompson identified the ways in which this landed class acted in a politically responsible manner, albeit after 1832 on sufferance from the middle classes.[6] In this, he extended a theme expounded by Sir John Habakkuk, his own supervisor, 'who originated modern work in the field'; a theme that was developed in the parallel but fundamentally eighteenth-century studies of Gordon Mingay and surveyed in the more recent general study by John Beckett.[7]

One key symptom of this attitude of responsibility lay in the approach of the British landed élite to taxation. In words that one can see as central to this thinking, Sir John Habakkuk was able to highlight this as one of the critical characteristics distinguishing the British aristocracy from the bulk of their European neighbours:

But the most important single fact about the English nobility is that they were, in the locality and the centre, the politically effective class, and therefore felt a responsibility for the way things went. They were prepared to tax themselves, and in the two great wars against France to tax themselves heavily. The Hammonds conclude a sustained indictment of the activities of the enclosing English landlords with this reluctant tribute: 'The other European aristocracies crumbled at once before Napoleon: the English aristocracy amid all its blunders and errors kept its character for endurance and fortitude'.[8]

While the case is far from absolutely proven, it would also appear that this distinctive fiscal responsibility combined with the benefits of the eighteenth-century financial revolution to establish in Britain a major international comparative advantage in public finance, something strategically critical to its emergence as dominant world power in the period.[9]

The political economy of British taxation had already proven its mettle by 1730, being able to raise revenues in the context of stabilised public finance out of all proportion to the capacity of its European neighbours. In at least one analysis, by Mathias and O'Brien, political stability and an at least implicit general assent to taxation, coupled with the extensive and growing urban nature of England, combined to make it far more heavily taxed than contemporary France, but at strikingly lower political cost.[10] From the middle years of the century, this had been developed through a more complex framework of approaches to raising revenues. Whereas the staple sources of revenues remained the Land Tax, the Excise and the Customs, the second half of the century saw imaginative discussions of ways to broaden the fiscal base, and the general acceptance among political economists that the taxation of luxuries was a desirable addition to the tradition of universal obligation to tax inherited from the years after 1660.[11]

Pamphleteers such as Francis Fauquier, espousing the rejection of the absurd notion of taxing the poor in 1756 found wider echoes, and between the onset of the Seven Years' and the American Wars, this became one of the four governing precepts of UK fiscal theory. The other principles also pointed clearly to the directions fiscal policy was increasingly to take: avoidance of direct assessment of means; the taxation of luxury as both self-assessed and essentially voluntary; and taxation of luxury as also sumptuary in impact, and hence representing a self-regulating curb on excess.[12] This shift received canonisation in *The Wealth of Nations* in 1776, where Adam Smith noted his general approval of the taxation of luxury:

Every man's contribution is altogether voluntary; it being altogether in his power either to consume or not to consume the commodity taxed. Where such taxes, therefore, are properly assessed and upon proper commodities, they are paid with less grumbling than any other.[13]

When Lord North introduced the tax in his budget speech in May 1777, then, the principle of the taxation of luxury and its essentially 'voluntary' nature had been well established, and clearly incorporated into established politics. The proposition to tax manservants, fitting so well into these precepts, had apparently much to commend it. Moreover, such a tax had been suggested by George Townshend as an appropriate response to the expense of the Seven Years' War, in 1756; it had been a long established feature of England's fiscal mentors, the Netherlands; and was to be proposed, by Silhouette, in France in 1759, and promulgated by edict.[14] Accordingly, the taxes proposed in 1777 met little opposition in the Commons and were described by Jenkinson, evidently ambitious for the office he was soon to achieve, as 'not only judiciously, but equitably laid'.[15]

The Servants Tax of 1777 introduced a flat rate payment from the year beginning 5 July 1777, to be made within six months of Lady Day each year, of one guinea for each manservant employed in any of the following roles:

Maitre d'Hotel; House-steward; Master of the Horse; Groom of the Chamber; Valet de Chambre; Butler; Under-Butler; Clerk of the Kitchen; Confectioner; Cook; House porter; footman; running footman; coachman; groom; positilion; stable boy; and the respective helpers in the duties of such coachman, groom or postilion; or in the capacity of a gardener (not being a day-labourer); park-keeper; game keeper, huntsman; [and] whipper-in.[16]

As with its twentieth-century successor, the tax specifically exempted those employed *bona fide* 'for the purposes of husbandry or manufacture, or . . . any trade or calling by which the master or masters of such servant earn a livelihood or profit'[17] For the first year, payment was stepped down proportionately to 15*s.* and the commissioners were empowered to relieve those with servants employed in several locations to pay in only one, exemption being granted elsewhere on exhibition of the receipt. Double tax was to be levied for any identified omission from a return.[18]

The tax was expected to raise a gross £105,000, North's officials advising him that it was reasonable to assume a population of 100,000 such servants in the country. This figure accorded reasonably with Adam Smith's own estimates of their numbers: he assumed that a man with an income of £200 p.a. would keep but a single servant, and that numbers would peak at less than fifty for a £10,000 a year man.[19] Treating Smith's figures at face value, and attaching them to the social structure suggested by Joseph Massie's figures for 1760, then forty to fifty thousand households employing eighty to ninety thousand servants would not be an implausible figure for the later 1770s.[20] This suggests that around 3–4 per cent of just under 1.5 million households in England in the later 1770s were employers of such servants, and that about one-third of England's 'servants' were such luxury consumption goods.[21] The political arithmetic was immaculate, and the tax as designed should have targeted only this consumption in a manner that left those of modest means, and those employing servants only for 'productive' employments, untouched.

Like the Inhabited House Duty of 1778 however, the tax proved a consistent disappointment. Revenues did not in fact flow until 1778, though interest on the loans to which it had been apportioned had been paid in the year ending 25 March 1778.[22] In the first full year to March 1779, revenues fell far short of expectations, leading to the first explicit criticism from the opposition. Fox argued that this showed a nation reaching its fiscal limits, and unable to bear greater burdens; North countered by taking the view that the failings were primarily administrative, and sought to reform the processes.[23] In 1780, the year for which a full listing survives, tax was paid on only 50,000 servants by just under 25,000 employers, roughly half the expected return.[24] It was the 'failure of the taxes' because of flaws in collection that North used as the justification for further new or additional taxes in the 1780 budget.[25]

Governments remained attached to the tax, and perhaps mistook symptoms for causes. In 1781, administration was transferred to the Excise Office, with listings to be revised annually.[26] From July 1785, the former duty was repealed and replaced with a sliding scale of charges, together with a new duty for female servants, and the administration was returned to the Taxes Board. Rates commenced at £1 5*s* for each male servant, and ran to £3 each for units of eleven or more; and for females taxes began at 2*s* 6*d*. and reached 10*s* at units of three or more. Waiters in taverns now joined the lists of those taxed. Employers aged over twenty-one, who had never married, had to pay a surcharge of a further £1 5*s* for each male servant, and 10*s* for each female.[27]

That such a tax should be continued, reformed and extended by Pitt confirms that North's views in promoting it were those of broad consensus, at least among the policy formers. Pitt's extension of taxation to female servants was intensely unpopular, despite the exemption for households containing children under the age of fourteen, *pro rata* at one female servant per two such children.[28] Revenues cannot be interpreted with certainty in the later 1780s, but they suggest that the two taxes together produced little more than £100,000, the sum originally anticipated for male servants alone in 1777. In the first year, 1785/6, taxes on females generated around £30,000, and revenues stayed at or around this level to abolition in 1791.[29] Given that the scale of domestic establishments was almost certainly rising over this period, the tax was clearly falling in real yield.[30] Thus, a tax that exactly fitted the canons set by Adam Smith and many other political economists proved a failure. Its relative longevity indicated the strong degree of governmental attachment to it, but does not wholly remove anxieties about its presumptive quality as a source. However, with these strong caveats in mind, it is to the evidence that the returns provide that we can now turn.

II

The returns for the Servants Tax for 1780 survive in a single complete volume and can be analysed to examine its incidence, and what it can demonstrate about the structural and spatial patterns of domestic service. To what extent were these manservants evenly distributed among Lord North's 'high classes of life', or were they primarily taxed as part of the 'genteel establishments' of England's grandees?[31] If the latter, then can this be seen as another example of the way in which later eighteenth-century taxation bit relatively more on the resources of great landed society, than on the commercial and industrial communities of the growing towns? The returns for 1780 record tax being paid on a total of 50,044 servants in some 24,750 households. The evidence of the returns shows, however, that the provision to pay on all servants from only one location was not consistently followed, and the numbers of actual employers were slightly smaller than would at first appear. There is also inconsistency within the record, there being a slightly larger number of both masters and servants as derived from the breakdown by size unit, and some complete omissions, most notably Nottingham.[32]

As will be seen in the summary figures of Table 2.1, the vast majority of returns were for small units, of one or two servants, but more than half the manservants found themselves employed in larger households. If fewer than one-third of the servants found themselves employed in the 60 per cent single-servant households, rather more were to be found in groups of five or more, and one in nine in units of ten and above. These simple statistics almost certainly understate the degree of such concentration. Making due allowance for some under-declaration, widely discussed by contemporaries, and perhaps at least doubling the taxable number to allow for women servants and for others who, by the definition of the statute, may have been deemed sources of 'profit', however tangentially, it is very clear that the larger households, and even some of those of middling rank, were already relatively large units of employment by the standards of the time.[34] Certainly there were large industrial and commercial plants by the late 1770s, but the great majority of employ-

Table 2.1 Summary distribution of taxed manservants, 1780[33]

servants per household	*number of households*	*percentage of households*	*number of servants*	*percentage of servants*
1	14959	60.4	14959	29.9
2	4661	18.8	9322	18.6
3	2134	8.6	6402	12.8
4	1048	4.2	4192	8.4
5–9	1554	6.3	9586	19.2
10–19	357	1.4	4563	9.1
20–29	29	0.1	672	1.3
30+	8	0.0	348	0.7
Total	24750	100.0	50044	100.0

ment remained in the small workshop, the cottage of protoindustry or the farm, and the large, multi-servant household, evident when these figures are grossed up to allow for likely omissions, was exceptional in this context. That, clearly, was the source of the elaborate hierarchies of organisation and authority that had long characterised the establishments of the landed grandees, and which was being increasingly emulated by others.

This becomes all the more striking when one considers the returns for the very largest units, the leading ten units of taxpaying in 1780, listed in Table 2.2. The names and the seats represent very clearly the expected élite, but there are also some surprises in that they were not wholly aristocratic. To some extent, however, this simple ranking of the largest individual units paying tax is misleading, and a number of grandees would appear if their several returns were aggregated: for example, Lord Grosvenor paid tax on fifty-nine servants in seven locations, and the Duke of Portland paid on only fourteen at Welbeck but another thirty-nine at his two London addresses, Privy Gardens and Piccadilly. This dispersal makes the source difficult to employ direct from the record, and is a matter discussed further below.

Not surprisingly, the tax was also quite concentrated in its geographical impact. In both absolute share and in the share of the larger concentrations, some parts of the country stood out from the rest. Above all, the incidence of the tax was primarily metropolitan. Both in the share of masters (14.3 per cent) and of servants (17.5 per cent), the metropolitan region, defined crudely as London, Westminster and Southwark, significantly exceeded its proportionate share of England's population,

Table 2.2 The ten leading payers of the Servants Tax, 1780

rank	*taxpayer*	*place*	*number of servants*
1	Marquess of Rockingham	Wentworth (Yorks, WR)	62
2	Earl of Egremont	Petworth (Sussex)	55
3	Duke of Rutland	Belvoir (Leics)	49
4 =	Sir Henry Harpur	Upper Grosvenor Street, Westminster	42
4 =	Earl Spencer	Brington (Northants)	42
6	Earl of Stamford	Dunham Massey (Cheshire)	34
7	Duke of Beaufort	Badminton (Gloucs)	33
8	Duke of Ancaster	Eresby (Lincs)	31
9 =	Sir James Lowther	Lowther (Northumberland)	29
9 =	Charles Anderson Pelham	Arlington Street, Westminster	29

which in 1780 was around ten per cent.[35] Greater London may, of course, held a rather greater relative share of national wealth, leaving its servants as underrated in comparative terms, but the definitional and data problems in assessing this issue preclude an answer in the present study.[36]

More surprising, perhaps, was the relatively small degree of difference between non-metropolitan counties, and between England and Wales. For the country as a whole, there were on average 2.03 servants per master, estimated from the slightly different aggregate figures derived from the county-by-county breakdown in the record. For non-metropolitan England, the mean was 1.96, and for Wales 1.85. Metropolitan England, as defined above, clearly stood out on this measure, at 2.49. This crude ratio can also be applied to assess where there were relatively greater clusters of servants per houshold return than elsewhere. We might perhaps financially call this a measure of 'best-seated' counties, on the assumption that the key variable in this was the share of the returns from grandees in the county. Taking a significant difference fairly arbitrarily at ten per cent above the average, seven English counties displayed larger average clusters of servants per taxpaying household than the rest. These were, in descending order, Buckinghamshire (2.51), Rutland (2.39), Chester (2.31), Hertfordshire (2.25), Yorkshire (2.21), Sussex (2.20) and Westmorland (2.18). All had something of a reputation for being the counties of gentry seats, but much the same would also have been said of Northamptonshire or Norfolk, the first of which was almost exactly on the average, and the latter somewhat below.

Much more startling than these differences were those observed within our metropolitan zone of London, Southwark and Westminster. The differentness of greater London was on this measure wholly attributable to the City of Westminster, which displayed a ratio of 3.08, where Southwark was on the mean at 2.45, and London far below at 1.55. Clearly this reinforces the impression that this may have been a tax effectively targeted upon luxury 'consumption' of servants where this usage was most obvious and easiest to define. In Westminster, above all, ostentation and social aspiration may have proved powerful forces in generating substantial returns, and may also have proved effective disincentives to evasion or avoidance. Could a £5,000-a-year-man, even one struggling to make his actual income match its reputed level, afford to be seen to be quibbling over the odd pound per servant on such a public platform? Equally, perhaps, more focused concerns with hard-nosed business may explain London's low ratio.[37] Conspicuous consumption may not have been so prevalent a social norm in the City.

The final general conclusion to be drawn from these data disaggregated to county level is that already implicit in the above: there were striking differences between counties in their clusters of larger taxpaying units, here defined arbitrarily as those in the 5–9 and 10+ ranges. As one can see from the figures of Table 2.3, metropolitan England showed a significant concentration of larger households and units of servants, but again this was primarily attributable to the impact of Westminster and Southwark. Wales, perhaps surprisingly in view of contemporary views about its detachment from England, displayed a remarkably similar pattern to that of non-metropolitan England in the middle ranges, though with a rather greater proportion of the smallest, and a smaller proportion of the largest units.[38] On these summary figures, the fundamental difference revealed was between the metropolitan region and the rest of England and Wales.

When disaggregated fully to the county level, some striking contrasts again emerge from these data. In the figures of Table 2.4, the differences within the metropolitan region are again revealed, with Westminster still more clearly contrasted with the City. Southwark too had a greater concentration of larger household units and of servants than the City. Different patterns too are revealed between the other 'selected counties', those already noted above as having a significantly greater number of servants per taxpaying household than the average.[39] Even then, the patterns of distribution differed significantly. Buckinghamshire clearly had a great preponderance of larger units, assessed by both household size and the numbers of servants, whereas counties with small aggregate returns, such as Rutland, were severely distorted by the largest taxpayers (Lord Gainsborough at Exton). Hertfordshire, Surrey, and Middlesex

Table 2.3 Percentage distributions of households and servants, 1780

	households				*servants*			
servants per household	*1*	*2–4*	*5–9*	*10+*	*1*	*2–4*	*5–9*	*10+*
non-metropolitan England	61.5	31.1	6.1	1.2	31.5	40.3	19.4	8.9
metropolitan England	52.4	34.9	7.0	5.6	21.0	36.1	17.4	25.5
Wales	63.1	30.2	6.1	0.7	34.1	40.8	20.1	5.1

Table 2.4 Percentage distributions of households and servants, selected counties, 1780

	households				*servants*			
	1	*2–4*	*5–9*	*10+*	*1*	*2–4*	*5–9*	*10+*
Berkshire	53.4	37.1	8.4	1.1	25.0	43.5	24.8	6.7
Buckinghamshire	53.5	32.7	9.7	4.1	21.3	34.4	23.9	20.4
Cheshire	54.4	35.8	7.7	2.2	23.5	38.6	22.9	15.0
Hertfordshire	50.2	39.1	9.2	1.6	22.3	43.9	24.2	9.6
Middlesex	54.5	39.3	5.3	0.9	27.1	51.0	15.9	6.0
Norfolk	63.0	31.7	4.9	0.5	35.7	43.4	17.2	3.8
Northamptonshire	67.4	24.3	6.9	1.4	34.2	29.8	22.2	13.8
Rutland	61.4	29.8	3.5	5.3	25.7	33.8	11.8	28.7
Surrey	49.6	41.8	8.1	0.4	23.2	51.6	22.6	2.6
Sussex	60.5	30.7	6.2	2.5	27.5	34.5	17.8	20.2
Westmorland	67.5	27.5	2.5	2.5	31.0	32.2	5.7	31.0
Yorkshire	60.7	28.8	8.3	2.2	27.6	33.6	23.8	15.2
London	66.4	31.6	1.9	0.2	42.8	49.2	6.8	1.3
Southwark	68.1	24.3	0.0	7.6	27.8	22.4	0.0	49.8
Westminster	42.3	38.1	10.9	8.8	13.8	33.2	22.1	30.9

showed an unusually high concentration in the middle bands, perhaps pointing to the early impact of suburban and villa developments, with their service retinues. Surprisingly, the last displayed a distinct peak only in the second size interval, and a distribution of servants per unit little different from the average for non-metropolitan England. Its mixed character of the metropolitan and the suburban, combined with intensive agricultural production, perhaps explain this outcome. Our 'best-seated'

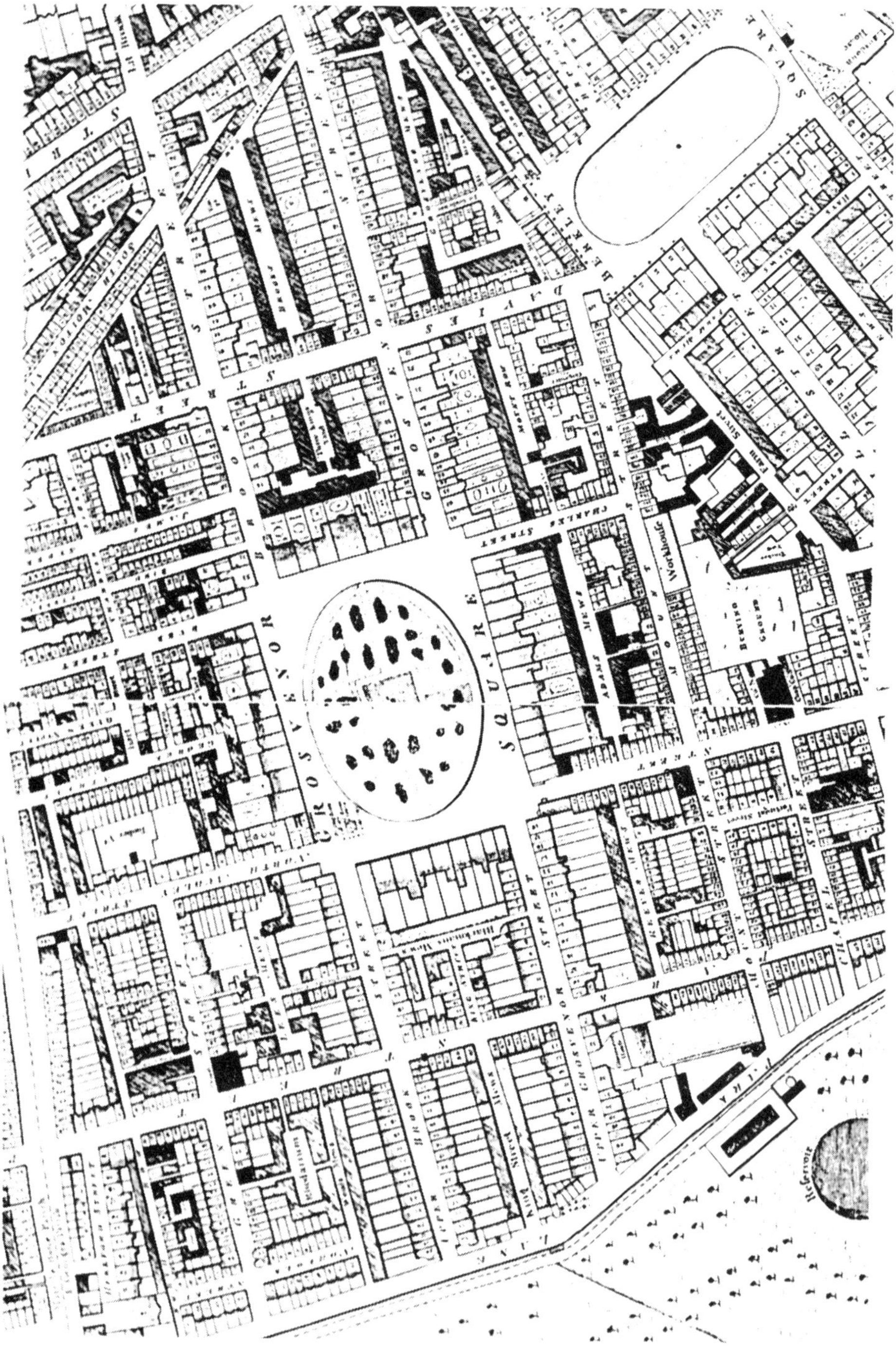
GROSVENOR
SQUARE
CHARLES STREET
Workhouse
Reservoir

Householder	*Servants*
GREEN STREET	
Lord Viscount Hampden	10
Major Madden	3
Mrs Dorothy Palmer	3
Twelve other servants	
UPPER BROOK STREET	
Sir Francis Sykes	12
William Sheldon	8
John Chetwynd Talbot	8
Lady Brown	7
Hon Col Conway	5
Bishop of Gloucester	5
Mr Henry Lascelles	5
Lady Frances Coningsby	4
Rev Mr Fullerton	4
Countess of Glasgow	4
Dowager Lady Grosvenor	4
Barbara Wright	4
Hon Miss Byng	3
Hon Ann Charges	3
Hon Miss Herbert	3
Mrs Sarah Johnson	3
Thomas Ramsden	3
Twenty-six other servants	
UPPER GROSVENOR STREET	
Sir Henry Harpur	42
Earl of Clarendon	13
Duke of Montrose	11
Mr Bernard Brocers	8
Bishop of Norwich	8
Sir Thomas Cave	6
John Radcliffe	6
Lady Vincent	6
Mr John Wyndham Bowyer	5
Mr Charles Carter	4
Williams Fellows	4
Mr Mumby Gouldbourne	4
Lady Fitzwilliams	3
Peregrine Furey	3
Mr Edward Monkton	3
John Rust	3
Twenty other servants	
PARK STREET	
Lord Harrowby	9
Mr Thomas Bowlby	4
Mr Alexander Gray	4
Countess of Moreton	4
Mrs Strachey	4
Mr William Cooper	3
Sir Thomas Head	3
Seventeen other servants	
MOUNT STREET	
Lady Mary Coke	6
Mr Richard Nevil	3
Six other servants	
AUDLEY STREET	
Sir James Pennyman	14
Lord Algernon Percy	11
Sir George Howard	10
Sir John Mordant	10
Earl Legonier	8
Mrs Hewers	7
John Wells	6
Francis Boscawen	5
Lord Gen Johnson	5
Mr Richard Mitchell	5
Hon Seymour Conway	4
Hon Capt Hanger	4
Mr Thomas Hunt	4
Mathew Arnot	3
Mr Richard Coffin	3
Mr Fitzpatrick	3
Mrs Hallett	3
Sixteen other servants	
GROSVENOR SQUARE	
Duke of Buccleugh	22
Mr Peters Delme	17
Mr William Aislabie	16
Early of Derby	13
Lord Grosvenor	13
Earl of Abercorn	12
Lord Robert Manners	12
Marquess of Carmarthen	12
Mr Thomas Duncombe	11
Bishop of Worcester	10
Sir Gilbert Heathcoat	10
Charles Baldwin	8
Earl Percy	6
Sir Richard Heron	6
Countess Shaftesbury	6
Lord Sonds	6
Sir Robert Rich	6
Duke of Chandos	5
Mr William Jennings	5
Lady Jerningham	4
Countess of Northington	4
Lady Stouverton	4
Three other servants	
DUKE STREET	
Countess of Suffolk	16
William Webber	4
Hon Mrs Yorke	4
Mrs Hutton	3
Mrs Mary Harrison	3
Nineteen other servants	
CHARLES STREET	
Lord Downe	12
Earl of Dartmouth	12
Marquess of Lothian	9
Sir George Pocock	9
Countess of Essex	8
Mr Burke	5
Lord Frederick Cavendish	5
Mrs Elizabeth Coke	4
General Cowper	4
Mr Edward Lewis	4
Colonel Francis Ramsden	4
Mr William Blair	3
Sir John Chapman	3
Lady Gallway	3
Lady Gray	3
Mr John Leveson Gore	3
Lady Hesketh	3
Mr Horton James	3
Nineteen other servants	
GROSVENOR STREET	
Earl of Hertford	15
Earl of Ludlow	13
Lady Aylesford	12
Sir James Peachy	12
Francis John Tyson	10
Mr Charles Churchill	6
Countess of Radnor	6
Col William Egerton	5
Lady Featherstonehaugh	5
Catherine Stapleton	5
Col Buckley	4
Mr Ralph Gowland	4
Mr John Lawson	4
Elizabeth Starkie	4
John Seare	4
Nineteen other servants	
BERKELEY SQUARE	
Hon Edward Bouverie	13
Duke of Beaufort	12
Earl of Shelburn	12
Lord Bulkeley	10
Earl of Darnley	10
Countess Talbot	10
Lady Clive	8
Mrs Amelia Burrell	7
Lady Albermarle	6
Duchess of Ancaster	6
Thomas Thornhill	6
Lord Claremount	5
Lord Robert Spencer	5
Hon John Yorke	5
Mr Theodore Crowley	4
Lord George Cavendish	3
Sir Charles Frederick	3
Edward Stanley	3
George Thornhill	3
Nine other servants	

Figure 2.1 Servants Tax by West End streets, 1780, superimposed with Horwood's plans of London and Westminster, 1792–99

counties, Cheshire, Sussex, and Yorkshire, displayed the smoothest gradation across the three largest cells.

Overall, then, the summary data of the Servants Tax returns indicate a high degree of concentration in the impact of the tax. They suggest that the largest establishments of the gentry and aristocracy may have been still among the larger units of employment in the industrialising economy. The tax's impact was heavily concentrated onto the metropolitan region, above all on Westminster, where no doubt the rest of the country believed superfluity to exist and fully to deserve taxation. There were also, outside greater London, some counties in which there appeared significantly greater average households of manservants, and the closer examination of these pointed to significant differences within that set. Clearly, the tax contains patterns which may puzzle, and which will repay closer examination.

III

In the first of three brief examinations of some of the data in detail, the striking contrasts within greater London become all the more clear. Above all, when placed on the map of the expanding city, the data for the 'west end' of the City of Westminster provide a striking reminder of the importance of service in the city. Nowhere else in the country displayed so great a concentration of such clusters of manservants upon whom tax was paid. The point is best made by reference to the descriptive map of their distribution (see figure 2.1). This maps some of the principal 'quality' residential streets of the West End, and lists in parallel the tax returns, street by street. It confirms some of the earlier suggestions, but also has some perhaps surprising implications.

The first conclusion to be drawn is that there were some of the principal streets in which were clustered the great magnates. Part of their impressive strutting on the London stage consisted in their ostentatious retinues of servants. On these figures, and making due allowance for omissions and for the as yet untaxed but probably more numerous females, servants must have comprised the larger part of the resident and working population of such areas. In areas such as this, and even in parts of Westminster such as Soho Square, where 'quality' was not quite so undiluted, the presence of the great establishments was an overwhelming feature of the employment patterns of the city.[40] Evidently, living cheek-by-jowl with such grandees as the Hampdens, Howards or Harrowbys, let alone the huge establishments of Sir Henry Harpur or the Duke of Buccleuch, the householders paying tax on a mere one or two manservants must have been very sensitive to their relative inferiority of place.

What was so different about these grand streets of Westminster was their scale. This was in striking contrast to the City, where as we have seen there was a predominance of single manservant households (see table 2.4), notable even by comparison with the national average. This, however, in combination with a much more intensive land use within the confines of the old City walls, means that the density of servants may have been little different. The servant was ubiquitous within greater London, but their experiences within the city could differ very radically. In the great houses of much of the West End, and to some degree in Southwark, service clearly took place within a large and hierarchical household, with units of employment in excess of twenty being relatively common. In the City, by contrast, servants appeared in ones and twos, and their employers, perhaps more concerned with Mammon than display, may have been perhaps both more restrained in their 'consumption' and more adept at their redefinition of servants towards 'profitable' ends.[41]

Two other factors help to explain these West End differences, both of which need further investigation before very firm conclusions can be drawn. The first is the evident pattern throughout the whole of the tax, and particularly visible in London, for many of the 'quality' to maintain separate households for husband and wife. For some this meant a 'city' wife and a 'country' husband, and for others two separate establishments within the city, plus a seat or seats outside. Sir Matthew Featherstonehaugh, for example, was returned for fifteen manservants at Harting (Sussex), and Lady Featherstonehaugh for five in Grosvenor Street (see figure 2.1); and Mr Thomas Arthington paid on four each at his Yorkshire home, Arthington, and at the Adelphi, while Mrs Arthington, perhaps his wife, paid on one in Leeds.[42] Until the complete record is fully collated and probable family units matched with certainty, these must be regarded as but preliminary associations, but the tax appears to offer a route to identify family patterns of residence through their declared servants. It may thus be possible to draw further inferences about the nature of family relationships, though clearly these will remain somewhat speculative.[43]

The final comment to be made on this general pattern of distribution follows directly from this, in that our earlier comments on the largest taxpaying units is misleading as a representation of the rankings of the grandees by their manservants. Only when all of the entries for each seat of each employer are put together can one draw the full comparison, and even within Westminster, some at least had more than one household, which, when aggregated, place them much higher in the relative rankings. Once again, the full consideration of the impact of such factors on the relative standing and overall incidence of the tax must await its fuller analysis, but some examples are summarized in Table 2.5.

Table 2.5 Aggregated manservants for selected employers, 1780

total	*employer*	*locations*
69	Earl of Egremont	Petworth (Sx) 55; Piccadilly 12; Newport (Ex) 2
67	Marquess of Rockingham	Wentworth (Yo) 62 [plus 1 separately listed]; Newmarket (Sk) 2; Great Garrowden (Nh) 1; Grosvenor Square 1
66	Duke of Rutland	Belvoir (Le) 49; Cheveley (Cb) 17
59	Lord Grosvenor	Dullingham (Cb) 19; Swaffham Bulbeck (Cb) 13; Grosvenor Square 13; West Watling (Cb) 5; Newmarket (Sk) 3; Eaton (Ch) 5; Great Abingdon (Cb) 1
54	Duke of Portland	Piccadilly 22; Privy Gardens 17; Clipston Welbeck (Nt) 14 [plus 1 separately listed]
54	Earl of Stamford	Dunham Massey (Ch) 34; Enville (St) 8; Charles Street 12
52	Duke of Devonshire	Piccadilly 25; Edensor (Db) 19; Newmarket (Sk) 5; Londesbrough (Yo) 2; Beamsley (Yo) 1
46	Earl Spencer	Brington (Nh) 42; Stanton Bury (Bu) 2; St Albans (Ht) 1; Dunston (Li) 1
45	Duke of Beaufort	Badminton (Gl) 33; Berkeley Square 12
43	Lord Beaulieu	Weakly (Nh) 20; Dover Street 20; Stoke Poges (Bu) 3
42	Sir Henry Harpur	Upper Grosvenor Street 42
38	Duke of Ancaster	Grimsthorpe (Li) 31; Newmarket (Sk) 1; [Duchess of Ancaster, Berkeley Square 6]
36	Sir James Lowther	Lowther (Nb) 29; Swillington (Yo) 6; Whitehaven (Cu) 1
32	Lord Scarsdale	Kedleston (Db) 16; Mansfield Street (Mx) 16
26	Duke of Northumberland	Charing Cross 18; Alnwick (Nb) 3; Isleworth (Mc) 3; Werrington (Dv) 2
20	Lord North	Downing Street 18; Hampton (Mx) 2
16	Duke of Bridgewater	Cleveland Row 15; Worsley (La) 1

The rank revealed by this preliminary aggregation is broadly compatible with that suggested by table 2.2, but with some significant changes.

Several of the great families of the land that were absent from the top ten individual returns are to be found high in this overall ranking. None of Grosvenor, Portland, Devonshire or Beaulieu appeared in the earlier listing, but clearly maintained substantial establishments at several locations in the country, and spread their returns accordingly. At a lower level, the same could be argued for Lord Scarsdale and the Duke of Northumberland, although in the former example, as with Lord Beaulieu and a number of others, it is not altogether certain that the two numerically identical returns really signify distinct establishments: these may be examples of duplications. The Prime Minister set a fair example to his fellow grandees by paying on the eighteen manservants at Downing Street. Many other large aggregated establishments may emerge from the full analysis of the record.

For nearly all of this group of leading taxpayers, even those who like Lord Grosvenor spread the portfolio of manservants across a number of seats, the Westminster presence was always substantial. Of the peers in this listing, only Rockingham, Rutland and Spencer felt able to maintain a relatively small household in London, and only Sir James Lowther, by their standards a representative of relatively new wealth, remained wholly 'provincial' in his tax returns. The spiritual peers, also showed mixed patterns: Durham paid for 2 servants at North Bailey in Durham, 4 at Bishop Auckland and 12 in Albermarle Street; Exeter only 6 at Dean Street; Ely 10 at Dover Street; and St Asaph, 7 at Bolton Road. This simple point, replicated by many others of lesser scale, explains the fundamental difference of the Westminster returns within London, and explains its great difference from those of the rest of England and Wales.

IV

This perhaps suggests that the grandees of the country were more likely to be caught in the net of this tax than the representatives of the growing commercial and industrial wealth. In part, as suggested earlier, this may have been the definitional consequence of the drafting of the statute. It may have been easier to classify servants as sources of profit for those in business. It also clearly refected a preference for status and ostentation that were displayed in the houses and domestic establishments of the grandees. The striking contrast between Westminster and the City of London suggests that there may have been some real differences between Westminster and other urban centres, and between them and the remainder of the country, and in this final section, this issue is explored by reference to the leading towns of England *c.* 1750. In exploring their records, it may be possible to draw some inferences about the relative incidence of this tax between the three principal categories of the wealthy.

For this purpose, the data from the principal eighteen provincial towns, selected as the leading towns defined by estimated population in 1750, have been analysed, and compared with the overall pattern for the residue of the county within which they were located.[44] Of that leading group, described below in table 2.6, several at the lower end of the distribution produced such small returns as to look dubious, and for that reason Sheffield and Chatham have been excluded from the present exercise.[45]

Table 2.6 Major urban returns to Servants Tax, 1780, compared with their county context (ranked by number of manservants per town on whom tax was paid)

	returns by town			*returns for residue of county*		
	masters	*servants*	*ratio*	*masters*	*servants*	*ratio*
Newcastle-upon-Tyne	126	219	1.74	275	520	1.89
York	138	210	1.52	1289	3021	2.34
Bristol	152	205	1.35	498	795	1.60
Chester	117	186	1.59	249	661	2.65
Norwich	115	173	1.50	698	1280	1.83
Liverpool	121	149	1.23	438	837	1.91
Manchester	107	141	1.32	438	837	1.91
Birmingham	99	134	1.35	265	527	1.99
Leeds	84	119	1.42	1289	3021	2.34
Exeter	63	79	1.25	463	825	1.78
Worcester	53	66	1.25	302	510	1.69
Plymouth	50	58	1.16	463	825	1.78
Coventry	45	55	1.22	265	527	1.99
Portsmouth	42	53	1.26	587	1234	2.10
Yarmouth	30	36	1.20	698	1280	1.83
Sunderland	20	21	1.05	288	611	2.12
total	1362	1904	1.40	5352	10821	2.02

The figures of table 2.6 certainly appear to offer support to the inferences drawn earlier from the contrasts of Westminster and London. Overall, this sub-set of urban returns displays a strikingly lower ratio of manservants per household than that of the county within which each of these towns was located. At just above two-thirds of their 'county' context, this contrast was less striking than the comparison of London with Westminster, the latter standing at roughly double the level of the former (3.07 to 1.55), but the number of manservants was distinctly closer to the London ratio than to that of the rest of the country. The urban pattern of the distribution of manservants, revealed by these towns and the City of London, was clearly distinct.

As is implicit in these figures, this group of towns also displayed a higher proportion of single-manservant households than the country as a whole. Overall, only a quarter of households in these towns contained more than one taxpaying servant, compared with the 40 per cent for the country as a whole, and only 45 per cent of manservants, in towns were employed alongside one or more other manservants compared with the 70 per cent for England and Wales.[46] In this respect, too, these observations indicate a pattern closer to that of London. None of these corporate towns generated proportions of multiple-servant households greater than that of the national average, and only Newcastle, Chester and Norwich (at 39.4, 37.6 and 37.4 per cent respectively) even approached that level.

This arbitrary exploratory technique thus reveals significant differences between the larger towns and the country as a whole, and appears to provide strong confirmation of our earlier inference, that the tax bit harder on non-urban wealth, which was more likely to be displayed in the form of 'consumption', servants. Westminster in this context represented an extreme form of the non-urban consumption pattern. The further consequence of the exercise conducted in table 2.6 is to further elevate the position of two counties within the group identified in table 2.4 as having unusually high mean units of servants. By deducting their large towns from the reckoning, Cheshire and Yorkshire rise to first and third in our ranking of 'best-seated' counties.[47]

Two problems remain to be resolved in this preliminary analysis: what was different about the three towns which were closer to the national average; and what sort of people were the larger urban taxpayers, whose relative rarity made the servant pattern of towns so different? Both questions can be approached, albeit crudely, through simple record linkage. More sophisticated subsequent work will be required fully to sustain the case made. For the set of towns considered, the records of the tax paid on units of three or more servants have been compared with the nearest consistent and comprehensive source, the *Universal British Directory* of 1793–98. Inevitably, information derived from a directory published so long after the compilation of the tax record is unlikely to yield many satisfactory linkages, but it does suggest answers to both issues, which may be further refined in subsequent research, and through links to other sources.

The three towns that deviated from the general urban pattern most clearly help directly with both problems. York, while not unusual in its share of masters with two or more servants, *was* unusual in the proportion of those employed in multiple-servant households, and this may yield a further clue.[48] All possessed an unusual number of large units, and these can be broadly characterised as the households of the urban gentry.[49] Fewer than half of the employers in such towns can at present be identified with absolute certainty from the *Universal British Directory*, but in each case those listed under the 'gentry', the political leaders (normally the members of the aldermanic bench or the common council), the lawyers and the leading surgeons predominated. Two coal-fitter families, part of the town's mercantile élite, George Colpits Esq and Matthew Bell, were observable in Newcastle where the largest single return, for 11 servants, was made in the name of Mr William Fenwick. Chester, Norwich and York provided largely undiluted evidence of urban gentry among its largest returns. The other towns in our selected group differed in having a far lower proportion of these largest units, and perhaps had a correspondingly smaller population of such urban gentry. None of our others, with the possible exception of Exeter, shared with this group the characteristics of provincial legal and ecclesiastical capital that may have helped to reinforce these differences.

Here perhaps lies the answer to the minor conundrum. The largest units, in some provincial towns, in Westminster, and perhaps in the country as a whole, were those fundamentally of 'genteel' or 'grandee' character. By the late eighteenth century, these were relatively less well represented among the wealthier strata of the leading provincial towns, where commerce and industry was already coming to dominate. Perhaps it was thus only in those towns that best preserved the characteristics of the old social élite that such households were to be found in any number. The net effect is to point strongly to the view that here was a tax which, for a variety of reasons, was socially selective and fell more heavily on the old rather than the newer economic élite, those who, by their patterns of life, residence and behaviour, effectively volunteered to pay it.

V

This has been merely a preliminary excursion into the backstairs, attics and basements of later eighteenth-century England and Wales. It has been based largely on a single source, with the objective of exploring how far it can be made to yield interesting conclusions on the nature of the tax itself, on its incidence, and on features of service for the manservants it covered. On the basis of such a sketch, our conclusions should be modest, but still those that relate closely to the writings of Michael Thompson, and perhaps also to those of his own mentor, Professor Habakkuk.

Like its twentieth-century successor, SET, the Servants Tax appeared to have everything going for it at its introduction. It had the broad approval of contemporary economic and political opinion, it had been successfully piloted in the Netherlands, and it was both voluntary and self-enforcing. Who but a cheapskate would jibe at a modest guinea per head per annum? Yet it failed. It did so probably because the extent of 'consumption' (as distinct from 'profit') servants was overestimated; because the nature of the schedules drawn may have permitted avoidance; and because the attempt to tighten the net to include female servants after 1786 brought intense political resistance. Disappointing from the beginning in its yields, no better than half that anticipated by Lord North, it also proved increasingly expensive to collect, largely because of the assessment processes involved, which required a better bureaucracy than was available even in the Excise Office. Additionally, in its intrusive nature it proved increasingly costly in political terms. Thus an excellent even popular scheme came to grief.

Despite this, we can still draw some useful conclusions from its surviving records. It looks as though, on all of the tests that have been applied here, the genteel, Lord North's 'high classes of life', did pay the greater burden, and that the commercial and industrial, largely urban, wealthy, contributed rather less. This strongly suggests, following Michael Thompson's own arguments, that not all of this genteel consumption expenditure was conspicuous waste.[50] It provided employment, probably on a much wider scale than captured by the tax, with significant multiplier effects. Albeit marginally, through its differential incidence the tax may have sheltered some of industry and commerce from some of the short-term financial costs of the American War. From its records we may perhaps infer the existence of some fundamental differences in the social patterns of behaviour between these groups, noting some support for a contrast between the ostentatious gentry and the more canny new industrial and commercial orders.

Yet, in the end, the evidence of this tax does not support unrestricted suggestions of fiscal self-sacrifice by England's landed élite. We know from the work of Michael Thompson and others that the tax was being levied in a period that was characterized by rising domestic establishments. But it fell in gross and real yield over time, it proved an inelastic source of revenue, and was withdrawn by Pitt as soon as circumstances permitted, in the early 1790s. Much as opinion in the late 1770s appeared to endorse the taxation of 'the elegant conveniencies of life', the outward show of which was a growing feature of English landed society, they ultimately proved inadequate as a means of extending the fiscal base. Even so, allowing for the dangers of employing a failed tax as a source, it can offer the historian valuable and intriguing insights on a society in transition.

Notes

1 The quotation is from Charles Jenkinson, later the first Earl of Liverpool, who became Secretary-at-War in the North administration in 1778: J. Almon, *The Parliamentary Register, or History of the proceedings and debates of the House of Commons*, VII, 1777, p. 192 (14 May 1777).

2 Lord North, 14 May 1777, introducing the budget in the context of the growing expense of the American War: Almon, *Parliamentary Register*, VII, pp. 183–5.

3 Mr James Callaghan, Chancellor of the Exchequer, introducing Selective Employment Tax in the 1966 budget statement, 3 May 1966: *Parliamentary debates, Commons*, 5th ser., 727, 1453–4.

4 *The Economist*, CCXIX, 6402, 7 May 1966, pp. 559–61.

5 This tax is discussed briefly by J. J. Hecht, *The Domestic servant class in eighteenth-century England*, 1956, p. 33, where its quality as a record is dismissed. Hecht's dismissal appears not to be based upon an actual reading of the returns, which are only cited through secondary sources, and is an assertion rather than a considered judgement. Clear evidence of such citation may be found in note 3, p. 8, despite the presence of the returns for Yorkshire in print: J. J. Cartwright, 'List of persons who paid the tax on male servants in 1780', *Yorkshire Archaeological Journal*, XIX, 1898, pp. 65–80.

6 See, for example, the discussions in Thompson's *English landed society in the nineteenth century*, 1963, Chapter X, esp. pp. 272–9.

7 I quote Thompson, *ibid.*, p. viii; G. E. Mingay, *English landed society in the eighteenth-century*, 1963, *The Gentry*, 1976, and many subsequent works; J. V. Beckett, *The aristocracy in England 1660–1914*, Oxford, 1986.

8 H. J. Habakkuk, 'England', in A. Goodwin (ed.), *The European nobility in the eighteenth century: Studies of the nobilities of the major European states in the pre-reform era*, 1953, p. 21.

9 P. G. M. Dickson, *The financial revolution*, 1967; P. K. O'Brien, 'Political preconditions for the Industrial Revolution', in O'Brien and R. Quinault (eds) *The Industrial Revolution and British society*, Cambridge, 1993, esp. pp. 135–49.

10 P. Mathias and P. K. O'Brien, 'Taxation in England and France, 1715–1810', *Journal of European Economic History*, V, 1976. See also P. K. O'Brien, 'The political economy of British taxation, 1660–1815', *Econ. Hist. Rev.*, 2nd ser., XLI, 1988, pp. 1–32, and J. V. Beckett and M. E. Turner, 'Taxation and economic growth in eighteenth-century England', *Econ. Hist. Rev.*, 2nd ser., XLII, 1990, pp. 377–403.

11 This aspect of the political economy of taxation seems to have attracted remarkably little interest among economic historians in recent years, as they have looked to evaluate its macroeconomic impact, but is discussed extensively by W. Kennedy, *English taxation 1640–1799: an essay on policy and opinion*, 1913, esp. Ch. VI, pp. 95–112, and VII, 113–50, which provides an interesting survey of opinion leading up to Adam Smith.

12 Kennedy, *English taxation*, pp. 130–1.

13 Adam Smith, *An inquiry into the nature and causes of the wealth of nations*, 5th edn, 1789, Book V, Chapter II, III, p. 374.

14 J. E. D. Binney, *British public finance and administration 1774–92*, Oxford, 1958, pp. 68–9; Stephen Dowell, *A history of taxation and taxes in England from the earliest times to the year 1885*, 2nd ed., 1888, III, pp. 215–8.

15 The other key innovation of the period was the Inhabited House Duty in 1778, perhaps inspired directly by Adam Smith, *Wealth of Nations*, Book V, Chapter II,

III, pp. 284–5. Binney, *British public finance*, argued that Smith was rewarded for his suggestion by appointment to the Scottish Customs Board.

16 17 George III cap. XXXIX, I.

17 *Ibid.*, II.

18 *Ibid.*, I, X, XVI.

19 Smith, *Wealth of Nations*, Book V, Chapter II, III, p. 310.

20 My reworking of Smith's propositions, a linear 1:200 ratio, across Massie's social tables as reproduced in P. Mathias, 'The social structure in the eighteenth century: a calculation by Joseph Massie', *Econ. Hist. Rev.*, 2nd ser., X, 1957, pp. 30–45. Hecht, *Domestic servant class*, pp. 33–4, also discusses these numbers, and reaches broadly similar conclusions, while noting that female servants probably greatly exceeded their male counterparts in number.

21 This could appear to be implausibly low: Peter Laslett, 'Mean household size in England since the sixteenth century', in Laslett and R. Wall (eds) *Household and family in past time*, Cambridge, 1972, p. 157, put the proportion of households with resident servants at around 13 per cent. Many of these would of course have been female and many more, definitionally, 'production' servants, rather than the objects of consumption targeted by the tax. On a base of 13 per cent of households with resident servants, there would have been around 200–250,000 servants in the later 1770s, with a taxable proportion between 30 and 40 per cent.

22 Almon, *Parliamentary Register*, IX, 1778, Lord North, 6 March 1778, p. 2.

23 *Ibid.*, XII, 1779, 1 March 1779, pp. 12–13, 20.

24 The principal document studied in this chapter, PRO, T/47/8.

25 *Parliamentary Register*, XVII, 1780, 6 March 1780, pp. 200–1 and 15 March 1780, pp. 337–46.

26 21 George III, cap. XXXI, 1781, III.

27 25 George III, cap. 43, 1785, III and V.

28 25 George III cap. LXX, 1785; on the unpopularity of the extension, see Binney, *British Public Finance*, p. 69.

29 Figures have been extracted from parliamentary papers, reprinted in S. Lambert (ed.) *House of Commons Sessional Papers of the Eighteenth Century*, Wilmington, Delaware, 1975, 50, p. 145, 'An account of the gross produce of the undermentioned duties as far as the same can be made up . . .', 18 February 1786; 80, p. 257, 'An account of the annual net produce of the duties upon female servants . . . for four years, ending 5th April 1791', 15 February 1792.

30 Thompson, *English Landed Society*, pp. 188–9.

31 *Ibid.*, quoting the Farington diary for 1806, p. 188.

32 See below, n. 44.

33 Taken from the summary table in the listing, T/47/8, p. 1194. Percentages of households have been rounded to one decimal place; if given in full, they would total 100 per cent.

34 On the size of households of servants, see Hecht, *Domestic servant class*, pp. 1–8, which makes the obvious point that such retinues were smaller than many of those retained in earlier times.

35 Based at present upon their analysis of summary tables in T47/8 pp. 1189–91; England's population taken from E. A. Wrigley and R. S. Schofield, *The population history of England 1541–1871, a reconstruction*, 1981, p. 529, and London's population *c.* 1780 has been taken at 700,000.

36 I have suggested this in 'Food consumption and internal trade', in A. L. Beier and Roger Finlay (eds) *London 1500–1700: the making of the metropolis*, 1986, pp. 168–96.

37 This issue is discussed further below, p. 47.

38 Of course, what is required for a firm judgement of the meaning of these data is some comparative measure of real fiscal potential. Short of that, it is a reasonable assumption to reckon that such variations accorded with actuality, even if understating the real levels of domestic service.

39 See above, p. 41.

40 On servants, epecially the myriad female servants of the city, see M. D. George, *London life in the eighteenth century*, 1925 (Penguin edition, 1966), pp. 119–20, L. D. Schwarz, *London in the age of industrialisation: entrepreneurs, labour force and living conditions, 1700–1850*, Cambridge, 1992, pp. 45–8; and Hecht, *Domestic servant class, passim.*

41 Based upon an as yet incomplete reshuffling of the records of the tax into the city streets and wards. The issue of relative impact and possible inferential evidence of avoidance is discussed below, pp. 49–51.

42 Inferences drawn from the full listing of the tax record, now being collated in a machine-readable database. I am grateful for this and other extraction of data to Mr Jon Knox, and to Nick Steele and Katy Lyall, who input most of the data; the record was read from PRO microfilm, and I am very grateful to the School of Business & Economic Studies research initiative fund, and to Professor Christopher Elrington and the Victoria County History, who contributed to the funding of the filming. Mrs Arthington may have been the widow of Robert Arthington, brewer.

43 This requires a much fuller analysis of the data before wider conclusions can be drawn, but it does relate to some of Lawrence Stone's conclusions on the nature of gentry and aristocratic marriage in the period, as set out in his initial study, *The family, sex and marriage in England 1500–1800*, London 1977, and the later *Uncertain unions: marriage in England 1600–1753*, Oxford, 1992: neither provides a full assessment of the extent of this practice.

44 Taken from E. A. Wrigley, 'Urban growth and agricultural change: England and the continent in the early modern period', *Journal of Interdisciplinary History*, XV, 1985, pp. 683–728, table 7.1, as reprinted in Wrigley, *People, cities and wealth*, Oxford, 1987, pp. 160–1 reworking some of C. M. Law's original figures. There should, of course, have been nineteen towns in this group, excluding London, but, for reasons that are not yet clear, Nottingham returns appear not to have been consolidated into the records of the tax.

45 They produced 15 and 8 masters, and 16 and 11 servants respectively. Their returns have been excluded, as very questionable, also from the 'residue of county' columns.

46 The figures, precisely, were 25.8 per cent by households, and 44.7 per cent by servants, compared with the 39.6 per cent and 70.1 per cent derived from table 2.3.

47 Compared with the figures on p. 43, above.

48 On this measure, York joined the other three towns in the range of 55–60 per cent of servants thus employed, well below the national average for all taxpayers, but again very close to the London percentage (see above, table 2.4, p. ?).

49 T/47/8, *passim*, and *The Universal British Directory of trade, commerce, and manufacture*, 2nd edn, 1793–98, II, pp. 707 f. and IV, pp. 9 f., 29 f., 971f.

50 F. M. L. Thompson, 'Landownership and economic growth in England in the eighteenth century', in E. L. Jones and S. J. Woolf (eds), *Agrarian change and economic development: the historical problems*, 1969, pp. 41–60, esp. pp. 57–8.

3

AGRICULTURAL HAND TOOLS AND THE INDUSTRIAL REVOLUTION

E. J. T. COLLINS

One of the quainter anachronisms of rural life, surviving in most parts of the country up to and beyond the Second World War, was the astonishing variety of patterns of hand tools in use on English farms. There were not only large numbers of individual patterns, but the differences between one pattern and another were often so slight as to be barely perceptible to the casual eye, and to have had little or no effect on operational efficiency or method of use. Many of these are what are termed 'local' patterns, that is patterns which were peculiar to a specific locality, and which were denoted in makers' lists by the name of the region, county, town, even village, for which they were prescribed. Local patterns were most numerous among the so-called 'edge tools', herein defined as cutting tools made traditionally of iron with a steel cutting edge, such as axes, hatchets, billhooks, slashers, weeding hoes, digging hoes, sickles, scythes, reap hooks, spades and hay knives.

Folklore insists that local patterns are of great antiquity. They are widely believed to have been formulated in the remote past on the anvils of local smiths and to have survived into modern times due to the force of custom. Thus, long after the Industrial Revolution, manufacturers are said to have eschewed standardisation out of respect for the farm workers' attachment to traditional forms of tool. At the root of this belief are various assumptions about tool manufacture and pattern development in the pre-industrial period. But, in fact, most of our knowledge about the physiognomy and geography of tools is of much more recent date, being derived from museum collections of mainly nineteenth and early twentieth century tools, and manufacturers' literature.

The earliest known example of an illustrated agricultural tool catalogue is Joseph Smith's celebrated *Sheffield Key*, published in 1816,[1] but the first really authoritative record, relating specific patterns to specific places, is the outwork pattern books of the firms of Fussell of Mells and Isaac Nash of Stourbridge (*c.* 1840–96), which depict upwards of 150 named patterns of hooks, scythes and bills.[2] Ranges of local patterns were shown at the Great Exhibition of 1851. H. W. Slagg of Ford in Derbyshire, for instance, displayed the patterns of sickles and reap hooks suited, it was claimed, to the needs of the various 'neighbourhoods' in England and Wales.[3] The earliest individual makers' catalogues, however, date from about 1870, much later than for other tool-manufacturing trades, some of which were publishing illustrated lists in the late eighteenth century. By 1890 all first-rate houses and, by the time of the Great War, even the small makers were issuing them on a regular basis.

Various manufacturers' lists, catalogues and pattern books have been analysed in table 3.1 to show the distribution by region of 377 local patterns of 11 types of edge tool, during the period between approximately 1840 and 1950. As sources of information they are by no means infallible. Identical patterns were accorded different names by different manufacturers, just as patterns with the same name were not necessarily all the same shape. They provide, though, a reasonably complete inventory of the output of this branch of the hardware manufacturing trades, and allow a number of generalisations to be made about the production and distribution of local patterns in the nineteenth and early twentieth centuries.[4]

Local patterns form only a proportion of the total patterns produced. Tools were made in a range of sizes, normally four or five, but in the case of scythes as many as 29, ranging in length from 30 to 64 inches (0.75–1.60 m); in a range of haftings which could be tanged, socketed or strapped; and a range of finishes – black, bright, half-bright, self-coloured or painted red, blue or green. There were also several different styles of handles. About 1900 Nash of Stourbridge made three types of spade handle with eight different types of hand-grip, and three bill hook handles – turned, pistol-grip and caulked, with further variations in the shape of the foot.

There were patterns also which were classified according to other characteristics than shape: form of construction, type of material, mode of operation, function or application. For instance, in addition to 36 local patterns, there were 25 other patterns of weeding hoe: forged and riveted; swan neck, crane neck, short neck, long neck; half-moon, torpedo, short-shoulders, triangular, chisel, fork-end; onion, thistle, turnip, potato, wheat, bean; push, pull; singling, blocking. There were

Table 3.1 Regional distribution of local tool patterns

	axes	*shovels*	*mattocks*	*forks*	*spades*	*hoes*	*bagging hooks**	*scythes*	*reap hooks**	*sickles†*	*bills*	*totals*
London & South-east	4	–	2	1	1	6	6	3	5	2	12	42
South Central England (and Channel Islands)	3	–	1	2	3	3	10	2	7	1	25	57
South-west England	1	5	1	2	3	4	33	5	2	1	8	65
Eastern England	2	–	–	–	3	7	–	4	4	3	22	45
East Midlands	–	–	–	–	–	–	2	–	–	4	10	16
South Midlands	1	–	–	–	–	2	3	1	2	1	9	19
West Midlands	–	–	1	1	1	2	6	–	–	–	6	17
North Midlands	–	–	–	2	1	2	5	2	2	5	17	36
Northern England (and IoM)	2	–	–	1	4	1	–	6	4	4	8	30
Wales	1	2	3	–	2	1	10	3	7	2	19	50
totals	14	7	8	9	18	28	75	26	33	23	136	377

* This division of smooth hooks into bagging hooks and reap hooks is arbitrary, as to an extent these were interchangeable.

† Numbers of sickle patterns would be far fewer (about 14) if the Sheffield lists of 1861, 1871 and 1880 were interpreted differently.

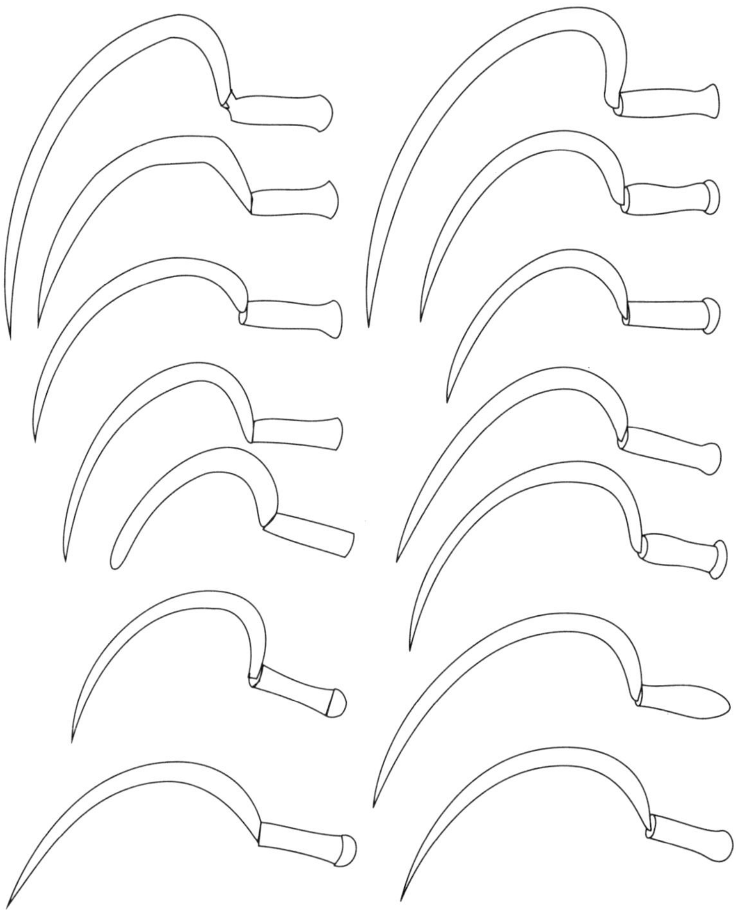

Figure 3.1 Sickle patterns: Smith's *Sheffield Key*, 1816

various other types of scythe: crown, patent, cast, riveted, solid, corn, bean, lawn, briar. The result was a prodigious number of individual models. It has been calculated from trade catalogues that, in the period 1919–39, the various companies comprising the Spear and Jackson Group offered 1,278 different sizes and patterns of hooks and slashers.[5] In the 1920s C. T. Skelton of Sheffield listed 746 different forks and spades, and Edward Elwell of Wednesbury, Staffs. sold 800 different harvesting and wood-cutting tools.[6]

The geographical distribution of local patterns was uneven. Table 3.1 shows far fewer in the north, the Midlands and East Anglia than in the south, south-west and Wales. In the north, especially, a single pattern

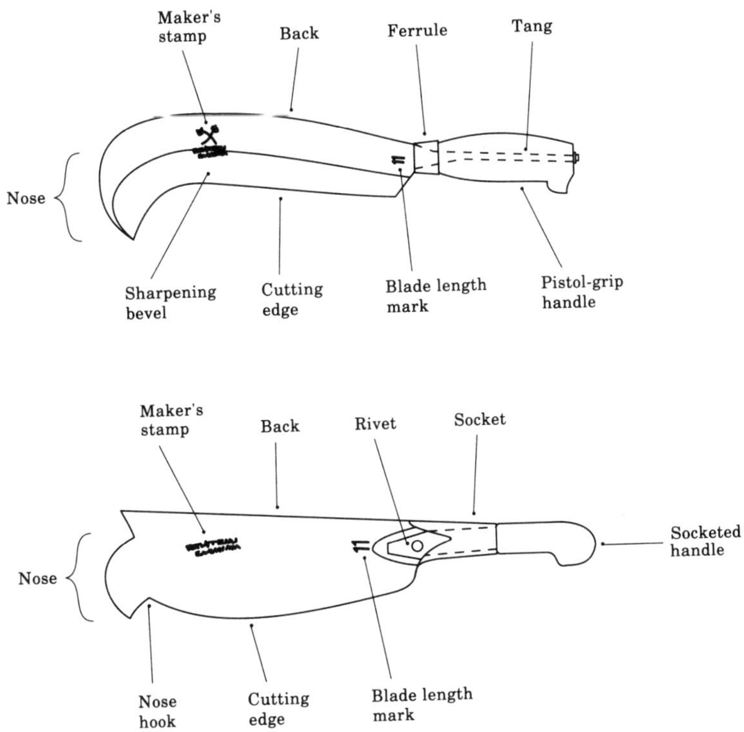

Figure 3.2 Bill-hook patterns: after R. Tabor, 'English bill-hook patterns', *Trades and Tool History Society Newsletter*, no. 11, 1985, p. 12

often served several counties, or an entire region. Local patterns were most numerous in Devon, Somerset, Wiltshire and mid-Wales, and least so in Durham, Cumberland, Lancashire, Cheshire, Norfolk and Essex.

There were more local patterns of some tools than others. This is shown in table 3.1, which lists 136 different named billhooks and likewise 108 bagging and reap books, but fewer than 20 mattocks, spades and axes. Local patterns, though, were often used outside their named localities. Ironmongers would normally have stocked at least three or four, and sometimes as many as ten named patterns of billhook. Patterns such as the Kent axe, London spade, Berkshire fagging hook, Yorkshire bill, and Bristol reap hook became 'universal patterns' used over a wide area, and especially popular in the urban centres where they were used for non-agricultural purposes, and where tool preferences were much weaker than in the countryside.

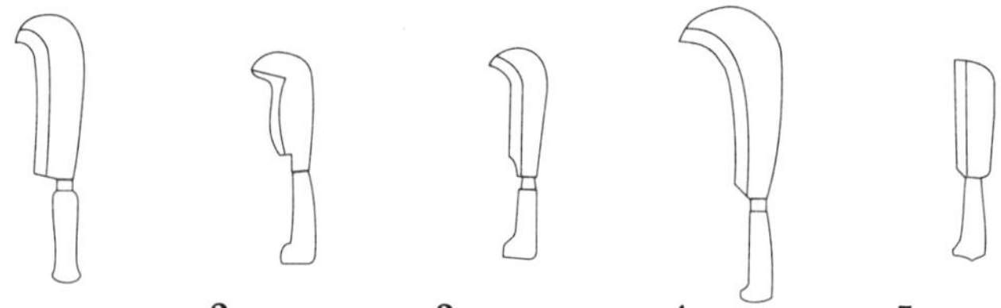

	1 Kent	2 Bristol	3 Knighton	4 Oxford	5 Rutland
nose	short	short	short	long	—
curvature	concave	convex	straight	concave	straight
nose-hook	sharp	sharp	sharp	sharp	—
cutting edges	one	one	one	one	one
hook°	—	—	—	—	—
handle	tanged	tanged	tanged	tanged	tanged

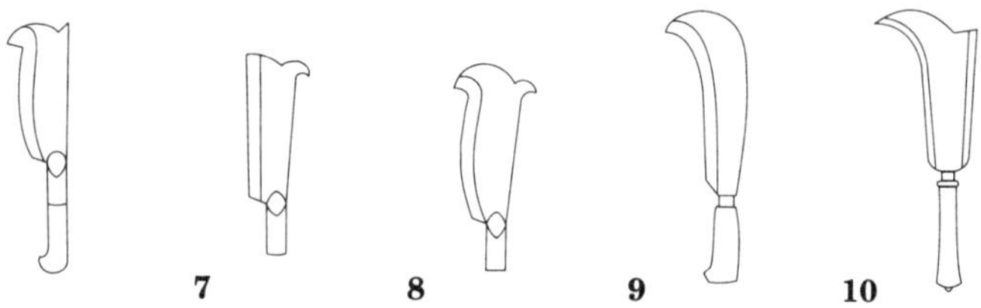

	6 Suffolk	7 Hertford	8 Offley	9 Shropshire	10 Yorkshire
nose	short	—	short	short	long
curvature	convex	straight	convex	concave	concave
nose-hook	sharp	—	sharp	open	open
cutting edges	one	one	one	one	double
hook°	180°	90°	90°	—	—
handle	socketed	socketed	socketed	tanged	tanged

Figure 3.3 Bill-hooks, key types.

Total numbers of local patterns seemingly increased over the nineteenth century and declined after 1920, at first gently and from 1950 precipitously, following a decision by leading makers to reduce product lines to a handful of universal and broad regional patterns. Numbers of sizes and patterns of spades, forks, shovels, hooks and slashers advertised by the Spear and Jackson companies fell from over 2,000 in 1919–39 to 150 in 1985.[7] Different tools exhibited, though, different trends. Sheffield sickle makers produced only about five patterns for the home market in 1914 compared with 12–14 in the early nineteenth century. Types of bill hooks, on the other hand, rose continuously up to the Great War or after. As an approximation, the variety of sickles began to contract from about 1850, reap hooks from 1870, scythes from 1900, and hoes, bill hooks and slashers from the 1930s. There was a relationship, albeit imprecise, between numbers of patterns and the size of the market. Thus the narrowing output of small hand harvesting tools after 1850 is linked to their gradual replacement by the bagging hook and scythe, then by reaping machines. Output of hoes and bill hooks held up well until after the Second World War, when chemical sprays obviated the need for hand weeding, and several factors – mechanisation, the demise of coppicing, hedgerow removal – diminished the demand for traditional wood-cutting tools.

I

Ethnographers and historians have assumed that the local patterns existing in the nineteenth century belonged to a craft tradition unbroken since medieval or even pre-historic times. 'The wide range of patterns', wrote Professor Allen, 'was due to the fact that in the days when no edge-tool industry in the modern sense existed, the village smiths of each agricultural district had been responsible for the evolution of the particular type of implement used there; and so, when agriculturists came to rely on industrial centres, they still demanded the special kind of tool to which traditional use had accustomed them'.[8] Others see the process as one of gradual coalescence, in which the patterns anciently produced by village blacksmiths merged to form regional patterns, whilst retaining numerous minor original features.[9] Local patterns are believed to have been ubiquitous to the point where, according to some historians, every county in Britain had a spade with a differently shaped blade, and every county its own bill hook.[10]

The basic forms of agricultural tools and key-types are clearly very old. Archaeology demonstrates that the balanced sickle, long and short scythe, bill hook, axe, hoe, mattock and spade, for instance, were in place by the end of the Roman Occupation.[11] There is a close resemblance between prehistoric and modern configurations of bill hook. Those excavated at Glastonbury are very similar to the present-day South of England pattern and one, with a cut-away nose, to the modern Devon, while a socketed example from Colchester is identical to the modern Suffolk. Manuscript evidence confirms that the five main forms of spade hand-grip had evolved by the later Middle Ages.[12]

Clearly, many of the basic design forms, or key-types, were formalised at an early stage but, as has already been shown, prior to the eighteenth century there is little evidence for the existence of local patterns as such. In Roman Britain the correlation between patterns and places is slight, at best inconclusive, it being possible to state only that certain shapes appear to have been more common in some regions than others while most occur widely. Depictions in medieval manuscripts are stylised and have no clear provenance. In the early modern period, references in probate inventories to stocks of tools on makers' premises distinguish only at the level of long, short or Scottish, as to scythes, or black or bright as to finish. There are few examples of medieval or early modern agricultural tools in museums, and few records pertaining to the early history of edge-tool manufacture. Yet it can be reasoned that had the local patterns produced in the nineteenth century descended from a craft tradition, there should be a correspondence between the geographical distribution of edge-tool makers in the pre-industrial period and that of local patterns in the modern period.

It is widely held that village smiths made all manner of agricultural tools. The folklorist, George Ewart Evans, states that the highest accolade that could be applied to a tool in East Anglia villages was 'blacksmith made'[13] A recent study of hedging states that bill hooks were once made by the local blacksmith to the user's specification.[14] Evidence, however, suggests that for all their versatility, very few smiths were adept at making edge-tools, and that before the Industrial Revolution, probably even in Roman times, tool manufacture was a highly skilled trade carried on mainly by specialists. Indeed, prior to the seventeenth century, smiths of any kind were rare; according to one analysis, even in economically advanced regions such as East Anglia fewer than one in ten villages could boast one.[15]

In medieval times the making of a durable edge may just have been within the competence of general smiths due to the particular quality of some bloomery irons, it being claimed that a steely iron made from certain ores could be work-hardened into a serviceable edge. In the 1960s in Nigeria, Professor Tylecote observed local smiths working crude iron of the same carbon content as Indian *wootz* steel into hoes and axes.[16] A high-phosphorus iron could be made into an edge as good as on any bronze tool. Steely edges could also be formed by case-hardening, where iron tools were packed in charcoal and re-heated in order to raise the level of carbon and so increase the hardness at the surface of the blade. These technical possibilities are still a matter of debate among metallurgical historians, but the balance of evidence – the rarity in Britain of ores rich in manganese and phosphorus, the slowness of the carbonising process and, not least, scientific analysis of the tools themselves – points to the likelihood that, from the high Middle Ages onwards, the majority of cutting tools were faced with steel. In the post-medieval period the types of iron produced by the indirect process, even after refining, were suitable only for tool bodies.[17]

Edge-tool manufacture was a difficult art. The commonest method was to forge-weld a small strip of steel between two plates of iron and beat out to form an edge.[18] The blade was then hardened, tempered and finally ground to a sharpness on a stone. All these operations required skill and fine judgement. Iron and steel having different melting heats, the two had to be brought together at an exact moment to make the bond. Steel burnt and was ruined if overheated. Many steels were of uneven quality and had to be re-forged to render them uniform and even then, the edges often were uneven and went soft. The hardener relied on an exact eye to recognise the heat of the metal by its colour and so determine the correct temperature at which to cool the blade by rapid quenching. Tempering was reckoned the most difficult art of all. Traditional 'blister', even high quality 'crucible' steels, had a variable carbon content, enough to affect the after-treatment of the blade, which often necessitated the testing of each individual piece to determine the proper tempering heat. Gaius Carley, who worked as an assistant to one of the last edge-tool smiths in Sussex, was never allowed to watch him tempering.[19] Likewise, at Cornard forge in west Surrey, the tempering of axe blades, for which the Moss brothers enjoyed a considerable local reputation, was a closely guarded secret.[20]

Given time and aptitude it was not impossible for a general smith to make a passable edge-tool but his work output was, in most cases, very low. The last maker in Hampshire, Henry Willis of Bramley, a blacksmith, made hooks and bills when trade was slack at the rate of 2–3 a day, and never more than 150 tools a year.[21] Willis, in fact, had shown as a boy a rare ability to shape a hook, but from old steel rasps, not by the traditional method of forge-welding steel onto iron. Sheet steel and iron and steel laminate became available in the second half of the nineteenth century, but were said not to weld as well as blister steel onto Swedish iron. Patent steels enabled some blacksmiths to specialise in the manufacture of weeding hoes, but the heavier tools such as spades and hooks remained the preserve of specialist makers. Up to the Second World War, when hand-forging ceased, the hook-smiths had been the aristocrats of the workforce in the factory firms, ahead of the spade and shovel makers. The making of solid (cf. riveted) scythes was generally reckoned the most skilled work of all, on account of the difficulty in maintaining an even heat over a large area of blade during welding and tempering.[22]

The trades of edge-tool maker and blacksmith were normally quite separate. Blacksmiths' accounts contain numerous references to sharpening, repointing and very occasionally re-steeling but, apart from weeding hoes, seldom if ever to manufacture. As far as can be discovered virtually none, or very few, of the edge-tool firms extant in the nineteenth century were founded by blacksmiths. Contrary to a misleading but often quoted statement by the naturalist Plot, edge-tools were not made by whitesmiths.[23] Whitesmiths rather made articles such as bolts, screws and spindles, not by forging but with the aid of files, lathes and rivets.[24] Spade-making was also a separate trade, carried on in different shops from the making of the crescentic tools. Of the 72 spade works operating in Ireland from the mid-eighteenth century, only three made scythes or hooks.[25]

In 1760 edge-tool manufacturing was a highly concentrated trade, centred around Sheffield and Birmingham. The former's pre-eminence dated from the Middle Ages[26] and by the late seventeenth century there were 600 smiths in the area, carrying on a large and rapidly expanding business with northern England, Scotland, the east Midlands and, not least, London, the entrepôt for southern and central England, and the south coast.[27] By 1750 aggressive marketing by the Sheffield masters or their factors had all but destroyed the traditional industry in East Anglia.[28] Birmingham and the Black Country, on the other hand, looked to the west and south Midlands, Wales and south-west England for its principal markets, although Worcestershire scythesmiths were already selling in Eton and Cambridge in the sixteenth century.[29] Little is known about the early history of the industry in Gloucestershire and Somerset, which emerged as a third centre, rivalling the west Midlands during the eighteenth century. Competition between manufacturing regions was fiercest in the north Midlands, Wales and the West Country, and the Home Counties.

Manufacturing activity outside these main areas appears, on the face of it, thin, inferring that by 1700 or earlier, edge-tool production had very largely ceased over much of the country. This is a rash assertion, but one that is lent weight by the results of a survey of the indexes of trades and occupations in local record offices, which suggest the following pattern of industrial distribution.[30] Few makers are recorded in south and south-east England or, apart from around Birmingham and Sheffield, over most of the north and midlands. Makers are at all common only in central southern and south-west England, and parts of East Anglia. Essex, for instance, records 21 makers in 12 towns and villages in the period 1588–1758, mostly around Chelmsford and Bishop's Stortford; and Suffolk records about a dozen, in and around Bury St Edmunds. Otherwise, there are relatively high densities in Wiltshire, around

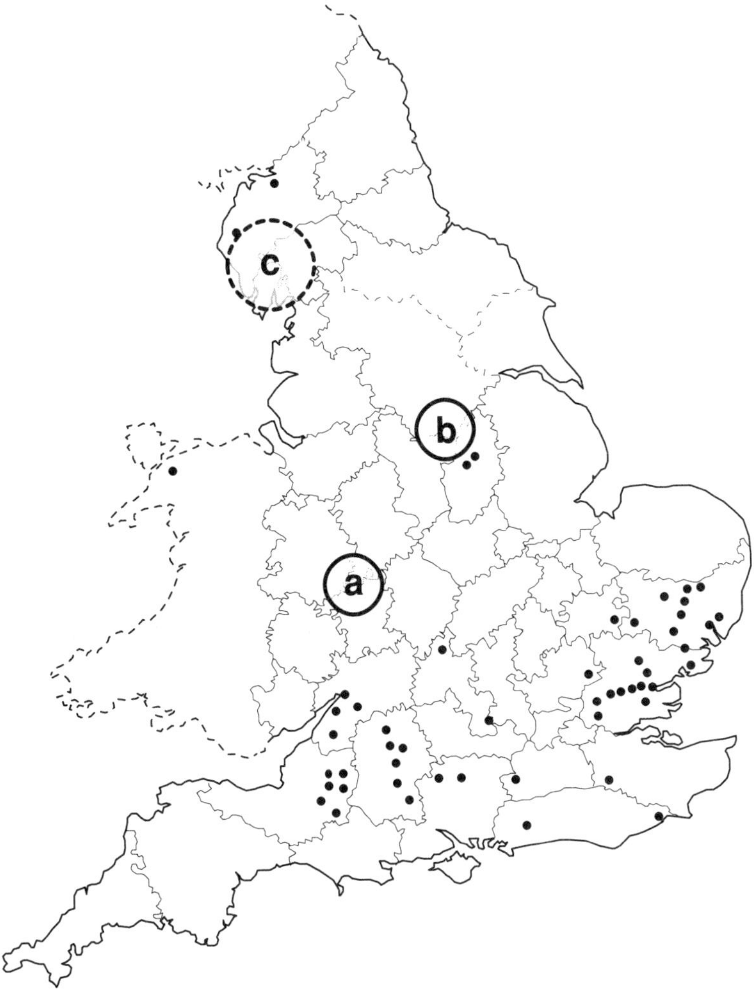

Figure 3.4 Location of edge-tool makers, *c.* 1550–1800
a West Midlands region; b Sheffield region;
c Lakeland and Furness

Salisbury; in Gloucestershire at several points including Gloucester and Cirencester; and in Somerset, mostly between Frome and Shepton Mallet.

Comparing the regional distribution of patterns in table 3.1 with that of manufacturers in figure 3.4 prompts the following conclusions: in the north and midlands, few local makers and few local patterns; in East Anglia, few local patterns but large numbers of local makers; in west central England, large numbers of both. There appears to have been little continuity of manufacture in the old medieval cutlery centres of Chester, Derby, Godalming, Hereford, Thaxted, Nottingham, Woodstock or London. In Salisbury the industry survived into the seventeenth century while, elsewhere in the county, at Mere and Netheravon for example, agricultural edge tools in a variety of local patterns continued to be produced up to the 1890s.[31] It is tempting to attribute the dearth of patterns in the north and midlands to the dominance of the Sheffield and west Midlands makers and, over the centuries, the coalescence of local into regional patterns. On the other hand, in Essex and Suffolk, where there was a flourishing local industry up to the mid-eighteenth century, the legacy was meagre: one hoe and five bill hooks. Why, in the nineteenth century, there should have been such large numbers of patterns in south and south-west England and Wales is still to be explained.

II

Local patterns are, by definition, formalised patterns, and a crucial question is at what stage of development the dimensions were fixed, and by whom. It seems unlikely that this would have been done by the local smith who, it will be argued, saw little benefit in producing standardised patterns. A possible sequence of events is suggested by his modern counterpart, a local smith forging edge-tools on an anvil from sheet steel in an industrial village near Izmir in western Turkey, observed by the author during fieldwork in 1980. Though all of the same key-type, no two tools were identical. Bill hooks, for instance, displayed a remarkable diversity as to the degree of curvature of the blade and the angle and size of the nose. Variation, the smith explained, was essential to meet the varying needs of his customers, for whom balance and weight rather than shape were the most important considerations in the choice of tool. Yet standardised patterns were obtainable in a nearby iron-monger's shop, which carried a stock of identical bills, cheaper than the smith's, but less robust, made by a factory firm in Ankara.

Thus it may have been that local patterns were formalised, not by small local makers producing generalised patterns for a local market, but by large makers producing fixed patterns for distant markets. This happened, perhaps, over much of northern and central Britain when, in the early modern period, Sheffield and West Midland makers or their factors, began to widen their markets. Where the merchandising was controlled by a relatively few firms of factors, who supplied the small masters and independent workmen with their patterns, there was opportunity for standardisation or, at any rate, some narrowing of patterns once

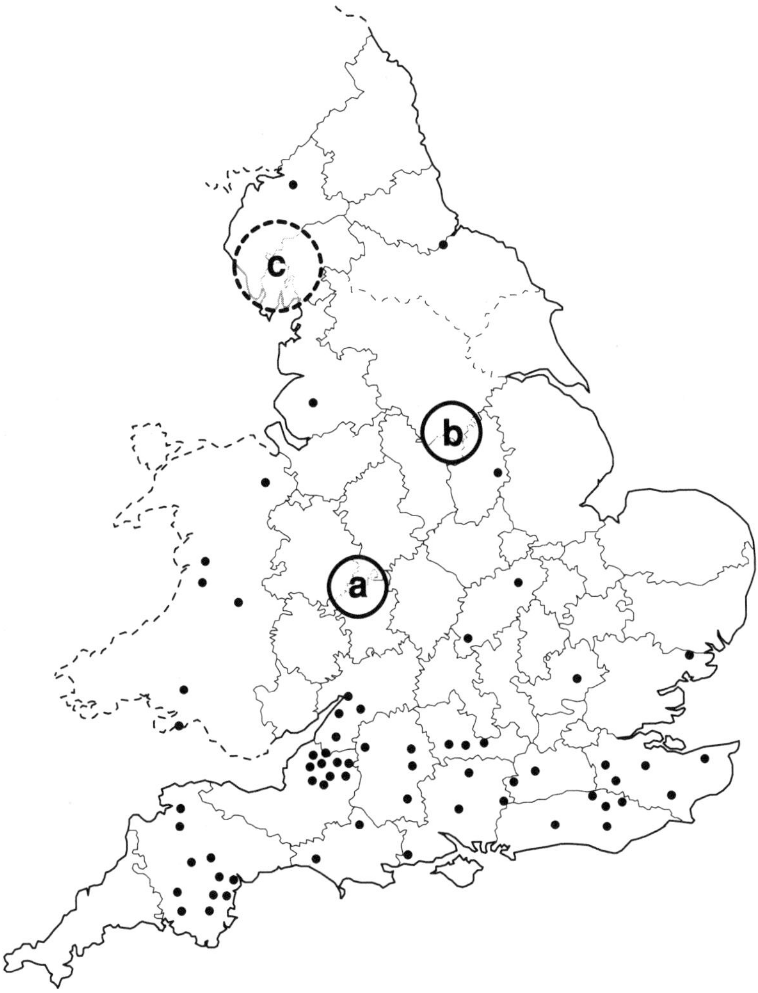

Figure 3.5 Location of edge-tool makers, *c.* 1800–1939
a West Midlands region; b Sheffield region;
c Lakeland and Furness

the local opposition had been eliminated. By this reasoning a large proportion of the 17 or so patterns of reap hooks and sickles represented in the *Sheffield Key* of 1816 had been formalised, probably, in the seventeenth and eighteenth centuries. This, though, accounts for only some of the patterns existing in the nineteenth century. It does not explain their multiplicity in the south and west, where their numbers increased, nor the many local patterns of tools, such as the bagging hook, weeding hoe and all-iron spade, the use and manufacture of which became widespread only after the mid-eighteenth century. The answer would seem to lie, not in the pre-industrial era, but in the Industrial Revolution itself, in the changes then taking place in the structure and organisation of the edge-tool manufacturing trades.

The proliferation of local patterns in south and south-west England and Wales was linked to, or a direct result of, the development there of an edge-tool manufacturing industry from the mid-eighteenth century, parts of which survived up to 1900, or in exceptional cases up to the Second World War (see figure 3.5). Manufacturing activity was especially vigorous in the south-west, in Gloucestershire, Somerset and Devon. The most famous of the firms, Fussell of Mells, established in 1744, rose to become one of the largest and, for a time, most technologically advanced in the country, the leading supplier of agricultural and industrial edge-tools not just to the south-west but adjoining regions, as far east as Berkshire, and with a good trade in London and the south midlands.[32] On account of their large and expanding trade with south Wales and the Marcher counties, firms such as Fussell and the Coaley Ironworks were regarded by Birmingham and Black Country makers as a far greater threat than Sheffield.

The West Country industry was highly innovative, being the first to use water-powered tilt hammers for the steeling and plating of edge-tools, operations previously performed by manual labour. This gave it a temporary advantage over its northern competitors who, up to the eighteenth and early nineteenth centuries, used water-power principally for grinding. Gloucestershire, indeed, is said to have supplied key workers to the Black Country. Works were set up on the fast-flowing streams around Dartmoor from the early nineteenth century, and in central and south Wales around 1850, often in converted corn or textile mills. In contrast to the West Country with its abundant water-power, firms in southern England, some established in the eighteenth century, others after 1850, and one as late as 1920, were pre-industrial. Of the 17 or so makers so far identified, all were very small, some with just a single workman, and used primitive methods: hammer and anvil, and grindstones driven by hand, foot-treadle, horse or donkey.[33]

A decline set in about 1840, after which the industry became increasingly dominated by a hierarchy of integrated factory firms. The occupational census for 1841 shows Sheffield and the West Midlands with just over 80 per cent of all edge-tool workers, but, surprisingly as many as 15 per cent in south-west England. After half a century of recurrent crises and steadily falling output, the once mighty firm of Fussell finally went under, with the result that by 1890 all but a tiny proportion of the national output was produced by the northern and midland firms. The point though is that over a broad sweep of England, from Kent, through Wiltshire and Somerset to Devon, as well as over large parts of Wales, there existed in the early nineteenth century a viable edge-tool industry which succeeded in stemming, and for a time perhaps even reversing, the seemingly irresistible advance of the Sheffield and Midland makers. In 1914 there were in those regions about 20 firms and in 1925 about 10, mainly in Devon, where electric motors had begun to supplement or replace the original water-wheels. In the south-west especially, there was intense three-way competition, between local, regional and national manufacturers, and a complex process of copy, counter-copy and invention, out of which arose the multiplicity of local patterns. There is a clear correlation between the distribution of manufacturers in figure 3.5, and of patterns in table 3.1.[34]

III

A feature of the edge-tool industry in the nineteenth century was the breadth and depth of its products, which vastly exceeded the technical needs of its customers, and the minute segmentation of the market. Edge-tools, though, were neither mass-produced nor mass-marketed. Up to the late eighteenth century edge-tool making was a small workshop trade. Tools were sold by itinerant salesmen in fairs and markets or, in the case of local makers, by custom, from market stalls or door-to-door. Radical changes in production and marketing occurred from 1750. Production was increasingly dominated by national and regional firms while, in distribution, the central figure was now the ironmonger. The aim of the larger manufacturers was to increase market share through a strategy based on quality, promotion of the trade mark and customer goodwill. The emphasis was on marketing rather than production, on diversified not standardised products, and on segmented as against mass markets.

Manufacturers competed on the basis not of price but of quality and service. In such a system, the ironmonger played a key role. He selected his suppliers and decided which patterns to stock. Indeed he could demand, and first-rate houses would usually ask him to submit patterns to his own specification. The Fussell pattern books (*supra*) confirm that a large proportion of local patterns was supplied by local ironmongers in the form of drawings or cut-outs. Patterns were classified by town or village, and the name of the ironmonger or factor who originated them, viz., 'Milverton Hewing Stephen's Pattern 1849', 'Speenhamland Berks Bagging Mr C. Wheeler's patterns for 1854', and 'Southam Bean Turner's pattern 1860'. Many of these patterns were subsequently incorporated in the firm's printed catalogues. Most patterns were copies of existing patterns by other manufacturers, or chosen from the outputs of local makers. Thus is is reasoned, competition between the different types of manufacturer, and of marketing systems, led to the multiplication of local patterns. The supplying of exclusive patterns was part of the strategy for expanding and consolidating dealer networks and strengthening brand loyalty. That in the same town or district, different ironmongers were supplied by different manufacturers, could account for variations within the local pattern, for example, the six or so different shapes of Suffolk bill hook.

Why were firms apparently so loathe to standardise their products, even when the market for agricultural edge-tools was static or declining? Of the 91 different patterns of bill hook produced by Elwell of Wednesbury in the 1930s, most were turned out in batches of fewer than 200, and sales were sometimes less than a dozen a season. Obsession with multiformity achieved its ultimate expression just prior to the First World War when John Redford of Sheffield made 10,000 varieties of engineers' files, not to mention needle files, saw files, and rasps; a source of wonder to be sure, but a phenomenon that has never been satisfactorily explained in business terms.[35]

What is clear is that by the late nineteenth century the leading houses measured success in terms of their ability to extend a product to the very limits of its niche, an objective in the furthering of which trade catalogues played an increasingly important role. Lavish productions of up to 150 pages, they depicted the entire range of patterns, many of which we know to have been produced in minute quantities. Sometimes as many as 8–10 pages were devoted to bill hooks, to which were attached a significance far exceeding their agricultural, still less commercial, importance. One retired warehouse manager confided that the invention of bill hook patterns was something of a game between the great houses before the war.[36] Despite machine tools, economies of scale were elusive; the production of short runs could always be justified even in the largest and best equipped firms. Only certain operations, mainly in the initial stages of production, were fully mechanised. Steam-powered hammers, flys, presses, shears and grindstones were standard in all large firms by the 1870s, but steel-faced tools were still forge-welded on individual hearths and hardened and tempered by eye.[37]

In short, there was no mass production in the true sense; there was little standardisation and the small maker was able to compete with the factory firm. There was some rationalisation, mainly of reap hooks and sickles in the late nineteenth century, and further limitation between the wars. One manufacturer claimed that, between 1917 and 1927, he had reduced his output of 300 patterns to 75 regular and 25 intermediary, with the result that machines could be set to run for three weeks where previously they might have to be re-set two or even three times a day.[38] In the Second World War the Ministry of Supply secured further reductions. However, the major turning point was the early 1950s, when a cartel of leading manufacturers decided to delete the majority of patterns from their lists and restrict production to a narrow range of 'universal' or regional types. Progressive reductions have occurred in the face of, on the one hand, more automated production systems and a switch from forge-welded to stamped tools and, on the other, agricultural mechanisation and revolutionary changes in tool retailing which is now largely channelled through DIY shops and garden centres. In other European countries the pruning has been less drastic. One Italian manufacturer still advertises 98 different patterns of bill hook![39]

IV

We have been concerned with the manufacture of hand tools rather than with their use, and have not so far mentioned the agricultural worker whose fierce attachment to traditional patterns is believed to have been an obstacle to standardisation. The relationship between the worker and his tools is intimate and complex and when, as was the case in the nineteenth century, work was often paid for by the piece, income could be directly related to working efficiency. Fieldwork suggests, however, that land workers were more particular about the weight and balance of a tool, and its size, than about its shape, which, as long as it resembled more or less the approved key-type, was of little consequence. When asked why they used specific patterns, they replied that these were the ones stocked by the local ironmonger and, being efficient, they saw no need to change them. Brand loyalty, though, was strong. In southern England the name Fussell of Mells is still highly esteemed, even though the firm went out of business in 1890, and its trade marks, subsequently acquired by Nash of Stourbridge, were last used in the 1950s. Berkshire woodmen had a special affection for the bill hooks made in the traditional manner by Pike of Thatcham, who gave up in the Great War, but whose tools are still remembered for their wonderful balance and razor-sharpness. Indicatively, there was little reaction when, in the early 1950s, hundreds of local patterns were deleted at a stroke. Apart from a question in Parliament in 1941, querying the decision by the Ministry of Supply to stop the production of the Ormskirk spade, the demise inside less than a decade of almost the entire national inventory of local tool patterns created little stir.

In conclusion: it is contended that whereas key-types probably evolved in pre-historic times, formalised patterns, local or otherwise, are of much more recent origin, some seventeenth and eighteenth but the majority nineteenth century, and evolved out of changes in manufacture and marketing. There is little which connects nineteenth-century patterns and pre-industrial village smiths. The former were most numerous in those areas, notably southern and south-west England, where there was a thriving edge-tool industry in the nineteenth century, in competition with Sheffield and the West Midlands. Another reason for doubting the conventional wisdom as to origins, is that not just ancient tools, but tools which only came into general use in the eighteenth and early nineteenth centuries had local patterns. The all-iron spade, for example, which gave rise to innumerable local patterns in Ireland, replaced the traditional wood and iron-sheath spade only after 1750.[40] Similarly, the bagging hook, which took over from the reap hook and sickle for harvesting wheat over much of south and west Britain, was used in only a very few areas – south Devon, the London area and Hereford – up to 1800;[41] likewise the hand-hoe, which entered general husbandry only in the eighteenth century with the spread of the turnip and market garden crops.

I have offered an economic explanation of what is often regarded as an ethnographic phenomenon. The social anthropologist, Clifford Geertz might have regarded the development of edge-tools as an interesting example of 'cultural involution', that is, progressive internal complication, which takes over from inventiveness once the limits of utility have been reached.[42] Local patterns though, like traditions, can be invented, a process which Professor Hobsbawm has described as one of 'formalisation characterised by references to the past, if only by imposing repetition'.[43] The development of patterns was a highly complex process, the exact nature of which can only be guessed at. Within the broad frame of agricultural history, hand tools may deserve only a footnote but, like another anachronism, Professor F. M. L. Thompson's urban horse,[44] it is an example of how, in the age of industrialism, old and new technologies expand simultaneously.

Notes

The author wishes to acknowledge the financial support of the ESRC; the firms of Spear and Jackson Ltd., Bulldog Tools Ltd. and ex-employees for information about the modern industry, and the many archivists who kindly searched through their indices for reference to early edge-tool makers.

1 Joseph Smith, *Explanation or Key to the various manufacturers of Sheffield* (ed. J. S. Kebabian), Early American Industries Association, 1975.

2 There are altogether five books, four (one Nash, three Fussell) deposited with the Hampshire County Museums Service, Winchester, and one (Fussell) at the Institute of Agricultural History, University of Reading.

3 *Official description and illustrated catalogue of the Great Exhibition*, London 1851, vol.

II, class 22, p. 610. Most of the tools exhibited by Slagg and other northern makers were for regions or groups of counties (Kent and the Isle of Wight the principal exceptions). The west midlands and south-west England on the other hand made large numbers of individual county and town patterns.

4 Sources are trade catalogues of the following firms: Isaac Nash & Sons (1899, 1940), Edward Elwell (*c.* 1930, 1955), Wm. Hunt & Sons (1915), A. Morris & Sons (*c.* 1950), Bullock and Sons (*c.* 1940s), C. T. Skelton (1914–15), Whitehouse Brothers (1904), Brades, Tyzack and Nash (1955), Spear and Jackson (1880), Chas. Thomas & Co. (1900), John Yates & Co. (*c.* 1920), J. Knapman (*c.* 1920), W. Gilpin (*c.* 1870), A. F. Parkes (*c.* 1970), T. Staniforth (1922), Cornelius Whitehouse (1952), Finch Brothers (*c.* 1914); Other sources: pattern books of Fussell & Sons (1844–73),. Isaac Nash & Co. (1881–96), *Official guide to the Great Exhibition* (1851); Sheffield Standard Lists (1816 & subsequent editions, esp. 1880).

5 K. Hawley 'Calling a spade a b. . . . y shovel' *Trades and Tool History Society Newsletter*, no. 23 (1988), p. 30.

6 *Ibid.*, p. 23.

8 G. C. Allen, *The industrial development of Birmingham and the Black Country 1860–1927*, 1929, p. 67.

9 R. Tabor, 'English bill-hook patterns', *Trades and Tool History Society Newsletter*, no. 11 (1985), p. 4. Hawley, 'Calling a spade . . .', p. 27 takes a similar position, i.e. that 'each pattern and size served a particular purpose', many of which were initially developed by local blacksmiths.

10 A. Huxley, 'Digging through the centuries', *Jnl. Royal Horticultural Society*, vol. III (1986), p. 483; A. Brooks, *Hedging*, 2nd rev, Wallingford, 1984, p. 33.

11 The most up-to-date and comprehensive study of ancient British tools is Sian E. Rees, *Agricultural implements in pre-historic and Roman Britain*, BAR, British Series, 69 (ii), 1979, pts 1 & 2. See also K. D. White, *Agricultural implements of the Roman world*, Cambridge, 1975; For spades, see W. D. Hassall, 'Notes on medieval spades', in A. Gailey and S. Fenton (eds), *The spade*, Belfast, 1970; W. H. Manning, 'Mattocks, hoes, spades and related tools in Roman Britain', in *Ibid.*

12 Tabor, 'English bill-hook pattterns', p. 11; R. G. Burgess, 'A load of old billhooks', *Tools and Trades History Society Newsletter*, no. 20 (1988), pp. 27–9.

13 G. E. Evans, *The farm and the village*, 1969, p. 134.

14 Brooks, *Hedging*, p. 34.

15 J. Patten, 'Urban occupations in pre-industrial England', *Trans. Inst. British Geographers*, no. 2 (1977), pp. 296–317.

16 R. F. Tylecote, 'Iron smelting in pre-industrial communities', *Trans. Iron and Steel Institute*, April 1965, pp. 340–58.

17 On this topic see R. F. Tylecote, 'The medieval smith and his methods' in D. W. Crossley (ed.), *Medieval industry*, CBA Research Report no. 40, 1981, p. 42 ff; H. R. Schubert, *History of the British Iron and Steel Industry*, 1957, p. 120; J. Harvey, *Medieval craftsmen* 1975, p. 176; R. A. Barron, *The Finch Foundry Trust and Sticklepath Museum of Rural Industry*, n.d., Sticklepath, Devon; H. Cleere and D. Crossley, *The iron-industry of the Weald*, Leicester Univ. Press, Leicester 1985, p. 104; K. C. Barraclough, *Sheffield Steel*, Buxton, 1975, pp. 10–11; W. R. Childs, 'England's iron trade in the fifteenth century', *Econ. Hist. Rev.*, 2nd ser., vol. XXXIV, 1981, p. 43.

18 For techniques, see A. W. Beaver, *The art of blacksmithing*, New York, 1976; Barron, *The Finch Foundry Trust*; M. Schofield, 'Five centuries of scythe making', *Country Life*, 5 December 1952; D. Tresner, *The scythe book*, Brattleboro, Vermont, 1981, pp. 5–11; Lloyd, *The cutlery trades*, 1913, pp. 30–63; Sheffield City Museums, *Information Sheet*, '3: Scythe-making at Abbeydale'; C. A. Turner, *A Sheffield Heritage*, Sheffield, 1973.

19 G. Carley, *The memoirs of Gaius Carley, a Sussex blacksmith*, Chichester, 1964, p. 20.

20 *Ex inform* Mr S. Moss, Tunbridge Crescent, Liphook; Mr L. G. Giles, Hollycombe Close, Liphook (3 October 1984).

21 *Ex inform* Mr A. H. Willis, Bramley, Hants (6 March 1985).

22 *Ex inform* Mr F. Ellis, Bridgnorth Road, Wollaston, Stourbridge, (15 September 1985).

23 Quoted in E. J. Homeshaw, 'Edge tools', *VCH Staffs* (1967), vol. II, p. 259.

24 Rev. Dionysius Lardner, *A treatise on ... manufacturers in metal*, 1833, vol. II, chap. 6.

25 Gailey, *Spade making in Ireland*, Ulster Folk and Transport Museum, 1982, pp. 49–79.

26 The best accounts of the Sheffield trades are D. Hey, 'The origins and early growth of the Hallamshire cutlery and allied 'trades', in J. Chartres and D. Hey (eds), *English rural society: essays in honour of Joan Thirsk*, Cambridge, 1990, pp. 343–67; D. Hey, *The rural metal workers of the Sheffield region*, Department of Local History, University of Leicester, 1972; G. I. Lloyd, *The cutlery trades* 1913; D. H. Blackwell, *The growth and decline of the scythe/sickle (shear) trade in Hallamshire*, unpub. Ph.D. thesis, University of Sheffield, 1973.

27 Blackwell, *Growth and decline of the scythe trade*, vol. I, pp. 65 ff; A. McPhee, *The growth of the cutlery and allied trades up to 1814*, typescript, Sheffield Public Libraries, 1939, *passim*; Hey, *Rural metal workers*; D. Hey, *Sheffield and its region 1660–1800*, nd., typesecript, with the compliments of the author, pp. 8–9.

28 A. H. Whitehead, *Garretts of Leiston*, 1964, pp. 8–9.

29 For edge-tool making in the West Midlands, see: Homeshaw, 'Edge tools', pp. 259–62; Allen, *Industrial development of Birmingham*, pp. 67–8; S. Timmins (ed.), *The resource, products and industrial history of Birmingham and the Midland Hardware district*, 1886, p. 657; M. B. Rowlands, *Masters and men ...*, Manchester University Press, 1975, pp. 8–32; W. H. B. Court, *The rise of midland industry*, 1938, pp. 37 ff; P. M. Frost, *The growth and localization of rural industry in south Staffordshire 1560–1720*, unpublished Ph.D. thesis, University of Birmingham, 1973, pp. 453–502.

30 The survey was, of necessity, limited. In many cases, either county record officers did not possess comprehensive indices of trades and occupations, or wills and inventories were located elsewhere. There was a problem too of nomenclature, edge-tool craftsmen being variously described as shearman, sheersmith, sickle smith, scythe smith, edge-tool maker, edge-tool smith, etc. The following county offices held detailed listings: Bedford, Bucks, Cambridge, Cumbria, Dorset, Essex, Hampshire, Hereford and Worcester, Kent, Lincoln, Norfolk, Nottingham, Notts, Oxon, Suffolk, E & W Sussex, Wiltshire.

31 C. Haskins, *The ancient trade guilds and companies of Salisbury*, Salisbury, 1919, pp. 370–1, 375; *Kelly's directory*, Wiltshire, 1855–1915.

32 On Fussell and other Somerset firms, see Burgess, 'A load of old bill-hooks', pp. 30–3; R. Athill, *Old Mendip*, Newton Abbot, 1964, pp. 79 ff; private communication, Robert Athill, 5 August 1985; R. Athill, *Mendip: a new study*, Newton Abbot, 1976, pp. 67 ff; *The Somerset Year Book 1934*, pp. 63–5. For Devon, see: Barron *The Finch Foundry Trust*; D. Gordon, 'Industry in a Devon village', *Country Life*, 14 January 1944; and private communications from: R. A. Barron, Sticklepath; Mrs Nora Peters, Hanham Rd, Salisbury; Dr Gregory Finch, Lawn Rd, Exmouth; Mr Morris, Iron Mills, Dunsford.

33 An illustration is the Moss brothers of Cornard forge, Liphook where all forging was done by hand (the smith working the light hammer, his assistant the sledge), and all grinding done by horse-wheel. The Mosses made, chiefly, hooks, bills and axes for sale in the Guildford district. Their advantage was their skill in tempering the steel. Their tools were heavier and contained more iron than factory-made tools. *Ex inform* Mr S. Moss and L.C. Giles (see n. 20).

34 Figure 3.5 is based mainly on directory evidence (e.g., Pigot, Kelly) and, for the early nineteenth century, the invaluable *Biennial directory ... for the brass, copper and metal trades in London and 480 towns*, 1816–17. For Wales I am grateful for the advice of Mr Elfyn Scourfield of the Welsh Folk Museum. The map omits various possible sites in Lakeland and Furness. Some purely spade mills (e.g., Dalston and Cleator) were erected from the late eighteenth century. According to J. D.

Marshall and M. Davies-Shiel there were over twenty mills and forges engaged in the manufacture of 'sickles, spades and edge-tools' in the region (*The industrial archaeology of the Lake Counties*, 2nd rev. edn 1977, p. 100). There were very few nineteenth-century local patterns for Cumbria and N. Lancashire.

35 Hawley, 'Calling a spade . . .', p. 23; *ex inform* Mr F. Ellis (see n. 22).

36 *Ex inform* Mr F. Ellis (see n. 22).

37 For nineteenth-century technical developments, see: Lardner, *A treatise*, vols I–II *passim*; Timmins, *Resource and industrial history of Birmingham*, p. 657; Blackwell, *Growth and decline of the scythe trade*, vol. I, pp. 138–65; *Implement and Machinery Review* (features on manufacturing firms), II (1877), pp. 822–23 (Elwell); IV (1878), pp. 186–90 (Spear and Jackson); XX (1894) pp. 184–9 (C. T. Skelton); Other firms in R. Morgan, *Farm tools, implements and machines in Britain: pre-history to 1945: a bibliography*, Institute of Agricultural History, University of Reading, 1984, pp. 38 ff.

38 A. Spencer, 'Production methods', *System* (February 1927), pp. 75 7.

39 *Private communication*, Leonelli Cav. Lanfranco & C. s.n.c., Castelraimondo, Macerata, Italy (4 July 1988).

40 Gailey, *Spade making*.

41 E. J. T. Collins, 'Harvest technology and labour supply, 1790–1870', *Economic History Review* (2nd ser.), XXII (1969), p. 456.

42 Clifford Geertz, *Agricultural involution*, University of California Press, Berkeley, Cal., 1966, pp. 80–1 and *passim*.

43 E. Hobsbawm, 'Introduction: inventing tradition', in E. Hobsbawm and T. Ranger (eds), *The invention of tradition*, Cambridge, 1983, p. 4.

44 F. M. L. Thompson, 'Nineteenth-century horse sense', *Economic History Review* (2nd ser.), XXIX (1976).

4

FOREIGN FARMING IN BRITISH EYES

AVNER OFFER

Some of the names are well-known: Arthur Young, James Caird, Rider Haggard, Seebohm Rowntree; all of them wrote at length about overseas agriculture.[1] Others come as a surprise: Florence Nightingale's sister Parthenope, Lady Verney, Bertrand Russell, Trebitsch Lincoln. This last was a Jew who came to Britain from Hungary. He organized a survey of Belgian farming for Seebohm Rowntree, then became a Liberal member of Parliament, a double agent in the First World War, a political operator in Shanghai between the wars and finally a Buddhist abbot in the same city.[2] Some of these writers undertook laborious travels, others never stirred beyond their armchairs. Edward Gibbon Wakefield published a compelling account of his travails as a gentleman farmer in the Australian bush before he ever left Britain. He wrote it in Newgate Prison, where he was serving time for eloping with an under-age heiress.[3] For all their detail of foreign practice, these writers were also participating in a sustained debate about *English* landed society, which Michael Thompson has done so much to illuminate.

Two themes run through this literature: the perennial one of national ascendancy and decline, which is brought out by foreign comparisons; and the topic of this paper which is largely the second theme, the interaction between economic efficiency, social equity and personal dignity. There were two distinctive paradigms of overseas farming: on the one hand the frontier settlers of North America and Australia; on the other, the peasant farmers of continental Europe, of Belgium and Holland, France and Germany, Norway, Switzerland and Italy. The trans-oceanic paradigm was predominantly a 'macro' perspective, highlighting the global dynamics of migration and trade. Writers on continental agriculture contemplated the 'micro' economics of the peasant plot, and its peculiar psychology.

These two traditions had something in common: an approach to farming that went beyond its efficiency in producing corn and beef. Farming also produces psychic and moral goods. Some of these goods are final products, like the satisfactions of social approbation, status, autonomy and dignity. Others make up the intermediate goods of human capital: enterprise, initiative, frugality, sobriety, sexual prudence, attention to detail, manual dexterity, technical knowledge. The two classes of goods are mutually dependent: motivation and skill (human capital) are nurtured on dignity and external recognition. Together, these attributes of farming as a vocation contribute (as Amartya Sen has termed them) to the satisfactions of 'being' and of 'doing'.[4] 'Being' is largely a matter of social standing. According to Fred Hirsch, the craving for social standing cannot be satisfied merely by an equal increase of wealth for all, because the goods that impart status are in short supply by definition. Room at the top is limited: this constitutes the 'social limits to growth'.[5] Of these positional goods, land is a prime example, and its possession was the basis of social status in pre-industrial Britain.

I

Take the trans-oceanic tradition first. As with much else, a good place to begin is with Adam Smith. The engine of modern economic growth was still in first gear, but Smith had already perceived some of its limitations. Material abundance in Britain led to *positional* scarcity. Overseas however, in the new settler societies, land was not scarce, so neither was status. In Britain, Smith wrote, 'rent and profit eat up wages, and the two superior orders of people oppress the inferior ones, but in new colonies, the interest of the two superior orders obliges them to treat the inferior one with more generosity and humanity.'[6] This blissful state of affairs arises from the abundance of land and from its occupation and cultivation by working owners. The system of tenure was crucial. In contrast with the colonies of France and Spain, the engrossment of land in British settler colonies had been more restrained, entails were less common, and there was a more active land market. Cheap land was conducive to social freedom.[7] There is, in Smith, a streak of pessimism about growth: what benefits people as consumers, can often diminish their dignity and autonomy as producers. Mass production, which requires the division of labour, also reduces the scope for individual enterprise and skill: 'The man whose whole life is spent in performing a few simple operations ... generally becomes as stupid and ignorant as it is possible for a human creature to become.' Such is the effect of the division of labour, which is the source of economic growth.[8] This was also the effect of the engrossment of land.

A generation later, Smith's editor and intellectual disciple Edward Gibbon Wakefield was more of a social conservative, and he saw things the other way round. In a series of books published between 1829 and 1849, Wakefield argued that over-accumulation at home was creating serious social pressures. Immigration was a safety valve, but frontier settlers were likely to acquire independence far too easily and early, at the expense of optimal growth and social deference. Like Smith, Wakefield thought that free land would dissolve the bonds of hierarchy. Karl Marx gives a graphic description, loosely based on Wakefield, of the wealthy Thomas Peel (a cousin of Sir Robert), who obtained 500,000 acres of empty land in Western Australia and emigrated to the Swan River with £50,000 and a full complement of servants. All of them deserted shortly, and he was left with no-one even to prepare his cup of tea.[9]

According to Wakefield, premature settlement by owner-occupiers was harmful, because economic development required not only the *division* of labour, but also its *combination*:

> There are numerous operations of so simple a kind as not to admit of a division into parts, which cannot be performed without the co-operation of many pairs of hands. I would instance the lifting of a large tree onto a wain, keeping down weeds in a large field of growing crop, shearing a large flock of sheep at the right time, gathering a harvest of corn at the time when it is ripe enough and not too ripe, moving any great weight; everything, in short, which cannot be done unless a good many pairs of hands help each other in the same undivided employment, and at the same time.[10]

But mere combination was not enough. Workers also had to be combined for a sufficient time: 'If the harvest cannot be gathered, the whole outlay in making it grow has been thrown away . . . constancy is a no less important principle than combination of labour.'[11]

All these considerations led Wakefield to propose the creation of an artificial scarcity of land, setting its price (the 'sufficient price') 'as to give the cheapest land a market value that would have the effect of compelling labourers to work some considerable time for wages before they could become landowners.'[12] Karl Marx saw this scheme for what it was, an attempt to accelerate the formation of capitalist relations of production.[13]

James Caird earned a reputation as a commentator on British agriculture in 1851 with his book on *English Agriculture in 1850–51.* In 1858 he travelled along the grain frontier in Illinois, Minnesota and Ohio. An early champion of high farming in Britain, by the end of the 1850s he could already perceive its coming crisis, which he blamed on two factors:

land scarcity and overseas competition. Land prices were bid up too high for farming by competition from 'men who, having made money in other pursuits, wish to retire to the more pleasurable occupations of a country life ... Great Britain is the most attractive place of residence on the surface of the globe, whether we regard its equable and healthy climate, its varied scenery and field sports, the almost sacred character of the rights of property in the eyes of its people, and the admirable combination of liberty and order which is preserved under its constitution. Men will pay for these advantages, when they can afford it, a price which is not measured by the ordinary rate of profit.' In Illinois you could buy land for about as much as it took to rent it for a year in Scotland.

Caird was not inclined to blame the social order alone: he also invoked the superior fertility of prairie soil. Caird also noted the different social climate generated by different land systems. He admired the efficiency, and the absence of pomp and ceremony among public officials. He deplored the lack of ceremony in the meals of ordinary people, and their nasty habit of chewing and spitting tobacco. The entrepreneurial farmer was not inclined to give himself any airs and graces.[14] As with Wakefield, Caird's solution to congestion at home was emigration: 'The time seems thus to have arrived when the farmers must thin the ranks of home competition by sending off the young and enterprising to countries where they may become the owners of a fertile soil, and profitably contribute to supply the wants of the old country, whose land can no longer meet the demands of her dense population.'[15]

By the 1880s, the decline of British farming was an accomplished fact. In a book on *The British Farmer and his Competitors*, William Bear denied that there was anything wrong with British soil and climate, and placed the blame squarely on the positional value of land, which kept rents too high. Good farming required security and independence; motivation, enterprise and skills would follow.[16] There is also, in this tradition, a sub-literature of practical inquiry, investigating the competitive failure of British grain: it is crammed with the facts and details of practical farming. It shares with the macro model a perception of overseas agriculture as an outlet for emigration, and the search for the particular factor (in land, fertility, labour costs) that explains why the overseas farmer can compete so well with British agriculture, supposedly the best in the world.[17]

II

In the macro approach, labourers and farmers behave like capitalists, to maximise their money returns. The positional payoff is a bonus. In the other tradition, British writers questioned whether the laws of political economy applied in the same way to European peasants. Just as British landowners paid over the odds for the status of landownership, European peasants *also* paid over the odds for the satisfactions of ownership. To pay for the land, they economised on everything else, and pushed cultivation to the edge of the most barren margins. Arthur Young, travelling in France in 1792, reported: 'I saw nothing respectable on small properties, except the most unremitting industry . . . the husbandry I met with, in a great variety of instances on little properties, was as bad as can well be conceived, yet the industry of the possessors was so conspicuous, and so meritorious, that no commendations would be too great for it. It was sufficient to prove, that property in land is, of all others, the most active instigator to severe and incessant labour.'[18]

One of the most imaginative and sweeping accounts of overseas systems of farming was published by political economist Richard Jones in 1831. Jones made a distinction between 'peasant' and 'farmer' rents; essentially between subsistence and more capital-intensive and market-orientated agriculture, between the share-cropping peasants of Eastern Europe, India and Ireland, and the wage-labour agricultures of Western and Northern Europe.[19] The Indian and Irish peasantry figured large in the literature of classical political economy, which in its turn, had some influence on agrarian administration in Ireland and the Indian Empire.[20]

John Stuart Mill gave the issue a much wider currency in British social and political discourse. He took up the subject during the Irish famine crisis of 1846; his solution for the crisis was not alms, but a redistribution of land to the cottiers, setting them up as independent farmers on waste lands. In 1846 he published more than 50 unsigned editorials in the daily *Morning Chronicle* about the Irish question. These articles held up the European peasantry as a model. Late in 1846 the *Quarterly Review* published a very critical article on peasant agriculture in France;[21] Mill responded with four editorials in the *Morning Chronicle*. Long sections of this journalism found its way, verbatim, into Mill's *Principles of Political Economy*, where it formed the core of a distinctive chunk of five chapters, a scattering of shorter sections, and a long appendix.[22]

In the process of making his argument, Mill unfolded the riches of rural travelogue and analysis, quoting at length from British and continental writers, with glowing accounts of rural society in Norway, Germany, Switzerland, Italy, France and Flanders.[23] He then carefully analysed the advantages of a rural society of peasant owner-occupiers: this peasant society is quite as efficient as any other system of agriculture; but more importantly,

> that no other existing state of agricultural economy has so beneficial an effect on the industry, the intelligence, the frugality and the prudence of the population, nor tends on the whole so much to discourage an improvident

increase in their numbers; and that no existing state, therefore, is on the whole so favourable both to their moral and their physical welfare. Compared with the English system of cultivation by hired labour, it must be regarded as eminently beneficial to the labouring class.[24]

This was a challenge to the social order. Flanders and Tuscany, not England, had the best farming in the world. Their advantage was not a superior product, but a superior producer: self-sufficient, prudent, thrifty, very hard-working, intelligent, responsible. The role of property is to create economic democracy: to devolve responsibility to the people, and to endow them with skills. In a passage on productivity Mill writes, 'A thing not yet so well understood and recognised is the economical value of the general diffusion of intelligence among the people'. In another place he writes:

No improvements operate more directly upon the productiveness of labour, than those in the tenure of farms, and in the laws relating to landed property ... above all, the acquisition of a permanent interest in the soil by the cultivators of it; all these things are as real, and some of them as great, improvements in production, as the invention of the spinning-jenny or the steam engine. We may say the same of improvements in education ... there is hardly any source from which a more indefinite amount of improvement may be looked for in productive power, than by endowing with brains those who now have only hands.[25]

What counts here, I think, is not peasant property, or even ownership as such: it is taking fulfilment as a measure of success together with material output; and insisting on the link between self-esteem and economic productivity.

Mill provoked a swift reply from the leading conservative economist, John Ramsay MacCulloch. MacCulloch denied everything that Mill affirmed. The satisfactions of the peasant proprietor were merely the blinkered contentment 'of an oyster in his shell'. Subdivision in France was proceeding to the point at which inches and logarithms would soon be required to measure it. Peasants were lazy, inefficient, technically ignorant, uneducated, undermotivated. As a bulwark of democracy, they formed a threat to good aristocratic government. There was no prospect of their ever co-operating for greater economic efficiency. The independence vaunted by Mill was shiftless insubordinate laziness, which undermined their character. They were impermeable to education.[26] The British system was best.

This was plausible, but history was soon to vindicate Mill and his acolytes. Owner-occupiers from across the Channel, the North Sea and the Atlantic, captured large parts of the British food market from the British tenant farmer. Wheat, butter, eggs, bacon, apples, even hay: all were imported in large quantities. Owner-occupiers overseas, working with their own hands, had a capacity for adaptation, learning and sacrifice which British tenant farmers on the whole did not.[27] By the 1880s, European peasant virtues were being projected onto American prairie farmers by despondent agrarians in Britain: Albert Pell and Clare Read, both of them conversative MPs, wrote a report on prairie agriculture for the Royal Commission on Agricultural Depression. The natural endowment of the prairie was not superior, they wrote, and distance was a disadvantage. The American farmer's main advantage was superior *motivation*:

> Few English farmers have any idea of the hard and constant work which falls to the lot of even well-to-do farmers in America. Save in the harvest, certainly no agricultural labourer in England expends anything like the same time and strength in his day's work ... He adds to all the mental cares of ownership the physical stress of manual labour of the severest description. No other class of men toil so unceasingly, enduring the life of savages for a while in order to conquer the backwood or civilize the prairie. The man, sedate and serious, is attempting almost single handed to perform the work of two, if not more, English labourers.

Another writer reporting from America added 'there runs through the society of the whole States ... a sort of nervous anxiety to be continually working. There is no idle class.'[28]

The Irish famine came and went, but Mill's vision of the peasant proprietor found another congenial context, in the 'land question' that emerged as one of the central issues of mid- and late-Victorian Britain.[29] The Liberal struggle against the landed ascendancy, rooted in the struggles of the first Reform Act and the Corn Law League, continued throughout the nineteenth century, from Mill through to Cobden, Henry George and Lloyd George. Jesse Collings used it as a plank for Joseph Chamberlain's 'unauthorised programme' in 1884–85.[30] Within this tradition, the European peasantry was invoked as a counterfactual, a standing reproach to the English system of estates. It was an odd model to choose, since rural drudgery was hardly a vision to inspire the suburban middle classes. The thread stretches unbroken from Joseph Kay through Cliffe Leslie, the Cobden Club essays, the Warden of Merton, George Brodrick, through Arthur Arnold and down to the land nationalisation society of Alfred Russell Wallace.[31] This Liberal commitment came to a somewhat incongruous climax when the Edwardian Liberals, in power at last, attempted to apply it literally, in their smallholding acts. Seebohm Rowntree was obsessed by the question, and published a fat volume on *Land and Labour: Lessons from Belgium.* He also administered the wide-ranging Liberal land inquiry of 1912–13. Another Liberal and obsessive ruralist, F. Robertson Scott, searched for similar lessons in Holland.[32]

III

MacCulloch found no real successors. By 1880, Caird already had serious doubts about high farming and English agriculture.[33] Arthur Balfour delivered an attack on French peasant proprietors and on their advocate Mill in 1885, but most of his invective was aimed at a more menacing target, the confiscatory proposals of Henry George.[34] With John Stuart Mill land reform entered into the Liberal bloodstream. As an additional attraction the case against landlordism could also be turned against socialism.[35] Conservatives increasingly regarded a contented hard-working peasantry, as Liberals had seen it before: not as an enemy of aristocracy, but as a rampart for property. Despite some misgivings, a conservative government implemented the first Smallholding Act in 1892.[36]

A decade later, in Ireland, Conservatives financed and implemented a massive transfer of land from its owners to its cultivators. After the turn of the century, as landowners become politically embattled, the European peasantry also began to fit in with the Conservatives' newly adopted policy of tariff protection. Now it was Conservative writers who held the Continental peasantry up for admiration.[37] Jesse Collings wrote in 1906:

> The owner of ten acres of land is as keen on the rights of property, and as watchful of the interests of his industry, as the owner of ten thousand acres. We see a landed aristocracy, in continental countries, which is not exposed to the disfavour and hostile criticism to which that order in England is subjected. The reason is, that it is not a class apart, separated from other classes of cultivators by a gulf which, under our present system, is well-nigh impassable. In these countries the landed aristocracy is intermingled with a landed democracy, and the two interests are not antagonistic, but identical. Hence it is that the rural economy of these countries is in the hands of a body diverse in character, but united in interest. Even the comparatively few labourers who are simply wage-receivers are in the same boat, because they can get land if they like to save and strive in order to do so. These classes, as a body, came to the conclusion that it was necessary to defend agriculture from foreign attacks, and for that purpose they not only proposed, but were strong enough to carry, legislation which imposed duties on imports of foreign corn.[38]

Just as interesting as this protectionism was an Edwardian streak of proto-Thatcherism, that picked up Mill's ideas about property, enterprise and human capital. Several conservatives advocated a reconstruction of

English agriculture on continental lines of ownership, education and co-operation. Leading the way was the *Times* journalist E. A. Pratt in 1905; better known perhaps is Rider Haggard's book on *Rural Denmark and its Lessons.* Just as interesting, is Henry Wolff's book on peasant initiatives in Europe, *Co-Operation in Agriculture.* Similar ideas were broached in confidential party documents.[39] Conservative and Liberal positions came very close during the Edwardian period.

Mill's insight into the motives and attitudes attaching to property is also echoed in the modern Conservative project to extend the ownership of houses and shares.[40] It is interesting to consider how this project differs from Mill's. Home ownership promises fulfilment through consumption and not production. Ownership does not involve the development of creative potential; on the contrary, it is meant to reconcile owners to the *lack* of control over their own lives as producers and citizens. Skill, character and creativity find little place in the conservative ideal of home ownership, apart from the delights of gardening and do-it-yourself. The lure of cheap borrowing and of windfall gains does not instil prudence and thrift. The Thatcherite small businessman is not a labouring yeoman, but more typically an employer, and as often a dealer as a maker.

Mill's analysis continues to resonate in other ways. The modern Conservative Party of the 1970s and the 1980s, in its belief in the stabilising and moderating effect of diffused ownership of real property, draws on this particular Victorian value. Victorian writers on peasant proprietors noted their willingness to pay more for land than a capitalist farmer would, and *much* more than its economic rate of return would justify. When the satisfactions are psychic rather than material, an economic price is difficult to estimate. Economic parameters (of risk and return) provide a yardstick for comparison between assets. But in the case of a peasant holding, or in the case of home ownership, this is not a valid procedure. Land ownership and home ownership are both positional goods, and their utility is not wholly captured by the flow of money income. Ownership of a plot, or of a home, is a *positional* necessity. The alternative to ownership can be social oblivion. Under such conditions, the constraint is not the productivity of the asset, but only the customer's capacity to pay. If the assets are in short supply, like land or houses, then social demand will bid their value up beyond anything justified by the imputed income flow alone.

This positional wealth competes with the productive economy. Positional investment partly accounted for the low level of accumulation in peasant France, and for the severity of agricultural depression in late-Victorian Britain. In 1980s Britain, through the relaxation of credit controls, soaring houses prices have created a bloated liquidity which has pushed up inflation, squeezed out investment, sucked in imports, and ravaged the economic project of Thatcherism.[41] Today, few social visions appear more dated than 'three acres and a cow'. But this obscure debate contains early pointers to the shape of our present institutions, and of our present discontents. In the rural landscape that Michael Thompson has so vividly described, landed property occupied the high ground of social esteem. The ideals and traditions of the landed aristocracy and gentry are still influential, but for those who reject them, on the right as well as on the left, the *critics* of landed society have an alternative vision to offer, a vision of possessive individualism derived from foreign institutions of land tenure, another vision that contemporary British society has inherited from the Victorians.

Notes

1 Arthur Young, *Travels in France during the years 1787, 1788 & 1789* (ed. C. Maxwell), Cambridge, 1950; James Caird, *Prairie farming in America*, London, 1859; Henry Rider Haggard, *Rural Denmark and its lessons*, London, 1911; B. S. Rowntree, *Land and labour, lessons from Belgium*, London, 1910.

2 Frances Parthenope, Lady Verney, *Cottier owners, little takes and peasant properties*, London, 1885; Lady Verney, *Peasant properties and other selected essays* (2 vols), London, 1885; Lady Verney, *How the peasant owner lives in parts of France, Germany, Italy, Russia*, London, 1888; Bertrand Russell, *German social democracy*, London, 1896, rep. 1965, Lecture 6; B. Wasserstein, *The secret lives of Trebitsch Lincoln*, New Haven, 1988, pp. 47–55; Rowntree, *Belgium*, p. xi.

3 E. G. Wakefield, *A letter from Sydney and other writings*, 1st publ. 1829, repr. London, 1929, pp. 6–14, 39–43. Other writers are referred to below, but the list is not comprehensive, and in particular it does not cover periodical literature. Ireland and India are also excluded.

4 These seem to be a development of the notion of self-actualisation, which is the prinnacle of the hierarchy of needs in the writings of the psychologist Abraham Maslow. See Amartya Sen (ed.), *The standard of living*, Cambridge, 1987, pp. 29 ff; A. Sen, 'Individual freedom as a social commitment', *New York Review of Books*, 14 June 1990, p. 52.

5 Fred Hirsch, *Social limits to growth*, London, 1977, ch. 3.

6 Adam Smith, *An inquiry into the nature and causes of the Wealth of Nations*, New York, Modern Library edn, 1937, bk. IV, ch. 7, pt. 2, p. 532.

7 Smith, *Wealth of Nations*, pp. 538–41.

8 Smith, *Wealth of Nations*, bk. V, pt. 3, art. 2, pp. 734–5.

9 These graphic details were contributed by Karl Marx, in a sarcastic account in *Capital*, vol. 1 (Moscow, 1954 edn), ch. 33, p. 717. The relevant passages are in Edward Gibbon Wakefield, *England and America*, New York, 1834, repr. 1967, pp. 259, 260, 273.

10 Edward Gibbon Wakefield, *A view of the art of colonization, in letters between a statesman and a colonist*, 1849, repr. Oxford 1914, p. 168.

11 Wakefield, *A view of the art of colonization*, p. 169.

12 Wakefield, *A view . . .*, p. 339.

13 Marx, *Capital*, vol. 1, ch. 33.

14 Caird, *Prairie farming*, pp. 2, 60–1, 73.

15 Caird, *Prairie farming*, p. 3.

16 William E. Bear, *The British farmer and his competitors*, Cobden Club, London, 1888, e.g., pp. 11–17 and ch. 9.

17 E.g., *Royal Commission on Agriculture* Joint Report of Mr Clare Read and Mr Albert

Pell MP [on United States Agriculture]; P.P. 1880, C. 2687, XVIII; *Royal Commission on Agriculture*, Further Report of Mr Clay, Junr. on American Agriculture; P.P. 1882, C. 3375, VI and XV, pp. 12–14; *Report of the Scottish Commission on Agriculture in Canada 1908*, Edinburgh, 1909, e.g., pp. 187–94 (John Sinclair, the Scottish Liberal MP and later Lord Pentland, who sponsored this informal inquiry also organised two earlier ones to Denmark and Ireland; see *ibid.*, p. 9).

18 Arthur Young, *Travels in France*, ed. C. Maxwell, Cambridge, 1950, p. 299.

19 Richard Jones, *An essay on the distribution of wealth*, 1831, repr. New York, 1956, *passim*, but esp. ch. 6.

20 W. J. Barber, *British economic thought and India*, Oxford, 1975; E. Stokes, *The English utilitarians and India*, Oxford, 1959; R. D. Collison Black, *Economic thought and the Irish question, 1817–1870*, Cambridge, 1960.

21 [John Wilson Croker], 'Agriculture in France', *Quarterly Review*, vol. 79 (Dec. 1846), pp. 202–38.

22 *Collected works of John Stuart Mill*, ed. A. P. Robson and J. M. Robson, vol. 24 (Newspaper Writings), Toronto, 1986, pp. 879–1078; nos. 355–8, pp. 1035–1058; Mill, *Principles of political economy with some of their applications to social philosophy*, Bk. 2, chs. 6–10 and appendix, *Collected works*, vol. 2, Toronto, 1965.

23 He cites (including later editions of the *Principles*) Bastiat, Chateauvieux, Howitt, Inglis, Kay, Laing, Lavergne, MacCulloch, Mounier, Rau, Rham, Sismondi, Thiers and Thornton. Full bibliographical details may be found in Mill, *Principles*, vol. 2, appendix 1, pp. 1096–1155.

24 Mill, *Principles*, vol. 1, pp. 295–6.

25 Mill,·*Principles*, vol. 1, pp. 183–4.

26 James R. MacCulloch, *A treatise on the succession to property vacant by death*, London, 1848, ch. 4.

27 George Gibson Richardson, *Corn and cattle producing districts in France*, London, 1877; Jesse Collings, *Land reform, occupying ownership, peasant proprietary and rural educationr*, London, 1906, pp. 190–91; most recently, this theme has been taken up by Patrick O'Brien and Caglar Keyder, *Economic growth in Britain and France 1780–1914: two paths to the twentieth century*, London, 1978, ch. 5.

28 Pell and Read, Report on United States Agriculture, pp. 5, 14; Clay, American Agriculture, p. 12.

29 From a large literature see, e.g., Clive Dewey, 'The rehabilitation of the peasant proprietor in nineteenth-century economic thought', *History of Political Economy*, vol. 6 (1974); Harold Perkin, 'Land reform and class conflict in Victorian Britain' in *The Victorians and social protest*, ed. J. Butt and I. F. Clarke, Newton Abbot, 1973; F. M. L. Thompson, 'Land and politics in England in the nineteenth century', *Transactions of the Royal Historical Society*, 5th ser., vol. 15 (1965); A. Offer, *Property and politics 1870–1914*, Cambridge, 1981.

30 Jesse Collings and J. Green, *The life of the Right Hon. Jesse Collings*, London, 1920, ch. 21; Collings, *Land reform*, chs. 14, 17.

31 Joseph Kay, *The social condition and education of the poor in England and Europe*, London, 1850, vol. 1, ch. 1, *passim*: T. E. Cliffe Leslie, 'The peasantry and farms of Belgium, 1867' in his *Land systems and industrial economy of Ireland, England & continential countries*, London, 1870, pp. 294–355; W. J. Probyn (ed.), *Essays on land tenure in various countries*, London, 1870, 2nd edn 1881; George Brodrick, *English land and English landlords*, London, 1881; Arthur Arnold, *Free land*, London, 1880; A. R. Wallace, 'How to cause wealth to be more equally distributed', *Industrial Remuneration Conference: The report of the proceedings and papers*, London, 1885, pp. 385–92; see also J. W. Burrow, 'The "village community" and the uses of history in late nineteenth-century England', in Neil McKendrick (ed.), *Historical perspectives: studies in English thought and society in honour of J. H. Plumb*, London, 1974.

32 Land Enquiry Committee, *The land*, vol. 1 (Rural), London, 1913; 'Home Counties'; [J. W. Robertson Scott], *A free farmer in a free state*, London, 1912.

33 J. Caird, *The landed interest and the supply of food*, 4th edn London, 1880, ch. 12.

34 A. J. Balfour, 'Land, land reform and the nation', *Industrial Remuneration Conference: The report of the proceedings and papers*, London, 1885, pp. 343 ff.
35 Kay, *Social conditions*, vol. 1, p. 149; Russel, *German social democracy*, Lecture 6.
36 Offer, *Property and politics*, pp. 352–4.
37 W. J. Ashley, *The progress of the German working classes in the last quarter of a century*, London, 1904, ch. 2.
38 Collings, *Land reform*, pp. 281–2.
39 E. A. Pratt, *The organization of agriculture*, London, 1905; Pratt, *Small holders: what they must do to succeed*, London, 1909; Henry Rider Haggard, *Rural Denmark and its lessons*, London, 1911; Henry W. Wolff, *Co-operation in agriculture*, London, 1912; Viscount Milner, see Offer, *Property and politics*, pp, 379–80.
40 See, e.g., Peter Saunders, *A nation of home owners*, London, 1990.
41 John Muellbauer, *The great British housing disaster*, London, 1990.

5

BUSINESSMEN INTO LANDOWNERS: THE QUESTION REVISITED

W. D. RUBINSTEIN

In 1981 I published an article in *Past and Present,* 'New men of wealth and the purchase of land in nineteenth-century Britain', which questioned the widely-held belief that the new ranks of businessmen and industrialists produced by the Industrial Revolution in Britain purchased land on any great scale.[1] Comparing all business and professional men who left £500,000 or more between 1840 and 1914 (together with a group of 'lesser wealthy' who left £250,000–£500,000 in 1850–69) with the authoritative entries in John Bateman's *Great Landowners of Great Britain and Ireland* (1883 edition), my study revealed that over 70 per cent of these wealth-holders owned less than 2,000 acres in Bateman's listing, with no more than 10–15 per cent owning more than this among certain decadal cohorts.[2] Only ten wealth-holders owned as much as 25,000 acres.[3] A second study, of a sample 300 landowners in Bateman's *Great Landowners* owning 5,000 acres or more, revealed that only 12 per cent represented families which had earned their fortunes after 1780, while 76 per cent represented pre-industrial fortunes.[4]

Not only did there appear from this to be convincing evidence that few post-industrial revolution magnates purchased significantly large landed estates, but more importantly these derisory totals must be placed in the context of the unprecedented growth of business and professional wealth and income after 1780, such that the *potential* for the acquisition of land by new businessmen was both unparalleled and enormous: national income earned in manufacturing, trade and related business activities, for instance, rose from £94 million in 1801 to £638 million in 1881, while between 1809 and 1880 about 3,430 individuals left £100,000 or more in personalty: if two-thirds of these were businessmen, leaving a median estate valued at £200,000, and half of this used to purchase land, the new class of business wealthy would have owned 6.9 million acres in England and Wales in 1883, more than the 5.4 million owned by the entire peerage.[5]

In actual fact, it would be surprising if the new wealthy in fact owned more than one million acres *in toto* in 1883, and arguably it was much less. The reasons for this failure to purchase land are varied and not easy to identify, but clearly include both negative and positive elements: on one hand, the lack of opportunities for land acquisition by royal decree, confiscation of the monasteries, enclosure or family dynastic alliance, together with the difficulties and expense of conveyancing, and the failure of even large-scale land purchase to lead automatically to a peerage or hereditary title; on the other hand, the higher yields, with complete security, of many stocks and bonds, the development of the West End and wealthy districts of the large provincial cities as a new type of Society which was a substitute for squiredom, and, perhaps, the alien and antipathetic nature of rural life for many Victorian businessmen.

Since these conclusions were firmly rooted in seemingly irrefutable objective evidence, I did not expect them to arouse any controversy whatsoever; indeed, since tracing these wealthy landowners and non-landowners is for me a rather enjoyable hobby, this all seemed a remarkably painless and straightforward way of publishing an article in *Past and Present.* In the inscrutable and unpredictable manner of academic debate, however, my article has attracted a steady stream of criticism and commentary. One reason for this continuing interest was that in 1984 Lawrence Stone and Jeanne C. Fawtier Stone published *An Open Elite? England, 1540–1880*, a 566-page study that uses very different sources to arrive at remarkably similar conclusions. The Stones studied 2,246 owners of 362 county seats and great landed estates in three counties, Hertfordshire, Northamptonshire and Northumberland, during the whole period 1540–1880, and concluded that only 6 per cent of all owners, and one-third of all purchasers of estates, were businessmen.[6] In so far as there was any 'symbiosis' at all between land and newcomers, it was between land and the professions – 'just as in the rest of Europe' – and not between land and businessmen.[7]

Much of the criticism of the viewpoint put forward independently by the Stones and myself has been specifically directed against the Stones' conclusions, especially their propensity to see low levels of social mobility in intergenerational figures of entry and sales which other historians take as, on the contrary, evidence of rapid mobility.[8] However, much of the criticism of this thesis is directed specifically at my work, and the purpose of this paper is to respond to the points raised by these critics and to offer fresh evidence on this question which will, I think, add considerable weight to the conclusions expressed in my previous article.

Before turning to these critics, it might be worth making some points about the difference in approach between the Stones and myself. My method has been to take all significant landowners in Britain at one point in time (1872–83) and compare them with the comprehensive and all-inclusive listing of wealthy businessmen and professionals provided by the probate records. This is possible because the two sources, the 1872 *Return* and Bateman's *Great Landowners* on the one hand, and the probate valuations for personalty, exist in this comprehensive form for these years. For an endeavour such as the Stones', which seeks to trace land purchase over several centuries, plainly these sources are not available and the historian must rely on other methods.[9]

Given the enormity of the task which the Stones undertook, probably something like their methodology was inevitable, and no one could have done this task with more skill. Nevertheless, their methodology is open to some serious doubts and questions, which must surely be fairly evident to any historian familiar with this question. The most obvious of all is their choice of three counties: although they have tried to choose three very different counties, no choice of three counties can ever be truly random. In particular, they have ignored any county containing a large city which grew mainly as a result of the post-1780 textile phase of the industrial revolution. Newcastle, while obviously a great industrial city, was already a legendary centre of colliery wealth long before 1780. Art is long but life is short, and no doubt to have included Lancashire or the West Riding would have proved an immensely daunting task; yet the impression remains that something is lacking in their choice of counties.

Secondly, the Stones mince no words that theirs is not a study of landed property as such, but of country houses above a minimum size (based upon a complex measurement system) standing in a ground above a minimum size: 'It cannot be emphasised too often that this is a study of owners of country property, not of landed property'.[10] This methodology is far from foolproof: the largest landowners in one of their counties, if they lacked a country house of sufficient size, would actually be excluded from their study. It would be quite possible to ascertain how often this happens, for 1873–83 at least, by comparing the list of seats (provided by the Stones in Appendix I, pp. 429–35) with the top acreage-owners in each county, according to the *Return*. Apparently the Stones have, regrettably, not undertaken this comparison in a direct way, although on p. 62 of their book they note the number of landowners in the *Return* with their main seat in one of the three counties *and* with 3,000 or more acres there, yielding a rent-roll of £3,000 p.a. or more: Hertfordshire, 64; Northamptonshire, 67; and Northumberland, 146 (the last figure they attribute to the significant number of colliery owners with substantial rentals from minerals). The number of houses in their study in existence in 1879 (their last year) amounts to about 97 in Hertfordshire, 70 in Northamptonshire and 63 in Northumberland. There is no discussion, so far as I can see, as to the anomalous families or houses – those with sufficient land but no house included in the study, or those with a house but insufficient land – and the relatively small number of houses in the Northumberland study, as the Springs point out in their *Canadian Journal of History* article (p. 340) may vitiate against a proper sample of newcomers.

However, the use of large landed seats as the touchstone for inclusion may have a second, more deleterious effect upon their findings, namely to exclude *nouveaux riches* who built on a less grandiose scale. The Stones of course include many country houses in their study built after 1780 – in Hertfordshire, to take one example, they include thirty-eight houses built between 1780 and 1880 – but they may well exclude many slightly less stately piles built by businessmen at this time; *Burke's Landed Gentry* and *Walford's County Families* are riddled with country houses, and their occupants, which were apparently of this type. The 1884 edition of *Walford's County Families*, for example, contains over 200 country-house owners in Hertfordshire,[11] more than twice as many as the 97 Hertfordshire houses in the Stones' sample which existed in 1879, the final year in their study. The Stones are also at pains to distinguish between the 'county' and 'parish' élites, but they have not demonstrated that all true members of the 'county' élite would be caught by their sample design. There is, finally, the probability of very transient country houses, occupied for only a few years; their number would, arguably, be greater in the nineteenth century, with its volatility of business fortunes, than before. The Stones' endeavour is much more directed to showing the creation and maintenance of a permanent county ruling élite, and the degree of generational entry into this permanent élite; their methodology may, however, be biased *a priori* against the type of wealth earned in post-Industrial Revolution England.

Nevertheless *An Open Elite?* is surely a formidable work in every respect. In its sweep and magisterial range of coverage, it may arguably be the most impressive book ever written on Britain's élites. For the purposes of my own research and its historical implications, it reinforces my conclusions and adds greatly to the confidence that can be placed in them, since the Stones employ an entirely different methodology.[12]

I

While both the Stones' and my work have been subject to criticism, some has been directed chiefly against my approach and my conclusions. The most thorough and full-blooded attack upon these conclusions is F. M. L. Thompson's paper, 'Business and landed élites in the nineteenth century', a contribution to Professor Habakkuk's *festschrift, Landowners, capitalists, and entrepreneurs.*[13] With unmatched erudition Professor Thompson has examined every nineteenth-century millionaire considered by me and concludes that there was much more land purchase than I have assumed, so much so in fact that Thompson believes the propensity for rich men in the nineteenth century to purchase land was arguably greater than in the past.[14] In reaching this conclusion, Thompson was able to use, and has used most extensively, two archival sources which were unavailable to me, the Legacy Duty Registers and the Succession Duty Registers (PRO I.R.26), which were closed to researchers when my research on wealth-holding was undertaken in 1972–76 and only became available in the early 1980s.

These registers record the eventual heir, *up to 150 years later*, of every testator, and from them Thompson and his research assistant J. M. Collinge were able to trace the eventual legatee of every millionaire estate. Thompson has, it seems, traced every millionaire estate in these sources[15] and he claims that my research methodology has missed land purchase among several categories of, in particular, the progeny of millionaires, in cases where the heirs of millionaires at the time of Bateman had a different surname from the original millionaire, and in those cases where the heirs of millionaires purchased land after the period 1872–83 when the *Return* and Bateman were compiled. Thompson apparently goes down to 1914 (and occasionally later) as the cut-off point to view the dynamic evolution of this pattern of land purchase; and he concludes, at least tentatively, that perhaps 90 per cent of millionaires and (with less certainty) that perhaps 50 per cent of the families of 150 half-millionaires deceased in this period had purchased some land.[16] (This half-millionaire figure of 50 per cent becoming landowners contrasts with the 20 per cent suggested by Bateman, but Thompson offers no further evidence on this matter.) In this exposition of his findings, it is hardly necessary to add that Professor Thompson combines a complete familiarity with the sources with an originality, cogency of purpose and felicity of style that are the sure hallmarks of the master historian.

An example of a millionaire, whose heir (a more distant relative) of another name noted by Thompson, is Philip Rundell, a goldsmith in the City, who left £1 million and no land. Unmarried and childless, much of his estate went to his nephew Joseph Neeld. Neeld and his heir (his brother John) spent much of this fortune on land purchase, John owning 13,812 acres yielding £20,761 in 1883.[17] An example of land purchase after 1872–83 is the case of George Carr Glynn, first Baron Wolverton, who according to Bateman owned about 700 acres. In the latter 1880s, after Bateman was compiled, Glynn's chief heir apparently purchased 3–4,000 acres of land.[18] It would seem clear at first glance that much of Professor Thompson's research must revise my original claims about land purchase, especially if it is considered as a dynamic process rather than a 'snapshot' at one point in time. Only an infinity of specific research on each wealthy family can trace the full extent of inheritance and succession, especially if there is a change in name, although transmission of property through heiresses, name-changing and the use of 'fictive kin', according to Thompson 'were aristocratic' games which some of the *nouveaux riches* learned how to play'.[19] It is also, of course, certainly the case that my study could not include land purchased after 1872–83.

Nevertheless, at second glance it is arguable that Thompson's claims are highly problematical, especially in the conceptual sense. The question we are investigating is whether businessmen (and very wealthy professionals) purchased land in quantity. If a distant kinsman of a millionaire succeeds to the property of his wealthy relative, there is one sense in which business money has been used to purchase land, but another sense, surely, in which it is not the case that a businessman has become a landowner; the more distantly one moves away from the original wealth accumulator, the more problematical such a claim becomes, especially if the heir is not himself a businessman and has done nothing to augment the original business fortune. Moreover, the further away from a wealthy businessman one moves, the more likely it is that the eventual heir does not come from the business classes but, regularly, from the gentry or the aristocracy by intermarriage.

A good example of the difficulties inherent in these claims is another case cited by Professor Thompson, that of William Joseph Denison, a millionaire City banker who died childless in 1849. Denison made his nephew Lord Albert Denison Conyngham his heir.[20] Obviously, Conyngham – the second son of the Irish peer, the first Marquess of Conyngham – was a scion of the aristocracy, not of the business classes, and any further land purchase cannot, surely, be attributed to a businessman–purchaser. Conyngham inherited Denison's 'considerable estates' – estates which, to be sure, were not noted by me – but Denison's 'vast personalty' was used to buy land, Conyngham eventually becoming Lord Londesborough, and his son the first Earl of Londesborough.[21] In 1883 this man owned an enormous landed estate of 52,655 acres yielding £67,876 p.a. There is no evidence in any biographical sketch that

Londesborough had any connection whatever with business life, and was certainly not a banker or active in trade.

The key question in all this is just how much new land purchase, beyond Bateman, the Legacy and Succession Duty Registers turn up. So far as I can see, only four millionaire businessmen left personalty to distant kinsmen, later transformed into land purchase, which was missed by my study because the eventual heir had a different, unsuspected surname – the cases of Rundell/Neeld and Denison/Londesborough, discussed above, and two further cases. These were the ironmaster William Henry Forman (d. 1869), whose fortune eventually found its way into land purchase by a nephew, Alexander Henry Browne, who in 1883 owned 5,797 acres yielded £7,162 p.a; and Samuel Eyres (d. 1868), a Leeds woollen manufacturer, whose wealth went to relatives named Kettlewell and eventually to the (re-named) Eyres-Monsell family, which in the interwar period produced Sir Bolton Eyres-Monsell, first Viscount Monsell (1881–1969), a Tory Cabinet minister. Charles Thomas Kettlewell, Eyres' son-in-law, is credited in Bateman with owning 4,183 acres worth £6,274 p.a.

Both cases illustrate the definitional problem noted earlier, of when or whether a businessman's money, *sans* businessman, should be counted as an example of a businessman-turned-landowner: Forman's nephew was already in the 'lesser gentry', according to Thompson, while Kettlewell was the son of an Anglican clergyman.[22] Again in neither case did the kinsman who, it seems, actually purchased the land have any apparent connection with business life. Most of the other cases discussed by Thompson are of relatively small land purchases, sometimes divided among several members of one family, but individually below the 2,000 acre minimum cut-off point in Bateman. A good example of this is the Crawshay family, which collectively owned over 5,000 acres in 1873 worth £17,000 p.a., but none of whom individually owned enough to be found in Bateman's *Great Landowners.*[23] Nevertheless, it should be kept in mind that most of the Crawshay iron fortune remained in stocks and shares and was not transformed into land, for six members of the Crawshay family left personal fortunes of £500,000 or more between 1810 and 1915, one of the largest number of individual wealth-holders in any wealthy British family. Indeed, the comprehensive nature of the sources employed by Professor Thompson, and the thoroughness with which he investigated this question, would seem to indicate as much as anything else that there really was no large-scale concealed transferral of business wealth into landed wealth during this period.

This last point is one which is perhaps central to this discussion and, as well, to Professor Thompson's corrections to my research, for again and again, both here and with other historians who have entered this debate, the fundamental question is just how much is a lot (of land purchase), and just when a businessman or his heirs become *bona fide* landowners, rather than businessmen with some land on the side, rather, I imagine, like an English tourist who claims to be Spanish on the basis of acquiring a suntan on the Costa Brava. The key matter to consider, it seems to me, is the proportion of total wealth a businessman invests in land purchase. Two things seem clear: that few if any nineteenth-century businessmen invested more than a small portion of their fortune in land purchase, and that the more land a businessman purchased, the wealthier he was likely to have been, so that, by and large, the most significant land accumulators among wealthy businessmen paradoxically retained the largest fortunes in non-landed sources of wealth. The Rothschilds are a prime example.[24] Thus, while Professor Thompson discerns a pattern wherein '80 per cent [of millionaires] succeeded in founding landed families'[25] it would be more accurate to point out that 95 per cent of the families of millionaires (at least) apparently retained the great bulk of their wealth in non-landed sources. *This* was the novelty, and, surely, the most striking aspect of nineteenth-century land purchase by its wealthy businessmen.

Professor David and Eileen Spring have offered a detailed critique of my work, together with a much longer criticism of what the Stones have to say about social mobility into the landed élite during the nineteenth century, in an article published in the *Canadian Journal of History* in 1986.[26] The Springs conclude that 'Tradition happens to be right about the openness of the English landed élite, however stale, flat and unprofitable it may be to say so'.[27]

The Springs' contention against my work is that I am actually discussing two separate questions which are not identical, 'the proportion *of the business community*, [which] chose to buy landed estates' and 'what proportion *of the landed élite* was of business origin'.[28] These two questions may have very different answers: for instance, it is quite possible, given the growth in business wealth after 1780, for a declining percentage of businessmen to have purchased land while, at the same time, the overall percentage of landowners with business backgrounds actually rose. Concerning the first point here, they contend that I have not shown that the percentage of notable businessmen who purchased land actually *declined*, since I offer no evidence on any pattern of land purchase before the nineteenth century. Concerning the second contention, they contend in effect, that my entry point for landed purchase is too high, since in this part of my work I set it at 5,000 acres. Their preference is for a much lower figure than either I or Bateman used, namely, 1,000 acres.[29]

The Springs are, of course, right to clarify the terms of the argument, and theirs is a useful exercise in common sense and clarity. It is perfectly true, of course, that my surmise that fewer businessmen purchased substantial landed estates in the nineteenth century than previously is only a supposition, although this is not really central to my argument. Nevertheless it is, I would contend, a reasonable one if, as the Stones' research seems to show, the rate of social mobility by businessmen into land was fairly steady over the lengthy period they have surveyed, since the effects of the industrial and commercial revolutions was vastly to increase the number of businessmen and business wealth.[30] The fact that the cost of land purchase per acre did not skyrocket is *ipso facto* evidence that demand was not enormous. Concerning the second point, any lower limit is arbitrary and (as with the Stones' research) limited by the time and resource constraints of the researcher. 5,000 acres of land, purchased at £30 per acre, is equivalent to 15 per cent of the total fortune of a millionaire or 30 per cent of a half-millionaire; once again, this debate seems to revolve around what is a lot and what is a little. In the second part of this paper, further evidence is presented which will explore this question down to a lower level of wealth and acreage, with strikingly similar results.

The arbitrary question of what is a lot and what is a little is also central to the critique of myself and the Stones offered by Professor Harold Perkin, who, like the Springs, disagrees with the thrust of our interpretation.[31] Rather like the Springs, Perkin regards the Stones' evidence of little social mobility into the landed aristocracy over the three centuries, as on the contrary, a great deal.[32] Concerning the nineteenth century, Perkin turns to two previous works of research on this subject which – according to him – demonstrate a contrary view. One is a little known and, regrettably, unpublished doctoral thesis by a former student of Perkin's, Robert O. Knapp, on 'The making of a landed élite: social mobility in Lancashire society with special reference to the social origins of landowners in the "Modern Domesday" Returns of 1873–76' (University of Lancaster, 1970).[33]

Knapp surveyed all 118 owners of more than 3,000 acres in Lancashire with seats in that county. He found that 55 of this total (46.6 per cent) 'had bought their way in' to the landowning élite after 1760.[34] Among this group of 55, a total of 41 (34.7 per cent) 'had gained their wealth from trade and industry, sometimes aided by marriage, but interestingly more by trade than by the new industry'.[35] If these figures are accurate, the apparent lack of businessmen-turned-landowners in a three-county survey like the Stones' becomes a possible anomaly and artefact of the choice of counties studied, although it should be noted that businessmen among the new entrants to Hertfordshire in their study reached 51 per cent of the total among their 1820–79 cohort.[36] Most of these new Lancashire business entrants must have been clustered toward the lower end of the acreage scale; I certainly found no evidence of a similar degree of penetration in my study. Nevertheless, like so much else in this debate, Knapp's figures can be turned on their head: *only* 55, out of all of the thousands of successful businessmen who prospered in Lancashire following industrialization, bought as much as 3,000 acres of land in that county; it must follow that the overwhelming majority of successful and wealthy Lancashire businessmen did not purchase land on that scale, at least locally. This is to me the more salient aspect of the interpretation of the facts.

Perkin also calls to arms Dr Anthony Howe's comprehensive and excellent analysis of 351 successful Lancashire cotton factory owners of the period 1830–60 studied in his monograph *The cotton masters 1830–1860.* According to Perkin, Howe shows that 'no less than 20 per cent' of his group of 351 Lancashire textile manufacturers bought sizeable estates, 'thus continuing the ancient tradition of new wealth emulating the landed life-style of the old'.[37] Perkin's employment of Howe to support his interpretation is curious in the highest degree.[38] In the first place, on the face of it 20 per cent is hardly a staggering percentage; that 80 per cent of successful Lancashire cotton masters did *not* buy large landed estates is plainly the central fact adduced by Howe. In the second place, the rarity rather than the frequency of land purchase is the point stressed by Howe himself in very clear terms. Howe notes, with great cogency, the crucial point that the *total* cost of land purchase by all the 351 cotton masters in his study amounted to '4 per cent of [the] total cotton capital in 1870'.[39] Only 39 of 351 cotton masters (11.1 per cent) achieved even 'minor gentry status', defined by Howe as ownership of 1,000 acres or more; only 13 (3.7 per cent) owned 3,000 acres or more.[40] The picture presented by Howe actually appears to duplicate both that presented by me, in my previous article and in the further research presented elsewhere in this paper, in every respect.

The most recent historian to treat this subject is Professor Martin Daunton who, in the midst of a wide-ranging attack on myself and other historians and sociologists who share my general outlook on the evolution of modern Britain, a viewpoint which in his words 'is the orthodoxy of British history . . . which has emerged since the mid-1970s' also attacks my claims on land purchase.[41] According to Daunton, who has exhaustively studied the Gibbs family of merchant bankers, land purchase by this family actually

> was designed to prevent overextension of the firm into more risky ventures, and to provide for members of the family who were not competent to run the business. The purchase of landed property was part of a strategy to keep the family *in* the City rather to provide an avenue for escape.[42]

Much the same motivation for land purchase existed in the case of the Greg family of cotton spinners, who bought land 'with the aim of offsetting the trade cycle in the cotton industry, providing a safe investment for surplus capital, [and] spreading risks'.[43]

This is plainly an ingenious suggestion (although perhaps not wholly original[44]), but one must express some doubt as to whether this was true for any more than a very limited number of cases. In the first place, there is no good reason for believing that there was any significant degree of land purchase: for instance, as we have seen, Dr Howe, who earlier put forward much the same idea as Professor Daunton, has found by careful statistical analysis that very few cotton-masters purchased any land. The case of the Gibbses – whose aristocratic pretensions were undeniable – was almost certainly highly untypical.

More basically, although land purchase by businessmen in previous ages may well have been undertaken on a wide scale because of the security provided by land, the nineteenth century differed from previous eras in that a wide range of safe non-landed investments became available which lacked the ancillary costs of land purchase such as conveyancing fees and estate improvement expenditure but which actually yielded as much or more. 'By the 1830s land had to compete with a growing array of outlets, the chief of which was railways'.[45] By 1875 the capital value of government stock, according to Robert Giffen, was £519 million, more than one-quarter of the capital value of all land in Britain.[46] Investment in very safe securities and stock issues, which undoubtedly formed an ever-increasing leitmotif to Victorian and Edwardian investment and inheritance patterns, might well be seen as a novel substitute for explicit entry into the gentry class of landowners by families who might have been able to afford this transmutation.

Professor Daunton's claim here also differs quite significantly from another one he makes in the same article, when he asks rhetorically

> how feasible was it both to pursue an active business career and to dispose of the fortune [by land purchase] within a single life, particularly if education and background had not provided the training for a rural life.[47]

This is a most curious point, for it appears to be a direct contradiction of his contention that land purchase was a deliberate policy of investment strategy; furthermore, if there was indeed an 'open élite' of land purchasers (as he seems to accept) and has been one throughout British history, this is just what has occurred down the ages. Nevertheless, the point is well-taken, for it *was* implausible that the nineteenth-century business élite would do this.

Within a very few years, there has been a variety of attacks upon the viewpoint of my article and the nineteenth-century component of the Stones' *Open Elite.* None of these attacks, it seems to me, has been particularly successful although they have clarified and extended our knowledge of this subject. In particular, none takes sufficient cognisance of the enormous and unprecedented *potential* investment which might have been directed into land purchase by the vast new business class created by the commercial and industrial revolutions, or the concomitant primary fact that so little actually went toward this end. Nevertheless, for the debate to advance beyond this stage, new evidence must be offered and more attention paid to questions of the self-perception of Victorian businessmen and of land purchase as a phase in the generational evolution of a wealthy family, matters to which we will now turn.

II

Whether well-taken or not, none of these points and considerations is a substitute for new evidence, and in this section of the paper more evidence on this matter will be offered. This consists of a very detailed examination of the landownership by everyone leaving £100,000 or more in England and Wales in 1873, 1874 and 1875, the years just after the *Return of Owners of Land* was compiled and, hence, the time period most likely to be completely accurate in terms of the *Return* and its comprehensiveness for each wealth-holder.[48] Furthermore, every wealth-holder was carefully traced in the *Return of Owners of Land* and his landowning down to less than one acre carefully noted.

A total of 391 persons left personal estates of £100,000 or more in England and Wales in the three years 1873–1874–1875.[49] Of this number, 54 were landowners – that is, persons whose ancestors had clearly owned large landed estates for at least three generations, and these have been excluded from any of the discussion. Most were landed aristocrats of long lineage or their close relatives, for example: Thomas, second Earl of Zetland (1795–1873), who left a personal estate of £250,000; Ulrick, first Marquess of Clanricarde (1802–74), £200,000; Arthur, fifth Marquess of Downshire (1844–74), £140,000. The majority of men and women in the sample – 337 in all – were business and professional men or their close relatives and not pre-existing landowners.[50] By occupation and business venue they were very typical of the nineteenth-century wealth élite. Although the northern industrial towns and manufacturing occupations were increasingly important as a source of large fortunes, the plurality were from commercial and financial trades in London, just as we have come to expect.

Among the estates probated in 1873, for instance, there were nine bankers, two stockbrokers and two shipowners, together with thirty-four miscellaneous merchants, including three timber merchants, five coal merchants, an orange merchant, a tool merchant, and a hosiery merchant – most situated in London – to set beside eight foreign merchants, active in or trading with Russia, the East and West Indies, and Australia. On the other side of the industry/commerce divide are ten cotton manufacturers, three colliery owners, three iron and steel masters, and manufacturers of worsteds, silk ties, tickets and underclothing. In tables 5.1 and 5.2, the occupations (by the Standard Industrial Classification) and business venues of non-landed wealth-holders probated in 1873 are detailed; there is no reason to believe this is not typical of the other two years.

In terms of renown, the wealth-holders in this study range from members of the Peel, Baring, Rothschild, Gibbs and Arkwright families through professionals like Sir Edwin Landseer (1802–73), the painter (who left £200,000), and Lord Westbury, the Lord Chancellor, to

Table 5.1 Occupations of known non-landed wealth-holders probated in 1873, by Standard Industrial Classification number in each category

1	coalmining	3	17	merchant banking	1
2	other minerals	0	18	other finance	0
3	iron & steel	3	19	foreign merchants	8
4	shipbuilding	0	20	retailing	2
5	engineering	2	21	other merchants	34
6	chemicals	1	22	insurance	2
7	cotton manufact.	10	23	stockbroking	0
8	woollen manufact.	1	24	shipowning	2
9	other textiles	0	25	other commerce	2
10	construction	1	26	newspapers	0
11	other manufact.	7	27	publishing	1
12	brewing	1	28	miscellaneous	1
13	distilling	1	29	professions – law	9
14	tobacco	0	30	other professions	3
15	foods	0	31	public administ.	3
16	banking	8	32	others	1

Summary, by sector

manufacturing	28	= 26.2%
food-drink-tobacco	2	= 1.9%
commerce-finance	60	= 56.1%
publishing	1	= 0.9%
professions and public administration	15	= 14.0%
other	1	= 0.9%
	107 *known*	

Table 5.2 Business venues of known non-landed wealth-holders probated in 1873

City of London	33	Hull	2
other London	23	York	1
other home counties	1	Otley	1
		Middlesborough	1
Lancashire (19)		*North-East (4)*	
Manchester	11	Newcastle-upon-Tyne	2
Bury	1	Darlington	1
Blackburn	1	Sunderland	1
Liverpool	6		
St Helens	1	*Midlands (5)*	
Cheshire (2)		Birmingham	1
Dukinfield	1	Wolverhampton	1
Stockport	1	Stoke-on-Trent	1
		Nottingham	2
Yorkshire (12)			
Leeds	1	Bristol	2
Bradford	1	Wales	2
Wakefield	1	Abroad	10
Halifax	1	UK total	103
Sheffield	1		
Saddleworth	1		

unknown and virtually untraceable local merchants and manufacturers.[51] The occupations and other biographical data on each figure were traced in a wide variety of sources at the Institute of Historical Research and the Society of Genealogists in London. Crucially for this study, the landowning of each wealth-holder was carefully traced in the *Return of Owners of Land.* The results here, it is fair to say, are as comprehensive and complete as we are ever likely to achieve, with the chronological gap between the *Return* of 1872 and any comprehensive listing of successful businessmen being reduced to the minimum. What, then, do we find?

The results are detailed in tables 5.3, 5.4 and 5.5 which set out, respectively, the acreages owned by the 337 non-landed wealth-holders in this study, the gross annual rental income from land owned by each, according to the *Return,* and the percentage of the total wealth of each wealth-holder held in landed wealth rather than otherwise. To compile the last of these, the gross annual rental income was multiplied by thirty to arrive at the approximate market value of the land; this figure was added to the personalty and the percentage of the overall total represented by land calculated.[52]

Table 5.3 Landed property owned by wealth-holders, 1873–75

	numbers of wealth-holders				
acreage	*1873*	*1874*	*1875*	*total*	*%*
10,000+	0	0	0	0	0.0
5,000–9,999	1	1	2	4	1.2
2,000–4,999	8	5	5	18	5.3
1,000–1,999	5	3	10	18	5.3
500–999	4	6	10	20	5.9
100–499	15	15	13	43	12.8
1–99	16	14	17	47	13.9
	49	44	57	150	44.5
less than 1	65	63	59	187	55.5
				337	100.0
landed	18	20	16	54	

Table 5.4 Gross annual landed income of non-landed wealth-holders, 1873–75

	numbers of wealth-holders				
income	*1873*	*1874*	*1875*	*total*	*%*
£5,000+	3	4	3	10	3.0
£2,000–4,999	11	6	15	32	9.5
£1,000–1,999	9	7	15	31	9.2
£500–999	8	8	9	25	7.4
£100–499	16	16	11	43	12.8
£1–99	2	3	4	9	2.6
	49	44	57	150	44.5
0	65	63	59	187	55.5
				337	100.0

Table 5.5 Percentage of total wealth held in land, among wealth-holders, 1873–75

	numbers of wealth-holders				
landed percentage	*1873*	*1874*	*1875*	*total*	*%*
50+	2	2	3	7	2.1
40.0–49.9	3	1	1	5	1.5
30.0–39.9	6	5	7	18	5.3
20.0–29.9	6	7	6	19	5.6
10.0–19.9	11	11	18	40	11.9
5.0–9.9	8	6	9	23	6.8
0.1–4.9	13	12	13	38	11.3
	49	44	57	150	44.5
0	65	64	58	187	55.5
				337	100.0

It will be strikingly obvious from a perusal of these tables that there is, in fact, not the slightest evidence of any disposition by business and professional wealth-holders to purchase land even in the most minimal amounts, let alone on a large scale. Less than 12 per cent of these 337 wealth-holders owned as much as 1,000 acres, with the majority owning nothing; only 21.7 per cent derived as much as £1,000 in annual income from land, a figure which almost certainly includes, in some cases, the rateable value of business premises; in only 14.5 per cent of cases did more than 20 per cent of a wealth-holder's assets consist of land, and in only 2.1 per cent of this sample – seven individuals out of 337 – was more than 50 per cent of their total assets invested in land. These figures are even lower than the acreage totals for millionaires and half-millionaires, and far from revealing a 'hidden' group of disguised businessmen-turned-landowners who sank their fortunes into land purchase and thus disappeared from the highest levels of the probate calendars – which record only personalty – this study, in going down to a lower level of wealth-holding, shows even less landowning among businessmen – just as one might expect.

Despite the paucity of examples of land purchase on a large scale by business or professional men, it might be useful to consider in more detail those wealth-holders who did purchase significant amounts of land, as judged by any of these categories. Four men owned 5,000 or more acres in the *Return*, an estate probably sufficient to place them, virtually automatically, among the great landowners. These were Thomas Baring (1799–1873) the great merchant banker and Conservative MP, who owned 8,058 acres in Hampshire; John Gerard Leigh (1821–75), heir to a Liverpool legal fortune accumulated by his father, the solicitor John Shaw Leigh (1791–1870), who owned 5,088 acres in Bedfordshire and Hampshire; and Peter Ormrod (1795–1875), a cotton spinner and banker in Bolton, who owned 5,290 acres in Lancashire.[53] All three were among the wealthiest men of their time in terms of their personal wealth, Baring leaving £1,500,000 and Leigh and Ormrod both leaving £700,000. It seems clear that their land purchases, even on so great a scale, did not represent more than a fraction of their wealth: for instance, Ormrod's 5,290 acres, at £30 per acre, would have cost about £159,000. Even if significant agricultural improvements and house-building have to be added to these figures, it is unlikely that any of the three spent more than one-quarter of their wealth on land purchase.

The fourth of the greatest acreage-accumulators in this sample illustrates the difficulties faced by the researcher in properly identifying or classifying putative business or professional men who might have turned landowners. This man was Thomas Henry Allen Poynder (1814–73) of Upper Brook Street, Grosvenor Square, and Hartham Park and

Hillmarton Manor, Wiltshire, a barrister who left £400,000 at his death. Although Poynder served as High Sheriff of Wiltshire in 1839, when he was only twenty-five, there is no direct evidence of any antecedent landownership in his family (although almost certainly there must have been for him to have obtained that position at so young an age). Poynder's father, Thomas Poynder of St George, Bloomsbury (1751–1837) proved almost impossibly elusive properly to identify. He is described in every published source as 'of Christ's Hospital', and indeed he served as Treasurer of the famous charity school from 1824 to 1835. Yet he plainly did not accumulate the £350,000 in personalty which he left at his death from any such pursuit; it seems conceivable that he was associated with either Thomas Poynder & Sons, builders, of Bishopsgate Within, or with Poynder and Hobson, lime and roman cement merchants of Blackfriars, listed in the 1823 London directory. The *Dictionary of National Biography* account of Poynder's collateral relative through his daughter's marriage, Sir John Poynder-Dickson, first Baron Islington (1866–1936) observes that 'his mother's family had made its mark in commerce and had attained considerable wealth in the East India trade'; this may be a reference to Thomas Poynder's mother Sarah, who was the daughter of Allen Cooper of the Hon. East India Company service, although there is no direct evidence for this. When, precisely, land first came into the family remains unclear: T. H. A. Poynder was educated at Charterhouse, in the latter 1820s, suggesting a distinctly London mercantile/professional origin, and then at Brasenose College, Oxford (and Lincoln's Inn) indicating, perhaps, more genteel family aspirations. Nor does what little is known of his wife, Mary Anne, daughter of Robert Edwards of Wrotham Place, Kent, shed any real light on when Poynder purchased 5,893 acres in Wiltshire and 47 acres in Middlesex.[54] When this family moved from commerce into the land – if, indeed, it did – remains unclear, illustrating the infinity of highly specific knowledge necessary for a proper study of this subject.

Ten wealth-holders possessed an income of £5,000 or more from their land, according to the *Return*, two in excess of £10,000: Leigh received £12,945 p.a. from his lands in Bedfordshire and Hertfordshire, and Poynder £11,975 from his estates in Wiltshire and Middlesex. The other great acreage-accumulators, Baring and Ormrod, also received very significant incomes from their lands, respectively £6,449 and £7,218. There were six other leaders in this category. Among the two wealthiest were the Nottingham and Derbyshire millionaire Francis Wright (1806–73), whose £1.4 million personal fortune was accumulated in the Butterley iron and steel works, extensive colliery interests, and a family bank, Lord Overstone being a distant relative, and also Baron Amschel de Rothschild. Wright, of Osmaston Manor, Derbyshire, also received

£5,267 p.a. from lands in Derby and Nottinghamshire. Baron Mayer Amschel de Rothschild (1818–74), of the Mentmore branch of the family, served as a Liberal MP from 1859 to 1874, and left £2.1 million at his death; the £6,885 he received in income from his Buckinghamshire estates, purchased in 1851, obviously represented only a minor portion of his princely income.

Osgood Hanbury (1794–1873), of the Lombard Street banking firm of Hanbury and Co., originally a Quaker family, received £5,118 annually from his estates in Essex and Suffolk. Hanbury left only £120,000 in personalty. Charles Thomas Naters Mather (1832–73) of Longridge House, Northumberland, and Newcastle-upon-Tyne, left £140,000 and owned 3,572 acres yielding £9,086 p.a. Mather's father, a Newcastle builder, in 1836 inherited a fortune of £200,000 from a shipowning kinsman in New York, apparently the basis of the family fortune.[55] Mark Philips (1800–73), who left £400,000, was a Manchester manufacturer and merchant, originally a Unitarian, and a well-known Radical MP for Manchester from 1832 to 1847. Curiously, this did not prevent him from owning 3,206 acres in Warwickshire and Lancashire yielding £5,933 including country houses like Welcombe, Warwickshire, and The Park, Prestwick, Lancashire.

In the case of the last man with a very high landed income, it is more controversial whether he should be classified here at all. William Grant (d. 1873), a cotton manufacturer in Bury whose family history is recounted by Samuel Smiles in *Self-Help* and who is said to have been one of the originals of the Cheeryble Brothers, left £250,000 in personalty. He owned 463 acres in Lancashire, which in the *Return* is given as yielding £6,493 p.a. It seems clear that most, and perhaps all, of this enormous income actually represents the rateable value of Grant's cotton factory. As noted, such cases have normally been excluded from these lists, but the relatively high figure of 463 acres owned by Grant would indicate that he owned some agricultural land; Grant certainly owned a country seat, Nuttall Hall, near Ramsbottom, Lancs.[56]

The third category of land purchasers requiring close attention are those, fifteen in number, whose landed wealth comprised roughly 40 per cent or more of their total wealth. This is, in many ways, the most significant of the three categories, for it is the propensity of businessmen and professionals to turn their personal wealth into landed holdings that we are, essentially, measuring: that a Baring or Rothschild held five or ten per cent of his total wealth in land, however substantial the holding, is probably not as good a measure of the movement of businessmen into the landed gentry as those cases where a much less wealthy businessman directed a far higher percentage of his overall assets towards land purchase.

Of these fifteen, four have been encountered already: Grant, Hanbury, Mather and Poynder, whose land holdings represented respectively 43.8, 59.6, 66.1 (the highest single percentage) and 46.5 per cent of their total holdings. Also above 50 per cent were Thomas Peers Williams (1795–1875), grandson of Thomas Williams the 'copper king', a banker, and a Conservative MP for forty-eight years, who left £100,000 as well as estates yielding £4,508 p.a; George Andrew (1821–73), a Manchester calico printer who left £100,000 but whose land – 299 acres yielding £4,132 p.a. – may well be artificially inflated by inclusion of the rateable value of his factories; Henry James Oakes (1796–1875), of an old-established banking family in Bury St Edmunds (£120,000; 2,840 acres worth £4,317); Sir James Duke, 1st Bt. (1792–1873), a City coal factor and insurance broker who served as Lord Mayor of London in 1848–9 and was additionally a long-serving Liberal MP (£120,000; 4,275 acres, £4,173 p.a.) and Frederic Arkwright (1806–74), gentry grandson of the cotton millionaire, from a family that probably retained no active business connections of any kind by the 1870s (£140,000; 1,728 acres, £4,795 p.a.).

With between 50.7 and 57.4 per cent of their total wealth in land, these five (with Hanbury and Mather for a total of seven) were the only business wealth-holders, out of 337, who had invested more than, roughly, 50 per cent of their assets in land. Between 40 and 50 per cent are found three other men, William Dickson (1799–1875), a Tyneside solicitor, banker and antiquary (£100,000; 1,049 acres, £3,275 p.a.); Coles William John Child (1813–73), a London dockside coal merchant who was – remarkably enough in an apparent reversal of the normal procession from trade to gentility – the son of the Clerk of the Cheque of the Yeomen of the Guards during the Reign of George III and George IV (£100,000; 259 acres, £2,886 p.a. – again, this may well be an inflated figure); and, finally, the Rev. John Metcalfe (1784–1873) of Ings House, Howes, Aysgarth, Yorks. N.R., (£140,000; 4,713 acres, £3,727 p.a.) who is counted here as of non-landed background chiefly because nothing could be traced of his father John Metcalfe, unlisted in any gentry genealogy, while the son's education at Appleby School (and Jesus College, Cambridge) at least suggests a middle-class origin.

Little or nothing, it would seem, can be inferred from this about the likelihood of any particular type of business or professional man buying land. As one would expect, most were, seemingly, Anglicans and Conservatives. Thomas Baring, for instance, was a Tory MP for thirty-five years who declined the Chancellorship of the Exchequer in 1852 and 1858, despite the close connection of the City in general and merchant bankers in particular with the Liberal Party and ideology. Similarly Peter Ormrod was an Anglican, a Church benefactor and a Conservative alderman, despite his position as a leading Bolton manufacturer, while calico spinner George Andrew's executors included an Anglican vicar. The families of Hanbury and Wright (originally Independent) had made the usual progression from Dissent to the Established Church, Wright being a prominent Evangelical Low Churchman. Although none of the men mentioned here was known to be a dissenter in adulthood, Rothschild, obviously, was one of the most prominent British Jews, while politically, several were Liberals, including the avowed radical Mark Philips. The pattern here seems similar to that found in John Foster's *Class Struggle in the Industrial Revolution*, with a nexus, where it existed, between Anglican businessmen and the local gentry, although there is once again no real evidence of any widespread landownership. These fifteen men, then, out of 337, are the *only* cases in which as much as 40 per cent of the total assets of these wealth-holders were in land rather than personalty; as we have seen, a careful examination of each case reveals that, if anything, these figures are probably exaggerated in some cases by the inclusion of participation by the wealth-holder in business life.

It might still be argued that the minimum cut-off point in this study, of £100,000 in personalty, still represents too high a minimum to catch all businessmen-turned-landowners. For this reason, a further random sample, of eighty persons leaving between £50,000 and £100,000 during the three years 1873–75, was extracted and the same biographical information obtained on each.[57] Of these eighty, eleven could definitely be classified as landowners of more than three generations standing, with the remaining sixty-nine being businessmen or professionals (those of

Table 5.6 Land ownership among a sample of wealth-holders leaving £50,000–£100,000, 1873–75

business/professional wealth acreage	*number of landowners*	*gross annual landed income*	*number of landowners*
10,000+	0		
5,000–9,999	2 (2.9%)	£5,000+	2 (2.9%)
2,000–4,999	1 (1.4%)	£2–5,000	1 (1.4%)
1,000–1,999	0	£1–2,000	0
500–999	1 (1.4%)	£500–1,000	1 (1.4%)
100–499	6 (8.7%)	£1–500	20 (30.0%)
1–99	14 (20.3%)	0	45 (65.2%)
less than 1	45 (65.2%)		
	69 (100%)		69 (100%)
inherited landed wealth	11		11
	80		80

unknown occupation were also classified here.) The statistics of this sample are extremely similar to those in the wealthier £100,000+ class, with 65.2 per cent owing no traceable land at all, and only three persons in this sample owning land on any considerable scale at all. These three were George Knollis Jarvis (1803–73, 4,720 acres yielding £5,824 p.a.), who inherited a Jamaica fortune and left £70,000 in personalty; Richard Meredith Richards (1821–73, 6,472 acres/£2,888 p.a.), who left £60,000, a grandson of a Lord Chief Baron of the Exchequer; and John Battersby Harford (1819–75, 7,561 acres/£7,661 p.a.), grandson of a wealthy Bristol banker. It will be noted that all three inherited their fortune; no 'self-made man' at this level both acquired a fortune and purchased significant amounts of land.

Returning to the original sample of those leaving £100,000 or more, another way of approaching this question of land purchase is to ascertain how many men in this sample became Justices of the Peace or Deputy-Lieutenants of counties. The figures which could be traced on this matter are probably understatements of the actual number, for there were surely some cases of men, unlisted in any biographical source employed by me, who held these positions; additionally, there may well have been a residual bias in such appointments against non-Anglicans and political radicals, while some wealthy businessmen were of course totally unsuitable for appointment to either judicial or ceremonial positions of this kind. On the other hand, by the 1870s appointees to the local bench, especially in Lancashire and London, no longer had necessarily to be landowners or socially acceptable to the squirearchy. For what they are worth, however, the figures are given in table 5.7.

Table 5.7 Non-landed wealth-holders in the 1873–75 sample known to have been a Justice of the Peace or Deputy-Lieutenant

	sample	*JP or DL*	%
1873	114	27	23.7
1874	107	16	15.0
1875	116	29	25.0
	337	72	*average* 21.6

Again, the striking impression made by these figures is, surely, the rareness with which wealthy businessmen could enter the ceremonial or judicial circle of the local establishment, akin to gentry status, despite the changes in the social bases of these positions which had already occurred in urban and industrial Britain. If there was a revolution in status and authority in late Victorian Britain, it had certainly not fully occurred by the mid-1870s.

It thus seems unarguable that this data provides clear confirmation of the general view put forward in my *Past and Present* article, by the Stones in *An Open Elite*, and by specialist social historians of groups of Victorian businessmen, like Anthony Howe; conversely there is nothing found here which contradicts this position. It is also most unlikely, given the fact that the *Return* of landowners was only compiled once in modern British history,[58] that more accurate coverage of a similarly comprehensive nature will ever appear.

III

A number of further points relating to the process of élite formation in modern Britain remain to be discussed here and these entail an examination of the dynastic process of gentrification, of which the 1873–75 'snapshot' sample may be only a single part; the notion of the landed élite as, increasingly, a 'caste' or 'caste-like' group, and the intention of those very wealthy businessmen who purchased land in significant amounts to enter the landed élite in a fully-fledged way.

Many of the historians who have examined this question have looked at the entry of a wealthy non-landed family into the landed élite as a two-step or multi-step process: in most cases the original wealth-holder enters the ranks of the minor gentry class by land purchase, but it is his son or grandson, or progeny even further down the line, who enters the true gentry class or the aristocracy by further land purchase, intermarriage and acquisition of the properties of that family, inheritance from distant kin, etc. on the one hand, and, on the other, true acceptance as a *bona-fide* landowner through the appropriate education of their children, socialisation into gentry mores, acceptance as a legitimate part of the 'County', acknowledgement through local office-holding, eventually a title, and listing in the appropriate 'snobs' directories.[59]

Obviously, something like this process happened innumerable times, although it is important to realise that it was at all times something of a lottery and that the conditions necessary for the appearance of many 'winners' – a national network of communication among the élite, internal political stability, the demographic likelihood of succession, a legal structure favouring property and primogeniture – existed in their most favourable form only after *c.* 1690. Conversely, both the rise of a new class of business wealthy after 1760 and the changes in British society which flowed from it may have presented a new set of obstacles to the continuation of this process in the nineteenth century. The rise of the public schools and the wider popularity of the university may well have created new networks of social reference from whose familial links marriage partners were drawn, while great wealth, landed or landless, almost always found an open door, as the example of the American millionaire heiresses on the English marriage market shows.

For the purposes of the discussion in this paper, however, there are two major considerations which are relevant. First, there is the question of motivation: how many business wealth-holders wished to begin this process of joining the landed classes? There is, secondly, the question of the continuation and evolution of this process and its *sui generis* features: in this case, the decline of English landed society in the twentieth century and in particular, the catastrophe of the First World War, which came just as the new business families of Victorian Britain should have become thoroughly integrated into the older landed élite.

From the 1873–75 data, as well as my previous research and the Stones', it can be suggested with confidence that the business élite of Victorian Britain was less likely to wish to begin this process of gentrification than its predecessors, given the unexampled increase in business wealth and the data presented above. However, a further yardstick in the process of gentrification presents itself by comparing the 1873–75 wealth-holders with *Burke's Landed Gentry* (and *Burke's Peerage*) for 1914, the last edition before the holocaust of landed society and at a distance of forty years after the deaths, and sixty or seventy years after the likely peak accumulative period, of this cohort.

Any such comparison is, clearly, not straightforward. Listing in *Burke's Landed Gentry* was totally arbitrary; many families of the 1873–75 wealth-holders would have died out or their fortunes been subsumed by distant kinsmen, virtually untraceable without herculean effort. Many wealth-holder families would have acquired titles, and thus be included in *Burke's Peerage and Baronetage* rather than the *Landed Gentry*, which encompassed only untitled landowners, but families acquiring titles might well have been landless, and little can be inferred about their merger with the landed aristocracy from this. Finally, since the *Landed Gentry* listed the genealogy of whole families, collateral relatives may have been the landowners, not the offspring of the wealth-holder in our cohort.

Nevertheless, for what it is worth, table 5.8 shows a comparison of the non-landed wealth-holders in the 1873–75 sample with listings for their families in *Burke's Landed Gentry* or *Burke's Peerage and Baronetage* for 1914. If anything, these percentages – small as they seem to be – *exaggerate* the number of progeny of the 1873–75 sample in *Burke's Landed Gentry* since many entries are clearly for collateral relatives; there are, similarly, unusual circumstances in other cases.[60] On the other hand, direct or indirect legatees of a number of these wealthy holders are doubtless

Table 5.8 Non-landed wealth-holders in the 1873–75 sample listed as gentry

	1873	*1874*	*1875*	*total*	
total non-landed	114	107	116	337	
Burke's Landed Gentry	26	12	16	54	(16.0%)
Burke's Peerage	10	7	8	25	(7.4%)

represented by distant kinsmen who were untraced, while, as noted, listing in *Burke's Landed Gentry* was rather arbitrary and capricious and not all-inclusive. Nevertheless the inference from these statistics seems fairly clear: just as few business wealth-holders sought to enter the landed élite, few families actually succeeded in doing so in a manner which would be recognised by the arbiters of gentry status as legitimate. There is thus little apparent evidence from this sample to suggest that the 'two-step' or 'multi-step' generational model of gentrification held true for Victoria's business élite, whatever had been the case in the past, while of course the watershed of 1914–18 would have played havoc with this pattern of evolution where it did occur.

Yet another way of viewing the entry of new men into the inner circle of landed society is that pursued by the Stones, and traces the building and ownership of suitable country houses, rather than any other criterion. Here, too, it is possible to adduce evidence from a fairly objective source which points still more strikingly in the same direction as the other data in this paper. In 1986 Michael Holmes of the National Art Library at the Victoria and Albert Museum published *The Country House Described: An Index to the Country Houses of Great Britain and Ireland* (Winchester, 1986), an alphabetical listing of over 4,000 country houses in the United Kingdom (including those now destroyed) which had been included in any of 135 guidebooks on architecture or county histories, or had been described in the monthly column on country houses in *Country Life* magazine, with bibliographical references to each place listed. A renowned stately home like Blenheim Palace or Warwick Castle often had twenty-five or more such references, ranging in date from the mid-eighteenth century through to the early 1980s, while hundreds of lesser-known houses referred to once in a single guidebook or county history were also listed.

Given the very large number of houses listed in Holmes' work, inclusion of a house owned by a wealthy Victorian businessman or professional should be a good test of the successful grafting of a new family onto the landed élite. Nevertheless, even here caveats are necessary: first, newer country houses would, presumably, have been included in many such sources chiefly for their architectural merit, but many second-rate Victorian piles such as would have been built or acquired by the new rich, especially below the millionaire level, were too undistinguished or unoriginal for notice; secondly, others possessed only a short, ephemeral existence before high taxes and death duties led to their destruction, or the inevitable conversion to use as a school, nursing home or 'loony bin'. Nevertheless, any family truly bent on acceptance by the country élite would presumably have acquired a suitable country seat as one of their highest priorities, and the figures based on Holmes' study should possess a certain real value. Here again is striking evidence of the lack of success – and, presumably, the lack of intention – of joining the landed élite.

Table 5.9 Non-landed wealth-holders in the 1873–75 sample known to have owned country houses

	1873	*1874*	*1875*	*total*	
total non-landed	114	107	116	337	
listed in Holmes	13	13	14	40	(11.9%)

Professor Thompson, in his article on 'Business and Landed Elites' has also commented on the true aspirations and self-identification of those millionaires and other wealthy men who did purchase land. Among the historians who have studied this subject there is no consensus about the aspirations and identity of the new magnates in terms of the old. The Stones and I have looked upon the landed and business élites as largely quite separate, certainly until the late Victorian period, while other historians have viewed these groups in very different terms. Pat Thane and José Harris proposed the term 'aristocratic bourgeoisie' to define the social position of the wealthiest Victorian merchant bankers, while F. M. L. Thompson, arguing for the ambiguity of class identity of the new Victorian rich, has claimed bluntly that 'the idea that there was a deep and widening social gulf between the top flight of new wealth and the old aristocracy is a myth'.[61] Harold Perkin, in his new sequel to *The Origins of Modern English Society*, has emphasised much the same view of old and new wealth as, essentially, linked and allied.[62]

Much of this debate, perhaps not surprisingly, has elements of the blind men and the elephant about it. It seems undeniable, for example, that the social gap between old and new wealth narrowed consistently from the 1880s onwards, and those who emphasise the narrowness or non-existence of this social gap chiefly refer to the late Victorian and Edwardian periods. It seems equally unarguable, to me at any rate, that the gap was enormously wider during the fifty years preceding the 1880s (just as, going back before the 1830s, it was less wide than it subsequently became) and that, as many historians have pointed out, the mid-nineteenth century was a period of the almost total ascendancy of the traditional landed aristocracy in national political terms. During this period – roughly from 1830 to 1885 – it seems extremely difficult to argue by example that more than a handful of genuine new men were accepted into the ranks of the landed aristocracy, while after 1885 there was, clearly, an increasing merger between land and business wealth, especially the magnates of the City and financial/commercial capitalism.

The notion that the landed aristocracy constituted, increasingly, a 'caste-like' group does not mean merely that newcomers were deliberately excluded from true acceptance by traditional landed society – although this occurred – but, much more, that the new business wealthy deliberately chose not to join the traditional landed aristocracy. Most new businessmen – as we have seen – made no efforts at all to join the landed élite in any sense whatever; in a significant minority of cases, although some land was purchased, the potential which their fortunes presented for purchasing land was certainly not realised and these men remained businessmen who, incidentally, owned a small landed property or estate, rather than landowners who began as businessmen. Only in the smallest and most unrepresentative number of cases were there a true exception to this pattern, that is, businessmen-turned-landowners in the true and traditional sense. At least this is what all the representative research known to me suggests: if this impression is false, it is up to those whose view of this evolution is different to provide valid evidence that they are right and, so far in this debate, no one has.

Notes

1 The article was originally published in *Past and Present* 92 (1981), pp. 125–48 and reprinted in my collection of essays, *Elites and the wealthy in modern British history*, Brighton, 1987, pp. 145–71.

2 Table 1 (table 6.1 in the reprint) in *Ibid.* Bateman's figures are revisions of the comprehensive national listing of landowners, *The return of owners of land*, compiled by Parliament in 1872–3.

3 'New men of wealth . . .' in *Elites and the wealthy*, p. 149.

4 *Ibid.*, table 6.2. The remainder (12 per cent) could not be identified.

5 *Ibid.* pp. 157, 163–4.

6 Lawrence Stone and Jeanne C. Fawtier Stone, *An open élite? England 1540–1880*, Oxford, Clarendon Press, 1984, p. 403.

7 *Ibid.*

8 See, e.g., Eileen Spring and David Spring, 'The English landed élite, 1540–1880: a review', Spring *Albion* 17 (1985), pp. 149–80; 'Social mobility and the English landed élite', *Canadian Journal of History*, XXI (December 1986), pp. 333–51; Harold Perkin, 'An open élite' (review of the Stones' book), *Journal of British Studies*, 24 (1985), pp. 496–501; for an excellent summary of the debate see 'Essays

in revision No. 2: social mobility and English landed society', *Social History Society Newsletter*, vol. 12, no. 2 (Autumn 1987).

9 The probate sources begin in a usable form in 1809; there was no parallel to the *Return* from the *Domesday Book* until 1873.

10 Stones', *An open élite?*, p. 11.

11 *Walford's county families*, 1894 edition, Index of names.

12 So far as I am aware, we conducted our research in complete isolation from one another, although I cite an earlier article by them on this subject and they cite one of mine. We did not meet, correspond or exchange information prior to publishing.

13 I am grateful to Professor Thompson for letting me have a copy of this paper in its unpublished form.

14 F. M. L. Thompson, 'Business and landed élites in the nineteenth century' in F. M. L. Thompson (ed) *Landowners, capitalists, and entrepreneurs*, Oxford, 1994, p. 165.

15 *Ibid.*, footnotes 18–47, *passim.*

16 *Ibid.*, and p. 165.

17 *Ibid.*, p. 147.

18 *Ibid.*, p. 154.

19 *Ibid.*, p. 153.

20 *Ibid.*, p. 148.

21 *Ibid.*, p. 148.

22 *Ibid.*, pp. 150–3.

23 *Ibid.*, pp. 163–4.

24 This is clearly noted in my article, e.g., Rubinstein, 'New men of wealth', pp. 149, 156–7, etc.

25 Thompson, 'Business and landed élites', p. 165.

26 Spring, 'Social mobility and the English landed élite', *Canadian Journal of History*, XXI (December 1986), pp. 333–51.

27 *Ibid.*, p. 351. The Springs have not employed any original research in their articles, it would seem, but focus on their perceived errors in the historians under attack.

28 *Ibid.*, p. 335 (italics as in original).

29 This summarizes *Ibid.*, pp. 335–7.

30 The percentage who had made their money in business, among purchasers of estates in the three counties surveyed by the Stones was 36 per cent in 1640–99, 27 per cent in 1700–59, 41 per cent in 1760–1819, and 43 per cent in 1820–79. (Stones, *An open élite?*, table 6.2)

31 Harold Perkin, 'An open élite?' (review of the Stones' book), *Journal of British Studies*, vol. 24, no. 4 (October, 1985), pp. 496–501.

32 *Ibid.*, p. 499.

33 I perused this thesis when I was Research Associate to Harold Perkin in 1974–5, but have not read or seen it since, and was unable to refer to it when writing this paper. The dates of the 'New Domesday' Returns in Knapp's title, 1873–6, refer to the years when the *Return* was published in the Parliamentary Papers, not when it was compiled.

34 Perkin, '*An open élite?*' (review), p. 500.

35 *Ibid.*

36 Stone, *An open élite?*, table 6.2.

37 Perkin, '*An open élite?*' (review), p. 499.

38 In fact Lawrence Stone has cited Howe's research to prove the opposite, that new industrialists did not buy land in quantity: Lawrence Stone, 'Spring back', *Albion* 17 (1985), p. 171.

39 Anthony Howe, *The cotton masters 1830–1860*, Clarendon Press, Oxford, 1984, p. 32.

40 *Ibid.*, pp. 29–30.

41 Daunton, 'Gentlemanly capitalism', p. 126. I responded to the points made in this

article with which I disagreed in '"Gentlemanly capitalism" and British industry, 1820–1914: a comment', *Past and Present* 132 (1991).

42 *Ibid.*, p. 131. Daunton has discussed the Gibbs family at greater length in his 'Inheritance and succession in the City of London in the nineteenth century', *Business History* XXX (1988).

43 *Ibid.*, citing M. B. Rose, 'Diversification of investment' by the Greg family, 1800–1914, *Business History* XXI (1979).

44 For instance, Howe suggests a similar motivation in his *Cotton Masters*, p. 30, as did F. M. L. Thompson in 'The land market in the nineteenth century', *Oxford Economic Papers*, 2nd ser., IX (1957).

45 Howe, *Cotton Masters*, p. 32.

46 Robert Giffen, *The growth of capital*, London, 1889, p. 30.

47 Daunton, 'Gentlemanly capitalism', p. 103.

48 Scottish and Irish estates were probated separately and are not included in this study. Printed Scottish Calendars of Confirmation date only from 1876 (rather than 1858 as in England and Wales), although manuscript probate calendars do exist for 1873–75 in Scotland.

49 Although I originally abstracted all such names, with their valuations, addresses, etc. from the probate calendars in 1972, in 1988 my research assistant in London, Carole Taylor, went through the laborious process of abstracting this information again; thus, so far as is humanly possible, the data collection is complete. The actual research on the occupations and landownership of these wealth-holders was undertaken by me alone however. This research is part of a much larger project to compile a biographical register of everyone leaving £100,000 or more during the nineteenth century. The valuation figure is that of the gross unsettled personalty of each testator, thus *excluding* the value of land, which has to be added in separately to ascertain the true value of his wealth at death.

50 There were about twenty wealthy women in this sample, mainly the widows or daughters of pre-existing wealth-holders. These have been categorised with the occupational category of their father or husband; for example, Hannah Brackenbury (d. 1873), £160,000, apparently the daughter or widow of a Manchester solicitor; Lady Elizabeth Cornwallis (d. 1874), £100,000; Sophia, 22nd Baroness de Clifford (1791–1874), £100,000.

51 The occupations (or any other information) of about fifteen of these persons, who were assumed to be business or professional in origin, could not be traced in any source. Two of the most difficult to find rejoiced in the names of William Gladstone and Horatio Nelson. Gladstone (1809–73) who left £120,000, proved to be a Russian merchant in London and St Petersburg; he was a cousin of the Prime Minister, but is omitted from most genealogies. Nelson (1800–17 October 1873) of Moorgate Villas, Clarborough, Nottinghamshire, who also left £120,000, was a surgeon turned paper manufacturer.

52 One point that should be noted is that a number of wealth-holders were listed in the *Return* as owning zero acres (*sic*) or a tiny landed holding, which, according to the *Return*, yielded a significant, even enormous, gross annual income: for example, Charles Augustus Stewart (d. 1873), merchant of Manchester, 0 acres, £475 income; George Greenwood Tetley (d. 1873), stuff merchant of Bradford, 7 acres, £2,770 income; Bryce Allan (1814–74), shipowner and merchant of Liverpool, 0 acres, £62 income. These figures represented the rateable value of the business premises or factories of these men (see the Introduction of the *Return*) and have not been included in the tables here. Almost certainly many gross annual incomes and acreages which *are* included here have been artificially inflated by the inclusion of the rateable value with the actual landed income. This should be kept in mind when considering these tables: the results almost certainly *exaggerate* the proportion of land purchased by these wealth-holders which was agricultural land.

53 Bateman credits the widows of Leigh and Ormrod with larger holdings a decade later, respectively 6,507 and 5,306 acres.

54 In Bateman, 'Poynder (late) of Hillarton Manor, Calne' is credited with owning

6,908 acres in six counties (5,913 in Wiltshire). Following Poynder's death the estates came to a collateral relative, Sir John Dickson, 6th Bt. who changed his name to Sir John Dickson-Poynder, served as a well-known Conservative MP for North-West Wiltshire from 1892–1910 and in several junior ministerial posts, and was created Baron Islington in 1910. This highly anomalous title for a Wiltshire squire was apparently a tribute to Poynder-Dickson's Chairmanship of the Board of the Royal Northern Hospital, Islington.

55 Mather's widow was remarried, to Hubert E. W. Jerningham, MP in 1874, and he apparently gained possession of Mather's lands, since he is credited in Bateman with owning precisely the same acreage and income as is Mather in the *Return.* The only information traceable on Mather, from *Walford's county families* for 1872, gave his father as 'C. Mathers' and his mother as Mary Naters. He does not appear in *Men of mark twixt Tyne and Tweed* or any other similar source.

56 Grant's estates passed at his death to his daughter Isabella, wife of Andrew Sherlock Lawson, and then to their son Sir John Grant Lawson, 1st Bt., MP (1856–1919).

57 This sample was obtained by turning to the fiftieth and 150th page in each volume of the English and Welsh probate calendars for the three years, and taking the first person thereafter to leave between £50,000 and £100,000.

58 Actually it was nearly done twice, for Lloyd George set in train the compilation of a similar catalogue for the purposes of expediting his land taxes during the term of the Asquith government. Apparently only half of Britain was surveyed and the surviving individual returns are extremely difficult to use.

59 See, e.g., the Stones, *An open élite,* especially Part 11 and Daunton, 'Gentlemanly capitalism', p. 130.

60 For example, James Alexander Guthrie (1823–73), a City banker and Director of the Bank of England, was also the hereditary laird of Craigie, Forfarshire, and his family is included in *Burke's Landed Gentry* on this basis.

61 Pat Thane and Jose Harris, 'British and European bankers, 1880–1914: an "Aristocratic Bourgeoisie"?' in Pat Thane, Geoffrey Crossick and Roderick Floud, (eds), *The power of the past,* Cambridge, 1984; F. M. L. Thompson, 'Business and landed élites', pp. 169–170.

62 Harold Perkin, *The rise of professional society,* London, 1989.

6

HODGE'S POLITICS: THE AGRICULTURAL LABOURERS AND THE THIRD REFORM ACT IN SUFFOLK

PETER CLARKE
WITH THE ASSISTANCE OF KEVIN LANGFORD[1]

Hick – the sort of hick who is wont to live in the sticks – is only a corruption of Richard. Hodge, as the typical name for an English agricultural labourer, likewise turns out to be nothing more than a medieval abbreviation of Roger, and Chaucer switched between the two forms at whim. But one way or another, Hodge has always had a bad name. Assimilated with the near-homophone *hotchpotch*, which, with its French derivation, comports a benign sense of mixing into our native plain cooking, the term *hodge-podge* carries contemptuous connotations – a clumsy gallimaufry of ingredients, fit to impress only the gullible. A dictionary of 1700 calls Hodge 'a country clown'. Poor Hodge: whatever did he know of politics? 'He knew nothing and desired as little', was how one Conservative commentator put it in 1885, trying to come to terms with the implementation of the third Reform Act. 'Nonetheless Hodge was enfranchised, much to his own surprise and his master's.'[2] What impact household suffrage had upon county politics continues to baffle historians as much as it surprised contemporaries. This essay offers some evidence from one English county upon these matters.

It was only in 1885 that the English agricultural counties suffered (or enjoyed) a real political awakening. Until then the structure of county politics was faithfully moulded upon its template: the structure of English landed society. As its historian has written, in terms which are still as valid as when they were first published: 'the rule of the landed interest was based on deference, on the whole voluntarily accorded, and not on outright power and coercion.'[3] Subsequent historiographical controversies over the intentions of those who reformed the electoral system in 1832 have not disturbed this judgment about the way that the structure actually functioned. It is clear that it was not radically affected by either the second Reform Act in 1867 or the Ballot Act in 1872. For the essential fact was that electoral power was left predominantly in the hands of the forty-shilling freeholders, or else of rural voters even less inclined to quarrel with the *status quo*, thus perpetuating the rule of a political class who could perfectly well be trusted to vote in secret. Their politics were a transparent amalgam of conceptions of 'independence' and 'deference', both deeply ingrained in peculiarly compatible ways so as to affirm the antique solidarity of the landed interest as a hierarchical community. The yeomen of England, whose forty-shilling freehold could be traced back to a statute of 1430, thus held sway for four-and-a-half centuries until the third Reform Act precipitately extended household suffrage, which was still a relative novelty in the boroughs, into the counties as well.[4]

Under the second Reform Act there were 172 English county divisions, of which the Conservatives won no less than 127 in 1868, 145 in their great victory of 1874, and still 118 amidst the Gladstonian triumph of 1880.[5] Little wonder that Disraeli had only been tempted to leap in the dark to the extent of fastening household suffrage upon the boroughs in 1867, and had prudently resolved to sit on his assets rather than meddle (in any fundamental way that went much beyond the usual gerrymandering) with the representation of the counties. The parliamentary strength of the English counties was increased by a third under the 1885 redistribution; but any notion that this was good news for the Conservatives was exploded by their sorry performance in the subsequent general election, when their share of this enhanced total of 234 seats dropped back to 101, leaving the Liberals for the first and last time holding the majority of English county constituencies.

Admittedly, this is partly a statistical effect, since 74 small boroughs, which in 1880 had returned 50 Liberals out of 87 members, had meanwhile been dissolved into their surrounding county divisions; and it should also be borne in mind that the actual Liberal majority was accumulated in northern county divisions, many of them mining and woollen textile seats. Even so, if the Conservatives still held 66 seats in the southern counties to the Liberals' 63, this was a decisive reversal of their overwhelming margin of superiority in 1880 (87 to 21).[6] The Conservatives, in short, were left with crumbs of comfort where once they had possessed an ample granary.

Michael Thompson once suggested that, to the extent that redistribution in 1885 ejected alien town elements from some rural seats, this had the effect of 'making the task of the landowners much less complicated, provided they could manage the agricultural labourers.'[7] In the long run, we shall suggest, this may have been true; but, at the time of the 1885 general election, many landowners would have spoken like good Keynesians in supposing that 'this *long run* is a misleading guide to current affairs.'[8] The fact was that they seemed unable to manage their own labourers. The landed interest seemed to have made the mistake of trusting that the unspoken assumptions of deference would work as well under the new franchise as under the old. 'The landlord and squire of the parish, who had always blanketed and coaled his poorer neighbours in the winter, and supplied cider in abundance at harvest time, thought – though no such intention had crossed his mind when he did it – that he would surely reap the harvest of his meritorious dealing at the polls', ran one Conservative account. 'The parish, led by the priest and the publican, would vote with him, and for him, in a body'; instead of which, the counting of the votes revealed the ungrateful Hodge to have 'set up the Gladstone statue on the plain of Dura. Its feet are composed of miry clay. At the base of the statue, as its pedestal and support, is the agricultural labourer.'[9]

There is nowhere better for an investigation of the miry clay than Suffolk. Its electoral history in the era between the Great Reform Act, which created its Suffolk's East and West divisions, and the third Reform Act of 1884–85, is rather like Tolstoy's concept of a happy marriage: in fifty uneventful years almost nothing happened to make it particularly interesting or unlike the run of English counties in general. In East Suffolk the Tories were careless enough to lose one of the seats in 1832 but never subsequently lapsed – though they were run fairly close in 1868, and even closer by a solitary Liberal challenger in 1880. In West Suffolk, likewise, the Conservatives had secured both seats from 1837 onward (with the qualification that Lord Jermyn sat for five years as a Peelite from 1859 before succeeding his father as Marquess of Bristol). This was the Constable country of pastoral politics: a tranquil scene, where ennui was tempered only by inanition.

A picturesque attachment to Old Corruption was a parallel theme in the surviving rural boroughs. Bury St Edmunds was jointly controlled by the (Whig) Duke of Grafton and the (Tory) Marquess of Bristol and was represented through four parliaments by their respective sons. Eye consisted of no less than eleven parishes, covering over thirty square miles, but could still only muster 253 registered voters in 1832. They were, moreover, usually spared the trouble of voting, returning Sir Edward Kerrison, Bt., unopposed in ten general elections running, with the first contest occurring only in 1874.[10] For activity we must look to Sudbury, a borough of which it can confidently be said that others may have been older, but none more corrupt.

While many rotten boroughs found themselves abolished in 1832, Sudbury continued to subsist in a state of deliquescent putrefaction for a further twelve years. The presence of 150 poverty-stricken handloom weavers as freemen voters matched temptation on the one side with opportunity on the other; they seized upon electoral bribery, which reached thirty pounds a head in 1835, as a more profitable cottage industry, but one which was also, alas, doomed to extinction. The system reached its climax in the 1841 election when each Liberal supporter was issued with one ticket which he could exchange for two guineas at the Black Boy on one side of the market square, where the hustings had been set up; and, having voted the right way, could collect a second ticket on the other side of the square at the Swan, where, installed in an upper room, an anonymous agent known only as 'the Redhaired Man', would receive the ticket through a slot in the door and dole out another two guineas in return.[11] Such were the civic traditions on which generations of electors had been raised; and it is evident that the political education of Hodge – marvelling at such tales as reached him while he dreamt of the franchise under the wide Suffolk sky – left a good deal to be desired.

I

The meaning of household suffrage is our first theme. Contemporaries spoke confidently of Hodge acquiring the parliamentary franchise as a result of the legislation of 1884–85. It needs to be queried whether their perception was well-founded, in view of the fact that recent historians have been more impressed with the extent to which household suffrage fell short of a fully democratic franchise. There are two relevant calculations which need to be made. One is to estimate what proportion of agricultural labourers had the vote; and the other is to estimate what proportion of the electorate were agricultural labourers.

For practical purposes it can be assumed that there were hardly any agricultural labourers on the Suffolk county register before 1884, since the number with an *ownership* franchise in 1885 was negligible. The point is that *ownership* (of property) took priority over *occupation* (of a house) as a qualification; so any householders who had previously qualified for the vote, irrespective of the introduction of household suffrage, would continue to have been classed as ownership voters. Finer evidence on the position after 1884 can be found by collating the new register for south Suffolk with the 1881 census enumerators' returns for a sample of six villages.[12]

What this immediately confirms is that, after 1884, this is truly a *household* suffrage and that the adult men who did not have votes were overwhelmingly those who were not 'householders'.[13] Even the ownership vote, in these rural areas, was largely limited to householders. Over 70 per cent of ownership voters were resident in the constituency, or, to put it another way, they comprised 6.2 per cent of the total electorate, whereas the non-resident ownership vote was only 2.7 per cent. Since ownership took priority as a qualification, this franchise can be regarded as being inflated by the registration of voters who would otherwise have qualified as occupiers, with the advantage for them of having to satisfy a residence period of only six months instead of twelve.

Given the importance of householder status in generating votes, the first task is to establish how many adult men were classified as householders in the 1881 census. (Women accounted for 9 per cent of householders in these villages, but were excluded from the parliamentary franchise.) This is shown in table 6.1, based on the ten-village sample.

Table 6.1 Men over 21 who were census householders (10 villages in south Suffolk)

	those over 21	*householders*	%
gentry, farmers etc.	146	122	84
traders, craftsmen	190	152	80
agricultural labourers	704	576	82
other farm employees	49	43	88
servants	44	28	63
others	94	52	55
totals	1227	973	*average* 79

The significant finding here is that agricultural labourers were as likely as their social superiors to emerge as householders in the eyes of the census. This was not, however, the same thing as securing the franchise. There were three checks upon the franchise, each of which prevented householders from getting onto the register. First, occupiers had to fulfil a *residence qualification* of twelve months (six for ownership voters) up to 15 July in order to appear on the register due to come into force the following 1 January. In fact, the 1885 register, as used in the general election in November and December, was an accelerated version of the register which would otherwise have become operative in January 1886, and which thus served also for the general election of July 1886. Second, the receipt of *poor relief* by any member of the household was a disqualification. In the third place, *inefficiency* took its toll.

In calculating the effect of the qualification period, one piece of information is crucial: what proportion of householders 'turned over' every year through removals and arrivals. It is not easy to establish the number of arrivals, which has to be approached indirectly, by tracking the names of occupiers on the 1885 register back to those listed as householders by the 1881 census. In principle this discloses how many of the 1885 electorate had arrived since 1881, and hence the annual rate of arrivals. The number of householders arriving in the course of a twelve-month period, of course, ought to be the number disqualified by a twelve-month residence stipulation. Thus we can estimate the impact of the first check, leaving the second and third as residual factors. The extent of the pauper disqualification can be ignored for the moment in calculations which work back from the 1885 register, since it is obvious that disqualified paupers, like all other omissions, were necessarily omitted.

In the six-village sample there were 476 occupier voters on the register in 1885, of whom 177 had not been listed as householders in the previous census. Thus in the 39 months from April 1881, when the census was taken, to July 1884, when the qualifying period for registration commenced, 'arrivals' (including men coming of age) were running at an annual rate of 36. In the course of the next twelve months, then, it is reasonable to assume that a further 36 householders would have arrived, in addition to the 476 who actually qualified. The grand total of householders for July 1885 is thus 512, of whom 36 (7 per cent) would have arrived too late to meet the residential requirement for the vote. This estimate for 'latecomers' needs to be borne in mind.

On closer inspection, a minor inconsistency emerges between the census enumerators' conception of a household and that of the revision courts. The discrepancy is not in itself surprising except, as it were, in direction. Far from the courts finding legal reasons to disfranchise men whom common sense could identify as 'householders', it was the census which adopted the more restrictive definition, especially when considering servants, who nonetheless sometimes crept on to the register as occupiers. The number of 'electoral householders' is thus understated by 2 per cent in the census. But it would be fallacious to adjust the estimate for arrivals from an annual rate of 7 per cent to 5 per cent. The 2 per cent of 'non-census householders' must be regarded as a once-for-all margin of error (say, 10 electors in this sample), reducing the true total for arrivals over the whole period from 117 to 107, and thus bringing the estimate of the annual rate down to 33. The net effect is marginal, in trimming the figure for annual arrivals to 6.6 per cent. Given the equilibrium, in which arrivals and removals were in balance, a realistic estimate for annual 'turnover' is somewhere between 6 and 7 per cent.

This figure needs to be established with some care because, whether measuring arrivals or removals (including deaths), it has further implications for our understanding of the structure of the franchise. Table 6.2 disaggregates the census householders of 1881 in the eight-village sample and shows how many of them failed to appear on the 1885 register.

Table 6.2 Occupation of adult male householders (8 villages in south Suffolk)

	1881 census	*not on 1885 register*	%
gentry, farmers, etc.	86	16	19
traders, craftsmen	96	26	27
agricultural labourers	398	116	29
other farm employees	27	10	37
servants	27	9	33
others	33	15	45
totals	667	192	29

Applying an estimate of 6–7 per cent annual turnover would give a putative norm for removals over the whole period April 1881–July 1885 in the range 24–28 per cent. This can be compared with the deficiency of 19 per cent actually shown for gentry and farmers, who were admittedly less mobile than other classes. Table 6.2 thus suggests that virtually all the rural upper crust who fulfilled the qualifying period of residence ended up on the register, which is only to be expected. Rather less predictable is the inference that, after making an allowance of 24–28 per cent for 'removals', this only leaves a residual shortfall of something between 1 per cent and 5 per cent of unenfranchised agricultural labourers. This can, of course, be explained by noting that these were men who had been householders since at least 1881 and who must have remained disfranchised in 1885 for the residual reasons of the pauper disqualification or administrative inefficiency. If this residual category of 1–5 per cent comprised the only 1885 householders excluded from the register, it would imply that 95–99 per cent were included. But this is to overlook the number of arrivals during the period July 1884–July 1885, which means allowing for an additional 6–7 per cent of 'latecomers'. With an increment of 6 per cent, it would need to be added to the 5 per cent residuals generated by that assumption; and similarly with an increment of 7 per cent, it would need to be added to the corresponding estimate of 1 per cent residuals.

Either way, the total is much the same. This suggests that around ten per cent of those agricultural labourers who were householders failed to appear on the electoral register. These necessarily intricate calculations, which may seem wearisome and arcane, have now yielded findings which can be more simply expressed. All told, it seems likely that over eighty per cent of adult male agricultural labourers were householders and, in turn, that over ninety per cent of these were registered. This implies that about 75 per cent of adult male agricultural labourers had the vote.

Applying this estimate to the occupational census totals is not straightforward. The snag here is that no figure is given for adults within the total for male agricultural labourers in Suffolk (35,515). The national aggregate for agricultural labourers, however, is broken down by age, indicating that 70 per cent were over the age of twenty-one. It is reasonable to apply this age-distribution to the Suffolk total, giving an estimate for the county of nearly 25,000 adult agricultural labourers.[14]

This chain of reasoning gives an estimate of 18,665 agricultural labourers on the electoral register for the county divisions of Suffolk in 1885. It also provides an elegant way to express the general relationship between what we actually know and what we want to know. What is actually given is a census total for male agricultural labourers for each county. The inference that – on the most conservative assumptions – at least half of them were enfranchised can be derived from applying three simple proportions: 0.7 (adults) × 0.8 (householders) × 0.9 (registration) = 0.5 (enfranchised labourers).

This gearing may have been more favourable towards agricultural labourers than towards other workingmen who had less chance of forming a settled household. In Suffolk as a whole the 1885 electorate was 76.7 per cent of the number of adult males in the 1881 census. This compares with national figures suggesting that 60–70 per cent of adult males were registered to vote in this period. The proportion of British men able to vote was substantially lower in working-class districts of cities but was not far short of the Suffolk figure in other counties of England and Wales as a whole (73.2 per cent of adult men were enfranchised in 1891/1892).[15] Whatever its other deficiencies, however, household suffrage did not discriminate against Hodge simply because he was poor.

Having estimated the proportion of agricultural labourers who qualified to vote, what proportion of the electorate did they constitute? Given that over half the agricultural labourers recorded in the 1881 census for each county were enfranchised after 1884, they formed 34 per cent of the electorate in Suffolk. For comparison, this was about the same proportion as in Norfolk and Oxfordshire. Only Cambridgeshire exceeded it, with 38 per cent; and in other rural counties, like Bedfordshire, Hampshire, Sussex and Northamptonshire, agricultural labourers accounted for between 25 and 30 per cent of the county electorate. It is also possible to break down figures for the five county divisions into which Suffolk was carved in 1885. Moreover, the proportion of the electorate who were agricultural labourers and the Liberal share of the vote in 1885 can be tabulated, as in table 6.3.[16]

Table 6.3 Suffolk county divisions 1885

	agricultural vote (%)	*Liberal poll (%)*
North East (Eye)	45	61.5
North West (Stowmarket)	42	57.0
South East (Woodbridge)	35	50.9
South (Sudbury)	34	58.7
North (Lowestoft)	18	53.6

This table is suggestive rather than conclusive on two linked points: the extent to which the agricultural labourers dominated the situation and the relationship between their enfranchisement and the Liberal breakthrough in a county which had previously been solidly Conservative. It is apparent that Hodge was not omnipotent in the absolute sense that the miners were in the eleven constituencies in England and Wales where they constituted over half the electorate. His position was more like that of the cotton workers in the archetypal mill towns, Blackburn and Burnley, where they were prominent and easily identifiable yet comprised less than one third of the electorate.[17] The agricultural labourers were not in a majority even in the Suffolk North East division; and since this included the dissolved borough of Eye, where household suffrage had been in force in the villages since 1867, there is direct evidence from the local press during the 1874 General Election of the presence of agricultural labourers on the Conservative side – showing that Liberal support among this class was by no means axiomatic. More needs to be said about the politics of the period to make better sense of this picture.

II

There is a broad historiographical consensus nowadays that the course of politics cannot simply be read off from, or explained away by, structural factors. Thus it is recognised that political consciousness is not predetermined in its forms but is shaped by popular values, traditions, perceptions, and actions, sometimes spontaneously and sometimes in response to particular sorts of leadership. The history of nineteenth-century radicalism is being rewritten in such terms.[18] In Suffolk what needs to be recaptured is the political context which mediated the effect of three influences: economic conditions, trade union organisation and religious affiliation.

The Suffolk labourers had the lowest agricultural wages in England. Bowley's index for Suffolk wages (1881=100) shows a sharp drop in the early years of the decade: to 89 in 1882 and then fluctuating around 84 for the next five years. But since Bowley's price index shows a fall of ten per cent between 1883 and 1885, the unfavourable impact on real wages came in 1881–83, with an improvement of 5 per cent both in 1884 and in 1885.[19] It would be bold – or crude – to read off a simple political response from these economic indicators. It is not immediately obvious why they should have helped the Liberals; nor is there a simple economic explanation of the remarkable revival of the National Agricultural Labourers' Union.

The union reached its maximum strength in the early 1870s, enlisting up to one in four agricultural labourers in East Anglia, though probably fewer in Suffolk than in Norfolk or Essex. The 1874 lockout, which prompted its decline, began at Exning in Suffolk; but, even so, union activity was maintained in an impressively resilient way.[20] One of the two districts administering Suffolk, that for 'West Suffolk', underwent an internal crisis in the summer of 1884, when its secretary was accused of embezzlement. Reliable figures for membership of the union, therefore, only survive for the 'Suffolk' district, where there was a minimum of 1,100 paid-up members in February 1884, plus an unspecified number of others in arrears.[21]

The Suffolk district records show that in the five months before the 1884 harvest the union held 88 meetings in the villages, which produced a total of about 120 recruits (24 per month). In August there were no meetings, and in September only eight. In the next five months, organisational activity was resumed at much the same level as previously with 93 meetings. This was a few more – but only a few – than in the March to July period. The impact, however, was wholly transformed, as seed which had once fallen upon stony ground now produced its own harvest – not an hundredfold, admittedly, but getting on for sevenfold. Total recruitment from October 1884 to February 1885 was 762 (152 per month). Most of them joined in October and November. The increase, moreover, came in the trade contributions, not those for sickness benefit, surely a sign of militant rather than prudential motives. Growth slackened after February 1885, but contributions to the union held up until after the general election in December.

It would be difficult to deny this phenomenon a strong political connotation; it clearly has to be read as an indication of political radicalism. The political context was one dominated by the fate of Gladstone's Bill to harmonise the franchise in counties and boroughs alike on the basis of household suffrage. The Bill was carried on its second reading by the Liberal majority in the Commons in June 1884, only to be defeated in the House of Lords in July. 'What a suicidal act of the Lords!' Gladstone commented in his diary.[22] While the harvest was gathered that summer, a political crisis unfolded in which the Conservatives insisted on a redistribution measure as the price of compromise, while the Liberals noisily championed the cause of the agricultural labourers, as expressed through the People's House, against the obstruction posed by an overweening territorial aristocracy. In August Gladstone assured the Queen that 'it is indisputable that the Liberal party, and the great open, & open-air, meetings which it has promoted, have very generally, in consequence of the Franchise Bill, demanded organic change in the House of Lords.'[23] Here was the veiled threat to the constitution and the hereditary principle which was to be the means of unlocking the crisis. In high politics, this meant royal mediation and a compromise settlement, linking the passage of the Franchise Act with an agreed scheme of redistribution of seats. In the fields of Suffolk, a simpler view prevailed as the Liberals prepared to reap the political dividend.

The National Agricultural Labourers' Union, under the leadership of Joseph Arch, now emerged as a virtual adjunct to the Liberal Party. Arch himself was to be the victorious Liberal candidate in Norfolk North West in 1885. From the beginning of 1885 it was increasingly difficult to distinguish between union and Liberal meetings; union speakers frequently held practice ballots which invariably produced near-unanimity in the Liberal cause. There was a transparent connection between union activity, parish by parish, and overt Liberal support. The comments most frequently hurled at Conservative speakers spoke for themselves: 'Who gave us the franchise?' and 'You didn't give us the vote.'[24] The Conservative candidate for North East Suffolk began his campaign with a disquisition on political theory in which he explained that 'the labourer has no more natural rights than cows or sucking pigs'. He spent the rest of the election vainly attempting to extenuate this comment and finished with less than 40 per cent of the poll. The Liberals meanwhile circulated a pamphlet entitled, 'Fear ye not, ye have as much value as cows and pigs', and on polling day carried a pig through the streets of Eye.[25]

Such appeals were eloquent among a class whom, it was agreed on both sides, newspapers did not reach. In the villages of rural east Suffolk, illiteracy levels of 20 per cent were commonly found, and in west Suffolk of 30 per cent – twice as high as the level of illiteracy measured in the urban areas.[26] For many illiterate labourers, the meetings of 1884–85, whether initially held under union auspices, or convened to demonstrate feeling over the franchise, or straightforwardly organised in support of Liberal candidates, were a breakthrough into socialisation of a novel kind. Hitherto, election meetings in the counties had only taken place in the towns. The air of a revivalist crusade becomes apparent as the Red Vans of the Land Restoration League began to penetrate into darkest Suffolk to preach their gospel and proselytise for the Liberal Party.

Religious affiliation needs to be considered in its own right, for the direct links with Nonconformity were, of course, significant. The great majority of agricultural union leaders had connections with Methodism, with its current post-millenialist doctrinal effusions raising enthusiasm to an unusually high pitch.[27] It should be recalled that 1881–83 formed the penultimate peak in the range of religious revivals during the period 1840 to 1914, the final peak being that of 1904–6.[28] There is an obvious coincidence here with the electoral fortunes of the Liberal Party. In eighteen rural villages which can be identified from press reports as predominantly Liberal, Nonconformity had 42.3 per cent of the attendances in the 1851 religious census; in five Conservative villages the Nonconformist share was 27.6 per cent in 1851. Likewise in nine more urbanised districts, the four that were Liberal showed a figure of 49.0 per cent Nonconformist in 1851, while the five that were Conservative showed 32.6 per cent.[29] Dissent thus acted on a spiritual level as a feeder into Liberal activity and commitment, in much the same way as the union did on a material level.

It becomes difficult to see how the Liberals could lose in 1885, with both God and mammon on their side, not to mention Mr Gladstone. For the genius of Gladstone's leadership surely lay in the way his moral populism mobilised the inchoate animus of social resentment behind a rationally ordered political agenda. His charismatic appeal was uniquely capable of rallying the Liberal coalition. Opponents conceded as much, bemoaning 'the vast power of a great name' in tones which offer a more convincing tribute than those of fulsome Gladstonian adulation. 'Around it is cast the glamour of a prestige second to none in the annals of English history, the weight of an intellect among the first and greatest in the world of to-day, and the force of a personal enthusiasm which for years has had an electric effect on the masses of his countrymen.'[30]

The appeal of the People's William, which had been potently demonstrated among urban workingmen for twenty years, was now given a rural dimension as Hodge too was welcomed as 'our own flesh and blood' within the pale of the constitution. It was a Liberal parson in Warwickshire who recalled saying to a farmer, 'I doubt if these men ever heard of Gladstone', and then testing the effect by mentioning his name early in an election speech. 'It met with rapturous response here and everywhere', he reported; 'All over England the rustic belief in him was pathetic; he was in the words of Virgil's Nisus, the god of their desires; they believed that he would come like Elias to restore all things; holding in his hands free education, parish councils, three acres and cow. His name, and his name alone, won the rural constituencies, and created the parliamentary majority . . .'[31]

Indications to this effect can be paralleled in Suffolk. It was not Joseph Chamberlain's unauthorised programme which succeeded in tapping the springs of rural radicalism. His slogan, 'Three Acres and A Cow', was ridiculed by the Conservatives and disowned by the Liberals.[32] Yet the land remained a central issue – or symbol, perhaps – on the Liberal side. What Arch stressed, with a strong local resonance, was compulsory cultivation, which he called 'doubtless the FIRST duty of the next parliament which we shall help elect'.[33] The area under crops in Suffolk had declined from its 1874 level by 5 per cent in the mid 1880s; between then and 1892 it declined a further 5 per cent.[34] That there was a real problem here is indisputable; what is more doubtful is whether the union or the Liberals – whether Arch or Chamberlain or Mr Gladstone himself – had a real remedy. The fruits of victory after 1885 were hence rather insubstantial; and subsequent disillusion must be part of the explanation for the fact that the Liberal triumph in the counties was shortly to be reversed and never to be repeated.

III

Yet there was no mere reversion to the old politics of deference in Suffolk. Instead, a new Unionist politics of opinion and organisation was created, partly as a response to the shock at the grassroots in 1885 and partly as a result of the fracture in high politics over Irish Home Rule in 1886. The primacy of the Home Rule issue in restructuring allegiances seems inescapable. It was the subject of 88 per cent of Unionist and of 82 per cent of Liberal speeches in 1886, with its nearest challenge coming from the land in 22 per cent of Liberal and 10 per cent of Unionist speeches.[35] Moreover, in 1892 there was an inverse correlation between the number of Liberal speeches which mentioned Ireland and the Liberal poll in the four Suffolk divisions where sufficient evidence can be tabulated.[36] Cause and effect can, of course, be disputed in this relationship, but it hardly affects the central point, that it was issues and leadership, propaganda and persuasion, that mattered now.

An anthropomorphic view of Hodge behaving 'splendidly' in the Liberal interest in 1885, only to become as 'true as steel' to the Conservatives in 1892, was common at the time.[37] It should be remembered that, over the whole of Suffolk, only one in six of the 1885 Liberal voters had become Unionist by 1892 – five-sixths had not – though in the South or Sudbury division the proportion may have been as high as one in three. Such differences served to split the representation of the county in an interesting way. Though the Gladstonian Liberals succeeded in holding only Suffolk North East (Eye) in 1886, by 1892 they had won back the North West (Stowmarket) and South East (Woodbridge) divisions as well. The two divisions that were Unionist in 1892 were thus South

(Sudbury) and North (Lowestoft). Moreover, this was a fair reflection of the swing in votes. Between 1885 and 1892 there was a drop of over twenty per cent in the Liberal poll in Sudbury and ten per cent in Lowestoft, as compared with six per cent in Stowmarket, four per cent in Eye and an increase of three per cent in Woodbridge. What distinguished Sudbury and Lowestoft from the rest was the fact that in both of these divisions the Liberal candidate of 1885 stood as a Liberal Unionist in 1886 (and was in each case unopposed).

The impact of these two defections might, in principle, suggest that the assumptions of a deference community lived on, either if the constituencies took their lead from their notables with dumb loyalty, or if the candidates responded with instinctive solidarity to the feelings of their supporters. The fact is, however, that none of the constituency Liberal parties in Suffolk broke with Gladstone over Home Rule, so there is no reason to impute influence from the constituency activists upon their candidates; nor were the electoral majorities of those Liberal MPs who became Unionist particularly precarious, thus ruling out an obvious electoral motive. Moreover, examination of candidates' nomination papers and attendance at meetings suggest that there was no significant defection of Liberal notables on anything like the same scale as the turnover of votes in these divisions. Only in Woodbridge were there subsequent complaints about a lack of middle-class organisers in the villages; yet this went along with a net increase in the Liberal vote between 1885 and 1892. There is, in short, little to suggest that Unionist politics simply reasserted the power of the old élites through a reversion to traditional mechanisms of social control.

Liberal Unionism swelled the Conservative tide but also introduced awkward cross-currents which first had to be navigated. In the divisions where there was no Liberal Unionist presence the turnout fell by no more than would be explained by the age of the register, suggesting few abstentions in a straight choice between Gladstonian and Conservative candidates. In Eye, however, where a genuine Liberal Unionist candidate was brought in against the sitting Gladstonian member, there is clear evidence of abstentions among Conservative electors, reluctant to adopt a 'Unionist' identity. In Lowestoft and Sudbury, despite the defection of the sitting Liberal MPs, Sir S. B. Crossley and W. C. Quilter, this particular conflict of loyalties was not put to the test because both were unopposed either by Gladstonian or Conservative candidates. By 1892 Crossley had retired and his place was taken in Lowestoft by a Conservative candidate, who comfortably held the seat. In Sudbury, however, Quilter was to battle on for twenty years, establishing a strong local position as an unrepentantly *Liberal* Unionist. He continued to print all his bills on the Liberals' yellow paper, and the Conservative press published his addresses of 1885 and 1892 side by side to demonstrate his consistency – a double-edged quality in the circumstances. Only on temperance and disestablishment did he trim to his new political allegiance.[38] The vast personal popularity of Sir Cuthbert Quilter (as he became in 1897) was thus for years a major factor in Sudbury, but even this could not save him from defeat in the great Liberal landslide of 1906.

Such tactical successes for Unionism, however, were less important than the development of an effective electoral strategy. Reinvigorated with a popular cry against Home Rule, the Unionists successfully adapted to a kind of new politics which had initially been a Gladstonian preserve. They did so, however, in a significantly lower key, so as to capitalise upon their natural advantages – gently and tactfully, but persistently and purposefully. Some Conservatives had seen the way forward in the immediate aftermath of the 1885 results, writing of the need to mobilise the thinking classes into new feats of organisation and propaganda. 'At the last election the farmers almost universally tried insolent coercion', it was observed; 'They no more thought of bringing reason to bear on their labourers than they would upon their stock.' The lesson drawn was that it was now vital to nurture 'the tie of propinquity, of long association, of benefits given and received', with the aim 'that the new vote, instead of being an occasion of severance, should become an added bond of union.'[39] What was called for, in short, was not a direct emulation of the radical style but some cognisance of how old wine might be decanted into new bottles.

True, in 1891 there were still Conservative speakers in Suffolk ready to advise the labourers that 'the only plot of land they will get is six feet by two'.[40] But in general a more hospitable manner was affected. Both sides now used magic lantern shows, not least to make the Irish question more vivid. There was a changed pattern of meetings, with candidates now attending three or four every night instead of the one which had been normal in 1885. By 1892 the Primrose League had become a major focus of activity, paralleling Liberal networks like the Friendly Societies and trade unions. The Unionists held smoking concerts in the villages, where there would be a programme of popular songs and other similar acts, while the candidate would be expected to do his turn in the interval. It was a Liberal paper which commented that 'people were delighted that the monotonous routine of village life had been so agreeably broken'.[41] But the Liberals now knew that they did not have a monopoly on the best songs.

In surveying the agricultural vote, Henry Pelling has concluded that 'one cannot but be impressed by the constant and unyielding influence of the large landowners, and the weakness and apathy of the labourers.'[42] Yet an important question remains about how such influence was mediated, given that household suffrage had created a broad-based electorate, wide open to pressure from below. The evidence from Suffolk suggests that the old Tory interest never recovered from the rebuff it met in 1885; but the intelligent, accommodating, responsive Unionism which Salisbury helped to fashion after 1886 laid the basis for a resilient Conservatism which could hold its own in town and country alike. It was not just the Villa Toryism of the suburbs which needed organisation, as Salisbury's well-known phrase had it; the authentically popular politics which household suffrage brought to the English counties also demanded attention. In Suffolk this entailed a change in political style which was, in the end, more significant than those of party allegiance. Hodge now expected to be flattered and cajoled at election times, not told to tug his forelock.

Notes

1 The original research for this essay largely derives from the dissertation completed by Kevin Langford, under the supervision of Peter Clarke, for Part Two of the 1985 Cambridge Historical Tripos, on Liberal electoral performance in East Anglia, with special reference to Suffolk. I am also grateful to Duncan Tanner for his comments.

2 'The political education of the country voter', *Fortnightly Review*, n.s., xl (1886), pp. 36–48, at p. 38. This is a well-informed anonymous article which is highly germane to the points discussed below.

3 F. M. L. Thompson, *English landed society in the nineteenth century*, London, 1963, p. 272.

4 Charles Seymour, *Electoral reform in England and Wales* (Yale, 1915; reprinted Newton Abbot, 1970), p. 10. I am in general much indebted to the fruitful historiographical debate about nineteenth century electoral behaviour, notably David Cresap Moore, *The politics of deference*, Hassocks, 1976 and Richard W. Davis, *Political change and continuity, 1760–1885: a Buckinghamshire study*, Newton Abbot, 1972.

5 J. Vincent and M. Stenton (eds), *McCalmont's parliamentary poll book, 1832–1919*, Brighton, 1971, p. xxi.

6 Michael Barker, *Gladstone and Radicalism, 1885–94*, Hassocks, 1975, App. A.

7 *English landed society*, p. 276.

8 J. M. Keynes, *A tract on monetary reform*, Collected Writings, 30 vols, London, 1971–89, vol. iv, p. 65.

9 'The political education of the country voter', pp. 37–8.

10 See Norman Gash, *Politics in the age of Peel*, London, 1953, esp. p. 217 for Bury and App. B for Eye; H. J. Hanham, *Elections and party management*, London, 1959, esp. App. III for Eye; Vincent and Stenton (eds), *McCalmont*, *passim*.

11 Gash, *Politics in the age of Peel*, pp. 161–2.

12 The *six-village sample* comprises: Acton, Alpheton, Denston, Edwardstone, Kersey and Stradishall. In the figures used below it has sometimes been possible to produce an *eight-village sample* by adding Cowlinge and Somerton; or a *ten-village sample* by adding also Cockfield and Kedington.

13 These findings corroborate the interpretation of Duncan Tanner, first presented in 'The parliamentary electoral system, the "Fourth" Reform Act and the rise of Labour in England and Wales', *Bulletin of the Institute of Historical Research*, lvi (1983), pp. 205–19; see also Tanner, *Political Change and the Labour Party, 1900–1918*, Cambridge, 1990, ch. 4. The definition of a householder had not always been unambiguous but it is not the main point here.

14 1881 Census, vol. iii, Summary Table 5 gives occupations by quinquennial age cohorts: men aged 20–21 were taken as one-fifth of those aged 20–25; thus 70 per cent of agricultural labourers were aged 21 and over. The age distribution for all males aged 15 and over in Suffolk, as given in Division IV, Table 1, is congruent with this.

15 See Neal Blewett, 'The franchise in the United Kingdom, 1885 1918', *Past and Present*, 32 (December 1965), pp. 27–56; H. C. G. Matthew, R. I. McKibbin and J. A. Kay, 'The franchise factor in the rise of the Labour Party', *English Historical Review*, xci (1976), pp. 723–52, esp. Table IV at p. 730; and cf. Table III showing enfranchisement levels around 80 per cent in four agricultural counties in 1911.

16 All electoral statistics from F. W. S. Craig, *British parliamentary election results, 1885–1918*, London, 1974. The electorate for 'urban' and 'rural' areas was apportioned for each division according to their respective population in the 1881 census. The total number of agricultural labourers enfranchised was estimated, on assumptions justified above, at 18,665, comprising about half the 'rural' vote, which was thus halved for each division.

17 Roy Gregory, *The miners and British politics, 1906–1914*, Oxford, 1968, App. B; P. F. Clarke, *Lancashire and the new Liberalism*, Cambridge, 1971, p. 78.

18 Two seminal essays are Gareth Stedman Jones, 'Rethinking Chartism' in *Languages of class*, Cambridge, 1983 and Ross McKibbin, 'Why was there no Marxism in Great Britain' in *The Ideologies of Class*, Oxford, 1990. The major work in this field is now Eugenio F. Biagini and Alastair J. Reid (eds), *Currents of radicalism*, Cambridge, 1991, which contains several highly pertinent essays.

19 All derived from A. L. Bowley, 'The statistics of wages in the United Kingdom during the last hundred years (Part 1 – agricultural wages)', *Journal of the Royal Statistical Society*, lxi (1898), pp. 702–22.

20 See Pamela Horn, *Labouring life in the Victorian countryside*, Dublin, 1976; and, for an interpretation which minimises the effect of the 1874 setback upon locally-based unionism, Alun Howkins, *Poor labouring men: rural radicalism in Norfolk, 1870–1923*, 1985.

21 Figures for subscriptions and meetings are taken from the secretary's reports given weekly in the *English Labourers' Chronicle* for 1884–5.

22 H. C. G. Matthew (ed.), *The Gladstone diaries*, xi, Oxford, 1990, p. 171 (8 July 1884).

23 *Ibid.*, pp. 191–2 (19 August 1884).

24 *Bury Free Press*, 18 July 1884, 12 September 1885; see also 1 August 1885 and *East Anglian Daily Times*, 22 September 1885.

25 Hunter Rodwell, *East Anglian Daily Times*, 23 November 1885; F. S. Stevenson scrapbook, Ipswich Record Office, qS 324; *Bury and Norwich Post*, 8 December 1885.

26 Illiteracy figures are derived from the number of men signing the marriage register with a mark: *Annual Reports of the Registrar General*, P.P., 1884–5, xvii, 121; 1886, xvii, 125. The following Poor Law Unions comprise rural east Suffolk: Bosmere and Claydon, Samford, Woodbridge, Plomesgate, Blything and Wangford (20.0 per cent illiterate); rural west Suffolk: Risbridge, Sudbury, Cosford, Thingoe, Mildenhall, Stowmarket, Hartismere and Hoxne (29.1 per cent); urban Suffolk: Bury St Edmunds, Ipswich, Mutford and Lothingland (13.5 per cent).

27 For an interpretation laying stress on this factor see Nigel Scotland, *Methodism and the revolt of the field*, Gloucester, 1981.

28 A. D. Gilbert, *Religion and society in industrial England*, London, 1976, p. 192.

29 Figures for religious affiliation are derived from the returns for the Ecclesiastical Census of 1851, microfilm in Bury St Edmunds Record Office and Ipswich Record Office. Attendance was counted for the largest congregation of the day in each place of worship. Liberal non-urban districts, based on newspaper reports, were: Brampton, Debenham, Finningham, Framsden, Framlingham, Fressingfield, Mendlesham, Stradbrooke, Walpole, Yoxford, Aldeburgh, Clayton, Barrow, Lakenheath, Walsham-le-Willows, Woolpit, Assington and Bildeston (18,000

Anglicans, 13,200 Nonconformists). Conservative non-urban districts were: Hintlesham, Holbrook, East Bergholt, Needham Market, Stoke by Nayland (7,750 Anglicans, 2,950 Nonconformists). Urbanised Liberal districts were: Beccles, Wickham Market, Stowmarket and Haverhill (6,350 Anglicans, 6,000 Nonconformists). Urbanised Conservative districts were: Gorleston, Saxmundham, Woodbridge, Bury St Edmunds and Newmarket (11,700 Anglicans, 5,650 Nonconformists).

30 'The political education of the country voter', p. 44.

31 F. E. Green, *A history of the English agricultural labourer, 1870–1920*, London, 1920, pp. 85–6, quoting Rev. W. Tuckwell, *The reminiscences of a radical parson.*

32 For example, *East Anglian Daily Times*, 23 September 1885, 28 October 1885; see also Barker, *Gladstone and Radicalism*, pp. 35–6, and Henry Pelling, *Social geography of British elections, 1885–1910*, London, 1967, p. 16.

33 *English Labourers' Chronicle*, 7 March 1885.

34 P.P., 1874, lxix; 1884–85, lxxxiv; 1886, lxx, 1892, lxxxviii.

35 Based on an analysis of 49 Conservative and 50 Liberal speeches in the local press.

36 The range is from Woodbridge (+2.9 per cent Liberal poll) where only 4 of 18 Liberal speeches mentioned Ireland; through Stowmarket (–6.0 per cent), 15 out of 42; and Lowestoft (–10.2 per cent), 9 out of 20; to Sudbury (–22.5 per cent), 10 out of 25.

37 *Bury Free Press*, 12 December 1885; *South West Suffolk Echo*, 16 July 1892.

38 *South West Suffolk Echo*, 2 July 1892.

39 'The political education of the country voter', p. 42.

40 *Stowmarket Reporter*, 4 May 1891.

41 *East Anglian Daily Times*, 12 July 1892; cf. Martin Pugh, *The Tories and the people, 1880–1935*, Oxford, 1985, pp. 110–13 and App. X at pp. 230–31.

42 Pelling, *Social geography*, p. 428.

7

THE POLITICAL ECONOMY OF DEATH DUTIES: HARCOURT'S BUDGET OF 1894

M. J. DAUNTON

Your great Budget of 1894 will ever stand out as the ablest, most far-reaching, wisest, most courageous and sound financial proposal upon a just basis which has been propounded for a quarter of a century at least. That Budget and those proposals will tend to strengthen our whole fiscal system and your name will ever be remembered as that of a statesman who had the wisdom to evolve and the courage to propose changes so essential to the well-being of the state.

(*Henry Burdett, 1895*)[1]

Sir William Harcourt's budget of 1894, with its reform and graduation of the death duties, could, claimed T. H. Farrer, 'rank with the great efforts of Sir R. Peel and Mr Gladstone'. It would, he argued, 'properly take its place amongst the great measures which have helped to reconcile capital and labour; have adapted the demands of government to the altered circumstances of society; and have advanced the welfare of the people'.[2] Perhaps there was, after all, life for Liberals after the retirement of Gladstone earlier in 1894. 'You have given to the Liberal party . . . a new lease of life', one radical MP assured Harcourt. 'It will be a really popular budget because it has put burdens on strong shoulders instead of weak ones.'[3] The sentiment was shared by Thomas Ellis, who informed Harcourt that 'People are realising more and more the hugeness of the Budget. You would be astonished at its tremendous popularity if you faced a great audience in an industrial centre'.[4] But hope soon turned to disappointment, for the Liberal government fell in 1895, and Harcourt lost his own seat at Derby. Not all industrial centres were so enamoured of a Chancellor who had increased the duty on beer and proposed 'local option' in control of the drink trade as well as reforming the death duties.

The budget of 1894 created alarm amongst landowners as well as hope amongst radicals. It was, remarked the *Morning Post*, 'introduced with the levity of a schoolboy whose knowledge of finance is limited to some Socialist manual',[5] and Harcourt received a schoolmistress's admonition from Queen Victoria. His actions, she warned, 'cannot fail to cripple all landowners' and dissolve the social order:

> Many properties are now only kept afloat at considerable loss to the proprietors who, if the Budget becomes law, may be driven to still further curtail their expenditure. This must inevitably affect the poorer classes, especially the agricultural community, numbers of whom will be thrown out of work altogether. Then again country seats will be unoccupied and charities throughout the country be denuded of support. Where again will be the inducement to owners of property to effect improvements, when by so doing they know they are only encumbering their successors . . . Most earnestly does the Queen urge and hope that Sir William Harcourt may be able to modify these proposals, which she owns she thinks dangerous.[6]

Her fears were no better founded than the hopes of the radicals. Although the reforms of the death duties were, as Michael Thompson has noted, 'hailed as harbingers of ruin for agricultural landowners', their impact was in reality slight. These modest demands of the state could usually be met from annual income or insurance policies without the need for forced sales, and even when duties were increased in 1909, most sales took place for other reasons. Radical fiscal policies provided a convenient justification for the abandonment of ancestral acres, rather than the motivation.[7]

The hopes and fears of the budget of 1894 were soon dissipated, and some historians have played down its significance, viewing it as a modest and relatively uncontroversial measure of rationalisation, an attempt to sweep away the complications of the existing legacy, probate and succession duties: in this view, Harcourt's enemy was the luxuriant legal undergrowth rather than landowner. On the other hand, his budget has been seen as a precursor of Lloyd George's more radical attacks on the landed class in the People's Budget of 1909, marking a fundamental shift from the traditions of Gladstonian finance. Was it indeed his intention to destroy the great landowners by the introduction of graduated death duties? Alfred Milner, who played a major role in reforming the death duties as Chairman of the Inland Revenue, was able to defend the budget to the new Conservative Chancellor in 1895 as a means of *protecting* landed property. Prior to 1894, land was treated more favourably by the death duties, on the grounds that it was burdened by local taxation. This was, he argued, 'very injurious to the interests of land' which stood to lose more from its inability to secure a reduction in the burden of local taxation than it gained by 'clinging to its indefensible advantages in respect of Death Duties'. The net cost of the death duties on land would, Milner calculated, be no more than £600,000 a year, which was a price worth paying. 'If that sacrifice, by putting land for the first time on a footing of equality with other property in respect of burdens common to all enables it to make out a case for relief from burdens peculiar to itself, the sacrifice may after all turn out a blessing in disguise'.[8] Salisbury's administration did indeed remove some local burdens from the land.[9]

What precisely was Harcourt's own intention? Was he attempting to remove the radicals' criticism of the privileged position of landowners, in order to contain their demands which were threatening to destabilise the Liberal coalition? Or was he throwing himself into the radical campaign against landowners in an attempt to give a new lease of life to Liberalism, which was frustrated by the caution of civil servants such as Milner and the fears of the Prime Minister, Lord Rosebery? As well as these rival views, there is a third interpretation: that Harcourt's budget was part of a more far-reaching political strategy which differed in major respects both from Gladstone's great budget of 1853 and from Lloyd George's budget of 1909. The politics of Harcourt's budget need to be analysed on their own terms. He was not accepting the radical critique of landowners which was being pressed by, for example, the progressives on the London County Council as well as by a growing number of MPs. He was equalising duties on land and personalty, which removed a major grievance; but he was not proposing to take the further step of imposing specific and punitive duties, or of attacking the 'unearned increment' of rent. In this respect, he was taking a different stance from Lloyd George in his budget of 1909 and the land campaign.

What he *was* willing to accept, in a major departure from Gladstonian orthodoxy, was graduation of income tax. His strategy in 1894 was less the imposition of burdens on landowners and *rentiers*, in order to relieve the poor from the burdens of indirect taxation, than an attempt to reduce the incidence of income tax on the lower levels of income which fell within the reach of the Inland Revenue. Essentially, these were the modestly affluent members of the middle class: tradesmen, white-collar workers and professional men who were earning between £150 (the threshold for the payment of income tax) and £400 (the upper limit of abatement of income tax). He was adjusting Gladstone's ambition of 1853 to new circumstances, attempting to build from the middle out rather than to set one type of property or income against another. He aimed to remove the worst grievance against landed wealth rather than, as Lloyd George, to appeal to the land question as a means of constructing an alliance of interests against a common enemy. Harcourt's budget made little explicit appeal to labour: its main attraction was to the centre, as part of a strategy of building support in a crucial constituency.[10]

I

The need for rationalisation of the complicated and confused duties on the transfer of wealth at death was widely accepted by the early 1890s, by both Liberals and Conservatives. But it would be inaccurate to portray Harcourt's reform of the death duties as merely a measure of simplification and consolidation: what were criticised as anomalies and confusion in the early 1890s had been put in place in earlier budgets with deliberation and careful thought. The perception of the death duties changed from a coherent and rational system of balances to an incoherent and flawed system of favouritism: the acceptance of the need for reform was not simply the outcome of a desire for administrative convenience and legal clarity, but reflected a deeper shift in attitudes and assumptions.

When Harcourt introduced his budget in 1894, there were four separate death duties: probate, legacy, succession and estate (see table 7.1). Probate and legacy duties were both imposed on personal property, on different principles: the first was a sliding scale according to the total value of personal property left by the deceased; the second levied a varying rate of duty on the sum received by beneficiaries according to the 'consanguinity scale' of their relationship with the deceased. These two duties therefore favoured real property, which was not liable. Gladstone's budget of 1853 marked a major shift towards a tax system which was widely perceived to be fair between classes, forming the basis of the social contract of the mid-Victorian state.[11] This involved, amongst other changes, the creation of a new death duty to balance the fiscal system.

There was, Gladstone remarked, a widely expressed feeling that 'the operation of the income tax is severe upon intelligence and skill as compared with property'. The Financial Reform Association and many Liberal MPs argued that the income tax should be differentiated by the source of income, in order to fall more heavily on 'realised' or 'spontaneous' unearned incomes derived from investments than on 'precarious' earned incomes which involved the risks of trade or personal exertion. The former, it was argued, continued on the death of the owner; the latter depended on the good health and life of the individual who needed to put income aside to provide for his dependants. Gladstone opposed differentiation of the income tax, for he had grave doubts about the possibility of distinguishing between individuals and groups on such a basis, and defining 'lazy' versus 'industrious' incomes. Above all, such a strategy would destroy the basis of the income tax by setting one class against another, and he argued that the correct way of proceeding was to consider the tax system as a *whole* and to seek a remedy for the unequal incidence of the income tax elsewhere.[12]

The claim that 'intelligence and skill under our system of taxation pay too much, and property too little' could, Gladstone contended, be met through a 'safe, honourable and efficacious' mechanism: the adjustment of death duties by a new succession duty which extended the legacy duty to *all* successions.[13] This was, he told Edward Hamilton in 1888, the measure which had given him the most trouble, and on which he prided himself most: 'indeed, he only carried it, because hardly a soul could follow its provisions'.[14] The intention, however, was clear: to suggest that real property was bearing its fair share of national taxation; and to counter the complaint that the income tax fell too heavily on intelligence and skill compared with property. Generally, the taxation of property – for example, by a differentiated income tax – posed dangers which were avoided by the use of death duties:

> The greatest mischief of taxes upon property is the liability of a constant recurrence of those struggles of classes which are often associated with them. But in carrying into effect this increase in the legacy duty, you have this great advantage, that the liability to pay occurs only within the limitation which the laws of a higher power have ordained; that it only occurs once, on the death of a man.[15]

Real property should therefore pay death duties, but Gladstone did not accept that the rate should be the *same* as on personal property. Land and houses suffered from an additional burden of local taxation or rates, as well as paying land tax and income tax on the flow of rents. It was only fair, therefore, that less should be taken from rateable property than from property which did not pay these special burdens, and Gladstone concluded that the fairest method was to charge the successor on the life interest rather than the full capital value.[16] Personal property therefore paid legacy duty on the full capital value of the bequest, whereas real property received 'more tender consideration' and paid succession duty on the value of the life interest rather than the capitalised market value, with the right to pay over four years (see table 7.1, succession duty).[17] The inequality of death duties on real and personal property was deliberate, as a means of compensating for the burden of income tax on 'precarious' earned incomes which did not rest on the possession of personal or real property, and as a means of adjusting the incidence of duties on real and personal property to take account of the burden of local taxation.[18]

Gladstone promised in 1853 that the income tax would ultimately be abolished, and he hoped that the yield from the succession duty would contribute to this ambition. The revenue from the new duty did not, however, fulfil his expectations of £2m. a year; as late as 1885, the yield

Table 7.1 Death duties prior to the reforms of 1894

Probate Duty: 1694

levied on:	personalty
	to include everything which the deceased possessed of value, paid out of the estate before division
rate:	*ad valorem*, by the amount left
	1881 tariff: £1 per £50, up to £500 net
	£1 5*s* per £50, up to £1,000 net
	3% of value above £1,000 net

In 1888, half of the proceeds was paid to local authorities in aid of local taxation.

Legacy Duty: 1796

levied on:	personalty		
	paid by the individual on the property to which he/she succeeds, at the time of succession		
rate:	varied according to the relationship of the legatee to the deceased; levied on the saleable value on receipt of the legacy		
	1815 tariff:	widows	exempt
		lineal descendants	1%
		brothers, sisters and their descendants	3%
		uncles, aunts and their descendants	5%
		great uncles, aunts and their descendants	6%
		any other person	10%

In 1881, personal estates up to £300 were exempted; and lineals were relieved from the payment of legacy duty where probate duty had been paid (the level of probate duty was increased to protect revenue).

Succession Duty: 1853

levied on:	realty and settled personalty
	applied the legacy duty to bequests payable out of, or charged on, real estate; i.e., it taxed what was left untouched by the legacy duty
rate:	The rate of legacy duty was levied on the capitalised value of the 'years of enjoyment' or life interest. Assume a man aged 35 succeeded to 100 acres worth £5,000, with a net income of £150; the value of an annuity of £150 for a man aged 35 would be calculated from life tables, which gave £2,362. The tax on this sum could be paid in eight half yearly instalments, with the balance being remitted in the case of death.
	In 1888, the existing rate remained in force for property which was liable to probate duty as well as succession duty (for example, leaseholds); for other property, the rate was increased by 0.5 per cent where it passed to lineals and 1.5 per cent where it passed to non-lineals.

1888 tariff:	lineal descendants	1.5%
	brothers, sisters and their descendants	4.5%
	uncles, aunts and their descendants	6.5%
	great uncles, aunts and their descendants	7.5%
	any other person	11.5%

Estate Duty: 1889

levied on: realty and personalty

rate: 1% duty on all personal estates of £10,000 and above, however divided;

in the case of landed property and settled personalty, it was levied where the value received by a *single* heir amounted to £10,000, which was calculated on assumptions which placed it below the capital value.

Note: leaseholds were defined as personal property for the probate duty, and as real property for the legacy and succession duties.

Source: S. C. Buxton, *Finance and politics: an historical study, 1783–1885*, London, 1888, I, pp. 117–18 and II, pp. 292–8, 384–5; S. C. Buxton and G. S. Barnes, *A handbook to the death duties*, London, 1890, pp. 1–65.

was only £935,000.[19] Gladstone considered abolition of the income tax in 1862, 1863 and 1868 but was frustrated, as Hamilton remarked, because 'the country was not imbued with a real spirit of economy'.[20] However, the opportunity to redeem his pledge seemed to exist in 1874, when a surplus of £6m. was anticipated. The loss of revenue from the income tax could be met by

> the proposal to reconstruct and enlarge the death duties. Direct taxation of a kind most vexatious to trade and industry was to be removed; direct taxation, the least of all unfavourable to trade and industry, and going, as a direct tax should wherever possible go, straight to property, was to be imposed.[21]

He lost the election of 1874, and the opportunity passed, but it is clear that Gladstone viewed death duties as preferable to income tax in terms of their incidence on different types of income and the minimisation of social conflict.

During his second administration of 1880–85, Gladstone introduced some relatively minor changes to the level of probate and legacy duties in 1881,[22] and attempted a more sweeping reform in 1885 when an increase in revenue was required to prevent a large deficit. Gladstone proposed to increase the succession duty on real property; and to impose a 5 per cent income tax on corporations on the grounds that they, unlike an individual, did not pay death duties at intervals on their property.[23]

The budget was rejected, the Commons passing a motion that it 'declines to impose fresh taxation on real property' until ratepayers were offered relief 'in respect of local charges imposed on them for national services'.[24] The government resigned, and it was left to the Conservative Chancellor, George Goschen, to provide a solution.

By the 1880s, there was increasing concern about the level of local taxation, and Goschen placed central government support for local finance on a new basis in 1888, by handing to local authorities the revenue from certain licence duties and half the proceeds of the probate duty. He linked this concession to the rates (and hence real property) with a compensating addition of 0.5 per cent to the succession duty paid by lineals on real property, and 1.5 per cent by non-lineals (see table 7.1). He claimed, therefore, that he was preserving the balance in the fiscal system as a whole by a compensating adjustment of the local rates and death duties. Liberal politicians were concerned that Goschen's proposal was widely perceived as a means of relieving the burdens of urban rate payers, which undermined their support in towns.

But Henry Fowler assured Harcourt that the scheme was far from restoring balance to the fiscal system, which left room for the Liberals to launch a counter-offensive. There had been, he pointed out, two inequalities: in local taxation, realty paid in excess of its share; and in national taxation, realty paid less than its share. Goschen had more than met the first inequality, which meant that the Liberals should press for absolute equality in the second, now that there was no justification for more favourable treatment. Realty, he assumed, accounted for 45 per cent of all property, and personalty for 55 per cent; yet their respective contributions to the death duties were £1,420,000 and £6,970,000, or 17.1 per cent and 82.9 per cent. 'We must raise and fight this issue now', he insisted, 'It is a scheme in the interest of the landowner as against the ratepayer in towns and though in some respects it is good as far as it goes, it goes a very little way.'[25]

The point was seized upon by Gladstone, who moved an amendment to Goschen's measure, that 'the Duties accruing upon deaths should be so fixed as to equalize the charges upon real and personal property respectively'.[26] Gladstone was himself the author of the succession duties which he was now castigating as being in the interests of the landed class, but circumstances had changed:

> The present enormous disparity under the Death Duties, between the charge upon realty and the charge upon personalty, has only been tolerated because of the advantage enjoyed by personalty in respect of the limited contribution to the rates, and, in regard to a great portion of personalty, its not being liable to any contribution at all to the rates.[27]

Personalty was paying considerably more than realty (see table 7.2).

Table 7.2 Incidence of death duties on personalty and realty, 1887

type of property and value		*lineals*	*brothers*	*cousins*	*strangers*
land: net value £10,000; net rental £300; a successor aged 35 pays on £4,472 12 6d.		£47 4 9*d.*	£141 14 3*d.*	£236 3 9*d.*	£472 7 6*d.*
		(succession duty paid in 8 half-yearly instalments)			
		present value with payment over 4 years at 4%			
		£42 8 0*d.*	£127 4 0 *d.*	£212 0 0*d.*	£424 0 0*d.*
£10,000 charged on land / *£10,000 settled personalty*		£100	£300	£500	£1,000
			(legacy or succession duty)		
£10,000 personalty	*probate*	£300	£300	£300	£300
	legacy	—	£300	£500	£1,000

Source: Buxton, *Finance and politics*, II, appendix M, pp. 384–5.

The probate duty of 3 per cent fell on 'free' personalty but not on settled personalty such as marriage settlements, or on realty;[28] under the legacy duty, settled and free personalty paid 1 per cent on their full capital value in one lump sum, whereas under the succession duty, real property paid 1 per cent on the life interest in instalments which reduced the real rate as shown in table 7.2.[29] Goschen's proposals failed to adjust this inequality. He was transferring between £4m. and £5m. of revenue levied on personalty by the probate duty in order to assist the rates, which largely meant realty; and there still remained the inequality of the death duties in favour of real property, an inequality which had 'lost its whole and only justification'.[30] Gladstone calculated Goschen's scheme left a wide discrepancy in the death duties: personalty would pay $3\frac{5}{8}$ per cent compared with real property at $1\frac{1}{5}$ per cent.[31] But it was not enough to compare real and personal property, for the category of 'visible personalty' such as railways, mines, ironworks, leaseholds and occupiers' interests were particularly hard hit: they paid rates *and* were liable to the higher incidence of death duties on personalty.[32]

Although the enormous increase in the level of rates meant that all ratepayers had a strong claim to assistance, Gladstone felt that landowners had the weakest case. Indeed, he accused them of hypocrisy and deceit in pleading the cause of all forms of real property and appealing to urban MPs for support, without drawing attention to the incidence of taxation. 'The landed proprietors, in fact, posed as the sympathising friends of the urban communities', claiming a common grievance when they were deriving large profits from the expenditure of rates which fell on their tenants through increased rents. The claim of 'visible personalty' for relief was therefore greater, for the increase of rates largely fell on them. Yet Goschen ignored the claim: owners of visible personalty paid the probate duty from which the rates were compensated; landowners received their compensation from other people. Visible personalty was therefore liable to 'great inequality', contributing to its own compensation from the rates and paying three times as much in death duties as landowners.[33] The case for equalising the death duties was consequently accepted by Gladstone in 1888, as a necessary step to restore balance to the tax system.

Goschen made a further attempt at reform in 1889, when he introduced a completely new 'estate duty'. Rather than increasing the income tax, he proposed to tax 'the surplus which can be put by' in accumulated wealth. He justified his decision on grounds of proportionality, that individuals with large fortunes paid least in relation to their total income and property. He proposed to lay an additional tax on estates of £10,000 and above, which represented an income of £300 to £400 a year, in the form of a charge of 1 per cent on the capital value of both realty and personalty. He differed from Gladstone in arguing that the existing inequalities of the death duties were justified; his aim was to add a new tax which was equal between personalty and realty. He did not succeed, for the measure as implemented treated realty more favourably than personalty. The duty of 1 per cent was charged on the full capital value of personalty, whether it was left to one person or divided between several; and it was paid at once. On realty, it was charged only where an *individual* succession exceeded £10,000; it could be spread over four years; and it was imposed on a restricted value of land.[34] Despite Goschen's initial intention, the new estate duty in practice introduced a higher rate of tax on personal than real property, and so exacerbated the Liberal criticism that death duties did not fall sufficiently on realty, which had been relieved of its heavy burden of local taxation.[35]

Liberal critics of the death duties found a mass of inequalities and anomalies in the death duties as they had been left by Goschen in 1889. 'The history of Death Duties', remarked Buxton and Barnes, 'has been one long tale of tinkering and tacking', so creating 'subdivisions, eccentricities, and anomalies without end, and which together form a maze which no one who has not devoted much time and patient study to the subject can hope to unravel'.[36] But it was one thing to suggest that anomalies existed; it was another to propose a practical scheme for reform. Should the entire system of death duties be swept away and a new consolidated duty put in its place, or should there be a further adjustment to equalise the incidence? But, even more important, what was the intention: to restore balance within the tax system as a whole, or to use the death duties as a means of *increasing* the incidence on certain types of income and property?

Gladstone's strategy in 1853 was to adjust death duties to the precise level which compensated real property for its higher burden of local taxation, while at the same time ensuring that it paid sufficient to offset the differential impact of income tax on precarious and realised income. It was a clever and careful balancing act, which used the death duties to create a sense of equity and fairness in the tax system as a whole. The death duties were part of a system of *proportionate* taxation, by which each social group or type of income paid the same rate when all claims were taken together. By the 1880s, this approach was under threat. The level of local taxation had increased, and was continuing to increase, as a result of expenditure on education, public health measures, slum clearance, and the costs of poor relief and public order. Local sources of revenue were under strain, and the correct response became a matter of deep political division, within as well as between parties.

The Conservatives could, of course, argue that real property was bearing an increasing burden of rates and that it should be relieved, as in Goschen's scheme of 1888. The reaction of Gladstone and Fowler in 1888 was to argue that too much relief had been offered to land, and they continued to view the death duties as a device to balance the fiscal system as a whole, ensuring that land paid its fair share of the total tax bill from local rates, income tax and death duties. Their criticisms of the reforms of 1888 and 1889 continued to be based upon the assumptions of proportionate taxation. But a new view was emerging in the Liberal party, associated with Henry George's *Progress and poverty*: far from being overburdened by local taxes, land was escaping its proper contribution. In part, this was the result of the ability of landowners to shift the incidence of rates to tenants and occupiers through increased rent, but the case went much further. The increase in land values was a result of the enterprise of the community as a whole, and the investment in better roads and other infrastructure; it was socially created, and should therefore be taken by the community as its own. The burden of taxes on land should therefore be far higher, and Goschen's scheme of relieving the rates at the expense of national taxes was a retrograde step.[37] What was needed was an increase in the incidence of taxes on real property and unearned incomes.

How does Harcourt's budget of 1894 fit into this debate? Was Harcourt using the death duties to balance the fiscal system and to preserve proportionality, simply following Gladstone's approach of 1888 that relief to the rates and realty should be complemented by a full equalisation of death duties? A balanced tax system in the 1850s required a variation in the incidence of death duties, but subsequent shifts in other taxes meant that in the 1890s it required equalisation. On such an account, the aim remained constant: in order to keep the fiscal ship on an even keel, it was necessary to adjust the ballast. Or was Harcourt going a stage further, using the death duties to increase the tax burden on land, on the grounds that it had a greater capacity to pay? There could, however, be a third possibility, that Harcourt was moving away from Gladstonian fiscal orthodoxy, in order to pursue Gladstone's aim of using the tax system to maintain an integrated, legitimate social and political system which built outwards from the centre to the extremes, rather than setting groups against each other, in a way which mollified the radicals without launching an outright attack on landowners.

II

Harcourt faced a difficult task when he became Chancellor of the Exchequer in 1892, for there was the prospect of a budget deficit as a result of the Salisbury government's large naval building programme. In order to finance the naval programme, Goschen drew on the savings produced by the conversion of the national debt to a lower rate of interest in 1888, but he also needed to increase revenue by about £1.1m. from an increased duty on beer and the estate duty which would, complained Hamilton, make the present confusion more confounded. 'It is better', he remarked, 'to tread on the toes of our rich class than to run amuck against the commercial masses'.[38] The estate duty – 'rather a tinkering proposal' complained Hamilton – would raise £800,000 and the beer duty £300,000; Goschen also hoped to secure revenue from ground rents. It scarcely seemed equitable that £100,000 earned by Rothschild was all taxed as income, whereas the Duke of Westminster was not taxed on the same amount received from houses whose leases fell in and reverted to him, or from a fine for renewal. 'A small proposal of this kind', Hamilton believed, 'may stave off for some years the larger and thorny question of taxing ground rents'.[39] The Cabinet was not convinced, for it had already offended the brewers and caused alarm by the estate duty.[40] Goschen's proposals, Hamilton commented, 'were naturally more cheered on the opposition side than by his own friends. The fact is, it was a very Liberal Budget – indeed, had it come from the other side, it would have encountered great opposition from the Conservatives, and the Brewers whose wrath is partly suppressed would have been furious. The Estate Duty is the thin end of the wedge to a graduated system of taxation, which is pretty certain to be expanded in the future'.[41] It was, as Hamilton remarked, an uncomfortable experience for Goschen to gain support from the Liberals, and he 'does not like being taunted with Socialist tendencies'.[42]

Despite his best attempts to increase revenue, Goschen was forced to borrow to finance naval expansion, establishing a separate Naval Defence Fund in 1889. Hamilton was horrified at the 'great constitutional innovation' of the Naval Defence Bill which tied the hands of parliament to finance a building programme over five years, with £10m. from a special Naval Defence Fund paid out of taxes over seven years. This was, felt Hamilton, reducing the independence of parliament. 'It is mortgaging a part of the taxes too far ahead for expenditure of a kind over which Parliament likes to have annual control', and Hamilton was particularly concerned that expenditure was being charged to the capital account at a time when Britain was at peace, the income tax at a modest 6*d.* in the pound, revenue rising, and prosperity returning. 'A precedent set by a man of Mr Goschen's financial authority is a most dangerous precedent and one that heterodox financiers of the future . . . will not be slow to follow'.[43]

Gladstone opposed this expenditure and the recourse to a loan, and on the Liberals' return to power he and Harcourt attempted to rein back naval expansion and to place the loan on a more orthodox footing.[44] The result was serious tension in the Cabinet over naval expenditure, leading to conflict with the Admiralty, and providing the occasion for Gladstone's resignation.[45] Although Harcourt was able to pay the annual charges of the Naval Defence Fund from the surplus of the New Sinking Fund and the dividend on the shares of the Suez Canal,[46] there was nevertheless still a need to impose additional taxation, and further naval demands in late 1894 reduced him to despair. Hamilton recorded Harcourt's assurance that nothing 'would induce him to impose additional taxation again to meet those demands. He thinks (and rightly so) that we have come to the end of our taxation tether in times of peace'.[47] Naval expenditure, he insisted to Spencer, should 'be cut according to the financial cloth' and he opposed any further increases.[48] 'The maw of the Admiralty', complained Hamilton, 'is insatiable',[49] and Harcourt's main concern as Chancellor was an attempt to satisfy its hunger and to insist, with scant success, that it went on a diet.

It is not the case, as Brooks has suggested, that Harcourt was relinquishing 'the old Gladstonian imperative of combating increased public spending'.[50] In fact, he was using the death duties in order to shackle the state and to reduce the drive for military adventures, in much the same way as Gladstone argued that the income tax would make an expansive foreign policy unpopular. His position was expressed by Farrer, who remarked that the naval scare 'was due, not to the demands of those who consume the bulk of dutiable articles, but of naval men, of amateurs, of those who pay direct taxes'. The budget would, he believed, provide an 'excellent object lesson for those who wanted increased naval expenditure', for 'they have been taught that those who call the tune must pay the piper':[51]

> It is often said that direct taxation, and especially graduated direct taxation, is dangerous with a democracy, because the masses will, under such a system of taxation, have the excitement of spending the money without the burden of paying it. But in the case of naval and military expenditure it is not the masses, but the classes, who call for it; and, therefore, if we wish to keep it within limits it is upon the classes and not upon the masses, that the burden should fall.[52]

A second source of financial pressure came from local government, whose maw was scarcely less insatiable – and above all, from that other creation of the Salisbury government, the London County Council. In 1892, the progressives and Liberals held 83 of 118 seats on the LCC, but their hold on the parliamentary constituencies was less certain. In 1865, every London MP was a Liberal, but by 1886 the Conservatives held 47 of London's 59 seats.[53] In the election of 1892, the Liberals reduced the Conservatives to 36 seats, which the London Liberal and Radical Union argued was largely due to the expectation that a Liberal government would relieve the pressure on occupying ratepayers in the poorer areas of London.[54] There was, however, a tension in London Liberalism. The growth of unions in London, and the efflorescence of new radical and Liberal associations, contributed to the revival of metropolitan Liberalism; but the emphasis on land reform, housing, a more generous poor law, and other social expenditure threatened to alienate middle-class support. There was a split between radicals and progressives on the LCC and in the constituency parties, (men such as J. W. Benn and B. F. C. Costelloe) and older and more conservative figures (such as Rosebery, R. W. W. Lingen and T. H. Farrer) who criticised London Liberalism as 'faddist, schismatic, jealous, unorganised'.[55]

One of the deepest divisions was over metropolitan finance, which had arisen as soon as the LCC was elected in 1889. A Local Government and Taxation Committee was appointed under the chairmanship of Farrer, which was asked to consider whether the costs of permanent improvements in London should be borne by owners of property. The committee came to a somewhat vague recommendation that acts permitting the LCC to raise loans should contain a provision that interest charges and repayment should fall on the various classes of persons interested in London property, in such a manner as Parliament directs; and that no contract should allow owners of property to shift the burden to another person.[56] The question of *how* the charges should be allocated between different classes was not resolved. A divide started to open within the ranks of the Liberals, as the land question turned the radicals into interventionist progressives. 'A course of lessons in the "law of rent"', remarked Sidney Webb in 1890, 'will usually convert a mere Radical into something very like a Socialist.'[57]

Lingen, Farrer and Rosebery were defeated by the radicals who took control of the key positions on the council in 1892. Farrer was alarmed at the prospects. 'The feeling about taxing Owners is intense;' he warned Harcourt, 'and it is formidable because there the Labour party and the Ratepayers pull together. It would take very little to make an Irish land question in London'.[58] Farrer's preferred solution had two prongs. The first was to divide the rates between the owner and occupier. 'Our radicals don't care for this division of rates', he admitted, 'because, they say, the owner will get it back in rent. This is only partially true, and it will in all events be an advantage to make the tax *appear* to fall on the right shoulders.'[59] The division of rates, Farrer agreed, 'will not do enough: and the second thing is a municipal Death Tax. But this means a complete revision of the Succession Tax and of all the Death Duties ... I believe that the best course for the Government would be a bold one – viz., to undertake a revision of the Death Duties ... and to have it as a card in case of another Election'.[60] Such a municipal death duty was 'the most obvious fund out of which to help the groaning occupier'; the radical proposal of extracting the unearned increment was, by contrast, both absurd and impossible. Farrer's aim was, indeed, less the destruction of the landed interest than to remove a grievance and so 'render the title to land more stable'.[61]

Radicals such as Costelloe accepted the proposal for a municipal death duty, which was approved by the Select Committee on Town Holdings. The Inland Revenue should collect a supplementary local duty of up to 2.5 per cent: 'such a method, while fully solving the financial problem which presses on London, would meet the strong demand for a recognition of the equitable right of the community to some share in the accumulating increase of rental values which the cooperating industry of the community creates ...'[62] Radical policy was, however, soon to move beyond this position: a municipal death duty was accepted by the Council as merely a short-term measure; it resolved that the most equitable method of relief was taxation of ground values.[63] In January 1893, 35 Liberal MPs, 40 members of the LCC, and representatives of various Liberal and radical clubs, urged Harcourt to introduce the taxation of land values. This was, they argued, preferable to the reform of the death duties:

> It is said that in place of this cardinal reform, other measures are to be substituted, such as the increase of the probate duty and its application to land; this, however excellent in itself, would fail to meet the necessity of the case, as no sufficient amount can be raised by a death duty, which is operative on an average once only in twenty years, and which can easily be evaded. ... These proposals, therefor [*sic*], are manifestly an inadequate alternative for the direct Taxation of Ground Values; this impost alone can extract from land owners a sufficient contribution to meet the expenditure by which land values are created.[64]

Farrer expressed his concern to Harcourt: it was unlikely that the LCC would be able to frame a measure which Parliament would accept, and it was in any case unlikely that a Private Bill could introduce a significant shift in taxation. The result would be disappointment and ill-feeling to the government.[65] The problems of the LCC would, argued Farrer, react on the Liberal party in London when the Bill failed. 'Cannot you do something which will allay this feeling, and lay the foundation for future Liberal triumphs in London?'

Farrer recommended two policies, which would unite all sections of reformers and 'steer clear of the formidable Labour questions which are likely to produce a new cleavage in political parties'. One was the unification of the government of London, which would improve the efficiency of administration, join the dignity of the City to the LCC, as well as 'adding ballast to that somewhat eccentric and unstable body'. Harcourt had tried to unite London government in 1884, and he agreed that it would have been desirable if 'the existing Corporation with all its wealth, all its powers and all its traditions would have been stretched like a sheet of india rubber over the whole of the metropolis'. He was, however, not willing to try again. Farrer's second proposal was the reform of taxation. 'I do not believe you will get any wisdom out of the LCC: though you may get support. The matter must be dealt with in connection with a large reform of Imperial Taxation – which will itself be one of the best cards you can play in the political game of the future'.[66]

Harcourt had, therefore, to meet the pressures of the navy for money and to contain both the grievances of occupying ratepayers and also the policies of the London radicals for local taxation based upon an explicit attack on landowners and rent. To Farrer and Harcourt, death duties were the best solution to both problems: they raised money, and at the same time could show the radicals that some action was being taken against the landowners, without indulging in an explicit attack on the unearned increment. What was not clear, however, was whether the death duties should be part of a proportionate system of taxation. By the early 1890s, a new concept was emerging, of the ability or capacity to pay. Farrer was still loyal to the use of death duties to restore proportionality to the tax system: was Harcourt taking the same line, or was he shifting towards a tax regime based on capacity?

The selection of a tax structure was connected with the fundamental dilemma of the Liberal party from the late 1880s, the concern that it had lost moderate, middle-class support. The solution, in the opinion of Rosebery, was to reject sectional Liberalism, and to return to the 'old Liberal spirit which existed before the split of 1886'.[67] The intention of the Liberal Imperialists was to appeal in particular to the middle class which had been frightened away by 'faddists', the alliance with the Irish, and the critical attitude to the empire.[68] The strategy, as Haldane saw it in 1888, was 'to get back the support of that minority of the upper and middle class, which does naturally, but at present does not, vote with them'.[69] But, complained Beatrice Webb in 1901, this was to define the centre as the non-political voter, 'the capitalist or professional man who desires little social change and the Empire maintained'. What the Liberals should be doing, she urged, was to appeal to 'the great lower middle and working class'.[70]

Although Harcourt was sceptical of Gladstone's Irish policy, in other respects he was part of the problem as defined by the Liberal Imperialists. He was a 'faddist', who supported temperance, increases in the duties on beers and spirits, and local option; and he was a staunch opponent of expenditure on the navy and imperial adventures. It would also be easy to conclude that his budget was a further attack on property-owners, alienating them from the party and driving them into the arms of the Conservatives. This was certainly what Rosebery feared, and Lewis Harcourt reported that he was 'fighting like a demon' against the steepness of the graduation of death duties:

> R said 'We shall lose all the monied mercantile classes and what shall we do then at the Election? and how can we find money to fight it? The split in the Liberal Party will become horizontal and not vertical.[71]

Rosebery had feared in 1889 that Harcourt 'would be so easily squeezed by the extreme Radicals', but this was not entirely an accurate perception. Harcourt had 'little real sympathy with advanced men', noted Hamilton; 'to lead such a pack . . . would indeed be an ordeal'.[72] Harcourt's aim was to contain the radicals, by moving from Gladstone's obsession with Ireland and channelling their views on social questions in a way which was less harmful to the Liberal coalition. It was necessary, as Haldane argued, to develop a 'constructive policy' on social issues so that the Liberals did not 'have the wind taken out of their sails on these questions by the "Unionist party".'[73]

It was necessary to contain the Radicals and counter the Conservatives, but Harcourt's strategy was different from the Liberal Imperialists such as Haldane and Rosebery. His aim was to build support from the centre, which he defined as the lower levels of income tax payers. He was not appealing to them on the basis of imperialism, but through an astute strategy which offered them tax concessions. Harcourt was, then, attempting three things: the provision of funding for the navy, while reining in the excesses of the Admiralty and its supporters; the containment of the radicals' challenge in London, while convincing them that action was being taken; and an attempt to shape the tax system in the interests of the lower levels of income-tax payers, which is more striking and significant than the reform of death duties taken in isolation.

III

Action on the death duties was clearly necessary when the Liberals came to power, but it could have taken a number of forms. The first and most cautious was proposed by Gladstone, who informed Harcourt in July 1892 that he would proceed with an English programme as well as home rule for Ireland, and that something should be done to equalise the death duties. This could easily be justified on the grounds of proportionality, adjusting the incidence on different types of property to balance the tax system. Gladstone was not pressing for a graduated estate duty, and he had been concerned even by Goschen's 1 per cent on large estates in 1889:

> He admitted that the principle of graduated taxation had already been recognized by the income tax exemptions ... He (Mr G) was prepared to accept, in the abstract, graduated taxation, but it was attended with dangers; for where was it to stop? If pressed, it might amount to confiscation. There clearly must be a limitation; and the objection to the present proposal of Mr Goschen's was that there was no finality: it invited of itself indefinite extension.[74]

It was, however, possible to go a step further, graduating the death duties and using them as the main source of additional revenue on the ground that accumulations of wealth were better able to bear taxation and that death duties were more suited to both graduation and differentiation than the income tax.

This was the position of Sidney Buxton. He argued in favour of the death duties as a means of raising additional revenue, on psychological grounds: death duties, he claimed, were less unpopular than other forms of taxation, for liability arose with the accession of wealth and the heavier rates charged to non-lineals were more readily accepted because the bequest was more unexpected.[75] Death duties also had an economic advantage over other taxes, for 'their levy or increase does not in any way fetter or disturb trade or industry, or affect the spending power of existing incomes. In their effect they are neutral, and in this neutrality lies their greatest merit'.[76] He was rejecting the view that the death duties were a tax on capital, which would reduce the yield from other taxes by destroying capital. Rather, capital should be viewed as accumulated income: there was no essential difference between the surplus of income over expenditure in one year, and the invested surplus of past years.

Capital was not 'destroyed' so much as redistributed, and the revenue derived from death duties enabled the reduction of other taxes, which were more disruptive of trade.[77]

Buxton argued that the death duties could also be used to introduce graduation and differentiation in a way which balanced the tax system as a whole by complementing an income tax levied at a single rate on all levels and types of income. The income tax pressed on precarious incomes derived from intelligence and skill more heavily, he argued, than on permanent or spontaneous incomes from investments:

> the precarious income is taxed at an equal (and therefore at a proportionately heavier) rate as compared to the secure income. The objection to the present system of assessments is, that the tax is levied in the case of precarious incomes not only on income, but also partly on what is practically capital. The owner of a temporary income, not derived from capital, and depending wholly or in part on his own health and life, is bound to save and to invest a portion of his income; a necessity which cannot be said to exist to anything like the same degree in the case of the possessor of a permanent income derived from capital. One man is at liberty to spend the whole of his income without being in a worse position than before; another, if he does more than spend a portion, is practically consuming his capital; and yet the income tax is charged equally on the two.[78]

By taxing the capital from which permanent incomes were derived, the tax system would be more balanced.[79] Although it was difficult to draw an exact line between different classes of income, as Gladstone had argued in 1853, Buxton believed that the inability to secure absolute justice should not prevent an attempt to minimise injustice. Above all, the increased reliance of revenue on income tax meant that the 'necessity of placing the incidence of our principal source of *direct* taxation on a juster and therefore firmer basis becomes more urgent'.[80] Buxton was still concentrating on balancing the tax system between precarious and earned incomes in terms of proportionality. He was not going much beyond the position of Gladstone.

Harcourt was willing to go further than either Gladstone or Buxton, for two days after his meeting with the Prime Minister he requested Edward Hamilton not only to prepare for the equalisation of death duties, but also for the graduation of income tax. In 1863, Gladstone had warned against the dangers of graduating the income tax beyond exemption for small incomes: if 'you adopt it as a general rule of your legislation it merely means universal war – a universal scramble amongst all classes, every one endeavouring to relieve himself at the expense of his neighbour – and an end being put to all social peace and to any common principle on which the burdens of the state can be adjusted'.[81]

By the early 1890s, many Liberals were prepared to graduate the income tax, feeling that Gladstone was concentrating too much on Home Rule and neglecting the formulation of an attractive domestic policy. A deputation of MPs urged Harcourt that 'man cannot live by Home Rule alone', and pressed for a 'good English programme', including a Radical budget. Lewis Harcourt agreed, and pitied Gladstone for his naive belief that equalisation of the death duties was sufficient:

> Poor man! We should want a great deal more than that ... we must have a 'revolutionary' Budget next year. Graduated Income tax if possible and further reduction of the Inhabited [house] duty, and if it can be managed, something more off tea and cheap tobacco.[82]

How far were these ambitions realised?

Harcourt was under considerable pressure to overhaul the income tax as well as the death duties, and in January 1894 he received a memorial from 94 Liberal MPs who complained that

> the principle of adjusting the burden of taxation according to the ability to bear it is flagrantly violated in our present fiscal arrangements ... the weight of taxation, which is really felt as a severe burden, by persons of small means, ought to be diminished by a much heavier assessment upon persons of fortune who do not at present feel the burden at all, and whose share of taxation might be greatly increased without even then imposing upon them any substantial sacrifice.

This was a clear rejection of the principle of proportionate taxation for a stress upon 'capacity'. They urged the consolidation of death duties on realty and personalty, and the introduction of a graduated scale. It would, however, take some time to become fully effective so that it was necessary, they contended, to take other measures. The income tax should be graduated; small earned incomes should be relieved of taxation and a differential rate imposed on incomes from 'accumulated property'; and grants to local government from national taxation paid by the poor should be replaced by taxes on land values raised by a municipal tax or death duties. By raising additional revenue, it would then be possible to reduce taxes on tea, coffee and cocoa and introduce a 'free breakfast table'. 'For many years the budgets have been more or less rich men's budgets – it is time we should have a poor man's budget'.[83] Why were these radical ambitions disappointed, despite the sympathy of Harcourt for a graduated income tax?

The plan for the reform of the death duties was substantially complete by the beginning of 1893. The situation then changed. A budget deficit of £1.5m. was anticipated, which was the expected yield from the reform of the death duties. The danger, as Milner saw it, was that the Cabinet would 'shy' at the scheme because of the time needed for parliamentary debate. 'He thinks', remarked Harcourt's son, Loulou, 'we shall eventually come to what he calls "something simple" for raising the wind': the addition of 1*d.* to the income tax, which would yield £2m. The radical budget which had been expected in 1893 gave way to the reality of a 'very humdrum affair'.[84] The more the question of the death duties was looked at, remarked Harcourt, the more complicated it became, with endless opportunities for obstruction; and the yield was likely to be low in the early years at only £500,000. The 'young hyenas' might be 'longing to slake their thirst on the blood of landlordism', commented Harcourt; but they were not likely to get anything from agricultural land. 'The whole increased burthen will fall on personalty and real property in houses, and these are not feeble interests'. And London would get nothing from the death duties, for they would be retained at the centre.[85]

Even with the increase in the rate of income tax, a bare surplus of £4,000 was expected which was 'rather running the national finance too fine'. The financial situation had deteriorated by the end of 1893, for the revenue was in a 'deplorable state' and Harcourt was embroiled in a tussle with his colleagues over the spending plans of the government, particularly on the navy. 'It is a devil of a mess', remarked Loulou, 'and means much extra taxation'.[86] After discharging £2m. of the Naval Defence Loan from the sinking fund, a deficit of £3m. still had to be covered.[87] The crucial question was how to distribute the burden.

Harcourt's initial intention in January 1894 was to reform the death duties in order to raise an additional £1m. in the first year; the remainder was to come from a further 1*d.* on the income tax, and from raising the duty on beer and spirits. There were obvious political dangers in this package: it would be criticised for taxing the poor man's beer; it would provoke hostility from landed interests who faced higher death duties on realty; and there would be resentment at two successive increases in income tax. Harcourt therefore wished to adjust the burden of taxation in order to minimise opposition. Property owners would, he hoped, be reconciled to the reform of the death duties by a concession in the calculation of their income tax under schedule A: they should be taxed on net rather than gross earnings by a 15 per cent deduction to cover outgoings on repairs and maintenance.

He also proposed to adjust the limits of income tax exemptions and abatements in order to reduce the tax burden on smaller incomes. Incomes below £150 were not liable to income tax, and on incomes up to £400, an abatement of £120 was allowed. Harcourt proposed that an abatement of £150 should be allowed on incomes up to £500, which would consequently pay less with income tax at 8*d.* than they had previously incurred at 7*d.* The additional yield from income tax was reduced by these exemptions to £250,000, and he expected to produce £1.5m.

from beer and spirit duties.[88] Discussion of a graduated income tax had disappeared from the agenda, and Loulou went so far as to inform Labouchère that 'we must dismiss the nonsense of a graduated Income Tax (as graduation is popularly understood) as being quite impossible'.[89]

It was therefore to his 'great amazement' that the Chancellor was converted to his proposal for a graduated income surtax in January 1894; he was equally surprised that Milner was not opposed in principle so long as the present method of collection was retained for the bulk of the income tax. Loulou's scheme was that the 'normal' income tax of, say, 6*d.* or 7*d.* in the pound would be collected by the same methods as before, with a graduated surtax of ½*d.* in the pound on incomes above £5,000, rising by ½*d.* for each additional £5,000 up to £100,000. The Chancellor was, Loulou reported, 'getting enthusiastic over it and says that some powder is wanted to charge the gun if so heavy a projectile as our deficit is to be fired'.[90] The attraction of the scheme was clear:

> It is plain that with the increased and increasing expenditure Income Tax must be treated as a permanent tax. It is essential therefore to redress its admitted inequalities. It is generally felt that it presses too heavily on the lower and too lightly on the higher rates of income. You must therefore have what may be called a normal Income Tax with (1) alleviation at the lower end (This is effected by the allowances under £500) (2) You must also have enhancement at the upper end.

In other words, incomes below £500 would get allowances; between £500 and £5,000 they would pay the full normal rate; and above £5,000 they would also pay a graduated surtax. The issue was whether the yield on the surtax on higher incomes would more than compensate for the proposed allowances on incomes below £500.[91]

Harcourt had clearly become convinced that increased levels of expenditure had changed the politics of taxation: it was not expedient to impose more burdens on the poor through duties on beer; it was necessary to moderate the pressure of income tax on small incomes; and the only way in which this could be achieved was by imposing a surtax on large incomes. 'I <u>must</u> deal with the Income Tax as it would be impossible in the present state of opinion to raise the larger amount from indirect taxation, and if the Income Tax is to be continued as it clearly must at a high level it will be indispensable to reform it at both ends'.[92] Harcourt failed in his ambition to introduce a surtax, it was not until 1907 that the principle of a surtax was accepted by Asquith, and not until 1909 that a scheme was introduced by Lloyd George. There is one ready explanation for the retreat. 'It is a great disadvantage in these Radical days', Loulou confided to his journal, 'that E. Hamilton and A. Milner should regard themselves as the sentinels of the Landlord and Capitalist class'.[93]

The old guard at the Treasury and Inland Revenue were clearly formidable opponents of change, and the task of the next Liberal administration was eased by their replacement by a younger generation. Not only did Asquith and Lloyd George face less opposition within the civil service; they also had a clearer political choice. Unlike Harcourt, they could point to the alternative means of raising revenue proposed by the Conservatives: tariffs made a graduated income tax more acceptable. The delay to the introduction of graduation should not, however, be reduced to a simple story of administrative conservatism or class interest delaying reform to the fiscal system. The opposition of the Inland Revenue and Treasury to graduation was based upon a highly developed and articulate set of assumptions about the nature of the British fiscal system and the relationship between the state and taxpayers, which continued to inform policy after the introduction of graduation and differentiation.

The Inland Revenue's case against graduation was summarised by the deputy Chairman, F. L. Robinson, in 1891. He argued that there were theoretical objections: the attempt to arrive at equality of sacrifice was impossible to achieve; there was a danger that graduation would lead inexorably to confiscation; and the introduction of high rates would discourage industry.[94] These theoretical objections did not convince Milner, who was prepared to accept that the principle of graduation was sound.[95] The practical considerations did convince him that change was dangerous. The income tax, Robinson pointed out, was largely collected indirectly: tax was deducted from payments of rent, interest, and dividends at source rather than at their destination. The different sources of income fell into different 'schedules', and it was not necessary for the Inland Revenue to be aware of the total income received by any individual under each head. The introduction of a system of graduation would, argued Robinson and Milner, entail a major adjustment in the tax system. 'The Income Tax ... *lends itself ill to graduation,* because the material facts, on which such graduation is based, can only be supplied by the individual taxpayer, who has the strongest motive for, and infinite means of, concealment'. The clauses in the budget bill providing powers to collect the necessary information 'must be stringent, and their inquisitorial character is certain to provoke discussion'.

Objections to granting the Inland Revenue more inquisitorial powers would be as nothing compared with the unpopularity brought upon the Inland Revenue and government in using the powers. It would not simply be a matter of troubling 10,000 people who would ultimately pay the surtax, for it would be necessary to send forms to 100,000 people in order to discover who was liable. Eighty per cent would not reply, and it would not be possible to know whether this was because they did not have an income of £5,000 or because they were concealing their income. It would therefore be necessary to have powers of compulsion, despite the fact that in four cases out of five there would be nothing to tax.

The only alternative would be to guess: when the estimate was too low, it would be readily paid; when it was too high, there would be thousands of appeals, which would involve checking information on shares, settlements, mortgages. This would be costly, time-consuming and result in further aggravation of many people:

> The inquiries necessary to furnish us with even a small fraction of this information would bring us into collision with a vastly greater number of people than those we intend to tax. Experience shows, that the irritation caused by the inquiries of the taxgatherer is universal: it is not confined to the persons whom he is ultimately seeking to charge. We should be making 100 incidental enemies for every recalcitrant, or mendacious, plutocrat whom we were trying to run in.

The collection of taxes by direct assessment on professional fees or traders' profits already caused more trouble than the much larger sums collected at source; 'but the individual assessment of traders in respect of their trading profits is incomparably less difficult, and less invidious than the direct assessment of persons *upon the whole of their means*'. Change threatened compliance and consent:

> is the game worth the candle? Would this extra million a year not be dearly bought if it involved setting up a feud, so long happily avoided, between the public generally and the vast body of persons, often not very well-mannered or very literate, who are concerned in the collection of the taxes. This is not merely a question of *officials*. It must not be forgotten, what a vast amount of work is done in tax matters by the *unpaid Boards of Commissioners*, what great assistance they render to the Revenue, or how largely we are dependent on their cordial co-operation. Now this new business of assessing individuals on their whole incomes will be intensely distasteful to the Commissioners. It is not only that they are generally drawn from the class, whom the surcharge will hit, or at any rate, worry. They will dislike the kind of work which it involves. I am sure I am taking no superficial or departmental view, when I ask the question, whether the indirect injury done to the Revenue in the long run by the new departure is not likely to outweigh the meagre pecuniary result of it?[96]

Graduation of the income tax clearly required the tax authorities to know the *total* income of individuals in order to apply the correct rate of tax, and Robinson argued that there were two possible methods. The first was to reverse the system of assessment and to concentrate on the destination of income rather than its source, making a direct assessment of every person on his whole income. Robinson was sceptical, arguing that it had been tried when the income tax was first introduced in 1799 and abandoned in 1803. Milner agreed: direct assessment

> will not only be desperately unpopular, but will lead to every kind of fraud, evasion, and conflict between the Revenue authorities and the public. You would have to *graduate tremendously* if you wished to get even the present yield of the Duty by means of Direct Assessment. The great increase of yield resulting from the substitution of taxation 'at the fountain head' for Direct Assessment in the beginning of this century, and the experience of the American property tax are very instructive on this point. It is to be remembered, that almost all the friction, complaint, expense and unpopularity connected with the Income Tax at present arise out of the collection of that $\frac{1}{4}$th–$\frac{1}{3}$rd part of the tax which is got *directly*. The far greater sums indirectly collected give rise to hardly any dispute, and excite no odium against the impost.[97]

The alternative plan was no better: to continue to deduct tax at source, but to apply the highest rate and refund the difference. It would, remarked Robinson, entail 'enormous labour and the incessant irritation to the taxpayer involved in such a process are very obvious'.[98]

Milner was horrified. Suppose that tax at the highest rate was deducted from the dividends of a public company

> and all the hundreds of shareholders coming here for abatements at varying rates, each having, in order to obtain abatement, to state the whole of his income, from whatever sources, and to prove his statements. Imagine the expense of such a system, and, above all, imagine the passionate affection, which the hundreds of thousands of claimants, each struggling to fill up a schedule of his income and to answer 150 questions from this Department with respect to it, would feel for the Chancellor of the Exchequer, who had introduced this notable 'reform'.[99]

Milner had, he informed Harcourt, 'great administrative and I might almost say moral objections' to a surtax which required rich people to declare their income from all sources: 'It will lead to an amount of deliberate lying, which it is rather unpleasant to contemplate and which in nine out of ten cases it will be impossible to check. And the financial result will be very disappointing'.[100] Milner's fear, remarked Loulou in his journal, was that 'it would make the Income Tax so odious in its levy that it might have to be swept away. I don't believe a word of all this but it has produced its effect on Chex [Chancellor of the Exchequer] and I can see that he has in his own mind abandoned the idea for this year at least. Milner may have saved him financially but I am sure he has ruined him politically'.[101]

The income tax was so important to the revenue of the country, that nothing should be done to make it unpopular and jeopardise its collection. Indeed, the acceptance of the income tax in Britain was remarkable in comparison with other European countries, and the Inland Revenue and Treasury were convinced that this depended upon a high level of compliance. The taxpayer was not troubled by officious bureaucrats, and did not need to divulge all of his financial secrets; in cases of dispute, the adjudication was made by a lay commissioner who was drawn from the same type of person as the taxpayer. The attempt to graduate the income tax was dangerous; it was also unnecessary, for the graduation of estate duty was equivalent to a graduated and differentiated income tax, without its shortcomings. A personal estate of £37,500 would produce an income of £1,440, assuming a return of 4 per cent; the additional estate duty was equivalent to an income tax of 1.25*d.* On a personal estate of £200,000 producing an income of £7,680, the additional duty was equivalent to 6.25*d.* income tax; and on a personal estate of £1,200,000 producing an income of £45,080 to 10*d.*[102] A graduated estate duty was, argued Hamilton, easier to collect because it did not involve inquisition; it affected only incomes derived from capital, and exempted incomes from salaries which were dependent on the life of the individual who earned the income; it did not affect anyone with an income of less than £1,000 a year; it would not operate in the life of present owners; and it would yield £4m., equivalent to 2*d.* on the income tax which would fall on all incomes liable to the tax, unlike the estate duty which would only hit the better-off who derived income from the funds and other investments.[103]

Hamilton was clearly willing to support the estate duty as the lesser of two evils, preferable to differentiation and graduation of the income tax. It could also be supplemented, urged Milner, by a graduated inhabited house duty which could yield the necessary sum without the objections to the surtax, and would be borne by the same people: the assessments existed, and the money could be raised with 'no wholesale cultivation of perjury, no permanent feud between the tax-gatherers and a large section of the population – a war waged over the whole field of business and finance and incidentally harrassing everybody who either has, or has anything to do with money'. It was, argued Milner, not wise to embark on a 'financial revolution', at the same time as the 'gigantic task' of the graduated death duty, and in the absence of financial necessity, 'merely in order to affirm a principle, already sufficiently affirmed, for this year at any rate, by the graduation of the Death Duty up to 10 per cent, and, if necessary, by the graduation of the House Tax'.[104]

Although Harcourt bowed to pressure from Milner and Hamilton to drop the surtax from the budget of 1894, he emphasised that it was merely a tactical retreat. 'I still adhere strictly to the principle', he informed Milner, 'and though I recognise that I am not in a position to give effect to it, I shall not abandon the principle, but hope we shall one day find the means to carry it out'.[105] Milner responded that he was 'content to bow politely to the surtax *in theory*', provided that it was abandoned in practice for the present year, until he had time to consider how to obtain information without upsetting everyone and 'to state at greater length and elaboration (and perhaps calmness) the very strong objections I still have to the scheme in any form'.[106] Already in 1894, Harcourt was being urged by Reginald Welby of the Treasury to proceed on an experimental basis on a small number of very large incomes rather than to accept Milner's claims that the proposal was impossible to implement. The proposal should not, he agreed, be entertained if it entailed applications to as many as 100,000 with 'those hateful inquisitions', but 'I should be sorry ... to abandon altogether a policy which I think would be found in the long-run conservative'. Although the scheme proposed by Milner was impracticable, Welby felt that Harcourt could proceed experimentally with a higher starting point – say £50,000 – which involved fewer applications.[107] The case for graduation had, it seemed, been won by 1894.

Harcourt wished to introduce both a graduated estate duty and a graduated income tax; what he was not advocating was differentiation in order to impose a higher tax on 'unearned' or 'spontaneous' income than on earned or 'industrial' income. Milner was certainly sceptical:

> The idea of charging incomes from property and incomes from personal exertion at different rates, is as old as the hills. It is practically impossible of execution with the present Income Tax. It is conceivable, that some day Income Tax will be abolished and a Property Tax substituted. Perhaps this will be better, but it means a financial revolution of such magnitude, that it could not possibly be attempted at present. The idea that tinkering with the Income Tax will meet the difficulty is wholly misleading. Nothing else will meet the difficulty but sweeping the Income Tax right into the Thames and starting afresh.[108]

It could be argued that 'unearned' income derived from property was already more heavily taxed than 'earned' income. In part, this was the result of the method of collection of income tax, for 'spontaneous incomes are assessed at *their known amount*, the industrial incomes for the most part *on the amount declared by their recipients*'. This probably accounted for an abatement of 20 per cent: a man with £500 from investments paid on the whole amount at source; a small trader who earned £500 would report an income of £400, and would obtain an abatement of £120 so that he would pay on only £280.[109]

The property which produced 'unearned' or spontaneous income was also taxed by death duties; 'and if it does not pay sufficiently, the remedy lies in an increase of death duties, and not in the introduction of hopeless confusion into the income tax'. It was difficult to separate unearned from precarious incomes, but even it were possible, Milner doubted whether the result would be justice:

The true principle of taxation – if you can only get at it – is equality of sacrifice. But a differential income tax would, in hundreds of instances, put the heavier burden on the weaker shoulders, the lighter burden on the stronger ... Is the widow with £500 a year and 5 children to educate to be taxed at a heavier rate than the successful barrister or doctor or man of business earning £5,000 or £10,000 or £20,000?

The strongest case for differentiation was that income resting on the exertion of an individual ceased on his death, which meant that he had to save for his dependants; he should therefore pay a lower rate of tax on his income. This was, argued Milner, to identify taxable income with expenditure or what he *ought* to spend. The problems were insuperable, in Milner's opinion:

the moment a State attempts to determine, what every man *ought* to spend, in order to find out on how much of his income he ought to be taxed, it attempts a task with which no human ingenuity can grapple, and with which the machinery of the State, even if duplicated and triplicated, would be quite ludicrously inadequate to deal.

It was therefore necessary to fall back on a rough and ready method, that a person with an earned income should put aside a quarter or a third. Milner had doubts: some industrial incomes were less precarious than income from investment. What was needed was a distinction between precarious and *assured* incomes, which would be even more difficult. And it was not always the case that a man with a precarious income needed to save more than a man with an assured income: 'A person with a small fixed income and a growing family, is surely more bound to lay up something than the rich bachelor partner in a big commercial business'.

It is difficult enough, in all conscience, to find out what a man's income is. It is still harder to discover what his expenditure is. But to determine, *what his expenditure ought to be*, in the infinite variety of human circumstances, is a task which it would be absolutely futile to attempt, and the State would only make itself ridiculous by attempting it. The result would be to create a number of inequalities far greater, and to excite an outcry far more clamorous than any to which the present income tax, with all its admitted anomalies, has ever given rise.[110]

There is no indication that Harcourt disagreed with such an analysis, and he made no proposal for differentiation.

The outcome was that income tax was reduced on the lower level of incomes through an adjustment of the level of exemption and abatement, with an increase in the burden on large incomes through an increase in the rate. Milner estimated that the income tax in 1894/5 ought to yield £16,200,000 in order to balance the budget; he anticipated that an increase in the rate from 7*d.* to 8*d.* would produce £16,956,000, which left £750,000 for remissions; and he costed various proposals (see table 7.3).

Table 7.3 Cost of concessions on income tax 1894–5

I	raise abatement from £120 to £150 up to £400 income	£488,000
II	raise abatement from £120 to £150 up to £500 income	£824,000
III	raise abatement from £120 to £150 up to £400 income plus 10% off schedule A	£948,000
IV	raise abatement from £120 to £150 up to £500 income plus 10% off schedule A	£1,284,000
V	raise abatement from £120 to £150 up to £500 income plus 15% off schedule A	£1,513,000

Source: Bod. Lib., MS Harcourt dep. 70, fos. 144–67, Memo on various proposed changes in the income tax, A. Milner, 9 March 1894.

Milner was willing to accept that remissions I and II, and even III, were feasible within the limits of the budget estimates; the problem was offering concessions to Schedule A in options IV and V, which would require additional revenue from the surtax. This was expected to yield £500,000, which would almost cover IV and still leave a deficit on V.[111] Milner's own preference was to drop all concession to schedule A. It was, he remarked, simply a sop to landowners to mollify them for paying the same rate of death duties as personal estate.[112] The eventual outcome was to offer an abatement of £160 on incomes up to £400: the number of taxpayers involved in 1891/2 was 475,257. In addition, an abatement of £100 was granted to individuals with an income of between £400 and £500. Harcourt also allowed a deduction of 10 per cent from income from land and 15 per cent on houses in Schedule A. The thrust of the budget was to assist 'higher-paid workmen, clerks, struggling professional men, the smaller shopkeepers, manufacturers and agriculturalists'.[113]

IV

Harcourt's budget of 1894 was, therefore, more than a simple attack on the landed interest. Rosebery feared that it would be interpreted by landowners as a serious threat to their future, which would alienate the 'last relics' of property owners who would become 'an active and alarmed adversary'; it was, indeed, desirable to preserve the aristocracy, for 'a plutocracy of the American type would be a bad substitute for the landed class in Great Britain'. There was also a danger that capitalists would be driven from the party by a graduated scale on personalty. On the other hand, argued Rosebery, the budget would not secure additional support: those who possessed less than £500 were neither numerous nor grateful enough; and the masses did not give the Liberals the support which the party was entitled to expect. Above all, Rosebery was alarmed by 'the cleavage of classes in this country in which the Liberal party would rest on nothing but a working class support without the variety and richness and intellectual forces which used to make up that Party'.[114]

Harcourt reacted with his usual bluster. Rosebery's argument would, he remarked, 'have been thought extreme in its Toryism by Lord Eldon. There is nothing to do with such rubbish as this sort except to treat it with the contempt it deserves'.[115] The animosity of landowners, he informed Rosebery, he cheerfully accepted: they were simply being deprived of monopolies they should never have possessed. By contrast, incomes under £500 accounted for 90 per cent of the electors, and the only method of securing their support was by earning their gratitude. Any failure of the masses to support the party, he somewhat tactlessly informed Rosebery, was not the fault of the masses but of the leaders of the party; their support could not be secured 'by appearing as the defenders of fiscal privileges and exemptions of the wealthy which are universally condemned'.[116] What he did not point out to Rosebery was that he was giving concessions to the landed interests and small house owners through favourable treatment under Schedule A; and that he was containing the more radical attacks on landowners. He was in many ways pursuing the same end as Gladstone in 1853: to use the tax system to unite rather than divide classes. He was building from the middle out, offering concessions to the lower level of income tax payers. The increase in the death duties helped to contain the pressure from the radicals for an outright attack upon land, without mounting an onslaught on land as a separate fraction of capital which was, as Offer has remarked, 'a destructive worm in the apple of the New Liberalism'.[117]

Notes

1 Bodleian Library, MS Harcourt dep. 228, fos. 21–22, Henry Burdett to W. Harcourt, 14 July 1895. Burdett (1847–1920) was a leading hospital administrator and reformer: see F. K. Prochaska, *Philanthropy and the hospitals of London: the King's Fund, 1897–1990*, Oxford, 1992, p. 11.

2 T. H. Farrer, 'Sir William Harcourt's budget', *Contemporary Reivew* 66 (1894),

pp. 153, 164; see also Bodleian Library, MS Harcourt dep. 25, fos. 217–18, Farrer to Harcourt, 1 July 1894 where he referred to the budget as 'the most important Financial Reform since Peel's great changes'. Farrer (1819–99) had been a civil servant at the Board of Trade until 1886; in retirement, he became a member of the LCC from 1889 to 1898 (*Dictionary of national biography, supplement,* II, p. 201). R. B. Haldane and George Trevelyan both claimed that it was the greatest budget since 1853: Bod. Lib., MS Harcourt dep. 123, fos. 135–6 Haldane to Harcourt, 20 July 1894; MS Harcourt dep. 406, fo. 81, 30 March 1894).

3 Bod. Lib., MS Harcourt dep. 224, fos. 90–91, Fletcher Moulton to Harcourt, 16 April 1894.

4 Bod. Lib., MS Harcourt dep. 225, fos. 98–100, T. Ellis to Harcourt 27 October 1894.

5 Quoted in A. G. Gardiner, *The life of Sir William Harcourt,* II, London, 1923, p. 290.

6 Gardiner, *Life,* II, p. 298 quoting the queen's letter to Harcourt, 5 June 1894.

7 F. M. L. Thompson, *English landed society in the nineteenth century,* London, 1963, pp. 325, 329–30; on the development of insurance policies to cover death duties, see Bod. Lib., MS Harcourt dep. 137.

8 Public Record Office, IR74/2, Finance Act 1894. Experience of the first year of the new estate duty, A. Milner to Michael Hicks-Beach, 12 August 1895.

9 A. Offer, *Property and politics, 1870–1914: landownership, law, ideology and urban development in England,* Cambridge, 1981, chapter 14.

10 His approach was similar to the Conservatives in the interwar period: see R. McKibbin, *The ideologies of class: social relations in Britain, 1880–1950,* Oxford, 1990.

11 H. C. G. Matthew, 'Disraeli, Gladstone and the politics of the mid-Victorian budget', *Historical Journal,* vol. XXII (1979).

12 *Hansard,* 3rd ser., 125, 18 April 1853, col. 1386–7.

13 *Hansard,* 3rd ser., 125, col. 1394, 18 April 1853. Gladstone was not alone in his belief; in 1842 Lord John Russell opposed the introduction of the income tax and argued that the equalisation of the death duties was 'fairer, better and more just': *Hansard,* 26 April 1842, quoted in Buxton and Barnes, *Death duties,* pp. 19–20.

14 British Library Add. MSS 48,648, Edward Hamilton diaries, fo. 28, 25 February 1888.

15 *Hansard,* 3rd ser., 125, col. 1395, 18 April 1853.

16 *Hansard,* 3rd ser., 125, col. 1397, 18 April 1853.

17 Buxton, *Finance and politics,* I, p. 118.

18 Gladstone's strategy in 1853 is explained in S. Buxton, *Mr Gladstone as Chancellor of the Exchequer,* London, 1901, pp. 13–16, 122–3, 135–7. The succession duty was opposed by Disraeli as 'unsound in principle', both as a tax on capital and for leading to partition of estates which was 'a very great evil'. See Buxton and Barnes, *Death duties,* p. 21.

19 Buxton and Barnes, *Death duties,* pp. 22, 25–6.

20 BL Add. MS 48,654, fo. 57, 25 November 1890.

21 W. E. Gladstone, 'Lecky's History of England in the eighteenth century', *Nineteenth Century,* 21 (1887), pp. 934–5; see the exchange between Gladstone and Lecky which indicates that Gladstone did not make this intention public. He merely referred at the time to 'judicious adjustments' of taxes and the need to make them more equitable: W. E. H. Lecky, 'Mr Gladstone and the income tax', *Nineteenth Century,* 22 (1887), p. 54 and W. E. Gladstone, 'Mr Lecky and political morality', *Nineteenth Century,* 22 (1887), p. 281. See also Buxton, *Finance and politics,* II, pp. 166–7.

22 The rates of probate duty were simplified: the existing rates had been set in 1815, rising from 10s (on gross estates between £20 and £100) to £15,000 (on estates of £1m. and above); the steps were irregular and fell more heavily on small estates. The probate duty was increased and graduated, rising from £1 per £50 up to £500, to £1 5*s* per £50 up to £1,000, and amounting to 3 per cent above £1,000. The legacy duty of 1 per cent on lineal descendants was abolished where probate duty

was paid in order to remove the double payment; on small estates of up to £300, the legacy and probate duty was commuted to 30*s*. The details are in Buxton and Barnes, *Death duties*, pp. 7–11, 18–19.

23 This revived an earlier scheme of 1863, which was rejected because Gladstone had proposed to tax charities.

24 Buxton, *Finance and politics*, II, pp. 297, 314–16.

25 Bod. Lib., MS Harcourt dep. 23, fos. 203–9, Fowler to Harcourt, 4 April 1888.

26 *Hansard*, 3rd ser., 324, 9 April 1888, cols. 731–2, 735–6; and 325, 23 April 1888, cols. 190, 192.

27 *Hansard*, 3rd ser., 325, col. 192.

28 This meant, according to Buxton and Barnes, *Death duties*, p. 41, that 'a considerable encouragement is given to the undesirable practice of tying up stocks and shares in settlement, and to the creation of life renters'.

29 Buxton, *Finance and politics*, II, pp. 297, 384–5; Buxton and Barnes, *Death duties*, pp. 37–56.

30 *Hansard*, 3rd ser., 325, col. 199. In 1885, Gladstone had proposed to increase the death duty on real property *without* a compensating concession to the rates. See Buxton and Barnes, *Death duties*, pp. 27–8.

31 *Hansard*, 3rd ser., 325, cols. 204–5, 212.

32 *Hansard*, 3rd ser., 325, col. 205.

33 *Hansard*, 3rd ser., 325, 23 April 1888, cols. 206, 209–11.

34 This was a technical point: the sum on which duty was imposed was calculated from the annual value, and was not to exceed the amount charged on an annuity under the succession duty. The schedule of the succession duty provided values up to 95 years, whereas rent is a perpetual annuity. In other words, freehold land was valued as if it was leasehold. Further, building land was only charged at its agricultural value. See Buxton and Barnes, *Death duties*, pp. 31–33, 50.

35 Buxton and Barnes, *Death duties*, pp. 29–33.

36 Buxton and Barnes, *Death duties*, pp. 33–4.

37 This change in perceptions is analysed by Offer, *Property and politics 1870–1914*, chapters 12 and 13.

38 BL Add. MSS 48,650, Hamilton diaries, fos. 63–4, 26 February 1889; fo. 75, 12 March 1889; fo. 84, 26 March 1889; fo. 90, 2 April 1889.

39 BL Add. MSS 48,650, fos. 95–6, 11 April 1889.

40 BL Add. MSS 48,650, fo. 99, 15 April 1889; fo. 112, 30 April 1889.

41 BL Add. MSS 48,650, fos. 101–2, 16 April 1889.

42 BL Add. MSS 48,650, fos. 115–16, 4 May 1889.

43 BL Add. MSS 48,650, fo. 69, 5 February 1889; fos. 61–2, 24 February 1889; fo. 72, 9 March 1889.

44 See S. R. B. Smith, 'Public opinion, the navy and the City of London: the drive for British naval expansion in the late nineteenth century', *War and society*, 9 (1991), pp. 39–42.

45 This continued to be an issue: in 1895, the demands of the navy limited Harcourt's ability to offer tax concessions, and the government fell on a vote on the supply of cordite to the army which had been cut in order to pay for the navy. See D. Brooks (ed.), *The destruction of Lord Rosebery: from the diary of Sir Edward Hamilton, 1894–5*, London, 1986, pp. 82, 93, 110. See 5 March 1894, p. 117 where Hamilton reports a conversation with Gladstone. 'He referred again to the Navy question and denounced the proposals in as strong language as ever. "If", he said, "I stood alone in the world on this question, I could not be moved, so strongly am I convinced that this large increase to the Navy will lead to disaster in Europe – Europe is my watchword".' Also, on 22 March 1894 (p. 126), Hamilton reported that Gladstone 'broke out again on the subject in strong language. "I regard it", he said, "as the greatest and richest sacrifice ever made on the altar of militarism. It is absolute insanity. I can only apply my old phrase to the author of it 'mad or drunk'. I dread the effect which the proposals may have on Europe. The peace of Europe is my primary consideration. Financial considerations such as the

sounding of the death-knell to the Sinking Fund are merely secondary".'

46 Brooks (ed.), *Destruction*, p. 23.

47 Brooks (ed.), *Destruction*, (13 November 1894) p. 189.

48 Brooks (ed.), *Destruction*, (13 November 1894) p. 189; (28 November 1894) p. 193; (14 December 1894) p. 197; (11 January 1895) pp. 204–5.

49 Brooks (ed.), *Destruction*, (16 January 1895) p. 208.

50 Brooks (ed.), *Destruction*, p. 16.

51 Farrer, 'Sir William Harcourt's budget', pp. 153, 164.

52 T. H. Farrer, 'The imperial finance of the last four years', *Contemporary Review*, 58 (1890), p. 497.

53 K. Young, *Local politics and the rise of party*, Leicester, 1975, pp. 42, 223; P. Thompson, *Socialists, Liberals and Labour: the struggle for London, 1885–1914*, London, 1967, p. 90.

54 Bod. Lib. MS Harcourt dep. 187, fo. 126, memo by the executive committee of the London Liberal and Radical Union, 9 January 1893; and fos. 134–5, Resolutions passed at a meeting of the Council of the London Liberal and Radical Union, 8 May 1893.

55 Thompson, *Socialists, Liberals and Labour*, pp. 91–9; J. Davis, *Reforming London: the London government problem, 1855–1900*, Oxford, 1988, pp. 119–22.

56 LCC, Minutes of Proceedings, January–December 1889, Minutes of 21 May 1889, Report of the Local Government and Taxation Committee, 15 May 1889, pp. 352–3. The Report was drafted by Hobhouse and Farrer: see LCC/Min 8181. Minutes of 9 July 1889, Report of the Local Government and Taxation Committee, 26 June 1889, pp. 548–9.

57 Quoted in Davis, *Reforming London*, p. 122; see pp. 149–152 for the changes in the LCC.

58 Bod. Lib., MS Harcourt dep. 119, fos. 111–15, Farrer to Harcourt, 23 November 1892 and 11 November 1892 fos. 83–4; see also Farrer, 'Imperial finance', III, p. 924.

59 Bod. Lib. MS Harcourt dep. 119, fos. 111–15, Farrer to Harcourt, 23 November 1892; for Costelloe's doubts, see MS Harcourt dep. 187, B. F. C. Costelloe, 'memorandum as to the finance of the London County Council', October 1892, fos. 86–93.

60 MS Harcourt dep. 199, fos. 111–15, Farrer to Harcourt, 23 November 1892.

61 Farrer, 'Imperial finance', III, pp. 923–7.

62 Bod. Lib., MS Harcourt dep. 187, B. F. C. Costelloe, 'Memoranda as to the finance of the London County Council', October 1892, fos. 86–93; MS Harcourt dep. 187, fos. 18–19.

63 LCC Minutes of Proceedings July–December 1892, Adjourned Report of the Local Government and Taxation Committee, 16 November 1892, 29 November 1892, pp. 1122–5 and 1 December 1892, pp. 1142–4. The LCC continued to press for this policy, and in 1898 prepared a bill for submission to parliament: see LCC Minutes of Proceedings, July–December 1898, 12 July 1898, pp. 865–6; LCC Minutes of Proceedings, September–December 1900, 18 December 1900, pp. 1724–6.

64 Bod. Lib., MS Harcourt dep. 187, fos. 127–31, memorial to Harcourt, 23 January 1893.

65 Bod. Lib., MS Harcourt dep. 221, Farrer to Harcourt, 25 November 1892, fos. 87–8.

66 Bod. Lib., MS Harcourt dep. 221, Farrer to Harcourt, 25 December 1892, fos. 198–202; MS Harcourt dep. 119, Harcourt to Farrer, fos. 116–17, 24 November 1892 and fos. 203–4, 28 December 1892.

67 Rosebery, *The Times*, 6 May 1899, quoted in H. C. G. Matthew, *The Liberal imperialists: the ideas and politics of a post-Gladstonian élite*, Oxford, 1973, p. 130.

68 Matthew, *Liberal imperialists*, pp. 130–3.

69 R. B. Haldane, 'The Liberal party and its prospects', *Contemporary Review*, January 1888, quoted in Matthew, *Liberal imperialists*, p. 130.

70 B. Webb, *Our partnership*, p. 225, for 1 November 1901.
71 Bod. Lib., MS Harcourt dep. 406, fos. 88–90, 2 April 1894.
72 BL Add. MS 48,651, fo. 14, 15 June 1889; and 48,652, fo. 42, 26 January 1890.
73 BL Add. MS 48,651, fo. 95, 15 September 1889; 48,653, fo. 86, 25 July 1890.
74 BL Add. MS 48,650, fo. 114, 2 May 1889.
75 Buxton and Barnes, *Death duties*, p. 67.
76 Buxton and Barnes, *Death duties*, p. 68.
77 Buxton and Barnes, *Death duties*, pp. 69–70.
78 Buxton, *Finance and politics*, II, p. 173.
79 Buxton and Barnes, *Death duties*, p. 74.
80 Buxton, *Finance and politics*, II, p. 173.
81 *Hansard*, 5th ser., 170 col. 622, 26 April 1863.
82 Bod. Lib., MS Harcourt dep. 383, Lewis Harcourt journals, fos. 2–3, 19 July 1892 and fos. 20–2, 21 July 1892.
83 Bod. Lib., MS Harcourt dep. 122, fos. 21–7, Memorial to Sir William Harcourt, 12 January 1894. The 'free breakfast table' was dreaded by Hamilton, for 'innumerable electors now-a-days would go wholly untaxed ... The soundest of doctrines is that taxation should involve representation: not much less sound appears to me to be the inverse doctrine, representation should involve taxation (of some kind, however light)'. (BL Add. MS 48,652, fo. 23, 4 January 1890).
84 Bod. Lib., MS Harcourt dep. 383, fo. 22, 21 July 1892; 389, fos. 27–8, 4 January 1893, fo. 29, 5 January 1893; 391, fo. 33, 15 February 1893, fos. 45–6, 17 February 1893; 392, fo. 49, 11 March 1893, fos. 88–90, 24 March 1893; MS Harcourt dep. 222, fos. 42–3, memorandum to Cabinet, 3 March 1893.
85 Bod. Lib., MS Harcourt dep. 120, fos. 163–6, Harcourt to Buxton, 18 April 1893.
86 Bod. Lib., MS Harcourt dep. 392, fos. 96–7, 28 March 1893; 396, fos. 18–19, 25 October 1893, fos. 36–7, 3 November 1893; 397, fos. 97–9, 27 December 1893; 398, fos. 1–8, 27 December 1893.
87 Bod. Lib., MS Harcourt dep. 57, fos. 55–9, Harcourt to Rosebery, 23 March 1894.
88 Bod. Lib., MS Harcourt dep. 398, fo. 8, 27 December 1893, fo. 17, 1 January 1894; 399, fos. 27–8, 12 January 1894; dep. 57, fos. 55–9, Harcourt to Rosebery. By March 1894, he was proposing an allowance of £150 up to £400 and £100 between £400 and £500.
89 Bod. Lib., MS Harcourt dep. 399, fos. 43–4, 14 January 1894.
90 Bod. Lib., MS Harcourt dep. 399, fo. 24, 30 January 1894 and fos. 45–6, 7 February 1894.
91 Bod. Lib., MS Harcourt dep. 70, fos. 40–3, notes on surtax, 1 February 1894[?].
92 Bod. Lib., MS Harcourt dep. 70, fos. 56–7, Harcourt to Milner, 19 February 1894.
93 Bod. Lib., MS Harcourt dep. 406, fo. 21, 16 March 1894.
94 F. L. Robinson, *Some opinions on certain recently revived propositions suggested with a view to a more equal incidence of the income tax* (printed for official use, 1891).
95 Bod. Lib., MS Harcourt dep. 70, fo. 160, Memo on various proposed changes in the income tax.
96 Bod. Lib., MS Harcourt dep. 70, fos. 160–6, Memo on various proposed changes in the income tax.
97 Bod. Lib., MS Harcourt dep. 69, fos. 37–41, Milner to Harcourt, 15 April 1893.
98 Robinson, *Some opinions*, p. 13.
99 Bod. Lib., MS Harcourt dep. 69, fos. 37–41, Milner to Harcourt, 15 April 1893.
100 Bod. Lib., MS Harcourt dep. 70, fo. 63, Milner to Harcourt, 20 February 1894.
101 Bod. Lib., MS Harcourt dep. 405, fos. 57–8, 10 March 1894.
102 Bod. Lib., MS Harcourt dep. 65, fos. 1–4, E. Hamilton, 7 April 1894; he also made some 'rather fanciful' calculations for income from real property in MS Harcourt dep. 65, fos. 78–82, 13 April 1894. In 1906, the same point was still being made by H. W. Primrose of the Inland Revenue: PRO, IR74/11, 'Note as to methods of estimating the annual tax on property which would be equivalent to the present occasional taxes on transmission of property at death', 3 July 1906.
103 Bod. Lib., MS Harcourt dep. 65, fos. 1–4, 7 April 1894.

104 Bod. Lib., MS Harcourt dep. 70, Memo on various proposed changes in the income tax, fos. 166–7. Gladstone had proposed the use of a graduated house duty in the 1860s: see BL Add. MS 48,654, fo. 57, 25 November 1890. The case for the use of death duties as a means of graduation rather than using a declaration of total income was accepted by Buxton and Barnes, *Death duties*, pp. 72–4; and in 1890 the Political Economy Club accepted the principle of graduation, 'the fact being that the "Death duties" alone offer a field for its extension' (BL Add. MS 48,652, 8 March 1890, fos. 78–9). See also Farrer, 'Sir William Harcourt's budget', pp. 156, 158–60 where he argued that, failing graduation at an earlier stage, the death duty was a form of deferred income tax at the final stage.
105 Bod. Lib., MS Harcourt dep. 70, Harcourt to Milner, 10 March 1894.
106 Bod. Lib., MS Harcourt dep. 70, fos. 172–9, Milner to Harcourt, 12 March 1894.
107 Bod. Lib., MS Harcourt dep. 70, fos. 142–3, Welby to Harcourt, 11 March 1894.
108 Bod. Lib., MS Harcourt dep. 70, fos. 254–5, Milner to L. Harcourt, 30 March 1894.
109 Bod. Lib., MS Harcourt dep. 69, fos. 100–10, A. Milner, 30 April 1893.
110 Bod. Lib., MS Harcourt dep. 69, fos. 79–93, Note on differential income tax, A. Milner, 27 April 1893.
111 Bod. Lib., MS Harcourt dep. 70, fos. 144–67, Memo on various proposed changes in the income tax, A. Milner, 9 March 1894.
112 Bod. Lib., MS Harcourt dep. 70, fos. 186–201, Memo by A. Milner, 16 March 1894.
113 *Birmingham Daily Post*, 23 April 1894, quoted in Brooks, *Destruction*, p. 24.
114 Bod. Lib., MS Harcourt dep. 57, fos. 77–89, Rosebery, 3 April 1894.
115 Quoted in Gardiner, *Life*, II, p. 287.
116 Bod. Lib., MS Harcourt dep. 57, fos. 93–109, Harcourt, 4 April 1894.
117 Offer, *Property and politics*, p. 403.

8

WILLOUGHBY DE BROKE AND WALTER LONG: ENGLISH LANDED SOCIETY AND POLITICAL EXTREMISM, 1912–14

DAVID SPRING

Historians are agreed that extremism left its mark on English politics in the years 1912–14, and was most evident in the politics of the Conservative party. But there agreement would seem to end. Which individuals or groups (political and social) within the Conservative party perpetrated extremist acts has not been precisely ascertained – nor, for that matter, has the notion of political extremism been precisely defined. This paper does not thoroughly resolve these matters. Its main intention is a narrow one: to examine in detail the politics of two landed politicians, Willoughby de Broke and Walter Long, the latter in more detail than the former. A secondary intention is to throw some light on the nature and degree of political extremism to be found in English landed society. This part of the paper is both brief and tentative.

Of the two men, Willoughby de Broke and Walter Long, the former has the greater reputation among historians as an extremist. If the Radical Right (as extremism in the pre-World War I Conservative party is sometimes misleadingly designated) is assigned a leader, he is apt to be Willoughby de Broke. Walter Long, on the other hand, is apt to be judged as the more moderate in his politics.[1] The upshot of the paper will be to question this view, finding in Walter Long more of the extremist than in Willoughby de Broke, and venturing on the strength of this discovery some estimate of landed extremism generally.

I

Richard Grenville Verney, 19th Lord Willoughby de Broke (born 1869), succeeded his father in 1902, coming into possession of some 18,000 acres dispersed over seven English and Welsh counties, the principal estates being the home estate of Compton Verney of 12,621 acres in Warwickshire, and an outlying estate in Lincolnshire of about 3,000 acres.[2] Financially this large property was in some trouble in 1902 when Willoughby came into it. Precisely how much trouble is not clear; but enough, it would appear, to prompt renting the big house at Compton Verney to Sir Ernest Cassel, the Anglo-German financier, in 1895. Willoughby and his family did not return to the big house until 1910. How much of a restoration of the family fortunes this signified there is no way of knowing: not all that complete, it would seem, given the sale of the Lincolnshire estate in 1914.[3]

Much more is known about Willoughby the landed politician than about Willoughby the great landowner. During his lifetime his political masters found him useful: he was thought to have some gift for public speaking, as well as the makings of a good party whip (although he never became one).[4] After his death, historians in the 1930s like R. C. K. Ensor and George Dangerfield thought poorly of him. But more recently some historians have markedly enhanced Willoughby's reputation: one has seen him as 'a thoughtful and intelligent writer', another as a 'major political figure'.[5]

Contemporary opinion was probably closer to the truth. Take, for a start, Willoughby as a political thinker. Admittedly he had a minor journalistic talent, mainly deployed in Leo Maxse's spirited if sometimes outrageous *National Review*. But what he wrote was jejune, if occasionally not without charm or wit. Willoughby himself described his political thought as 'the crude views of a Tory visionary'.[6] A good deal of it went into calling for a new Tory philosophy without much in the way of explaining what that philosophy was. Again he put the matter correctly: his was a philosophy that did without 'the terrible thing called a programme, or even ... a concrete policy ... [but instead was] an appeal to the old British conception of Justice, Unity and Freedom'.[7] However, even Willoughby on occasion found it necessary to ventilate a programme, as he did once for Leo Maxse in 1910: 'Tariff Reform, Social Reform, Government by King, Lords and Commons, and a limited empire is a programme that is bound to prevail'.[8] But this bare recital said little about the strength of Willoughby's commitment – which in the case of both Tariff Reform and Social Reform was not striking – nor did it point to much in the way of extremism.

A better place to look for Willoughby's extremism, and where it has usually been found, is in the tactical pronouncements and performance of the party politician. Willoughby the party politician got off to a slow start. As a member of the House of Commons, 1895–1900, he spoke infrequently. As a member of the House of Lords after 1902, he spent his first five years there in almost as speechless a state. Then, in 1907, his political career came to life. The occasion was a contemplated reform of the House of Lords. Willoughby was hostile to any reform of the Lords, however moderate, even when advocated by a fellow Tory peer. For him the House of Lords was the chief bulwark against revolution, the sacred Ark of the Tory Covenant. Thus he had no hesitation in backing the Lords' rejection of Lloyd George's 1909 Budget; and equally decisive and even more energetic was his opposition to the 1911 Parliament Bill and its drastic limitation of the Lords' veto. The Parliament Bill prompted what was the most sustained political effort of Willoughby's life. As the Diehards' whip he would never work so hard again. Here it was that he won notice as an extremist – although it needs remarking that Willoughby the Diehard in 1911 stayed well within the bounds of the Constitution.

Willoughby, the founder in March 1913 of the British League for the Support of Ulster and the Union, did not. The purpose of his League was the strengthening of the illegal activities of Sir Edward Carson and his Ulster Covenanters in their resistance to the Liberal Government's third Home Rule bill of April 1912. The founding manifesto of the League announced that Irish Home Rule would harm not only Ulster but also Nationalist Ireland and the United Kingdom generally, fatal to the latter's 'safety' and to 'the consolidation of the Empire'. Attached to the manifesto was a list of the League's chief supporters, numbering 100 peers and 140 Members of Parliament.[9] By September 1913, according to Willoughby, agents for the League were to be found 'in practically every constituency in England, Scotland and Wales'; large meetings were being planned in Liverpool and London; and men were being enrolled 'who are ready to go over to Ireland, supposing the Bill passes without a general election'. He concluded defiantly that 'in the absence of the old Constitution the only thing left is physical force'.[10]

This recital of intention would satisfy most definitions of extremism. Yet on looking more closely at what Willoughby's League did in its first year, rather than noting what Willoughby said it would do, its significance as an agency of extremism diminishes appreciably. Large claims were made for the number of men enlisted: something like 10,000 by December 1913, it was said.[11] But whether most of these men were any more than names on a list, how many were armed and systematically instructed and drilled, remain unanswered questions. Some arms and men no doubt made their way to Ulster; and the League had a full-time Headquarters staff to arrange such matters. But both the Ulstermen and even some of Willoughby's associates found the League and its efforts unimpressive. A spokesman for the Ulstermen in December 1913 declared 'the British League [to be] of very little use ... We have had oceans of correspondence with them ... [but] we shall have to rely on ourselves for the most part'.[12] Basil Peto, one of Willoughby's chief associates, corroborated this judgment. He found the League 'inadequate to the situation and must be strengthened, developed and supported'.[13]

The League never became adequate to the situation. In 1914 it was supplanted, its work falling into much more capable hands. Some weeks earlier, F. S. Oliver, man of letters and man of business, had had occasion to comment on Willoughby's activities. He was explaining to a friend the several alternatives English Conservatives might resort to in the case of Irish Home Rule. A 'rising or rebellion' was one – but one that needed thought. 'My friends in Warwickshire and Worcestershire', he went on, 'tell me that Willoughby is circularising them all (as it might be Prince Rupert!) to get their horses ready and practice with firearms ... I rather suspect that nothing serious is being done at all. When you come to revolutions or even political campaigns genius and gallantry won't carry you very far, unless a certain number of quiet blokes have previously sat down and worked out things on the lines of Bradshaw and Mr Whiteley's emporium'.[14]

The 'quiet blokes' were about to sit down and work things out. They were Alfred, Lord Milner, once High Commissioner to South Africa, and Leo Amery, once *The Times* special correspondent to South Africa and now, in 1913, Member of Parliament for Birmingham South. Earlier in the year Amery's name was to be found in the list of Willoughby's supporters on the founding of the British League. Probably on Amery's instigation, Willoughby himself early in 1914 wrote to Milner, seeking his advice on how best to assist Carson and his Ulstermen. It so happened that some weeks earlier Milner had decided to set on foot a major enterprise with the same object in view. He and Amery had for some time been discussing the matter. Characteristically Milner took little time in deciding whether it was profitable to take Willoughby's offer of collaboration seriously. He decided not to. As he wrote to Amery about Willoughby and his associates:

> I have no confidence in the judgment of any of that crowd ... in their gassing around in a perfectly indefinite way, and pinning their faith on an absurd and impracticable expedient like sending a handful of men over to Ireland, when there are not nearly arms enough for men already there.[15]

Milner was in a hurry. He needed a ready-made organisation quickly. Instead of Willoughby's he chose Walter Long's Union Defence League, set up in 1907 to resist Home Rule for Ireland. Given Milner's needs his choice was a sensible one. He sensed quite rightly that Willoughby lacked seriousness: he lacked the stamina of the genuine political animal. He was at best the occasional politician, far more in love with the hunting field and English country life than he was with the daily grind of the professional politician. One has only to dip into Willoughby's incomplete autobiography, *The Passing Years*, to see this. The book is a moving lament for the waning of landed society, its life being slowly crushed, as Willoughby put it, 'by the new formidable symptoms of industrialism, and the untoward manifestations of the thing called democracy that were destined . . . to react so hideously upon the nation at large'.[16] In a list of the leading personages in landed society, arranged in order of importance, Willoughby chose to put the Master of Foxhounds and the agricultural landlords well before the Member of Parliament. That was no accident on his part. Walter Long would have chosen otherwise, although he was both foxhunter and landowner himself.

Thus Milner, Amery and Long set up a formidable alliance, that would shortly set in being Milner's League of British Covenanters. This was to be the working centre of Conservative extremism. Willoughby did not disband his own League, but it was never more than loosely associated with Milner's effort. Long, on the other hand, worked closely with Milner, from early in February 1914 until the coming of the European war.

II

Like Willoughby, Walter Long (born in 1854) inherited a great landed property, in Long's case of 15,404 acres, 13,829 in Wiltshire, at Rood Ashton the home estate.[17] Unlike Willoughby he had by 1914 sold off more than half of it, something like 9,000 acres. He had sold 1,300 acres as early as 1876, 150 acres in 1883, 3,800 acres in 1905, and the same amount again in 1911.[18] What informed this policy is not clear: probably a combination of indebtedness and a reluctance to be overburdened with landed property which became increasingly unattractive financially with the onset of agricultural depression. From the 1880s onwards Long had been in search of other forms of property – building sites and rentals in Canadian cities, for example.[19] He had also taken to picking up directorships in English firms, among them the Great Western Railway from 1894 to 1905. In short, he was still a *rentier* in 1914, but rather less a landed one, although the core of the Rood Ashton estate was still intact. Nor, if we take his memoirs (written in the 1920s) as evidence, did he offer himself to the world as anything other than a Wiltshire squire. Compared with Willoughby, however, it is clear that he was less rooted in the English countryside.

This phenomenon of landed transformation may also be traced in Long's political career. He entered Parliament in 1880, representing North Wiltshire, a member of what he designated the 'Country Gentleman Party'.[20] This species of politician he summed up aptly: they were amateurs, rooted in the locality, chiefly agrarian in outlook and interest, spoke rarely in the House, and were unambitious for office. Long soon left their company: he was ambitious, had energy and sought work. By 1885 he had become Parliamentary Secretary to the Local Government Board; by 1893 he had cut loose from the moorings of locality and landed influence, sitting for the West Derby division of Liverpool from 1893 to 1900, for South Bristol from 1900 to 1906, for South County Dublin from 1906 to 1910, and then for the Strand Division of Middlesex where he was still seated in 1914. By then, of 34 years in the House of Commons he had spent 21 not as a member of the 'Country Gentleman Party' but as a landowner-turned-professional politician. In this respect he differed much from Willoughby de Broke.

Long, the professional politician, not only loosened his ties to his ancestral acres and his Wiltshire background but also climbed to a place of power in the Tory party. On this he had set his heart early, again unlike Willoughby who seems not to have yearned for anything more than a backbencher's existence. Long was in the Conservative Cabinet at the relatively early age of 40, when in 1895 Lord Salisbury formed his third administration and appointed Long as President of the Board of Agriculture. In 1900 he became President of the Local Government Board, and in 1905 served briefly as Chief Secretary for Ireland. However brief his tenure, this office crystallised Long's deep involvement in Irish affairs and his intense opposition to Irish Home Rule.

In 1907 he founded the Union Defence League, an extra-parliamentary organisation devoted to preserving the union between England and Ireland, with its headquarters in London. The League revealed two things about Long the politician: first, the centrality of the Irish Question in his political agenda; and second, his flair for political organisation, an uncommon one to be found in a landed politician, and again a sign of his professional stance. He busied himself in a variety of extra-parliamentary associations, some of which he founded, some of which he joined, and in all of which he played a prominent part. There was the Union Defence League, the Budget Protest League of 1909, the Central Landowners' Association, the Primrose League, and the League of British Covenanters.

The Union Defence League took first place. It provided Long with a permanent power base in the Tory party, a prime vehicle for his political ambitions, which after 1906 included the party's leadership, and a necessary counterweight to his political rivals, the Chamberlains, who had as their power base the Tariff Reform League. Long on occasion confessed himself a moderate Tariff Reformer, but confessed as readily that Tariff Reform meant far less to him than did the union with Ireland: 'I believe that if we get financial Reform and lose the Union we shall be ten times worse off as an Empire than we are now', he once put it.[21] Accordingly Long's principal political card, to be flourished when needed, was the preservation of the union with Ireland, a cause for which he became a self-appointed public guardian, sharing this task with Sir Edward Carson and the sixth Lord Londonderry. He was not, however, like Carson an Irishman born and bred, nor like Londonderry a great Irish (Ulster) as well as English landowner. Indeed his Irishness was a bit tenuous, being limited to having an Irish mother and an Irish wife, and serving as Irish Chief Secretary for ten months and sitting for South Dublin for four years.

Long's Union Defence League came to the fore conspicuously once the Parliament Act of 1911 had passed and the imminence of another Irish Home Rule Bill was assured. Long had not joined the Diehards in the Parliament Bill crisis, remaining loyal (unlike Willoughby) to the leadership of Balfour and Lansdowne. Also unlike Willoughby, he seems to have relished the decks being cleared for the struggle over Ireland, to which he looked forward as one the Conservatives were bound to win. As he wrote to Lady Londonderry, 'I firmly believe that if our Parliament Bill is passed and Home Rule Bill produced I believe we can knock them [the Liberals] out in two years and save the whole situation'.[22]

Such was the scenario, described with Long's characteristic bluntness, that he was to act on until the coming of war in 1914. As early as the spring of 1911, months before the final act in the Parliament Bill struggle, Long began to rally the anti-Home Rule forces. Jointly with Carson, he obtained for his own Union Defence League monopoly power to manage the anti-Home Rule campaign outside of Ireland. The League held meetings, acted as a sort of think-tank on the Irish Question for Conservative Members of Parliament, and raised money, both for the League and Carson's Ulstermen.[23] By the end of 1911 and the start of 1912, Long and Carson set on foot a series of large meetings, at first in Lancashire and Cheshire, then most impressively of all a giant meeting at Balmoral in Ulster, some days before the Liberal Government introduced its Home Rule Bill. There, in a brief speech, Long managed to match even Bonar Law, the new party leader, in the intemperance of his remarks: 'If they [presumably the Government]', Long is reported to have declared, 'were going to put Sir Edward Carson and Lord Londonderry into the dock, they would have to find one large enough to hold the whole Unionist party'.[24]

This threatening note, the threat of illegal action, is to be found also in Long's private correspondence. It went hand in hand with a refusal to accept any compromise, such as the exclusion of parts of Ulster from the operation of the Home Rule Bill. Long was therefore much distressed by the private negotiations between Carson and Bonar Law, on the one hand, and Asquith, the Liberal Prime Minister, on the other, which ensued in the latter months of 1913. Long distrusted not only the Liberals but also Bonar Law, whom he rightly took to be growing uneasy with his own policy of extremism.

On 7 November 1913, Long wrote to Bonar Law the sort of letter he was in the habit of writing: a letter in which he portrayed himself as the voice of the Conservative party, which to a degree he was, given his assiduous cultivation of backbench opinion. 'I think I ought to let you know', he wrote, 'that I have seen a great many of our most reliable men and their unanimous opinion is that if Asquith makes any overtures and we accept them the result would be absolutely *fatal* to our party'.[25] A fortnight later, he was still 'very much alarmed at the prospect of some compromise being arrived at', and concluded that 'the only thing to do is to fight them in Parliament and out, to make their government of the country an impossibility, and to compel them to face the electors, as no doubt we could do if we decided to resort to this policy – a very serious step to take, but one which circumstances may easily justify'.[26]

By mid-January, if not earlier, Bonar Law concluded, much to Long's satisfaction, that negotiations with Asquith were getting nowhere. Both Bonar Law and Long thereupon decided to resort to other means, to make the 'government of the country an impossibility', as Long had put it. Bonar Law turned to considering the possibility of so amending the Army Annual Act as to force the Government to a general election. As a member of the Conservative Shadow Cabinet, Long was privy to this action which was taken up for consideration early in February 1914. At the same time he chose his own course of action. This was to work closely with Alfred Milner, the foremost architect of extremism, next to Sir Edward Carson.

By December 1913 Milner had finally decided to re-enter politics in a formidable fashion. Unlike Long, an intellectual and a visionary, and deeply hostile to the parliamentary game, he shared Long's conviction that Liberalism was the enemy and Irish Home Rule the issue best suited to defeat it. This he planned to do by strengthening Carson's Covenanters: he would bring them money to buy much-needed arms; he would sow disaffection in the Army to make impossible the enforcement of Home Rule; and he would organise a campaign in mainland Britain to educate public opinion on how and why Home Rule was to be vanquished. In all these efforts Long, already a veteran in the war against Home Rule, was Milner's natural ally.

His first task was to raise money, for Ulster as well as for the campaign closer to home. Through his Union Defence League he had already been raising money for Ulster. Now in February 1914 he redoubled his efforts, assisted by a highly unusual public meeting called by the City of London Conservative Association on whose platform foregathered Lord Rothschild, uncrowned king of the City, Arthur Balfour, one of two City Members of Parliament since 1906, and Sir Edward Carson. What an extraordinary scene this was: at the heart of the greatest financial centre in the world, the 'Ulster pirate' (as the American Ambassador to the Court of St James, Walter Hines Page, had called Carson) appealed to an audience of bankers for financial aid in resisting the will of His Majesty's Government. He explained that he had recently authorised an expenditure of sixty to eighty thousand pounds, presumably for arms, and he asked for their help in making possible such expenditure.[27]

Long's goal in February 1914 was to collect £250,000 to £300,000, a large sum even for the Conservative Central Office.[28] The story of his effort to amass it is an incomplete one. He kept a special account for what he called his 'Ulster Fund' with his bankers in the City of London, Cocks, Biddulph and Co.[29] Long's account was in the name of himself and the Hon. Thomas Egerton, a younger son of the Earl of Ellesmere and a partner in the bank. Unfortunately Cocks, Biddulph and Co. no longer exist, having been absorbed by Barclays in 1919. Their ledgers and private papers, however, do exist, in Barclays' possession but made inaccessible by a hundred-year prohibition.[30] The complete story of Long's fund therefore will not likely emerge until the year 2014. But some useful facts have been uncovered. Long had collected £170,000 by May 1914, if not earlier. He went on collecting substantial funds until the outbreak of war: enough to pay for the Larne gun-running and the forming of a special élite force of 3,000 men, stationed in Belfast and in receipt of regular pay. A *Manchester Guardian* correspondent guessed that the Ulster Volunteer Force cost over £5,000 a week to maintain.[31] All in all, although the need was large, it would seem that money was forthcoming, and that Long was satisfied it was well spent. As he observed in June 1914, 'it is the armed resistance of Ulster which is [delaying the Liberal Government in putting the Home Rule Bill on the Statute Book and] making the defeat of the Government possible'.[32]

Long also turned a calculating eye on another Army, that of His Majesty's Government. Like Carson's Army, it too might be used to resist Home Rule. Bonar Law's idea of amending the Army Annual Act was one way of doing so. What he had in mind was highly unusual: to so amend the Act in the House of Lords 'that the Government would be unable to use the Army in Ulster [to enforce Home Rule] until after a General Election'.[33] This proposal Bonar Law put before his Shadow Cabinet, of which Long was a member. On 12 March the Shadow Cabinet agreed provisionally to amend the Act, 'but to leave details and decision as to moment of acting to Lansdowne and [Bonar Law]'. Of the several members of the Shadow Cabinet, Walter Long seems to have been the most decided defender of such action, apart from Carson, although he 'deprecated precipitate action or announcement' on the ground that the Government's position was 'untenable, and their proposals impossible'.[34]

Perhaps Long sensed by 12 March – what was in fact to happen shortly – that the Army itself would declare its opposition to being asked to enforce Home Rule in Ulster. Something like this took place, of course, in the following week in the so-called Curragh Mutiny, better known now as the Curragh Incident, thus making unnecessary the amendment of the Army Act. Although what happened at the Curragh at the start was not technically a Mutiny, since officers disobeyed no orders, the Curragh brought to the surface and set on foot what has recently been described as 'an unprecedented attempt to bring the army into the political field as a counterweight to the elected house of Parliament'.[35] Here Walter Long played a leading part, inferior among politicians only to Milner, Carson and Bonar Law.

Milner had once unburdened himself – to Geoffrey Robinson (later Dawson), editor of *The Times* and earlier Milner's private secretary in South Africa – on what best to do with the Army. Milner had occasion to regret that Unionist leaders were soft on the Army, reluctant to say what needed saying.[36] He wrote:

> I wonder whether Unionists, who talk of 'supporting Ulster' if the Government proceed to extremities without an election have ever thought what they meant by these high-sounding declarations. Did they merely mean that they would hold indignation meetings, and write letters to the Press? What other *support* could they give the Ulstermen, if the Army were sent to shoot them, than to tell the Army that *it ought not to go*. The whole case is given away, when it is admitted that such orders to the Army could be 'lawful' orders in any but a technical sense.[37]

So far as the available evidence is concerned, Long did not vouchsafe posterity so blunt a statement. On the other hand, the available evidence would suggest that he was not averse to encouraging disaffection in the Army. If this was Milner's intention, it seems also to have been Long's. After all, he did, at a critical moment, assure Milner that 'I approve and will support anything you do'.[38]

Long, of course, being landed, slipped readily into the role. It was almost a family affair: the Army's way of life was landed, and many of its officers came of landed families.[39] Two of Long's brothers were Army officers, and so were a son-in-law and a son, the last being stationed at the

Curragh, serving in a cavalry regiment under Hubert Gough. The officers were traditionally law-abiding. But they were also inherently Conservative, thus facing a distressing prospect, that of putting down a rebellious Ulster, a Protestant and imperialist Ulster asking only to be left alone, free of subjection to a Catholic, anti-imperialist Dublin. By late 1913 the Army's distress had become a chronic malaise, known to the King, the Government and the Opposition. By November, Long was urging Carson to talk with his son about Ulster and the Army: 'if I may venture to say so, I think it would not be a waste of your time'.[40] Some days later, in reply to a brother who presumably had proposed some sort of anti-Government demonstration on the part of the Army, Long observed:

Am afraid it would not do. The action of the soldiers must be spontaneous, and if any action were taken such as you suggest, the cry would go up that we 'worked them'. I should like to have a talk with you about this – it is becoming *very* serious and will require *most* careful thinking out.[41]

Milner presumably did the thinking, and came up with his manifesto, the British Covenant, which was widely published in the British Press on 3 March 1914. It was sponsored by 20 non-political but eminent Englishmen. The British Covenant had two parts: the first was standard Tory criticism of Irish Home Rule; the second was an unusual declaration, intended as a mass collective statement, which citizens of the United Kingdom were invited to sign. This declaration, to Milner's mind the chief item in the Covenant, announced that a signatory

shall hold myself justified in taking or supporting any action that may be effective to prevent [the Home Rule Bill] being put into operation, and more particularly to prevent the armed forces of the Crown being used to deprive the people of Ulster of their rights as citizens of the United Kingdom.

Equally startling was the first name on the list of the Covenant's 20 sponsors – the name of the Earl Roberts, senior Field Marshal of the British Army, the most popular living soldier in 1914. No doubt it was a name meant by Milner to fix the Army's as well as civilian attention, to tell soldiers that they should not be asked to put down Ulstermen, as he had earlier written to Geoffrey Robinson.

From the start Walter Long vigorously promoted the Covenant through his Union Defence League, soliciting signatures, urging others to do so, seeking 'co-operation in making the "Declaration" widely known, so that we can obtain for it a vast number of signatures'.[42] By 6 March he reported to Carson a 'rush to sign the Covenant – we are really almost overpowered'.[43] When some of Milner's friends and sympathisers, among them F. S. Oliver, refused to sign, being put off by the Declaration concerning the Army, Long publicly hastened to allay their disquiet: signatories were only being asked, he contended (somewhat unconvincingly), to register their disapproval of Government policy.[44] He also assured a mass audience in Hyde Park, that if rioting occurred in Belfast, 'and if the soldiers were called upon to put them down, they would do their duty, and we should applaud them in the act . . .'[45]

But privately Long spoke otherwise. Some days after officers had resigned at the Curragh, he urged Bonar Law to announce that the Opposition would guarantee such officers the restoration of their rank and pension. It is interesting to note that Sir Edward Carson, when similarly enjoined, rejected such a step. Equally interesting is Long's justification: it is 'the least we can do for men who are, after all, only following the lead we have given them'.[46] How officers had interpreted this 'lead' may be gathered from the letters of Long's son, written from the Curragh on 26–27 March to his father. As the son put it on the 26th: 'The great point we were fighting for has been gained whatever happens and that is they cannot now ask the army to coerce Ulster'. On the 27th he wrote: 'We are now carrying on with everything exactly as if nothing had happened. The country now knows what the army thinks'.[47]

Although Milner's (and Long's) Covenant was not altogether responsible for the Army's knowing its mind, there is no doubt that young Long was correct – the Army would not obey its political masters if ordered 'to coerce Ulster'. Even so, however, there was no assurance that knowledge of this fact would persuade the Government to call a general election. In the probable event that it would not, and spurred on by the popularity of the Covenant, Milner set on foot his League of British Covenanters, of which Walter Long was Chairman. Milner's League worked closely with Long's Union Defence League, and both worked increasingly closely with the Conservative Central Office. The first act of the British Covenanters was to organise a national campaign of mass meetings to instruct the electorate in the iniquities of Irish Home Rule, chief of which was the predicament of Protestant Ulster, now declared to be in danger of extermination by a ruthless Liberal Government.

Long had eagerly joined Milner and Carson in the unprecedented work of stretching the limits of the Constitution and bringing the parliamentary machine to a standstill. All that was still needed to force a general election, he calculated, was a concerted drive not only by the League of British Covenanters but also by the leading lights of the Conservative Front Bench to persuade the British people that it was faced by a stark choice: a general election or civil war. This would be the object of numerous meetings, gathering momentum in May and June of 1914. Such meetings were held and, in a retrospective view in early July, Long looked back with satisfaction to what had been achieved. There had been some 239 meetings, 'addressed by all the chief speakers on the Unionist side', clearly demonstrating that what the country wanted was a general election: 'Never in all my long Parliamentary experience', he maintained, 'have I known the desire and demand for a general election so universal, so strong'.[48]

This strategy of forcing the Liberal Government to a general election – and of carefully avoiding any further negotiations with it – remained Long's until the coming of European war in August. He was therefore utterly hostile even to the last-ditch effort at compromise through negotiation, the Buckingham Palace Conference, sponsored by the King.[49] However, Asquith and his colleagues saw things differently. If they were resolved on anything in the summer of 1914, it was *not* to have an election. After all, they might well lose it, and their ambitious legislative agenda was not fully realised. And even if they won it, there was no guarantee of Ulster's acquiescence. Asquith therefore set his heart on settlement through negotiation, although by no means assured of a peaceful outcome.

Nonetheless Long persisted in pressing on, couching his language in military metaphor, by now widespread fashion in British parliamentary politics. If a campaign of mass meetings failed to bring the Liberals to the polls, he was all for forcing them there by more unusual means. Here Milner and Carson showed Long the way. Both heightened their posture of intimidation and threat. Carson, with Long at his side, in mid-July meetings in Ulster, demanded the exclusion from Home Rule of no less than all nine counties of Ulster – a demand which the House of Lords also made in its Amending Bill. More than that, Carson took a step closer to setting up his Provisional Government, which in effect would mean Ulster's seceding from the United Kingdom. By 11 July, the Ulster Unionist Council became the Ulster Provisional Government, with the latter's executive given unlimited power to act on its own initiative. The executive, however, gave no signal to secede.[50] In the last two weeks of July, Milner and Long were apparently nudging it to do so, Milner by raising more money, and Long looking to provide credit and an Ulster currency.[51] But the abrupt coming of war ended these efforts: Carson's Provisional Government was not to govern, and his Army died not in Belfast but on the Somme; and Asquith's Government remained undisturbed by the imminence of a general election.

Yet a Conservative victory of sorts was won, however little it was appreciated by the embattled Opposition at the time. In mid-September 1914, faced by the deadlock over Ireland, the Government enacted its Home Rule Bill, but postponed its operation and left the Ulster Question unresolved until after the war. The Government's compromise bought time. It also killed Home Rule.

III

A final question needs to be considered. How typical of great landowners similar to himself was Long's record of extremism? Before offering a tentative answer, we must be clear what Long's extremism amounted to. Admittedly he was not seeking to destroy parliamentary institutions. On occasion in a fit of petulance he declared his abhorrence of party politics – as in late May 1914, in a letter to Bonar Law, he announced: 'I am sick and tired of Politics, I really loathe the present House of Commons and modern form of Parliamentary tactics, and should be thankful to be quit of it all'.[52] But this was the outburst of an elderly man, recently ill, and at the best of times given to anger and carelessness with words. On the other hand, although the absolute subversion of Parliament was not his object, he was capable – to an extent, perhaps, never consciously defined – of damaging its working conventions. Strengthening Carson's finances and illegality, politicising the British Army, were ways of doing that. The coming of war may have forestalled other ways.

Unlike Willoughby's there is no reason to doubt the seriousness of Long's extremism. In some matters it outdid Milner's. Like Carson, he was a member of the Ulster Unionist Council. According to his own admission he was also a member of Carson's Ulster Volunteers which may account for the presence in his papers of copies of Battalion orders of the third Battalion, North Derry Regiment.[53] And last but not least, sometime in 1914 it was arranged that Long would take Carson's place in the event that the latter was arrested.[54] On 26 March 1914, he wrote to Carson warning him that 'warrants were signed for the arrest of political people, such as you and me ...'[55]

Given the genuineness of Long's commitment, it needs to be recognised that it was the commitment of a follower. The chief architects of Conservative political extremism, as we have noted, were not great landowners, but men like Carson and Milner, the one a barrister, the other a civil servant, both owning houses in the countryside, in Carson's case with 2 acres of land, in Milner's with perhaps 150 to 200. That such men provided the leadership was no accident. Organising the Covenanters, whether those of Ulster or those of Milner's British sort, was not work which great English landowners were disposed to undertake, or if some did, like Willoughby, they did not do it very well. The chief sources of their political and social influence they had always found, so to speak, in their visibility, in their ownership of great houses and much land and also in their willingness to undertake the obligations of local and national leadership. Theirs was more a face-to-face influence, rather than one of mass manipulation; mobilising public opinion was not work which came naturally to them. They were apt to leave it to others, to pseudogentry like Carson and Milner. That Long undertook it, and to the extent that he did, was probably something of a personal idiosyncrasy.

Moreover, in doing so, it would not seem that he spoke only for himself, or for some marginal, semi-conspiratorial element either in the Conservative party or in English society. Both he and Milner had the support of the Conservative leadership, that is, Bonar Law in the House of Commons and Lord Lansdowne in the House of Lords.[56] By early April, when the League of British Covenanters was founded and the first (and most impressive) of its mass meetings was held in London, the League also had the support of the Conservative Central Office, that is, the party machine.[57] Long, after all, stood high in the ranks of the Conservative leadership, a near miss as candidate for that leadership in 1911. Moreover, if anyone may be said to have spoken for the social group still influential in the Conservative party, that is, the great landowners, it was Walter Long.[58] Of course, like social groups generally, great landowners did not speak with one voice. Some, not many, were Liberal in their politics, and some of them were to be found in Asquith's Cabinet. Some, probably very few, declared no allegiance to either of the great parties. A more numerous body, nominally Conservative or Unionist, did not busy themselves conspicuously at Westminster, seemingly content with a desultory appearance in the Lords. Of these the sixth Duke of Portland is a good example. His life was devoted to horsebreeding, foxhunting and his estates; as he confessed, not until the third Home Rule Bill did he pay much attention to politics.[59]

Such landowners notwithstanding, landed society – especially in its topmost ranks and among an older generation – still displayed a relish for the pursuit of power, admittedly an exercise increasingly confined after 1880 to the Conservative party and its recent ally, the Liberal Unionists. These supplied a vehicle for a new phenomenon in landed politics, what may be called a party of resistance, armed with a rationale and strategy largely invented by the third Lord Salisbury, chief of Long's first cabinet, from whom it is likely Long learned much. Neither rationale nor party strategy, given that Salisbury's mind was capacious and powerful, were trumpery affairs.

His political strategy was rooted in what he once described as 'the great primeval subject-matter of all human conflict', the conflict over the ownership of property. This he saw emerging in its modern democratic form as early as the 1860s. It appeared as a 'struggle between the English constitution on the one hand, and the democratic forces that are labouring to subvert it on the other ... a struggle between those who have, to keep what they have got, and those who have not, to get it'.[60] The bearing of this insight for the landed élite's political strategy he once put in his own idiosyncratic way. As he explained the matter in the 1880s to Lord

Randolph Churchill, then in the guise of populist reformer, your 'course is to produce drastic, symmetrical measures hitting the classes hard, and consequently dispensing with their support, but trusting to public meetings and the democratic forces generally to carry you through. I think such a policy will fail. I do not mean that the classes will join issue with you on one of the measures which hits them hard and beat you on that. That is not the way they fight. They will select some matter on which they can appeal to prejudice and on which the masses will be indifferent, and on that they will upset you'.[61] Underlying this scenario was a note of tenacity, of landed prerogative, which Salisbury had also frankly confessed to as early as the 1860s. He had then written: 'There are many things which the great Revolution families have been willing to surrender for the sake of retaining political power; but there is one thing that they will not surrender – and that is political power itself'.[62]

Walter Long shared this imperative. For him, as for Salisbury and for his nephew, A. J. Balfour, the anti-landlord state was the enemy – in the case of Long and Balfour brought to life more menacingly than ever before in the policies and rhetoric of Lloyd George. Admittedly, to put in Salisbury's hard clear words what was in his mind, was beyond Long's powers. Nonetheless, however humdrum his mode of expression, however close it came at times to the incoherence of instinct, it drove him, as well as many of his fellow landowners, to take their last stand against a detested Liberal Government on the preservation of the Union between England and Ireland.

Apart from the Irish Question, both as tactic and ideology Salisbury's own creation, the great Conservative Prime Minister might well have been startled by much that was said and done by younger men. They relied much, to use his words, on 'public meetings and the democratic forces generally'. There were unusual goings-on about armies, England's and Carson's. There were strange pronouncements about the end of rule by parliamentary majority. Who can say what, had he been alive, Salisbury might have made of all this? Indeed, what might he have made of his nephew's dismissive rejection of Lloyd George's 1909 budget? Perhaps, had he lived in those stormy years, 1909–14, the speculation is not too fanciful that he would have fallen back on a sort of rueful moral complicity voiced by his nephew at a highly critical moment. That thoughtful man, Arthur Balfour, on learning in 1914 that the Conservative Shadow Cabinet was of a mind to amend the Army Annual Act replied: 'in revolutionary times I suppose revolutionary measures are necessary. I confess however that they are rather against the grain'.[63]

Adequate summing up is not easy, all the more so when it deals with a truncated episode. The coming of war left the story of political conflict in 1914 without a denouement, and thus without a full disclosure of its nature. What may be ventured, however, is that landed extremism was ambivalent: a mixture of conventional and unconventional politics. An historian has portrayed the latter as 'country house syndicalism' – a vivid but misleading phrase.[64] By it, he seems mainly to have meant the presence of an infectious and unthinking element. That no doubt existed in 1914. But the phrase is less appropriate if it conveys – as it is likely to do – what syndicalism normally conveys: a systematic effort from below to subvert society and government.

Landed extremism came from above. It left to the non-landed, Carson and Milner, the chief burdens of political organisation. It offered no genuine alternative either to parliamentary government or to current social arrangements. At the same time, it resorted to methods and rhetoric that blatantly defied its traditional concern with the preservation of law and order and challenged that system of government by parliament which they as much as anyone else had brought into being. It has been suggested by some historians that at bottom this was a demonstration of landed weakness. But can it be said that bringing the British Government to the verge of collapse was a demonstration of weakness? Might it not be better said that this was an impressive, admittedly somewhat diminished, and possibly the last, demonstration of landed political strength?[65]

Notes

1 Long, the moderate, tends to emerge in R. Murphy, *Walter Long and the Conservative Party, 1905–21*, unpublished doctoral dissertation, Bristol University, 1984, and in his 'Faction in the Conservative Party and the home rule crisis 1912–14', *History*, June 1986. Note, however, the brief reference to Long's being 'perhaps, as ardent as Lord Milner' in A. M. Gollin, *Proconsul in politics*, London, 1964, p. 194, footnote 1.

2 Estate size is drawn from J. Bateman, *Great landowners of Great Britain and Ireland*, London, 1883 edn.

3 R. E. Quinault, *Warwickshire landowners and parliamentary politics, circa 1841–1923*, unpublished doctoral dissertation, Oxford, 1975.

4 Sandars to Maxse, 7 December 1909, Maxse Papers, West Sussex Record Office.

5 J. R. Jones in H. Rogger and E. Weber (eds), *The European right: a historical profile*, Berkeley and Los Angeles, 1965, pp. 43–4; G. Phillips, 'Lord Willoughby de Broke and the politics of radical Toryism', *Journal of British Studies*, Fall 1980. Note, however, a less enthusiastic opinion of Willoughby in A. Sykes, 'The Radical right and the crisis of Conservatism before the First World War', *The Historical Journal*, September, 1983.

6 Willoughby to Maxse, 19 June 1910, Maxse Papers.

7 Willoughby to Law, 7 December 1912, Bonar Law Papers, House of Lords Record Office.

8 Willoughby to Maxse, 19 June 1910, Maxse Papers.

9 Both manifesto and list were published in the *Morning Post*, 27 March 1913.

10 Willoughby to Law, 11 September 1913, Bonar Law Papers.

11 *Morning Post*, 3 December 1913.

12 Col. McCammon to Greer, 10 December 1913, Ulster Volunteers Papers, 1327/4/21, Public Record Office of Northern Ireland. I am grateful to Dr Roderick Clifford for this reference.

13 Peto to Law, 13 December 1913, Bonar Law Papers.
14 Oliver to Craik, 10 October 1913, Oliver Papers, National Library of Scotland.
15 Milner to Amery, 8 January 1914, Amery Papers, in the possession of Mr Julian Amery. For Willoughby's letter to Milner, see Milner Papers, Bodleian Library, 6 January 1914. The valuable account of Milner and his relations with Willoughby's League in A. T. Q. Stewart, *The Ulster crisis*, London, 1967, chapter 11, omits mention of Milner's distrust, shared also by Leo Amery, of Willoughby and his associates.
16 Willoughby de Broke, *The passing years*, London, 1924, pp. 1–2.
17 Bateman, *Great landowners*, 1883 edn.
18 I am indebted to Dr Roderick Clifford for this information on Long's selling of land.
19 Viscount Long of Wraxall, *Memories*, London, 1923, pp. 331–2; Long's son to Long, 19 November 1911–24 March 1913, Long Papers, Wiltshire Record Office, 947/911, miscellaneous correspondence from Canada.
20 Long, *Memoirs*, p. 80.
21 Long to Balfour, 19 September 1908, Long Papers, British Library, Add. MS 62403.
22 Long to Lady Londonderry, 7 June 1911, Londonderry Papers, Durham County Record Office.
23 P. Buckland (ed.), *Irish Unionism 1885–1932*, Belfast, 1973, Memorandum of the Londonderry House Agreement, pp. 318–21.
24 *The Times*, 10 April 1912.
25 Long to Law, 7 November 1913, Long Papers, British Library, Add. MS 62404.
26 *Ibid.*, Long to Law, 21 November 1913.
27 *The Times*, 19 February 1914. Carson's expenditure was probably for the arms in the Larne gun-running.
28 Long to Gwynne, 21 May 1914, Gwynne Papers, Bodleian Library.
29 Information about Long's Ulster Fund is to be found in Gibbs Papers, Guildhall Library, London.
30 So I was assured some six years ago.
31 *Manchester Guardian*, 28 April 1914.
32 Memorandum on Amending Bill, 26 June 1914, Long Papers. British Library, Add. MS 62417.
33 R. Blake, *The unknown Prime Minister: the life and times of Andrew Bonar Law 1858–1923*, London, 1955, p. 174.
34 J. Vincent (ed.), *The Crawford Papers*, Manchester, 1984, pp. 328–9. Crawford, who was himself a member of the Shadow Cabinet, was of the opinion that the general feeling was opposed to such action.
35 C. Townshend, 'Military force and civil authority in the United Kingdom, 1914–21', *Journal of British Studies*, July 1989.
36 Actually it was Carson whom Milner had in mind; see Carson's speech at Manchester, *The Times*, 4 December 1913.
37 Milner to Dawson, 4 December 1913, Dawson Papers, Bodleian Library.
38 Long to Milner, 2 March 1914, Milner Papers.
39 See E. M. Spiers, chapter 2, in I. F. W. Beckett and K. Simpson (eds), *A nation in arms: a social study of the British army in the First World War*, Manchester, 1985, pp. 40–1.
40 I. Colvin, *Carson the statesman*, New York, 1935, p. 234.
41 Quoted in Sir C. Petrie, *Walter Long and his times*, London, 1936, p. 177.
42 Long to Cecil, 3 March 1914, Robert Cecil Papers, British Library, Add. MS 51072.
43 Quoted in Colvin, *Carson the statesman*, p. 291.
44 Oliver to Milner, 11 March 1914, Oliver Papers; see Long's letter, *Birmingham Daily Post*, 20 March 1914.
45 Long's speech reported in *The Times*, 6 April 1914.
46 Long to Law, 22 March 1914, Bonar Law Papers.
47 Long's son to Long, 26–27 March 1914, Long Papers, British Library, Add. MS 62417.

48 Long to Stamfordham, 2, 9 July 1914, Long Papers, British Library, Add. MS 62405.

49 *Ibid.*, Long to Lansdowne, 19 July 1914.

50 *Birmingham Daily Post*, 11 July 1914.

51 Frewen to Long, 16, 23 July 1914, Frewen Papers, Library of Congress.

52 Long to Law, 28 May 1914, Long Papers, British Library, Add. MS 62404.

53 These orders appeared January–June 1914; see Long Papers, British Library, Add. MS 62417. For Long's membership in the Volunteers, see his speech to the Primrose League in *The Times*, 1 May 1914.

54 According to Sir E. Wrench, *Alfred Lord Milner*, London, 1958, p. 281, it was Milner who was chosen to succeed Carson; but Wrench offers no supporting evidence. On the other hand, Sir Henry Wilson reports in the unpublished portion of his diaries that Walter Long informed him, 28 April 1914, that he, Long, would succeed if Carson were arrested; see Wilson Papers, Imperial War Museum. Wilson's version seems more plausible. Milner spoke poorly in public, and managing both Ulster and British Covenanters would have exceeded even his considerable energy.

55 Quoted in Colvin, *Carson the statesman*, p. 352.

56 Diaries, 24 February 1914, Milner Papers.

57 Both Arthur Steel-Maitland and Lord Edmund Talbot, respectively chairman and chief parliamentary whip of the Conservative party, attended this meeting. Such a connection existed earlier under Lord Balcarres.

58 See J. Ridley, *Leadership and management in the Conservative Party in Parliament 1906–14*, unpublished doctoral dissertation, Oxford, 1985, for a most useful prosopography of Conservative Members of Parliament.

59 Duke of Portland, *Memories of hunting and racing*, London, 1935; *Men, women and things*, London, 1937. For his confession about politics, see Portland to Roberts, 11 February 1914, Roberts Papers, National Army Museum.

60 Quoted by R. Stewart, in Lord Blake and H. Cecil (eds), *Salisbury: the man and his policies*, London, 1987, p. 99.

61 Quoted in W. S. Churchill, *Lord Randolph Churchill*, New York, 1906 (2 vols), II, 224.

62 Quoted by R. Stewart in Blake and Cecil, *Salisbury*, p. 112.

63 Balfour to Lansdowne, 13 March 1914, Balfour Papers, British Library, Add. MS 49730.

64 G. Searle, 'The "revolt from the right" in Victorian Britain' in P. Kennedy and A. Nichols (eds), *Nationalist and racial movements in Britain and Germany before 1914*, London, 1981, p. 27.

65 The summing-up ventured in this paper is an altered and amplified version of two previous summations: the first in the Introduction to D. Spring (ed.), *European landed élites in the nineteenth century*, Baltimore, 1977, p. 17; and second, D. Spring, 'Land and politics in Edwardian England', *Agricultural History*, January 1984. These exercises serve well to demonstrate the perils of summing-up. My most recent effort here is meant to be less exemplary in this respect.

9

GOLF AND EDWARDIAN POLITICS

ROLAND QUINAULT

In the late Victorian and Edwardian period the golf course became a common feature of the British landscape.[1] A game which had long been virtually restricted to the east coast of Scotland, suddenly spread throughout the United Kingdom. In 1860 there were under 20 golf clubs in Britain, virtually all of which were in Scotland. In 1913 there were over 1,200 golf clubs in Britain, of which about two-thirds were in England.[2] Golf became the favourite game of the British establishment and *Punch* observed in 1911 that those who did not play were 'outside the pale'. In the years before the First World War, all three leaders of the British parliamentary parties were keen golfers, as well as many Cabinet ministers and senior politicians.[3] Roy Jenkins has noted that 'golf was an almost essential accompaniment to Edwardian politics', but the reasons for that connection have not been investigated.[4] Historians of Edwardian sport have concentrated on football and cricket – which were favoured by the working classes – rather than golf, with the recent exception of John Lowerson.[5] Historians of Edwardian politics have been too high-minded, or too narrow-minded, to examine the sporting recreations of politicians.

Golf was an ideal game for Edwardian MPs, who were mostly middle-aged men with sedentary habits. Golf also offered particular advantages to the novice; help from caddies and professionals, and a handicap system which enabled them to compete with experienced players. A round of golf provided both outdoor exercise in pleasant surroundings and much opportunity for informal talk about politics. Since MPs were tied to Westminster for much of the year, they made particular use of the hundred or so golf courses around London. The railways and the motor car also gave them speedy access to the rapidly increasing number of golf courses throughout Britain.[6]

I

The popularity of golf with many MPs was fostered by their political and recreational connections with Scotland. Winston Churchill observed, in 1906, that 'Parliament is controlled by lawyers and Scotsmen'.[7] In that year, Campbell-Bannerman's Liberal Cabinet including seven Scots and four others who sat for Scottish seats. Many of those ministers represented constituencies on the east coast of Scotland: the traditional heartland of golf. During the summer and autumn many MPs joined what was jocularly known as the 'Golf stream' along the east coast of Scotland.[8] The first prominent politician to play golf regularly was a Scotsman who annually participated in the golf stream: Arthur Balfour.

Balfour's ancestral home, Whittinghame, in East Lothian, was close to the many golf courses on the south side of the Firth of Forth. His father had been a golfer, but Arthur was educated in England and he did not play golf as a boy.[9] However his mother, a sister of Lord Salisbury, gave him a distaste for hunting and shooting and he took up tennis and golf in the early 1870s.[10]

> It is not too much to say that my life at this time depended largely upon games and the social accompaniments of games. . . . About this period lawn tennis was invented, and golf underwent an expansion which amounted almost to a revolution. It is not easy from my point of view to exaggerate the importance of these events. they were, it is true, but games. . . . But in truth they have profoundly affected the social life of the period with which I am concerned, and are intimately connected with the generation to which I belong.[11]

Balfour's emphatic statement is significant because he was a central figure amongst the influential group known as the 'Souls'.

Balfour's enthusiasm for golf first attracted public attention when he was Irish Chief Secretary in the late 1880s. He regularly played golf with George Wyndham in Dublin although the ground was bad.[12] In 1890 Balfour wrote that whereas tennis was exercise, golf was an absorbing and philosophical game:

> With a fine sea view, and a clear course in front of him, the golfer should find no difficulty in dismissing all worries from his mind and regarding golf, even it may be very indifferent golf, as the true and adequate end of man's existence.[13]

When Balfour became First Lord of the Treasury and Leader of the

House of Commons, in 1891, the parliamentary reporter, Henry Lucy, wrote:

> Mr Arthur Balfour, in his lean leisure time plays golf; well enough in its way, but not, to the popular mind, an adequate set-off against Mr Gladstone's wood-cutting. Golf, like Wagner, is certainly growing in favour, but to the average person it is too much like Wagner to create a general wave of enthusiasm round any one of its votaries.[14]

For some time to come, golf was 'still scurvily treated by the newspapers except when Arthur Balfour went into a bunker'.[15] But Balfour's rapid political rise boosted golf's profile at Westminster.

In 1891 it was suggested that there should be a golf match between the two major parties, but the Liberals could not provide competent opposition. Therefore an individual Parliamentary Handicap – open to MPs and officers of Parliament – was arranged by the unlikely combination of Sir Herbert Maxwell, a Scottish Baronet and Henry Broadhurst, a former stone mason. The first tournament was played on Tooting Bec Common: 'a confined area intersected by numerous roads frequented by perambulator-wheeling nursemaids and also by loafers and tramps'. The hazards consisted largely of street lamps some of which were broken by the competitors. After another contest in the following year, the LCC banned further golf on the Common.[16] Balfour was unable to play in the first Parliamentary Handicap because he was piloting the Irish Land Purchase Bill through the Commons. But he won the Parliamentary Handicap in 1894 and 1897, and again in 1910, when he was sixty-two.

Balfour frequently patronised the new links established along the southern coast of England. In 1894 he wrote from Bembridge, on the Isle of Wight:

> I am beginning this letter in the club house surrounded by men attempting to dry themselves at a 'slow combustion stove' and speculating gloomily on the prospects of the afternoon which are, frankly speaking *bad* . . . but whatever the arbiter of our golfing destinies may have in store for us in the way of weather, at least Bembridge is better than the House of Commons.[17]

In 1895 Balfour was made captain of the new Rye golf club and in 1896 he wrote to George Curzon: 'I find it difficult to squeeze in the claims of both golf and politics into the 24 hours'.[18] His services to the game were acknowledged when he was made Captain of the Royal & Ancient Golf Club at St Andrews, in 1894.[19]

When Balfour helped to secure an improved water supply for the small coastal town of North Berwick he was made an honorary citizen of the town. From 1891 to 1914 he spent annual golfing holidays at North

Berwick which he described as 'the happiest hours of my life'.[20] Balfour golfed during the day and worked in the evenings either on his official papers, or his literary and philosophical studies. At weekends Balfour cycled over to his family at Whittinghame, where he built a miniature golf course on the terrace.

Balfour succeeded his uncle, Lord Salisbury, as Prime Minister in 1902. That year saw the introduction of the rubber cored 'Haskell ball' which could be easily mass produced and which went further than gutta percha balls. This further encouraged the craze for a sport which now had prime ministerial patronage. After the wearing parliamentary session of 1903, Balfour retired to North Berwick:

> I cannot quite understand why I am so happy here.... I am restricting my golf at present to one round a day. It requires some self-control, but it is worth it. It is better for my health: it is better for my work: and, not least, it is better for my golf. I am playing a fair game: and so far have won all my matches.[21]

His handicap fell to 8, despite the pressures of the premiership. Balfour's patronage boosted the popularity of North Berwick. In 1913 it was estimated that over 1,000 caddies were taken out, every fine day during the late summer season, on first-class courses within five miles of North Berwick.[22] These courses included Muirfield, at Gullane, where The Honourable Company of Edinburgh Golfers had migrated in 1891.

When Joseph Chamberlain resigned from the Cabinet to campaign for tariff reform, Balfour replaced him with his friend, Alfred Lyttelton. He had been a first-class cricketer and amateur tennis champion, but his friendship with Balfour led him to take up golf. In 1903 Lyttelton was living in a Lutyens-designed house next to the first tee at Muirfield. Lyttelton sold this house in 1906 – because it was too popular with his friends – but he then bought a house near the links at Rye, in Sussex, where he and Balfour had played in 1895.[23]

Balfour's resignation from the premiership and the 'Liberal landslide' of 1906 gave him more time for golf and he won the Dalrymple Cup at North Berwick in 1906.[24] This prompted accusations that Balfour cared more about golf than the Conservative party. In 1907 Rowland Hunt, the Tory MP for South Shropshire – not a golfing constituency – 'entreated their leader to come down from the Olympian heights of philosophy and golf'.[25] Balfour did not give up golf, but he eventually gave up the leadership. He was succeeded, as the Conservative leader in the Commons, by another keen Scots golfer: Andrew Bonar Law. He had spent nearly every holiday since 1891 near a golf course. In 1906 Bonar Law lost his Glasgow seat but was elected MP for Dulwich in the suburban 'golf belt' around London. In 1907 Law followed Balfour's example and won the Parliamentary Handicap. In 1911 Law only accepted the Tory leadership on the understanding that he did not have to forego his favourite recreation. 'I like my golf. It keeps me in good health and I don't mean to give it up'.[26] After the stressful parliamentary session of 1912–13, Law claimed that 'He did not know how he would have got on had it not been for his golf'.[27]

Both Balfour and Bonar Law were Scots and their love of golf partly reflected their nationality. The leader of the Liberal party from 1899 to 1908 was another Scot, Sir Henry Campbell-Bannerman. He was not a golfer, but in 1907 he opened a bazaar in aid of Montrose golf course. He contrasted the neglect of the course in his youth, when it was patronised by a couple of unemployed handloom weavers, with the current English and continental craze for golf.[28] In 1908 'C. B.' was succeeded as premier and Liberal leader by a golfing Englishman: Asquith. He had been introduced to the game when he visited St Andrews as a member of an Oxford reading party in 1875:

> In default of any other recognized form of athletic exercise, we Englishmen made acquaintance with the unknown and outlandish game of golf. The now world-famous links we often had in the afternoon almost to ourselves; and our clubs were carried for 1*s* or 1*s*. 6*d*. a round, by – amongst other eminent professionals – young Tommy Morris, then the open champion.[29]

Despite this marvellous initiation, Asquith did not touch a club again until his second wife, Margot Tennant – a Scot – encouraged him to take up the game.[30] From 1895 Asquith took golfing holidays, during the parliamentary recess, at St Andrews.[31] The town was adjacent to Asquith's constituency of East Fife, which included Elie, a small place which produced three of the outstanding professional golfers of the era: Douglas Rolland, his relative, James Braid, and Jack Simpson.

When Asquith spoke at a golf tournament in East Fife in 1896, he described golf as a most difficult accomplishment and confessed that for the past fortnight he had been endeavouring, mostly in vain, to cut a decent figure on the St Andrews links.[32] But Asquith's golf displayed some of the tactical skill which characterised his premiership. His 'prowess with the putter could not always compensate for an indifferent game through the green, though here want of length was within limits eked out by guile'. When playing with a suitably educated partner, Asquith produced Latin tags germane to the occasion, or Latin versions of the sayings of his Cabinet colleagues.[33] In 1912 Asquith was more excited by his match in the Treasury Golf Handicap than by the recent defeat of the government on an amendment to the Home Rule Bill.[34]

Asquith's enthusiam for golf was facilitated by the motor car. His first journey in a hired car – to the links at Cassiobury – was delayed by mechanical breakdowns and steep gradients and he was obliged to finish his round at sunset.[35] Nevertheless Asquith invariably used a car thereafter to reach golf courses across the length and breadth of Britain. He patronised the course at Huntercombe, near his country home at Sutton Courtney, and was Vice-President of Knebworth Golf Club.[36] During the autumn recess, Asquith joined the 'golf stream' along the east coast of Scotland. He was a member of the R. & A. at St Andrews and spent many holidays at Archerfield, his brother-in-law's house, near North Berwick.[37] Archerfield, in the words of his daughter, 'Was a lovely Adam mansion.... But what made it Paradise for my father was the possession of a perfect private golf-links stretching down to the sea'.[38] Asquith also patronised the links around the Moray Firth in north-east Scotland. In 1912 he was impressed by the Dornoch links and by the nearby home of the millionaire golfer, Andrew Carnegie.[39]

Golf featured in Asquith's epistolic affair with Venetia Stanley. He wrote to her in 1914: 'I am sorry your golf was so disappointing.... We must play together soon. You don't say what sort of course it is'.[40] He subsequently golfed with Venetia at Holyhead, while staying with her father at Penrhos, but they did not become regular partners. After the outbreak of war, Asquith wrote to her: 'I hope you haven't abandoned golf for good and all: it would be so delicious if we were able from time to time to play together'.[41] He returned to the subject in 1915: 'I do trust you will, when Providence permits, take to a little golf again: we had some quite good rounds just a year ago now at Delamere: do you remember?'[42]

John Grigg has observed that Lloyd George, more than any other politician of his time, epitomized the character and outlook of Edwardian Britain.[43] Certainly Lloyd George was typically Edwardian in his enthusiasm for golf. In 1912 he even contemplated retiring on his small private income and devoting himself to golf and literature.[44] Lloyd George first played golf on a family holiday in Scotland in 1895: just when Asquith was also taking up the game there. But he did not become a regular golfer until the later Edwardian period, by which time the game had spread to his homeland in north Wales. Lloyd George was MP for Carnarvon District which comprised the six coastal boroughs of (as they were then spelt) Carnarvon, Bangor, Conway, Pwllheli, Nevin and Criccieth. All these towns were increasingly dependent on tourists who were attracted by the beaches, the scenery and the golf. Lloyd George frequently played at Criccieth golf course, which was laid out on ground which had been part of his father-in-law's farm.[45] On one occasion, he partnered the village draper in a foursome with Churchill and the village cobbler.[46] In 1913 Lloyd George distributed the prizes at the Criccieth Golf Club summer tournament, when he recalled his greatest golfing moment: a hole-in-one over some olive trees in the south of France. He was quoted as observing that 'for middle-aged people pursuing a sedentary life like himself, golf was the greatest discovery of the age' since it provided good exercise all the year round.[47] In 1914 Lloyd George travelled from Criccieth to Holyhead, in Anglesey, where he won a foursome against the premier. Asquith reported that L. G. 'drives quite well and is not bad with his iron, but is an execrable putter'. During the match, the Chancellor talked about his land campaign.[48]

II

Lloyd George, when in London, golfed at Stoke Poges, Hanger Hill and at Walton Heath, where he became a member in 1907. By 1911 he was playing at Walton once, or twice, a week. The long course at Walton, high on the Surrey Downs, was specially designed for the new rubber-cored Haskell ball. It was described as 'wild and bleak and merciless . . . a vast tract of wind-swept heather'.[49] The prestige of Walton Heath was boosted by the prowess of the club professional, James Braid, who won the Open championship four times in six years.[50] But Braid never used the front door of the club house and only ate in the dining room by invitation, for in golf, as in cricket, there was still a social gulf between amateurs and professionals.[51]

Walton Heath had close connections with Westminster. The opening match, in 1904, was attended by several Tory MPs and several of the original Directors of the club were prominent Conservatives.[52] They included Cosmo Bonsor (who had been the Tory MP for Wimbledon); the Hon. A. E. Gathorne-Hardy (the son of the Tory elder statesman, Earl Cranbrook) and H. Mallaby-Deely (who became the Tory MP for Harrow in 1910). But the club was not exclusively Conservative, for the Earl of Crewe, a prominent Liberal, was a member of the committee throughout the Edwardian period. In November 1905 the club was taken over by a syndicate headed by George Riddell, who was part owner of the *News of the World* which had the largest weekly circulation in Britain.[53] Riddell introduced Lloyd George to the club and often took him there in his chauffeur-driven motor car.[54] Where the rising star of the Liberal party went, others followed. By 1913 the members of Walton Heath Golf Club included 6 Cabinet ministers (four of whom were on the Committee), 24 MPs, 21 lay peers and 2 bishops.[55] The select character of the membership was reflected in the entrance and subscription fees which were amongst the highest in the country.[56]

The popularity and prestige of the Walton Heath Golf Club raised the value of building land in the vicinity as high as £1,000 per acre.[57] Much of the land adjacent to the course was developed by Riddell who, in 1912, built a house for Lloyd George:

> L. G. is very anxious to take possession of the house I am building for him at Walton, so that he may spend Christmas there. He asked me to hurry up the builders.[58]

Lloyd George was very pleased with the house because it enabled him to indulge in his two latest passions: golf and his secretary-mistress, Frances Stevenson. The house was ideal for their liaison because it was beyond the village, well screened by thick hedges and not far from Wallington, where Frances still lived with her parents.[59] David and Frances spent much time together at Walton in the years before and during the First World War. His wife, Margaret, also liked the house at Walton, much preferring it to no. 11 Downing Street.[60] But Lloyd George thought that husband-and-wife golf was bad for both parties.[61]

Riddell let other houses at Walton to Charles Masterman, the Financial Secretary to the Treasury, and to John Simon, the Attorney-General. Simon had to spend long hours in the Commons, but kept fit by playing golf whenever he had the chance.[62] Other senior Liberals who played regularly at Walton included Isaacs, Seely, McKenna, Pease, Illingworth and the Master of Elibank. When Ellis Griffiths, the Liberal MP for Anglesey and Under-Secretary at Home Office, golfed with Lloyd George at Walton they debated what were the three best words in the Welsh language.[63] But politics was usually the favoured subject, as at a by-election in 1913, when Riddell noted:

> Golfed with L. G., Illingworth and Masterman. Going to the 7th hole, L. G. said to me, 'I am very apprehensive about Newmarket. I think we shall have a severe defeat'. At the 11th hole, a messenger arrived with a telegram containing the result – a win for the Conservatives by a large majority. This rather threw a gloom over the party.[64]

But political set-backs did not put Lloyd George off his golf. When he reached the final of the Treasury Handicap, he talked of nothing but the match on his return to the Commons.[65] A week later, Lloyd George and Isaacs defended their conduct in connection with the Marconi scandal. But on the following day, both men preferred to golf at Walton rather than to listen to the continuing parliamentary debate. Asquith was rather surprised to see Lloyd George dressed for golf, but the Chancellor promised to be back in time for the premier's speech that afternoon.[66] When the Marconi Inquiry Committee asked L. G. about his relations with the Master of Elibank (who had bought Marconi shares on behalf of the Liberal party), he truthfully, but economically, replied 'We were associated together at golf'.[67]

Another golfing partner of Lloyd George was Winston Churchill. Before his change of party, in 1904, Churchill's sporting interests had been largely confined to hunting, where his aristocratic connections came in handy, and polo, which he had played in the army. But in 1908 Churchill entered a Liberal Cabinet in which both the premier and the Chancellor were keen golfers. In the same year, Churchill followed in Asquith's footsteps, by choosing a Scottish wife, Clementine Hozier, and a Scottish east coast constituency, Dundee. Clementine enjoyed golf and Dundee was close to the famous links at St Andrews and Carnoustie. In 1910 Winston was elected a member of Walton Heath Golf Club and in 1911 he played there twice a week with Riddell, who considered him a charming companion, albeit one prone to 'more talk than golf'.[68] Clementine Churchill and the Duchess of Marlborough became lady members of the club. When Churchill stayed with the Asquiths at Archerfield, in 1911, he played a lot of indifferent, but enthusiastic, golf with the premier and his daughter, Violet.[69] One day, as they returned from the links, the premier offered Churchill the Admiralty, which he accepted with alacrity. At the Admiralty, Churchill singled out, for rapid promotion, David Beatty who was also a member at Walton Heath.[70] Churchill used the Admiralty yacht, HMS *Enchantress*, as a base from which he went ashore to golf on the coast of Britain and the Mediterranean. When Churchill feared that he might have to resign over the 1914 Naval estimates, he contemplated retiring to a small house at Carnoustie.[71]

Churchill's political alliance with Lloyd George was facilitated by their mutual enthusiasm for golf. L. G. invited Churchill to golf at Criccieth in 1910 and at Caernarfon in 1911.[72] On the Criccieth course, L. G. expounded to Churchill two alternative strategies: to form a coalition and govern the country on middle lines, or to carry through an advanced land and social reform policy. He later claimed that 'Winston forgot all about the game and has never forgotten out conversation'.[73] They also played together at Walton Heath where Churchill's handicap was 18: 3 higher than that of Lloyd George.[74] Churchill made up for his lack of skill by favouring a form of golf known as a 'greensome' – a four-ball competition which enabled him to partner Braid and win a fair proportion of matches.[75] On one occasion, when it was too hot to play, Winston showed L. G. the programme of the forthcoming investiture of the Prince of Wales at Caernafon. He later told the prince that he had learnt his lines for the investiture on the golf course.[76] On another occasion, when Churchill and L. G. arrived on the eighteenth green with the game undecided, Churchill allegedly said: 'Now I will putt you for the premiership'.[77]

Walton Heath never became a Liberal preserve, for the original Conservative element remained strong. The Tory members included Balfour, Bonar Law and the octagenarian diehard and former Lord

Chancellor, Lord Halsbury. He had been persuaded by his wife to take up golf as a less strenuous alternative to lawn tennis.[78] At Walton, one Tory MP made bets with Churchill and Lloyd George on the outcome of the December 1910 general election.[79] Newspaper editors and proprietors were also prominent in the Walton Heath membership lists. They included Riddell's partners, Emsley Carr, the Editor of the *News Of The World*, and Edward Hudson of *Country Life*, who both featured Walton Heath in their journals. The club was also patronised by Robertson Nicoll of the *British Weekly*, and Robert Donald, the Editor of the *Daily Chronicle*, which supported Lloyd George. It was said that a machine gun from a Walton Heath bunker on a Saturday morning would have changed the course of history, both in Downing Street and Fleet Street.[80]

Another journalist who occasionally golfed at Walton was Ramsay MacDonald. He was another Scot, but without the pedigree of Balfour or the wealth of Bonar Law. MacDonald was the illegitimate son of a farm worker, but his home town, Lossiemouth, became a fashionable seaside resort in the late Victorian period. Many of the visitors to the town were attracted by the golf links which were amongst the finest in north-east Scotland.[81] The Moray Golf Club was founded in 1889 and MacDonald was one of its earliest members. He revealed his enthusiasm for golf in a letter from Lossiemouth to his future wife:

> It has been pouring here of rain today and in a pause in the downpour I started a game of golf with my dear old schoolmaster to whom I owe so much. Shortly after we started it came in torrents and he begged me to give up the game. But he was beating me and I made up my mind to fight him out. For two hours we played in a downpour which drenched us from top to toe and I came out victor. The dear old man when he left the last hole put his hand in mine and with a lump in his throat said 'MacDonald, when I saw you first as a fat little boy I said you were either doomed to be hanged or something worth doing. Our game tonight has made me feel once again a babe in your hands'. I am telling you this because I really think he was right.[82]

Membership of the Moray Golf Club provided MacDonald with a wide social circle, especially during the summer holiday season. A few of the visitors were socialists, with whom MacDonald shared a taste for golf balls, tobacco and red ties. But his golfing partners also included a 'Dignified Dean' and a Professor of Church History. A prominent patron of the club was the large local landowner, Sir William Gordon Cumming, whose swears travelled further than his golf balls.[83] MacDonald regularly participated in the New Year golf tournament at the Moray Golf Club. In 1905 he won a prize which he took in the form of six 2*s* Haskell balls. When MacDonald returned to Lossiemouth after his election to Parliament in 1906, he was impatient for his luggage to arrive so that he could play golf.[84] In 1913, MacDonald engaged in a foursome, at Lossiemouth, with the Asquiths, who were staying nearby. Asquith wrote that his daughter, Violet, 'Rather lost her heart to the brindle-haired Labour leader'.[85]

III

For progressive Edwardian MPs golf was politically correct. Campbell-Bannerman observed that there was nothing aristocratic about golf: 'it was the game of all of them, it knit all classes of society'.[86] Balfour also believed that golf was 'a game for every class', but he thought that the game could only become truly popular if inland courses were developed.[87] Unfortunately, the creation of inland courses sometimes restricted public access to common land.[88] In the early 1890s, the development of golf courses at Chorley Wood and Mitcham led to disputes in which Balfour was indirectly involved.[89] But radical MPs – both Liberal and Conservative – focused their ire, not on golf courses, but on shooting estates.[90] By the Edwardian period, the Liberal leaders had tactfully deserted the grouse moors. Asquith did not shoot in Scotland after 1894 and Campbell-Bannerman regarded the shooting tenant and 'ghillie-dom' as 'the curse of Celtic Caledonia'.[91] Unlike shooting or hunting, golf did not involve killing or disputes with farmers over damage to crops and fences.

In 1913 Lloyd George launched his Land Campaign, in which he condemned agricultural landlords for putting sport before farming. His attacks prompted a Tory MP, E. G. Pretyman, to assert that Highland deer forests were no more unacceptable than golf courses. His remarks really got 'the goat's' goat and Lloyd George devoted a whole speech to a defence of golf. He pointed out that the Walton Heath course, which had previously been covered by useless heather and bracken, now employed 83 full-time and 110 part-time workers. The course was annually patronised by 3,000 people, mostly hard-working businessmen, but who also included 90 workmen who paid 2*s* 6*d*. a year to belong to the Village Club.[92] The club was actively supported by George Riddell and became the Artisans Club after the war.[93]

Golf was also acceptable to the Nonconformists who were so prominent in the Edwardian Liberal and Labour parties. Unlike horse racing, golf was not associated with organised betting. There were private bets between golfers, but the reliability of the handicap system ensured that limited money changed hands. Golf was also not associated with heavy drinking, despite the temptations of the 'nineteenth hole'. Bonar Law was a teetotaller and Riddell noted that Lloyd George, Isaacs and himself were 'all teetotallers, or nearly so'.[94] George Cadbury, the chocolate manufacturer, who was a vehement opponent of both betting and drink, was a keen golfer. The septuagenarian Cadbury spent the morning in his office at Bournville and the afternoon on his private links. He carried his own clubs, because he regarded caddying as 'blind alley' employment. Golf appealed to Cadbury 'not only as a physical recreation but as a moral tonic', yet he did not include a golf course amongst the extensive sporting facilities he provided for his workers at Bournville.[95]

The rapid growth in the popularity of golf attracted the interest of the press. The magazine *Golf* started publication in 1890 and became *Golf Illustrated* in 1899. It was owned by Leicester Harmsworth who became the Liberal MP for Caithness in 1900 and also one of the best golfers in the House of Commons. He and his golfing brother, Vivyan, persuaded their more influential brother, Alfred – Lord Northcliffe – to take up golf in 1910. Northcliffe laid out a private nine-hole course at his country home, Sutton Place and subscribed to more than twenty golf clubs. He also employed good golf writers: Bernard Leach on the *Daily Mail* and Bernard Darwin on *The Times*.[96] Frank Newnes, the son of George Newnes, who owned the *Westminster Gazette*, won the Parliamentary Handicap in 1906 when he was a Liberal MP.

Mutual enthusiasm for golf softened the asperity with which opposing politicians treated each other during the constitutional crisis of 1911–14. When Bonar Law became the Conservative leader, he decided to avoid friendly contacts with Lloyd George, whom he considered 'The most dangerous little man that ever lived'. In 1912, however, the two men met on the links and had a friendly chat. A year later, on the Riviera, Lloyd George played two rounds with Bonar Law, despite the current party deadlock over Irish Home Rule.[97] A few months later, while staying with the King at Balmoral, Bonar Law golfed with Churchill who 'left it to his sense of decency to fix the handicap I am to receive'.[98]

The principal ethical dilemma for golfing politicians was not whether to play with the opposition, but whether to play on Sundays. Ramsay MacDonald often golfed on Sunday because he thought it did him more good than going to a service.[99] But when Balfour stayed at a country house, in 1899, he only agreed to golf on Sunday, when he was assured that the course was entirely private. In the event, his game was observed by some villagers, who merely observed that he was 'a duffer at golf'.[100] By the later Edwardian period, both Balfour and Asquith often golfed on Sundays, on both private and public courses.[101] Lloyd George, however, still felt obliged to respect the strict sabbatarianism of Welsh Nonconformity and his Welsh wife. In 1913 he observed: 'It is hard that I cannot play golf on Sunday, but I shall walk round . . . and look at other people playing'.[102] When he was abroad, however, he did play on the sabbath and was inclined to let his sons do so.[103]

'The growth of women's golf has been extraordinary', wrote a leading practitioner in 1912. By then, the Ladies Golf Union had 409 affiliated clubs and there was a magazine specifically for women golfers.[104] Margot Asquith, the wife of the prime minister, presided over The Ladies Parliamentary Golf Association, which was open to the wives and female relatives of parliamentarians. Other members included Mrs McKenna, Mrs Ellis Griffith and Miss L. Pease.[105] Several Liberal ministers, including Asquith and Churchill, regularly played with female friends, or relatives, for mixed foursomes were very popular. But the failure of those minsiters to grant women the vote, prompted militant suffragettes to disrupt their golf.

In September 1909, three women members of the Women's Social and Political Union attacked Asquith at the door of the Littlestone golf club, but they were excluded from the premises by the Home Secretary, Herbert Gladstone.[106] In 1912, a woman who arrived at 11 Downing Street to interview Lloyd George about golf was mistaken for a suffragette. He refused to see her until she claimed that she would lose her job if he didn't agree to the interview. When Lloyd George golfed with Churchill at Walton, they agreed to use force, if it was absolutely necessary, to repel assaults by suffragettes.[107] In February 1913, the *Suffragette* newspaper exhorted golfers who met government ministers on the links, to give them a mandate for female suffrage, otherwise they would be 'Hopelessly stymied'.[108] Soon afterwards, suffragettes damaged golf greens at twelve courses from Sheringham, on the Norfolk coast, to Sandwich, on the Kent coast. They burnt slogans such as 'votes for women' and 'votes or war' onto the grass with vitriol. At Walton Heath the sixth to tenth greens were vandalised although the course had been guarded by 100 caddies specially selected for their strength. These attacks prompted Lloyd's Underwriters to offer 2 per cent premiums to cover eighteen-hole courses against malicious damage.[109]

Immediately after the vitriol attacks, suffragettes planted two bombs in the house being built for Lloyd George at Walton Heath. One went off, shortly before the builders were due to start work, and wrecked five rooms in the servants wing. Mrs Pankhurst claimed that the bomb had been intended to 'wake up' Lloyd George although he was out of the country at the time. She took personal responsibility for the deed and was duly sentenced to three years penal servitude at the Old Bailey.[110] The suffragettes were also active in the golfing areas of eastern Scotland. They caused considerable damage to property in and near St Andrews, but fears that they would damage the Old Course before the Championship were not realised.[111] In September 1913, Asquith was assaulted on the Lossiemouth links by two Scottish suffragettes, who grabbed him and knocked off his hat. The premier was armed with a formidable putter made of ancient applewood, but he relied on his daughter, Violet, to defend him until the detectives came up. The women were taken to the club house, where they were booed and Asquith was cheered when he completed his round.[112] The premier recorded that the wife of the Irish Chief Secretary 'hit a male suffragette (who was pouncing on her Augustine) with an umbrella on the head – much to Violet's envy, who now wishes she had used her cleek [a golf iron] upon my assailant'.[113] Violet later said that she had thrown away her club to avoid the temptation of using it.[114] Asquith continued to play at Lossiemouth – wearing a darker suit than was fashionable on the links – protected by two detectives who looked as if they were searching for balls.[115]

In 1914, the editor of the Unionist organ, the *Belfast Newsletter*, was assaulted by a suffragette after he had urged golfers to take the law into their own hands if they were attacked by suffragettes. A lady correspondent of the *Newsletter* attacked Lloyd George's politics, but admitted that he had a charming manner in the golf club at Walton Heath.[116] Golf was popular with many Irish Unionists, partly because it was the favoured game of businessmen and partly because of its Scottish connections. There were many golf links in the strongly Unionist county of Antrim, where the Portrush club produced two outstanding women golfers: Rhona Adair and May Hezlet. There were also some fine links along the coast of county Dublin: another Unionist bastion. In 1913 Bonar Law and two other Tory MPs spent a golfing holiday at Malahide, as the guest of the Unionist MP for Dublin University. They were preceded on the links by another strong Unionist, the Dean of the Dublin Chapel Royal, who suddenly died of a heart attack at the eighth hole.[117] Golf was not favoured by the Gaelic revivalists because it was not an ancient Irish game. Nevertheless many links were created in predominantly nationalist areas and the golf course at Tramore, near Waterford, was built by a friend and colleague of the Irish parliamentary leader John Redmond.[118] In May 1914, twelve Irish Nationalist MPs, including Joe Devlin and Willie Redmond, played a team from the London Irish Golfing Society at Walton Heath.[119]

IV

During the Edwardian period golf was exported to the rest of the English-speaking world and beyond. W. A. Watt, the premier of Victoria, who played at Walton Heath, described golf as 'the best game yet invented for the man who works above his eyebrows'.[120] The plans for New Delhi, drawn up in 1913, included space for a golf course to the south-west of the Viceroy's house.[121] After the Anglo-Russian agreement on Persia, it was assumed that golf would flourish in the British sphere of influence.

Golf advanced most rapidly in the United States, where it also became a favourite game of politicians. Two Presidents – Teddy Roosevelt and Woodrow Wilson – played golf in the Edwardian period.[122] Young Franklin Roosevelt became Secretary of the Campobello Golf Club in 1900 and golfed at St Andrews in 1905. His wife, Eleanor, was grieved that he preferred to golf on Sunday mornings rather than to attend church. Roosevelt's golfing was curtailed when he was crippled by polio, but he helped to design the course at Warm Springs, Georgia, where he went for treatment.[123]

In the summer of 1914 Asquith entertained the German Ambassador, Prince Lichnowsky, who recalled that the premier's 'Good health and excellent nerves were steeled by his devotion to golf'.[124] Certainly the European crisis did not put Asquith off his golf, for he played at Huntercombe only a week before Britain's declaration of war and a month later, at Littlestone.[125] From the end of 1914 until the end of 1916, Asquith spent many weekends at Walmer Castle, the official residence of the Lord Warden of the Cinque Ports. Walmer was close to several excellent golf courses including the Royal Cinque Ports, at Deal, and the Royal St George's, at Sandwich, which both hosted the Open Championship in the Edwardian period. When Asquith golfed at Deal, in 1915, there were only twelve holes to play on, because six had been commandeered by the army for shooting practice.[126] This was just as well because Asquith found his partner, the Lord Privy Seal, was a very slow player:

> Crewe tho' a very agreeable is a rather trying play-fellow, owing to the extraordinary deliberation of his methods. I calculated at last that I could have repeated to myself the Lord's Prayer and the Apostles' Creed between the time when he begins to address the ball on the tee and the final impact of the club upon it.[127]

Asquith's partiality for golf at Walmer played a part in his downfall. In December 1916 he insisted on going down to Walmer, despite the advice of his supporters that he should not leave London.

The new premier, Lloyd George, was no more willing than Asquith to foresake golf in wartime and he continued to play at Walton and at Criccieth when he had the opportunity. But Churchill's time and enthusiasm for golf waned during the war, and painting became his principal recreation. He told Balfour that painting could compete with either golf or philosophy.[128] Ramsay MacDonald's public opposition to the war prompted protests from several members of the Moray Golf Club in 1915.[129] A year later a resolution to remove MacDonald from membership of the club was endorsed by 73 votes to 24.[130] His friends considered that this was the hardest blow of all to him during the war. He never golfed on the Lossiemouth links again.[131]

Golf played a role in Lloyd George's downfall in 1922. At the Allied Conference at Cannes, convened to discuss German reparations, Lloyd George invited the French premier, Aristide Briand, and the Italian premier, Signor Bonomi, to try their untutored hands at golf. They were allowed to drive and putt, but their other shots were taken by the experienced British team: L. G., Bonar Law, Riddell and Grigg. Briand's first drive landed in a bunker and Bonomi left L. G. with such a difficult follow-up shot that he remarked, 'the question of reparations is difficult this time'. At the approach to the first green, Briand, instead of putting, drove the ball way beyond the hole.[132] The French press alleged that Lloyd George had deliberately made a fool of Briand, who was criticised in the Chamber and then resigned. That put paid to a reparations settlement and undermined Lloyd George's European policy. As the political outlook darkened for L. G., *Punch* transformed Walton Heath into the blasted heath of Shakespeare's *Macbeth*.[133] The fall of Lloyd George did not, however, lead to the end of prime ministerial golf, for the next two premiers were Bonar Law and MacDonald. Baldwin was the only premier between 1902 and 1935 who was not a keen golfer.

Why was golf so popular with Edwardian politicians? Many of them belonged to a generation, born in the 1850s and 1860s, who took up golf when it was rapidly expanding, like other kinds of organized games. But golf, unlike cricket, football or tennis, could be played at any time of the day and all the year round: a great advantage for busy politicians. Golf was also much less expensive than other élite recreations, like yachting and racing, and less socially exclusive than field sports. Thus it is tempting to regard the popularity of golf with MPs as evidence of the *embourgeoisement* of the political élite. However, Balfour – who initiated the link between golf and Westminster – came from the landed élite, whilst some archetypal middle-class politicians, such as the Chamberlains and Baldwin, were not golfers. Golf moreover, was not a team game and it was not taught in the public schools which largely catered for the sons of the professional classes.

Golf was played across the party spectrum from Tory diehards to radical Liberals and even some Socialists and Irish Nationalists. Mutual enthusiasm for golf helped to soften the asperities of party feeling, but seldom resulted in collusion between the parliamentary élite of the kind alleged by Chesterton and Belloc. Politicians generally golfed with members of their own parties and social circles. At Walton Heath, the only man who regularly golfed with politicians from all parties was the club professional, James Braid. He was reserved by nature and was left a small legacy by Riddell for 'his discretion'.[134] But for pressmen like Riddell, golf provided more opportunity for informal talk with MPs than was possible at Westminster. Hence the political gossip which enriches Riddell's diary.

For Edwardian politicians, golf was both a metropolitan and a provincial game. During the parliamentary recess, many MPs golfed on links in their constituencies or homelands. The golfing connections of Balfour with North Berwick, Asquith with St Andrews, Lloyd George with Criccieth and MacDonald with Lossiemouth, illustrated a more general phenomenon. George Hutchinson noted, in 1910, that many coastal resorts 'practically owe their existence to golf'.[135] When MPs were in London, they usually patronised select golf clubs, such as Walton Heath, which catered for the privileged and the wealthy. Nevertheless those golf clubs were less exclusive and less stately than the country houses which had been the recreational resorts of the Victorian political élite. Thus the popularity of golf with Edwardian politicians was a manifestation of social progressivism, as well as of relative privilege. By abandoning the grouse moor and the country house for the golf course and the club house, the Edwardian political élite acknowledged the changed political and social ethos of the age.

Notes

1 I wish to thank my brother, Dr Francis Quinault, Assistant Principal of the University of St Andrews, for providing the hospitality which inspired this study.
2 *Who's Who in Golf*, London, 1913.
3 *Punch*, 19 July 1911.
4 Roy Jenkins, *Asquith*, London, 1964, p. 26.
5 John Lowerson, *Sport and the English middle classes 1870–1914*, Manchester, 1993, pp. 125–53.
6 *Who's Who in Golf*, 1913.
7 Robert Rhodes James (ed.), *Winston Spencer Churchill: his complete speeches*, New York, 1974, 1. 694: 17 November 1906.
8 Lowerson, *Sport and middle classes*, p. 126.
9 Blanche E. Dugdale, *Arthur James Balfour* (2 vols), London, 1936, i. 23.
10 Kenneth Young, *Arthur James Balfour*, London, 1963, p. 133.
11 Arthur James, First Earl of Balfour, *Chapters of Autobiography* (ed. Mrs Edgar Dugdale), London, 1930, p. 224.
12 Dugdale, *Balfour*, i. 154.
13 The Rt. Hon. A. J. Balfour MP, 'The humours of golf' in: Horace G. Hutchinson (ed.) *Golf* [The Badminton Library of Sports and Pastimes], London, 1890, pp. 429–30.
14 Henry W. Lucy, *A diary of the Salisbury Parliament 1886–92*, London, 1892, p. 435.
15 Bernard Darwin, in *Fifty years' memories and contrasts 1882–1932*, by twenty-seven contributors to *The Times*, London, 1932, p. 206.
16 Sir Robert Speed, David Natzler and Lord Deedes, *The Parliamentary Golfing Society: a short history*, London, 1991, pp. 3–4.
17 Jane Ridley and Clayre Percy (eds), *The letters of Arthur Balfour and Lady Elcho 1885–1917*, 1992, p. 100: Balfour to Lady Elcho, 17 January 1894.
18 Quoted in: Kenneth Rose, *Curzon: A Most Superior Person*, London, 1985, p. 179.
19 *St Andrews Citizen*, 7 August 1897.
20 Balfour, *Chapters of Autobiography*, p. 228.
21 Dugdale, *Balfour*, i. 351: Balfour to Lady Elcho, 9 August 1903.
22 *The Times*, 2 October 1913.
23 Edith Lyttelton, *Alfred Lyttelton*, London, 1917, pp. 229, 287, 341.

24 Dugdale, *Balfour*, i. 194.
25 *The Times*, 21 February 1907. I am indebted for this reference to Ewen Green.
26 Lord Riddell, *More Pages From My Diary 1908–14*, London, 1934, p. 28.
27 Riddell, *Diary*, p. 122: 9 February 1913.
28 *The Times*, 27 September 1907.
29 The Earl of Oxford and Asquith, *Memories and Reflections 1852–1927* (2 vols), London, 1928, i. 22–3.
30 Herbert Asquith, *Moments of Memory*, London, (n.d.), p. 131.
31 *The St Andrews Citizen*, 10 July 1897, etc.
32 J. P. Alderson, *Mr Asquith* London, 1905, p. 218.
33 J. A. Spender and Cyril Asquith, *Life of Herbert Henry Asquith, Lord Oxford and Asquith* (2 vols), London, 1932, i. 215.
34 Riddell, *Diary*, p. 101: 16 November, 1912.
35 Asquith, *Moments of memory*, p. 131–2.
36 *Who's Who in Golf* 1913.
37 Spender and Asquith, *Life of Asquith*, i. 193.
38 Violet Bonham Carter, *Winston Churchill as I knew him*, London, 1965, p. 234.
39 Michael & Eleanor Brock (eds), *H. H. Asquith, letters to Venetia Stanley*, Oxford, 1982, p. 23: 14 September 1912.
40 Brock, *Asquith Letters*, p. 49: 16 February 1914.
41 Brock, *Asquith Letters*, p. 188: 22 August 1914.
42 Brock, *Asquith Letters*, p. 366: 9 January 1915.
43 John Grigg, *Lloyd George: the people's champion 1902–11*, 1978, p. 15.
44 Riddell, *Diary*, p. 95: October 1912.
45 John Grigg, *The Young Lloyd George*, London, 1978 edn, p. 225. M. J. B. Baddeley and C. S. Ward, *North Wales: part I* London, 1902 edn, p. 157.
46 W. Watkin Davies, *Lloyd George 1863–1914*, 1939, p. 439.
47 *The Times*, 25 August, 1913.
48 Spender and Asquith, *Life of Asquith*, ii. 50–51: H. H. A. to Margot Asquith, 4 June 1914.
49 Bernard Darwin, *Golf Courses of the British Isles*, London, 1910 pp. 11–12.
50 Cyril Hewertson, *Walton Heath Golf Club – the story of the first seventy-five years*, London, 1979, p. 8.
51 Bernard Darwin, *Braid*, London, 1952, pp. 171, 174.
52 *Golf Illustrated*, 20 May 1904. I am indebted for information about Walton Heath Golf Club to P. A. Truett (Captain, 1993) and to the club's assistant secretary, Mrs Janice Owen.
53 Hewertson, *Walton Heath Golf Club*, pp. 13–14.
54 J. M. McEwen (ed.), *The Riddell Diaries 1908–23*, 1986, p. 9.
55 *Walton Heath Golf Club: Rules and List of Members 1913–14* (privately printed). Hewertson, *Walton Heath Golf Club*, p. 18.
56 *Who's Who in Golf*, 1913.
57 Horace G. Hutchinson, *Quarterly Review*, ccxii (1910), 106.
58 Riddell, *Diary*, p. 95: 26 October 1912.
59 Frank Owen, *Tempestuous journey: Lloyd George, his life and times*, London 1954, p. 219.
60 Owen, *Tempestuous journey*, p. 221.
61 Riddell, *Diary*, p. 163: 26 June 1913.
62 A. P. Nicholson, *The real men in public life*, London, 1928, p. 181.
63 Riddell, *Diary*, p. 99.
64 Riddell, *Diary*, p. 150: 17 May 1913.
65 Ridell, *Diary*, p. 160: 13 June 1913.
66 Ridell, *Diary*, p. 163: 20 June 1913.
67 Owen, *Tempestuous journey*, p. 221.
68 Riddell, *Diary*, pp. 24, 37.
69 Bonham Carter, *Winston Churchill*, pp. 235–6.
70 Winston S. Churchill, *The world crisis, 1911–18*, London, 1931 edn, pp. 62, 72–3.

71 Riddell, *Diary*, p. 197: 18 January 1914.
72 Randolph S. Churchill, *Winston S. Churchill*, Companion volume ii, part 2, London, 1969, pp. 1023, 1253.
73 Riddell, *Diary*, p. 77: 2 July 1912.
74 *Walton Heath Golf Club: List of Members 1913–14.*
75 Darwin, *Braid*, 1952, pp. 148, 179.
76 Riddell, *Diary*, p. 19: June 1911.
77 Hewertson, *Walton Heath Golf Club*, p. 20.
78 A. Wilson-Fox, *The Earl of Halsbury*, London, 1929, p. 145.
79 R.S. Churchill, *W. S. Churchill*, Companion vol. ii, part 2, pp. 1027–8: Sir Joseph Lawrence to J. S. Sandars, 20 November 1910.
80 Thomas Jones, *Lloyd George*, London, 1951, pp. 62–3.
81 *Black's Guide to Scotland*, London, 1903 edn, p. 258.
82 Jane Cox (ed.), *A singular marriage: A Labour love story in letters and diaries of Ramsay and Margaret MacDonald*, London, 1988 [from: MacDonald Papers PRO 30/69] pp. 68–9: MacDonald to Miss Gladstone, 29 June 1896.
83 Cox, *Singular marriage*, pp. 52, 78, 88: MacDonald to Miss Gladstone: 9 August 1895: 6, 13 July 1896.
84 Cox, *Singular marriage*, pp. 291, 305, 363–4.
85 Brock, *Asquith letters*, p. 33: H. H. Asquith to V. Stanley, 21 August 1913.
86 *The Times*, 27 September 1907.
87 *Golfing*, 15 November 1900. I am indebted for this reference to Mr R. A. L. Burnet of St Andrews.
88 Donald Read, *Edwardian England 1901–15*, London, 1972, p. 47.
89 Lowerson, *Sport and middle clases*, pp. 144–51.
90 R. L. Outhwaite, 'The land of the pheasant – a manless countryside', *Daily News*, 1 February 1909; Christopher Turnor, *Land problems and national welfare*, London, 1911, pp. 17–18.
91 Asquith, *Moments of memory*, pp. 89–9; John Wilson, *CB: a life of Sir Henry Campbell-Bannerman*, London, 1973, p. 155.
92 *The Times*, 23 October 1913: Lloyd George's speech at Swindon.
93 Hewertson, *Walton Heath Golf Club*, p. 16.
94 Riddell, *Diary*, p. 120: 7 February 1913.
95 A. G. Gardiner, *Life of George Cadbury*, London, 1923, pp. 107, 253.
96 Reginal Pound and Geoffrey Harmsworth, *Northcliffe*, London, 1959, pp. 264, 400–401.
97 Riddell, *Diary*, pp. 27, 38, 123–4.
98 R. S. Churchill, *W. S. Churchill*, Companion vol. ii, part 3, p. 1778: W. S. C. to Clementine Churchill, 1 September 1913.
99 Cox, *Singular marriage*, p. 72.
100 Sir Henry Lucy, *The diary of a journalist*, London, 1920, p. 137.
101 Asquith, *Moments of memory*, pp. 149–50.
102 Riddell, *Diary*, p. 138: 12 April 1913.
103 Owen, *Tempestuous journey*, pp. 216–17.
104 Mrs Ross (née Miss May Hezlet), 'From the Ladies' Point of View' in: Horace G. Hutchinson (ed.), *The new book of golf*, London, 1912, p. 267.
105 *The Times*, 28, 29 November 1912.
106 *The Times*, 8 September 1909; Asquith, *Moments of memory*, pp. 156–7.
107 Riddell, *Diary*, pp. 77, 107.
108 Quoted in *Golf Illustrated*, 28 February 1913.
109 *The Times*, 17, 19 February 1913.
110 *The Times*, 20 February, 2 April 1913.
111 *Golf Illustrated*, 28 February 1913.
112 *The Times*, 29 August 1913; Asquith, *Moments of memory*, p. 155.
113 Brock, *Asquith Letters*, p. 34: 3 September 1913.
114 *The Observer*, 22 November 1969.
115 *Golf Illustrated*, 19 September 1913.

116 Riddell, *Diary*, p. 117: 18 January 1913.
117 *The Times*, 19 May 1913.
118 Stephen Gwynn, *Ireland*, London, 1927, p. 156.
119 *The Times*, 6 May 1914.
120 Riddell, *Diary*, p. 140.
121 Robert Grant Irving, *Indian Summer: Lutyens, Baker and Imperial Delhi*, London, 1982, p. 75.
122 *Golf Illustrated*, 4 July 1913.
123 Frank Freidel, *Franklin D. Roosevelt: The Apprenticeship*, Boston, 1952, p. 49; Geoffrey C. Ward, *A First-Class Temperament: The Emergence of Franklin Roosevelt*, New York, 1989, pp. 37, 53, 256.
124 Quoted in Brock, *Asquith Letters*, p. 86, note 1.
125 Brock, *Asquith Letters*, p. 126: 26 July 1914; p. 188: 22 August 1914.
126 Brock, *Asquith Letters*, p. 366: 9 January 1915.
127 Brock, *Asquith Letters*, pp. 549–50: 17 April 1915.
128 Scottish Record Office, Balfour MSS, GD 433/2/19: Churchill to Balfour, 11 September 1920.
129 *The Times*, 18 September 1915.
130 *The Times*, 2 September 1916.
131 David Marquand, *Ramsay MacDonald*, London, 1977, pp. 192–3.
132 *The Times*, 10 January 1922.
133 *Punch*, 1 February 1922.
134 Darwin, *Braid*, pp. 171, 174.
135 Hutchinson, *Quarterly Review*, ccxii, 103.

10

AFTER THE HORSE: NOBILITY AND MOBILITY IN MODERN BRITAIN

DAVID CANNADINE

For as long as the horse and carriage were the symbols of social standing, and possession of stables and grooms the sign of a prosperous competence, the English landed aristocracy retained its predominant place. The power of horse and aristocrat was challenged by the railway, but both learned to recognise an ally as well as a rival in its influence. Both were vanquished by the horseless carriage of the twentieth century. From steam to motor, both showed great tenacity in survival, and the power of the aristocracy disappeared no sooner than the last, anachronistic cavalry charges of the First World War. The landed aristocracy survives into our own times with great social prestige; and the horse survives also, dignified and recreational, rather than functional. *(F. M. L. Thompson, English landed society in the nineteenth century, 1963, p. 1)*

In traditional western societies, the horse was the very emblem of aristocratic wealth, power and status. 'All pre-eminence', an Arab emir noted of the Franks, 'belongs to horsemen. They are in truth the only men who count. Theirs is to give counsel; theirs to render justice'.[1] And for more than a millenium, this remained essentially the case: the ownership of horses was largely confined to the patrician élite, their dependants and their servants. From the Norman Conquest to the nineteenth century, an English gentleman who did not possess a safe seat in the saddle was almost a contradiction in terms. The breeding and racing of horses were quintessentially aristocratic hobbies, and fox-hunting became a favourite recreation of most landowners. The limits to county society were set by the distance a horse could comfortably travel in a day, and until the early twentieth century, it was the cavalry, not the infantry, which was the most glamorous and aristocratic element in the army. The horse was thus an essential symbol of a rural, ordered, hierarchical and aristocratic world, and the 'men on horseback' towered above the rest of society, in their material resources, in their political power and in their enjoyment of life.[2]

But as Professor Thompson's words rightly remind us, the transport revolution which eclipsed the horse was itself an integral part of those broader economic, political and social changes which undermined and eventually marginalised the aristocracy. For in the long run, the advent of the train, then of the motor, and finally of the aeroplane, helped consolidate the triumph of the town over the country, of the mass over the élite, of industrial riches over landed wealth, and of speed over repose. As Lord Brabazon of Tara recorded in his autobiography, the two most significant developments during his lifetime had been changes in what he called 'mechanical things', and 'the complete revolution in the social structure of our country'.[3] But the impact of these developments in transport on aristocratic decline was more varied and more nuanced than it is often fashionable to suppose, and the changing relationship between the traditional landed élite and the railway, the automobile, and the heavier-than-air machine deserves more detailed and sustained examination than, for the most part, it has thus far received.

I

In a famous and oft-quoted remark, Thomas Arnold welcomed the steam railway as 'heralding the downfall of the aristocracy', and he continued, 'I rejoice to see it, and think that feudality is gone for ever'. As Headmaster of Rugby School (once disparagingly dismissed by Lord Peter Wimsey as little more than a railway junction), Arnold may well have been making a virtue of a necessity. But in essence he was correct: the railway brought noise and smoke into the sequestered quietude of the countryside; its lines compulsorily crossed lands considered inviolate by their owners; and it enabled masses of ordinary people to travel distances hitherto undreamed of. It was the most potent symbol of the new age of the industrial revolution, and it portended major changes in the structure of business and of wealth-holding.[4] It also cut down the aristocracy to size: as Walter Bagehot observed, 'our companies, our railways, our debentures, our shares' had 'come up', while 'the aristocracy have come down'. In the old days, grandees had journeyed in magnificent carriage processions, while landladies and waiters bowed before them. But on the trains, they were virtually indistinguishable from other wealthy travellers, and at railway stations went almost unnoticed.[5]

During the first phase of railway building, when the major trunk lines were being constructed betwen 1825 and 1850, many landowners did all they could to protect their parks and their estates from what they regarded as this new and 'outrageous' invasion of their privacy. When the Liverpool and Manchester Railway was first promoted, it was opposed by Lords Derby and Sefton on just these the grounds, and in 1830 the line of the London and Birmingham Railway was resisted by Lords Clarendon and Essex for precisely the same reason.[6] The Great Northern Railway (GNR) was criticised by Lord Exeter, because it went too near Burleigh, and by Lord Fitzwilliam 'to prevent the separation of some woods [near Peterborough] which in a hunting point of view are inseparable'. The Duke of Wellington, having initially insisted that there should be no railway station within five miles of Stratfield Saye, eventually relented and allowed one at Mortimer, fully three miles distant. Some grandees carried their opposition to yet further lengths. Even after the London to Norwich line had been completed, Lady Suffield always drove from Blickling to town in her carriage, 'rather than rub shoulders with other people in trains'.[7]

But it was not just the privacy of their parks and houses that patricians sought to protect from the intrusion of the railway: it was also their high-class building estates in London and their suburban developments in the provinces. The Bedfords succeeded in keeping the London and North-Western Railway (LNWR) out of their Bloomsbury estate, but the amount of traffic generated by the nearby Euston station nevertheless led to a marked decline in the social tone of the area. During the 1870s and early 1880s, the Calthorpes sought unavailingly to prevent the construction of a main line from Birmingham to Bristol through Edgbaston, but had to settle for restrictions on sidings, and a total ban on factory buildings adjacent to the line.[8] At Folkestone, the Earl of Radnor was more successful in preventing the South Eastern Railway (SER) from promoting an extension scheme which would have undermined his attempts to develop a high-class resort. When the Great Central Railway (GCR) came to Marylebone in the 1890s, Lord Portman imposed 'burdensome and expensive restrictions': the track was to be put in tunnels or concealed behind high walls; there were to be no advertisements or working-class housing close to the main line; all coal yards had to be roofed in; and all buildings were to be seemly and ornamented.[9]

Nevertheless, as the British aristocracy was well aware, there were occasions when timely concession could be more profitable than intransigent opposition, and the attraction of selling agricultural land to railway companies at written-up, development value, was undoubtedly considerable. Indeed, Robert Stephenson believed that 'the charge for land was greatly augmented by the enormous and unreasonable compensation required by some proprietors beyond the correct value of the land', and recent research has once again confirmed this opinion.[10] The most famous example was Lord Petre, who received £120,000 from the Eastern Counties Railway for lands reputedly worth £5,000. This seems to have been an exception; but other landowners clearly did well for themselves. The Marquess of Ailesbury obtained £19,000 from the Great Western, and George Lane-Fox, an indebted Yorkshire country gentleman, was happy to sell off land to fourteen English and Irish railway companies.[11] Sales of urban land could be even more lucrative. Between 1864 and 1892, the Derbys obtained £483,408, and this was for small plots of land in Liverpool, after the major sales had been made; and in London, families like the Camdens, Somers, Southamptons and Westminsters also obtained large sums of money from the same source.[12]

From the late 1840s onwards, many landowners were prepared to take a more positive view of local railway lines, as an essential instrument in the exploitation of their non-agricultural estate resources. The earls of Dudley were keen promotors of mineral lines in the West Midlands, and the marquesses of Bute supported the Rhymney Railway as a means to bring their Glamorgan coal to their Cardiff docks. Earl Fitzwilliam supported the South Yorkshire Railway, because it would help his collieries, the Duke of Northumberland invested in the Border Counties line because it opened up his iron ore at Bellingham and his coal at Plashetts, and the Duke of Norfolk built a branch line to link Glossop with the Manchester and Sheffield Railway.[13] Sir Peter Hesketh-Fleetwood promoted the Preston and Wyre Railway in the hope it would lead to the growth of the resort to which he gave his name, and the Earl of Burlington (the future seventh Duke of Devonshire) persuaded the Brighton and Hastings Railway to build a branch line to Eastbourne; and in collaboration with the Duke of Buccleuch, he was a founding father of the Furness Railway, which later became the most profitable mineral line in the country.[14]

By the mid-Victorian period, it was also clear that branch lines could greatly enhance the value of agricultural estates, and landowners began to support local railways, out of a traditional sense of *noblesse oblige* mingled with self-interest. The earls of Yarborough encouraged lines in Lincolnshire, and the earls of Leicester invested in the Wells and Fakenham Railway and the West Norfolk Junction Railway. In Northumberland, the Wansbeck Valley Railway was almost entirely financed by two local landowners, Sir Walter Trevelyan and the Earl of Carlisle.[15] On a larger scale, the Duke of Devonshire invested heavily in the Lismore and Dungarvan Railway, in the hope that it would benefit his Irish estates: by 1873, his shareholdings were £117,810, and by 1885 they had almost doubled. The third Duke of Sutherland was even more lavish in his expenditure, laying out £266,000 on the construction of railways in his highland fiefdom. He was, notes Eric Richards, a man 'besotted by steam trains, fire engines and gadgets', who was 'guided by anachronistic notions of a Highland princedom to such an extent that they became extensions of the aristocratic ego'.[16]

Inevitably, this meant that by the mid-Victorian period, it was 'quite common for members of the peerage to appear on the boards of railway companies, though these were usually lines of local importance to particular estates'.[17] Having invested heavily in the South Yorkshire Railway, it seemed only natural that Earl Fitzwilliam should eventually become its chairman. The Duke of Devonshire was chairman of the Furness Railway, and most of his co-directors were Cavendishes or Buccleuchs, or their associates. The Duke of Sutherland was chairman of the Sutherland and Caithness Railway, the Earl of Mansfield of the Perth and Dunkeld line, the Earl of Carlisle of the Malton and Driffield Junction Railway, and the Earl of Yarborough of the Manchester, Sheffield and Lincolnshire. Untitled country gentlemen were also to be found occupying the same position. From 1847 to 1865, the chairman of the Bristol and Exeter Railway was James Wentworth Buller, a West Country squire, who was followed by the twelfth Earl of Devon.[18]

During the first three-quarters of the nineteenth century, aristocratic involvement with railways thus followed a recognisable pattern. On the whole, they were not especially enthusiastic about main lines and trunk routes: they regarded them as dangerous speculations, indulged in by irresponsible financiers who had no interest in the countryside they were crossing.[19] As a result, patrician investment was relatively meagre: the massive holding by the Dukes of Sutherland in the LNWR was the exception which proved the rule – it derived from their early investment in the Liverpool and Manchester Railway, itself the product of local considerations.[20] Their main concern was in fostering branch lines, which sometimes paid handsomely, if they were mineral-bearing, but which often did not. They were happy to become chairmen, but this was out of a sense of local obligation, rather than because of any desire to 'go' into business. Once again, the few exceptions prove the rule. From 1853 to 1861, the third Duke of Buckingham was chairman of the LNWR: but this was partly because he urgently needed to repair the family fortunes, and partly because the directors wanted an appropriate counterpoise to the excessive influence of the Duke of Sutherland in the company's affairs. From 1868 to 1872, Lord Cranborne (later Lord Salisbury, and Queen Victoria's last Prime Minister) was chairman of the Great Eastern Railway

(GER). Like Buckingham, he needed the salary but he, too, did well. He took over an ailing company, was determined to nurse it back to health, showed a firm grasp of business essentials, and did much to restore confidence.[21]

During the last quarter of the nineteenth century, the relationship between the landowners and the railways changed fundamentally, and in a variety of ways. As the engineering profession became more respectable, a small trickle of patricians began to go into the railway workshops.[22] G. J. Churchward's ancestors had been squires of Stoke Gabriel in South Devon since 1457. But after an apprenticeship on the South Devon Railway, he spent his life in the service of the Great Western. From 1902 to 1921, he was Superintendent of Locomotives and Carriages, and designed both the *Stars* and the *Saints*, the prototypical Great Western 4-6-0s, as well as the only Pacific ever built by the GWR, the *Great Bear*.[23] Even more patrician was the second Lord Montagu of Beaulieu, who was sent down from New College, Oxford, and was apprenticed at the London and South-Western Railway (LSWR) workshop at Nine Elms, where he was known as John Douglas, and earned 11*s* 6*d*. for a forty-eight hour week. For a time he drove expresses on the London to Bournemouth line, and he did so again during the strikes of 1919 and 1926. 'I'm glad', one railwayman remarked to him, 'that you're driving the train, my lord – I know that you will return it in perfect condition'. And so he did: at the end of one of these journeys, a passenger gave him sixpence: 'Well done, young man', he observed, 'I am so glad you are defying your union'.[24]

More generally, many aristocrats now began to see the railway companies of Britain as appropriate places in which to place extensive investments. The amalgamations of the mid-Victorian years meant that, by 1900, the biggest railway companies were among the largest and (at least in the case of preference and debenture shares) most secure businesses in the land. As aristocrats began to move into the stock market, such railway shares beckoned alluringly – initially at home, and subsequently abroad.[25] Before 1870, the railway investments of the earls of Leicester had been confined to the £15,000 they had placed in local, Norfolk lines. But during the 1870s, they invested £50,000 in the North Eastern (NER), the GER, the GWR and the LNWR, as well as £40,000 in Indian lines; and in the next decade, they bought a further £110,000 worth of British railway shares, and also made extensive investments in lines in Canada, the United States and South America. By then, indeed, this was a general trend. During the 1880s, Lord Salisbury invested extensively in railway stock debentures; and during the following decades, other illustrious investors in such home and overseas companies included the dukes of Portland, Devonshire, Bedford and Sutherland.[26]

But it was not just as investors that grandees (and gentry, too) were associating themselves with railways in a new way: they were also joining the boards of these great companies with an alacrity that had been conspicuously absent in earlier years. Landowners hard hit by agricultural depression eagerly sought directors' fees, and to be on the board of a railway company was to join the most elect group of all – partly because of the size and stability of these great undertakings, partly because of their unique position as prototypical public utilities, and partly because directors enjoyed the right of free travel throughout the whole of the national rail network.[27] Again, local connections helped: the Earl of Dudley, whose Black Country collieries depended on the railway, was a Director of the Great Western, as was Walter Long, a Wiltshire country gentleman and Tory Party potentate. The North Eastern recruited its board even more assiduously from the local notability: at the turn of the century, its directors included Lords Grey, Wenlock and Londonderry, as well as Sir Matthew Ridley and Sir Edward Grey.[28]

This sudden proliferation of titled directors of great railway companies inevitably led to a marked increase in the number of titled chairmen. Among the longest serving were Lord Colville of Culross at the GNR (1879–95), Lord Cawdor at the GWR (1895–1905), Lord Stalbridge at the LNWR (1891–1912) and Lord Cottesloe at the London, Brighton and South Coast Railway or LBSCR (1896–1908). When Viscount Ridley died in 1904, after three years as chairman of the North Eastern, he was replaced by Sir Edward Grey, who felt obliged to resign when the Liberals gained office only two years later.[29] Other patrician chairmen in the decade before the First World War included Lord Bessborough (LBSCR), Lord Knaresborough (NER), Sir William Hart Dyke (London, Chatham and Dover Railway), Lord Stuart of Wortley (GCR), Viscount Churchill (GWR) and William Whitelaw (Highland Railway and North British Railway). But the most famous aristocratic chairman was probably Lord Claud Hamilton, second son of the first Duke of Abercorn. He became a director of the GER in 1872, at the age of twenty-nine; he was vice-chairman from 1874 to 1893; he was chairman from 1893 until the company disappeared in 1922; and he had named after him one of the loveliest class of locomotives ever built.[30]

Most of these patrician chairmen were younger sons or country gentlemen of limited resources: Sir Edward Grey, whose Fallodon estate yielded a mere £4,000 a year was certainly grateful for the £2,000 salary he briefly drew as chairman of the NER. The contribution that the railways made to aristocratic finances is clear: what the aristocracy did for the railways in return is rather less apparent. Coincidentally, the era of patrician predominance on the boards of these great companies was with a difficult period in railway history: reduced profits, declining dividends, rising costs, increased government regulation and growing labour troubles.[31] These problems were so deep rooted and so pervasive, that it seems unlikely that patrician (or even non-patrician?) management was primarily to blame. In any case, most companies were under the *de facto* control of the general manager: the North Eastern, though groaning with grandees, was effectively run (and very innovatively and efficiently run) by Sir George Gibb.[32]

Nevertheless, it was widely believed that patrician directors and chairmen did not know much about running a company. In a time of growing labour unrest, it was increasingly inappropriate that they should look on themselves as paternal employers, regard their staff as 'servants', and remain implacably hostile to trades unions.[33] When Lord Colville of Culross retired as chairman of the GNR, it was partly because the company's recent performance had been distinctly unimpressive, and he was replaced by W. L. Jackson, who was significantly described as 'a man of practical commercial training'. Lord Stuart of Wortley's motto was 'Hold fast by the past', and this also seems to have been his maxim as regards business practice.[34] In his later years, Lord Knaresborough increasingly felt 'that the times were out of joint, and that he had little in common with current trends'. Lord Claud Hamilton was equally inflexible and out of date, and was described by his *Times* obituarist as 'not a conspicuously able man of business, and his judgement was not infrequently at fault'.[35]

With the major re-grouping of 1921–3, the number of railway directors was drastically reduced, from 600 to 80, and the connection between the aristocracy and the railways was inevitably much weakened. Neither the LMS nor the Southern Railway opted for landed chairmen, although lords continued to appear on the board: Rockley, Clinton, Folkestone and Courthope in the case of the Southern.[36] But at the Great Western, Viscount Churchill continued as chairman until his death in 1934, and at the LNER, William Whitelaw took charge, when Sir Edward Grey made it plain that he would not accept. But again, it was the general managers who were very much the dominant figures, and the problems of air and motor competition, of inadequate capital and delayed electrification, largely passed the chairmen by. Churchill was 'perplexed and ill at ease' during the strike-ridden inter-war period, and was replaced by Viscount Horne, who had much more experience of business, politics and industry; and Sir Eric Geddes once dismissed Whitelaw as representing 'the bygone feudal system of railway management, when railway directors regarded the general manager much as they would their bailiff or gamekeeper'. Appropriately enough, Whitelaw resigned as chairman in 1938 in order to devote himself to his family estates in Scotland.[37]

But in a similar manner to Lord Claud Hamilton, these two patricians both received fitting recognition from the companies they had served. When the GWR decided that it would produce no more Pacific locomotives, Churchward's *Great Bear* was rebuilt as a 4-6-0, and was re-named *Viscount Churchill*; and one of Sir Nigel Gresley's famous A4 Pacifics was called *William Whitelaw* – at least the second engine which was named after the LNER chairman. Indeed, it was Gresley himself who most triumphantly sustained the dwindling tradition of patrician involvement with railways into the inter war years. He was the grandson of the Rev. Sir Nigel Gresley, ninth baronet, and the bearer of one of the oldest names in the country. In the 1890s, he trained at Crewe, and for most of the inter-war years, he was chief locomotive engineer of the LNER. In 1928, he made the *Flying Scotsman* a non-stop service from London to Edinburgh; in 1935 he put on the streamlined *Silver Jubilee* train; and in 1938 the *Mallard* became the fastest steam locomotive in the world. How different were Gresley's social origins from those of George Stephenson. As was remarked on his retirement, he was 'a great Englishman, whose ancestors fought at Agincourt'.[38]

II

In certain quarters, the aristocratic reaction to the motor car in the two decades before the First World War was even more hostile than it had been to the steam engine during the second quarter of the nineteenth century. Unlike the railway, the automobile was explicitly conceived as a horse substitute: not for nothing was it initially called the 'horseless carriage'. And firms like Mulliners, which had previously made carriages, soon turned to the building of motor-car bodies.[39] But the motor was also the most potent symbol of the irresponsible and corrosive plutocracy by which the patricians felt themselves threatened from the 1880s onwards. By definition, motorists were vulgar, selfish and inconsiderate, 'simply rich people enjoying a new excitment'. They drove 'recklessly, and without proper consideration for other users of the road'. As they hurtled through the countryside, indifferent to tradition or to locality, they seemed to epitomise 'wealth's intolerable arrogance'. They abused their privileges 'with an inconsiderate insolence' which merely served to demonstrate 'the extent to which the wealth of England, during the past half-century, has passed away from the hands of gentlemen'. If the horse was the apt symbol of landed supremacy, then the motor was the sure and certain sign that that supremacy was coming to an end.[40]

More precisely, the motor car threatened three of the landed élite's most cherished institutions. The first was the very ideal of the 'county community', which presupposed a settled and leisurely country existence.

But the car effectively destroyed this stable and self-sufficient mode of life, by making country houses more accessible, and by making possible that new, and quintessentially plutocratic custom, the 'weekend' house-party.[41] The second was fox-hunting, which was the most potent symbol of county solidarity. But the noise of the motor frightened the horses, and the smell put the hounds off the scent. Many hunt committees forbade their members from driving to meets in cars; one MFH described the motor as 'the invention of the evil one': and Lord Willoughby de Broke thought it was 'quite out of harmony with the sport of fox-hunting'.[42] The third institution which was undermined by the motor was the cavalry. By 1914, it was clearly anachronistic, and during the inter-war years, the British army was belatedly mechanised. Even as late as the 1930s, a patrician officer like Major General Howard-Vyse was prepared to defend the 'constant association' with 'that comparatively swift animal, the horse', because he thought it resulted in a 'quickness of thought and an elasticity of outlook which are almost second nature'. But by then, the battle had long since been lost.[43]

Not surprisingly, then, 'early motorists', as Lord Brabazon later recalled, '... were a community rather disliked by the horsey element, and had to stick together'.[44] But as in the case of the railway, there were some aristocrats who from the very outset were well-disposed to this new form of transport, especially among the super-rich, those landowners who most approximated to the new plutocracy in both their income and their outlook. Among famous owners of racehorses, both Lord Derby and Lord Rosebery were early motoring enthusiasts. So was Lord Lonsdale, arguably the most renowned horseman of his generation, who was President of the AA from 1910 until 1944.[45] Among the more restless landowners of Cheshire, the second Duke of Westminster, Lord Rocksavage, and the Hon. Maurice Egerton were eager motorists; and during the First World War, Westminster equipped at his own expense a unit of twelve armour-plated Rolls-Royces, which saw service on the Western Front, and in North Africa.[46] Arthur Balfour was the first motoring Prime Minister. He drove up from the country to attend cabinet meetings; when he resigned in November 1905, he used a car to move his chattels out of 10 Downing Street; and on his eightieth birthday, his friends bought him a new Rolls-Royce.[47]

But some patricians also played a more active part, in the early days of the motor car, as propagandists and publicists. The Hon. Evelyn Ellis was a younger son of the sixth Lord Howard de Walden, and brother of one of the courtiers of the Prince of Wales.[48] In 1894, he purchased a Panhard in Paris, and brought it to England in the following year, driving it from the south coast to the Cotswolds, passing through Windsor on the way. By making the first recorded motor journey in England, he aimed to draw attention to the unreasonable restrictions imposed by the Locomotive Acts of 1865 and 1878, which limited all road vehicles to four miles per hour, and required that a man should walk in front carrying a red flag. Ellis deliberately flouted this law, by dispensing with the red flag and driving above the speed limit, and so helped to bring about the Locomotives and Highways Act of 1896, which did away with the red flag, and raised the speed limit to fourteen miles per hour. And thanks to his courtly connections, he persuaded the Prince of Wales to take his first drive in a motor vehicle in 1896, at Warwick Castle.[49]

But Ellis was outshone by Lord Montagu of Beaulieu, who soon changed his interests from driving trains to driving cars, and energetically exploited his social and political contacts in support of this new cause. He bought his first car in 1896, and paid his first motoring fine three years later. In 1899 he became the first MP to appear in a motor in New Palace Yard; in the following year, he was the first MP to use a car in a general election campaign; and in 1902, he took Edward VII for his first drive as king. He contributed to the *Book of Motoring* in the *Badminton Library of Sports and Pastimes*, was chairman of the Parliamentary Automobile Committee, and did much to facilitate the passing of the 1903 Motor Bill, which raised the speed limit to 20 mph.[50] But Montagu's greatest impact was through his journalism. In 1902, he began to publish *Car Illustrated*, which boasted a message of support from Arthur Balfour, and ran a series of articles entitled 'Cars and Country Houses'; and as a friend of Alfred Harmsworth's, Montagu was a regular contributor to *The Times* and the *Daily Mail*, for whom he wrote a series of motoring articles on a wide range of subjects.[51]

The third major patrician propagandist in these early, pioneering years was Hugh Fortescue Locke-King, a country gentleman who owned a 3,500-acre estate at Brooklands near Weybridge in Surrey. In 1907, he opened a two-and-three-quarter mile race track, to publicise British cars, and to enable British drivers to reach much higher speeds than were allowed on the road.[52] Until the Second World War, Brooklands was the mecca for British motoring, and it long retained signs of its patrician origins. Hugh Allen of the Jockey Club was the starter, the entry fees and prize money were in sovereigns, and the results were run up on a telegraph board at the end of each race. In the early years the cars were un-numbered, like horses, and drivers wore coloured smocks, like jockeys, by which they expected to be identified. Even after this practice was abandoned, amateur drivers still talked of 'stabling their mounts' at garages near the track, and throughout the inter-war years, the club committee remained dominated by grandees.[53]

But although there were many motoring enthusiasts and propagandists among the patricians, few of them became closely involved in investment or in management. Before the First World War, four hundred companies had been set up to manufacture motor cars in Britain. Almost all of them operated on a very small scale, and by 1914, scarcely one-quarter of them were still in being. Compared with railway debentures or preference shares, these were decidedly risky undertakings, and there were very few instances of aristocratic investment.[54] In the early 1900s, the Hon. Evelyn Ellis invested £13,000 in Daimler debenture shares, and this infusion of capital probably kept the company from collapsing completely. Better documented is the connection between the Earl of Macclesfield and William Morris. They first met in a motor car collision in Oxford (where Macclesfield was an undergraduate) in 1905. In August 1912, Macclesfield invested £4,000 in preference shares in Morris's new company, and in 1919, when Morris re-organised his business, Macclesfield took £25,000 worth of seven per cent preference shares. Again, this support seems to have been crucial for the survival of Morris's earlier enterprises.[55]

Since aristocratic investment in the motor industry was minimal, aristocratic directors and chairmen were rarer still. In the investment boom of the mid-1890s, many companies were promoted connected with tyres, cycles and cars, especially by Harry Lawson and E. T. Hooley. One technique they employed to persuade the public to invest in their uncertain undertakings was to deck out their lists of directors with titled names. Lord de la Warr was chairman of Dunlop, and Lord Winchilsea was chairman of the Great Horseless Carriage Company.[56] Other peers who were involved in such companies, either as chairmen or directors, included Lords Aylesford, Lonsdale and Albemarle. But these men were among the more disreputable members of the peerage, who eagerly (and foolishly) accepted cash payments from Hooley and Lawson in exchange for allowing their names to be used. But when the companies collapsed, the result was public humiliation, and thereafter, titled directors in the car industry were very rare indeed. Before 1914, the most conspicuous exception was the Earl of Shrewsbury and Talbot, who in 1903 had become chairman of a syndicate formed to sell Clément cars in England, and which later sold Talbot cars, made in Ladbroke Grove, Kensington.[57]

The closest connection between the motor industry and the aristocracy was forged by the Hon. C. S. Rolls, younger son of Lord Llangattock, a Monmouthshire landowner. Rolls had bought his first car in 1896, and was one of the earliest patrician enthusiasts.[58] In 1902, he set himself up in London, selling high-class cars to high-class people, and by ruthlessly exploiting his aristocratic connections, established a reputation as a brilliant salesman and demonstrator. By 1903, he numbered Lotd Rosebery, Lord Willoughby d'Eresby and the Duke of Sutherland among his clients, and by the following year, his customers included four foreign princes, two dukes, two earls, one viscount, seven barons and three baronets. Initially, Rolls was obliged to sell foreign motors, but his ambition was to sell a high-class English car. In 1904, he met the engineer Henry Royce and two years later, the company of Rolls-Royce was registered, with Royce making the cars and Rolls making the sales.[59] By the time of Rolls's death in 1910, the Silver Ghost was already established as 'the best car in the world'. Only Daimler, with close royal connections which lasted until the death of Queen Mary, and with the early financial support provided by the Hon. Evelyn Ellis, offered any serious competition in this high-status market.[60]

By the inter-war years, the links between the aristocracy and the motor had become noticeably weaker. In part, this was because the sale of great estates and the increasing impoverishment of many landowners meant that they no longer made up such an important element in the quality market for cars as they once had. This, at least, was Lord Cottenham's opinion:

> A great deal of money has changed hands of late years, but not always for the better. Where the Rolls-Royce, the Daimler or the Sunbeam in days gone by might well have been occupied by those to whom the well-being of their tenants and their servants was as important as the upbringing of their own children, today, these cars are occupied far too often by the war profiteer, to whom, after the manner of their kind, the maintenance of their 'dignity' and the satisfying of their appetites alike are gods. The squire is constantly seen driving a little car, nowadays.[61]

And there were also major changes in the industry itself. It no longer meant sport for the few so much as transport for the many. Large firms like Morris and Austin bought out many of their rivals, and concentrated on mass-produced vehicles for a mass market.[62] But in this transformation, the aristocracy played no part. William Morris bought out Lord Macclesfield's shareholding in February 1922, and thereafter never had dealings with him again. Only at Rolls-Royce did the patrician connection linger, where Lord Herbert Scott, a younger son of the Duke of Buccleuch, was chairman between 1936 and 1944.[63]

But some notables continued in their self-appointed task as publicists and propagandists. From 1921 until his death in 1929, Lord Montagu was motoring correspondent of *The Times*, and in 1922–23, he vainly tried to set up a syndicate to construct a motorway network connecting all the major British towns.[64] The sixth Earl of Cottenham raced cars for Alvis and Sunbeam during the 1920s, and wrote a succession of books dealing with almost every aspect of the past, present and future of the car: *Motoring without fears* (1928), *Motoring today and tomorrow* (1928), and *Steering wheel papers* (1932). Thereafter, he became motoring adviser to the Metropolitan Police and the Home Office.[65] And Viscount Curzon, later fifth Earl Howe, took up competitive driving in 1928 at the age of forty-four, on the advice of a magistrate who was bored with fining him so often for speeding. He became president of the British Racing Driver's Club, and edited the volume on *Motor Racing* in the *Lonsdale Library*.[66]

But the most famous patrician motorist during the inter-war years was probably the Hon. Mrs Victor Bruce, the daughter of Lawrence Petre of Coptfold Hall in Essex, who married the fourth son of the second Lord Aberdare in 1926.[67] She was the first woman to ride a motor-cycle, the first to be in an accident, and the first to be summonsed for speeding. In 1927, she won the Ladies' Cup in the Monte Carlo Rally, having driven for seventy-two hours, non-stop. In the same year, she drove to the Arctic Circle and back (and was granted an audience by the King of Denmark on the way). With her husband, she drove non-stop round the track at Monthléry, covering 15,000 miles in ten days at an average of 68 mph. In 1929, she drove round the same track for twenty-four hours, at an average speed of 90 mph, establishing a new world record for the greatest non-stop run by a single-handed driver. True to her aristocratic origins, she always drove wearing a string of pearls, and in 1939 she came first in the open jumping class at the Royal Horse Show, Windsor. 'Speed', she recalled in her autobiography, 'has always fascinated me since my first pony bolted. Going slowly always makes me tired'.[68]

III

Compared with the train or the car, the aeroplane was less negatively viewed by the aristocracy, at least during its early years. Ever since the time of Sir George Cayley, patrician dilettanti had shown an interest in the problems of flight, and during the last quarter of the nineteenth century, ballooning had enjoyed extensive aristocratic patronage. 'To go up in a balloon', Lord Brabazon later recalled, 'is the only way to go into the air like a gentleman'.[69] Nor, in its pre-jet manifestation, did the aeroplane threaten the sanctity of landowners' broad acres, or the peace and quiet of the countryside, in the way that the train or the motor did. Above all, there was something appealingly chivalric about the early pioneers of powered flight. In peacetime, it was daring, dangerous, almost buccaneering, to take to the air in these frail and flimsy machines; and in wartime, these latter-day knights of the skies duelled and jousted in aerial tournaments, elevated above the earth-bound and plodding infantry in much the same way that the men on horseback had been in earlier eras.

For many patricians, interest in the aeroplane was the natural extension of their interest in the motor car. The Hon. C. S. Rolls was an ardent balloonist (he eventually made 170 ascents) and in 1903 he had founded the Aero Club to promote the sport, significantly described as 'the Jockey Club of flying'. He then shifted his attention to cars, but once Rolls-Royce was established, turned again to the air, this time as an eager champion of powered flight. In 1908, he visited Le Mans to study Wilbur Wright's aeroplane, and soon bought one of Wright's machines for his own use. In June 1910, he set a new record by flying the English Channel both ways in his Wright aeroplane. By this time, his reputation was at its peak, and he began to be concerned about the government's indifference to the military implications of flying, and the precarious finances of many of the British aeroplane producers.[70] But in July 1910, he took part in a flying tournament at Bournemouth, and was killed when his plane crashed following the collapse of the tail plane, thus becoming the first Englishman to be involved in a fatal aero accident.

Among Rolls's closest friends was J. T. C. Moore-Brabazon, scion of a famous Irish landed family, who, after leaving Cambridge where he had briefly read engineering, was apprenticed for a year as a mechanic at the Darracq company in Paris, and became an international racing driver. In 1907, he won the Circuit des Ardennes in a Minerva, but by then he had already taken up ballooning and soon turned his attention to flying. In May 1909, he became the first Englishman to make a powered flight in the United Kingdom. One the Isle of Sheppey, he flew a Voisin for a little over one minute and ended with a crash that nearly killed him. But, as a result, he obtained the first pilot's certificate given out by the Royal Aero Club (Rolls was given the second). In October of the same year, he piloted a Short Brothers machine, and won the £1,000 prize offered by the *Daily Mail* for the first English aircraft to fly one mile. Like Rolls, he began to establish himself as a pundit and propagandist, but after Rolls's fatal crash, he stopped flying altogether.[71]

Other patricians were not so easily deterred. Maurice Egerton, Sir Archibald Sinclair, Lord Edward Grosvenor, Lord George Wellesley and the Marquess of Tullibardine were among the earliest pilots to qualify in the years before 1914. Like the AA and the RAC, the Royal Aero Club was laden with grandees among its presidents and committee men. Hugh Locke-King made Brooklands into a centre for aviation, and Lord Montagu of Beaulieu opened a training school in the grounds of his country house.[72] He gave generous coverage to flying in *Car Illustrated*, and began to take an interest in the military implications of powered flight. In 1909, he established the Aerial Defence Committee, and initiated the first ever parliamentary debate on the subject. Until 1914, he was a severe critic of the government's lack of interest, and throughout the First World War, he campaigned vigorously for the amalgamation of the Royal Flying Corps and the Royal Naval Air Service, and for the setting up of a proper Air Ministry.[73]

With very few exceptions, this was sum of the aristocracy's involvement with flying in its formative years: adventure and propaganda, topped off with a little politicking. As with the motor industry, there was a large number of small producers, whose finances were exceptionally precarious.[74] But there are only two recorded cases of financial assistance along the lines of Ellis with Daimler, and Macclesfield with Morris. Lady Howard de Walden recalled that her husband helped to finance one such venture, although she does not specify which. It proved to be a failure, as the plane only flew once, briefly and unsuccessfully. But for years afterwards, the silk with which the wings had been covered 'produced shirts galore' for de Walden's 'various godsons'. More significant was the 'Blair Atholl Syndicate', which was created to support the efforts of John William Dunne. The Duke of Westminster, the Marquess of Tullibardine, Earl Fitzwilliam and Lord Rothschild each subscribed £1,000. But although initially his experiments prospered more than those of Lord Howard de Walden's unknown pioneer, Dunne eventually ran out of ideas, and left aviation for good in 1914.[75]

Under these circumstances, it is perhaps not surprising that the aristocratic contribution to the airborne war of 1914–18 was decidedly meagre. Moore-Brabazon joined the Royal Flying Corps, and became expert in aerial photography and reconnaissance. The young Oswald Mosley served briefly during 1915. Other patricians who flew include Lord Edward Grosvenor, Lord Hugh Cecil, and the Master of Sempill.[76] But the most famous British aces – Albert Ball, James McCudden and Mick Mannock – were from a much lower social stratum, while the high command was very much in the hands of Hugh Trenchard. Unlike the ground war on the western front, there was no 'lost generation' of doomed patrician flyers. And there was no English equivalent to the German ace, von Richthofen, a Prussian aristocrat with a passion for hunting who brought down eighty allied pilots. In Germany, he was idolised as a knight of the air, a chivalric crusader. And the British public shared this view: they christened him the Red Baron, and when he was finally shot down, in the spring of 1918, he was saluted by *The Aeroplane* as 'a brave man, a clean fighter, and . . . a courageous nobleman'.[77] But no such figure emerged from the thin ranks of Britain's flying aristocracy.

During the inter-war years the RAF was subjected to severe economies until 1934, Imperial Airways was starved of funds, and the plane makers suffered accordingly.[78] To the extent that aristocrats were still involved, their connection was the familiar amalgam of recreation and propaganda, topped off by politics. The 'Flying Duchess' of Bedford took to the air because she was stone deaf, and because the change in atmospheric pressure alleviated the buzzing in her ears. She qualified as a pilot in her sixties, and made much-publicised round trips to India and the Cape of

Good Hope. In March 1937, she took off from Woburn on a routine flight, and was never seen again. It was later discovered that the word WOBURN had been painted in large letters on the roof of the house, for her benefit, which proved a mild embarrassment when the secret service moved there during the Second World War.[79] Predictably more flamboyant was Mrs Victor Bruce, who embarked on a round-the-world solo flight in 1930, only eight weeks after having gained her pilot's licence. In order to lighten her plane, she dispensed with the parachute. She crashed in the Arabian desert, caught malaria in Indo-China, and when flying over Hong Kong on 11 November, stopped her engine in mid-air to observe the two minutes silence. She later joined a flying circus, and subsequently ran an air despatch company.[80]

The foreword to her account of her round-the-world flight was written by the Master of Sempill, who was as much a propagandist for air travel as Lord Cottesloe was for the motor car. After serving in the Royal Flying Corps, he undertook many overseas missions to advise other governments on the setting-up of their air forces. He competed each year for the King's Cup between 1924 and 1930, and made many long flights abroad. He was President of the Royal Aeronautical Society and of the Gliding Association, aviation correspondent of *The Field*, and in 1931 published *The air and the plain man*.[81] Even more adventurous was the Marquess of Clydesdale, who later became fourteenth Duke of Hamilton. In 1933, he successfully led an expedition to take the first photographs of the summit of Mount Everest, an adventure which he later described as 'the only one original flight worthwhile'.[82] Like Sempill, Clydesdale prided himself on being – in the language of the time – 'airminded'. In essence, this meant being well disposed to modernity and to technological progress. And for members of the inter-war aristocracy, constantly afraid that their day was done, the attractions of proclaiming their 'airmindedness' were very great indeed.[83]

This may partly explain why it was that during those inter-war years the Air Ministry was almost consistently in patrician hands. In 1919, the Secretary of State for War and Air was Winston Churchill; the Under-Secretary of State was his cousin, Lord Londonderry; and his Parliamentary Private Secretary was Moore-Brabazon. For almost the whole of the period 1922–9, the Secretary of State was Sir Samuel Hoare, a Norfolk country gentleman, who was one of the best shots in the land, and had married a daughter of Lord Beauchamp.[84] Between 1922 and 1924, Hoare's Under-Secretary was the Duke of Sutherland, one of the last dukes to hold high political office. From 1931 to 1935 the Air Ministry was held by Lord Londonderry, whose wife staged lavish receptions for the National Government at Londonderry House, and was a close friend of Ramsay Macdonald. Londonderry was followed by Philip Cunliffe-

Lister, another landowner, who soon went to the Lords as Viscount Swinton.[85]

At a time when the patrician contribution to politics was in steep decline, this disproportionate concentration in one ministry deserves attention. For much of the inter-war period, the Air Ministry was a marginal and low-spending department, and was thus an appropriate billet for second-ranking notables. And the patricians in charge of it were either lightweight or accident-prone, or both. Samuel Hoare was in the shadow of Trenchard, the Chief of Air Staff, and saw himself in the subordinate role as 'the prophet's interpreter to a world that did not always understand his dark sayings'.[86] Londonderry owed his job to Macdonald's favouritism, and was described by J. C. C. Davidson as 'not really equipped for thinking ... not really fit for Cabinet rank'. When the government's policy was abruptly changed in 1934–5, he was clearly out of his depth, and Baldwin soon got rid of him. By contrast, Swinton was a much more able minister, who drove ahead the re-armament programme with vigour and success. But he was a maladroit politician, ill at ease in the Commons, and then marginalised in the Lords, and he alienated Neville Chamberlain without conciliating the anti-appeasers.[87]

In fact, the major contribution of these patrician ministers was made at the social rather than the political level, as they used their connections and their prestige in promoting the cause of 'airmindedness'.[88] The Duke of Sutherland was 'a leading patron of aviation', endowed a prize for light aircraft, organised an International Air Congress in London, was chairman of the Royal Aero Club in 1924–25 and president of the Air League from 1921 to 1944. Sir Samuel Hoare did his utmost to interest the royal family in the RAF, visited India in 1926 to launch the new Imperial Airways route, and went to South Africa three years later.[89] The Marquess of Londonderry was the most 'ardent flying enthusiast' of them all. In order to identify himself with the RAF, he learned to fly at the age of fifty-five, thereby earning a letter from the king's private secretary which was revealing in the comparison it drew: 'It is a fine performance at your age', Sir Clive Wigram wrote, 'to pilot an aeroplane as well as you do a horse'. He went on extended tours of inspection overseas, promoted an airport in Northern Ireland, regularly flew his plane bebween his estates in Durham and County Down, and wrote and lectured extensively on aviation matters.[90]

The Second World War vividly demonstrated what remained of this patrician connection with flying. Throughout Churchill's great coalition, the Secretary of State for Air was another notable, Sir Archibald Sinclair, Lord Lieutenant of Caithness, MP for the county, and the direct descendant of the great agricultural innovator. For a short time, Moore-Brabazon was Minister of Aircraft Production, where his close contacts with the industry enabled him to restore order after the piratical idiosyncracies of Lord Beaverbrook's regime.[91] Senior commanders in the RAF included the Duke of Hamilton, the Earl of Bandon, and the future sixth Earl of Gosford. Three of Hamilton's brothers also served, and the Duke himself was the embarrassed object of Rudolph Hess's peace mission in 1941.[92] Lord Londonderry, embittered at his dismissal from power, encouraged flying in Northern Ireland. And after her aircraft had been requisitioned and her despatch-pilots called up, Mrs Victor Bruce set up a factory in Cardiff to repair battle-damaged plane wings. They were brought to the factory in converted horse boxes.[93]

But the weakness of the aristocratic–aeronautic link inevitably meant that the patrician contribution to the war in the air was distinctly limited. As Secretary of State, Sinclair failed to stand up to the Prime Minister or the service chiefs, and being what one admirer called 'a great gentleman with a total incapacity for departing from the rules of truth and honour' was a grave handicap in his dealings with Beaverbrook. After only a few months at the Ministry of Aircraft Production, Moore-Brabazon was obliged to resign, having made some indiscreet and uncomplimentary remarks about the Russians.[94] Among the RAF high command, Dowding, Portal, Harris and Tedder were distinctly non-patrician. Only Sholto Douglas could claim distant aristocratic ancestry, but when he was made a peer in 1948 he took the Labour whip. And among the pilots, there was no knightly cult of chivalry comparable to that which was deliberately fostered in the German and Japanese air forces. Even Churchill noted, with slight but pardonable exaggeration, that 'none of the aristocracy chose the RAF – they left it all to the lower middle classes'. As G. M. Trevelyan put it in his *English Social History*, the Battle of Britain was won, neither on the playing fields of Eton, nor the village greens of England, but in the primary and secondary schools of the great cities.[95]

IV

In the last decade of the nineteenth century, a Yorkshire breeder made this confident prediction:

> I don't think for one moment that all the cycles and motor cars in the world, after the novelty is gone, will ever cause our English gentry, or their sons and daughters, to turn their backs on a beautiful typical riding or driving horse.[96]

To the extent that many members of the aristocracy remain attached to the outdoor life and to country pursuits, this prophecy has undoubtedly been fulfilled. But at a deeper level, it has not been borne out by subsequent events: the horse has not survived as the pre-eminent mode of transport any more than the aristocracy has survived as the pre-eminent élite. In part this has been because what the Countess of Minto described as 'incessant motion, high-speed motor cars, perpetual rush and hurry', has inevitably undermined the stability and hierarchy so essential for the survival of a traditional territorial aristocracy.[97] And in part it is because the patricians themselves have not loomed large in the histories of the railway, the motor or the plane. Even as inter-war celebrities, Lord Cottenham, Lord Sempill and Mrs Victor Bruce could not compare with Seagrave, Campbell, Lindbergh or Amy Johnson.

But while recent developments in transport can be studied with virtually no reference to the aristocracy, it is clear that the history of the aristocracy should not ignore recent developments in transport. For, as so often in the history of the nineteenth- and twentieth-century aristocracy, these agents of decline were also the means of adaptation. In the case of the railways, the aristocracy came to a very profitable accommodation: not just through selling their land, but later as shareholders in the major companies, as directors and as chairmen. And some of them welcomed the motor and the plane with at least as much enthusiasm, partly because they genuinely saw these new machines as supercharged versions of the horse; partly because they provided new scope for aristocrats to display their traditional characteristics of bravery, foolhardiness and a sense of adventure; and partly because they offered opportunities for a declining and anachronistic class to present itself as modern and fully up-to-date. Not surprisingly, many notables viewed these innovations in transport with at least as much enthusiasm as regret. As Lord Dunraven once delightedly exclaimed: 'Goodness! What changes in locomotion I have seen'.[98]

Nor has this connection between nobility and mobility entirely disappeared in the years since the war. As a result of the Transport Act of 1953, Donald Cameron of Lochiel, bearer of one of the most historic names in Scotland, became a part-time Transport Commissioner and chairman of the Scottish Area Board of British Railways. Two of Mrs Thatcher's senior ministers, William Whitelaw and Nicholas Ridley, were the direct descendants of patricians who were chairmen of railway companies.[99] The Duke of Richmond built a motor race track in the grounds of Goodwood, and Lord Montagu of Beaulieu opened his vintage car museum at Beaulieu. Lord Carrington was once a trainee manager at de Havilland's, and the present Duke of Leinster runs a flying school near Oxford.[100] And for those who cannot afford to fly the Atlantic first class, but aspire to distinguish themselves from the mass of travellers going tourist, both British and American companies offer an intermediate category. The names by which it is known tell us much about the different cultures of these two countries, especially about the 'aristocratic embrace' in which, to this day, Britain remains in so many ways enfolded. Most American airlines describe it as Business Class; but on British Airways, it is called Club.[101]

Notes

1 M. Bloch, *Feudal society* (2 vols, trans. L. A. Manyon), London, 1965, vol. ii, *Social classes and political organisation*, pp. 290–91.
2 J. H. Kautsky, *The politics of aristocratic empires*, Chapel Hill, NC, 1982, pp. 203–5, 346, 371; H. J. Perkin, *The age of the railway*, London, 1971, pp. 35–6.
3 Lord Brabazon of Tara, *The Brabazon story*, London, 1956, pp. xii–xiv.
4 Perkin, *Age of the railway*, pp. 171–2; J. V. Beckett, *The aristocracy in England, 1660–1914*, Oxford, 1986, p. 243.
5 F. M. L. Thompson, *English landed society in the nineteenth century*, London, 1963, pp. 190–91; D. Spring, 'English landowners and nineteenth-century industrialism', in J. T. Ward and R. G. Wilson (eds), *Land and industry: the landed estate and the Industrial Revolution*, Newton Abbot, 1971, p. 53.
6 J. Simmons, *The railway in town and country, 1830–1914*, Newton Abbot, 1986, pp. 23–4; Spring, 'Landowners and nineteenth-century industrialism', pp. 19–21.
7 Thompson, *English landed society*, pp. 259–60.
8 J. R. Kellett, *The impact of railways on Victorian cities*, London, 1969, pp. 251–2; D. Cannadine, *Lords and landlords: the aristocracy and the towns, 1774–1967*, Leicester, 1980, pp. 176–80.
9 Simmons, *Railway in town and country*, pp. 245, 261–4; Kellett, *Impact of railways*, p. 253.
10 R. J. Irving, 'The capitalization of Britain's railways, 1830–1914', *Journal of Transport History*, 3rd ser., v (1984), pp. 6–8, 10–16; Beckett, *Aristocracy in England*, p. 246; Spring, 'Landowners and nineteenth-century industrialism', p. 23.
11 J. T. Ward, 'West Riding landowners and the railways', *Journal of Transport History*, iv (1959–60), pp. 243–44; Beckett, *Aristocracy in England*, p. 246.
12 Kellett, *Impact of Railways*, pp. 178–81, 246–7, 275–8; Spring, 'Landowners and nineteenth-century industrialism', p. 23.
13 T. J. Raybould, *The economic emergence of the Black Country: a study of the Dudley estate*, Newton Abbot, 1973, pp. 70–88; M. J. Daunton, 'Aristocrat and traders: the Bute Docks, 1839–1914', *Journal of Transport History*, new ser., iii (1975), pp. 68–9; Thompson, *English landed society*, p. 263.
14 Perkin, *Age of the railway*, pp. 126–30; Cannadine, *Lords and landlords*, pp. 237–8, 269–71; S. Pollard, 'Barrow-in-Furness and the seventh Duke of Devonshire', *Economic History Review*, 2nd ser., viii (1955–56), p. 214.
15 S. W. Martins, *A great estate at work: the Holkham estate and its inhabitants in the nineteenth century*, Cambridge, 1980, pp. 61–2; Simmons, *Railway in town and country*, pp. 24, 308–10; Thompson, *English landed society*, p. 257.
16 D. Cannadine, 'The landowner as millionaire: the finances of the Dukes of Devonshire, *c.*1800–1926', *Agricultural History Review*, xxv (1977), p. 94; E. Richards, 'An anatomy of the Sutherland fortune: income, consumption, investments and returns, 1780–1880', *Business History*, xxi (1979), pp. 54, 66–70.
17 Thompson, *English landed society*, p. 306.
18 Beckett, *Aristocracy in England*, p. 250; Simmons, *Railway in town and country*, pp. 311–12; Pollard, 'Barrow-in-Furness', p. 214.
19 Thompson, *English landed society*, p. 261; Beckett, *Aristocracy in England*, pp. 254–5.
20 Richards, 'Anatomy of the Sutherland fortune', pp. 51–3.
21 F. B. Heath, 'The Grenvilles in the nineteenth century: the emergence of commercial affiliations', *Huntingdon Library Quarterly*, xxv (1961), pp. 40–9; T. C. Barker, 'Lord Salisbury, Chairman of the Great Eastern Railway, 1868–72', in S. Marriner (ed.), *Business and businessmen: studies in banking, economics and accounting*, Liverpool, 1979, pp. 81–103.

22 For the general background, see R. A. Buchanan, 'Gentlemen engineers: the making of a profession', *Victorian Studies*, xxvi 1983, pp. 407–29.
23 H. C. B. Rogers, *G. J. Churchward: a locomotive biography*, London, 1975, pp. 17–19, 86, 118, 123–30.
24 Lady Troubridge and A. Marshall, *John, Lord Montagu of Beaulieu: a memoir*, London, 1930, pp. 39, 41, 288–9; Lord Montagu of Beaulieu, *The motoring Montagus*, London, 1959, pp. 3–5.
25 For the general background, see D. Cannadine, *The decline and fall of the British aristocracy*, London, 1990, pp. 133–5.
26 Martins, *A great agricultural estate*, pp. 61–5, 267–9; Thompson, *English landed society*, pp. 307–8.
27 Cannadine, *Decline and fall*, pp. 406–17; P. S. Bagwell, 'The railway interest: its organisation and influence, 1839–1914', *Journal of Transport History*, vii (1965), p. 82.
28 K. Hoole (ed.), *Tomlinson's North Eastern Railway: its rise and development*, Newton Abbot, 1967, pp. 768–71; R. J. Irving, *The North Eastern Railway Company, 1870–1914: an economic history*, Leicester, 1976, pp. 131–2.
29 Viscount Grey of Fallodon, *Twenty-five years, 1892–1916* (2 vols), London, 1925, i, pp. 58–60; G. M. Trevelyan, *Grey of Fallodon*, London, 1937, pp. 85, 157–8; K. Robbins, *Sir Edward Grey*, London, 1971, pp. 102–4, 140.
30 C. J. Allen, *The Great Eastern Railway* (3rd edn), London, 1961, pp. 83, 127–38.
31 D. H. Aldcroft, 'The efficiency and enterprise of British railways, 1870–1914', in D. H. Aldcroft, *Studies in British transport history, 1870–1970*, Newton Abbot, 1974, pp. 31–51; P. J. Cain, 'Railway combination and Government, 1900–1914', *Economic History Review*, 2nd ser., XXV (1972), pp. 623–41; R. J. Irving, 'The efficiency and enterprise of British railways, 1870–1914: an alternative hypothesis', *Economic History Review*, 2nd ser., XXXI (1978), pp. 46–66; P. J. Cain, 'Private enterprise or public utility? Output, pricing and investment on English and Welsh railways, 1870–1914', *Journal of Transport History*, 3rd ser., i (1980), pp. 9–28.
32 R. J. Irving, 'British railway investment and innovation, 1900–1914', *Business History*, xiii (1971), pp. 58–9.
33 G. Alderman, *The railway interest*, Leicester, 1973, p. 227.
34 C. H. Grinling, *History of the Great Northern Railway, 1845–1922*, London, 1966, pp. 425–7; Alderman, *Railway interest*, p. 193.
35 C. J. Allen, *The London and North Eastern Railway*, Middlesex, 1966, p. 23; *The Times*, 27 January 1925.
36 Bagwell, 'Railway interest', p. 82; Sir John Elliot, 'Early days of the Southern Railway', *Journal of Transport History*, iv (1960), pp. 200–8.
37 Robbins, *Edward Grey*, pp. 364–6; Allen, *London and North Eastern*, pp. 48–53, 60–1, 218–19; M. Bonavia, *The four great railways*, Newton Abbot, 1980, pp. 29, 50, 57–8, 72; F. Booker, *The Great Western Railway: a new history*, Newton Abbot, 1977, pp. 140–43.
38 Allen, *London and North Eastern*, pp. 27, 60.
39 F. M. L. Thompson, 'Nineteenth-century horse sense', *Economic History Review*, 2nd ser., XXIX (1976), p. 61.
40 H. Barty-King, *The AA: a history of the first seventy-five years of the Automobile Association, 1905–80*, Basingstoke, 1980, pp. 96–7; G. R. Searle, *Corruption in British politics, 1895–1930*, Oxford, 1987, p. 25; R. Carr, *English fox-hunting: a history*, London, 1976, p. 147.
41 Cannadine, *Decline and fall*, pp. 359–60.
42 H. Langrishe, 'Motor cars and horses', in Lord Northcliffe (ed.), *Motors and motor driving*, London, 1906 edn, pp. 344–9; Cannadine, *Decline and fall*, p. 363.
43 B. Bond, *British military policy between the two wars*, Oxford, 1980, pp. 64–6.
44 Brabazon of Tara, *The Brabazon story*, pp. 29–30.
45 T. R. Nicholson, *The birth of the British motor car, 1767–1897* (3 vols), London, 1982, vol. iii, *The last battle, 1894–97*, p. 372; D. Sutherland, *The Yellow Earl*, London, 1965, pp. 169–71; Barty-King, *The AA*, pp. 110, 190.

46 J. M. Lee, *Social leaders and public persons*, Oxford, 1963, pp. 42–3; M. Harrison, *Lord of London*, London, 1966, pp. 96–7, 162–82.
47 K. Young, *Arthur James Balfour*, London, 1963, pp. 459–60; K. Rose, *The later Cecils*, London, 1975, pp. 136, 254.
48 *The Times*, 8 September 1913.
49 Nicholson, *The last battle*, pp. 338, 356–7.
50 Lord Montagu of Beaulieu, 'The utility of motor vehicles', in Northcliffe, *Motors and motor driving*, pp. 25–37; P. Tritton, *John Montagu of Beaulieu, 1866–1929: motoring pioneer and prophet*, London 1985, pp. 48–97; W. Plowden, *The motor car and politics, 1896–1970, London, 1971, pp. 44–6.*
51 Troubridge and Marshall, *John, Lord Montagu*, pp. 91, 216; Montagu of Beaulieu, *The motoring Montagus*, pp. 10–12, 23–34.
52 W. Boddy, *The history of Brooklands motor course*, London, 1957, pp. 5–17, 295, 353.
53 K. Richardson, *The British motor industry, 1896–1939*, Hamden, Conn., 1977, pp. 122–31; W. Boddy, 'The motor course', in C. Gardner (ed.), *Fifty years of Brooklands*, London, 1956, pp. 18–19.
54 S. B. Saul, 'The motor industry in Britain to 1914', *Business History*, v (1962), pp. 22–44; R. Church, 'Markets and manufacturing in the British motor industry before 1914, with some French comparisons', *Journal of Transport History*, 3rd ser., iii (1982), pp. 1–20.
55 Richardson, *British motor industry*, pp. 29–30; *The Times*, 8 September 1913; P. W. S. Andrews and E. Brunner, *The life of Lord Nuffield: a study in enterprise and benevolence*, Oxford, 1955, pp. 66–67, 89.
56 Nicholson, *The last battle*, pp. 361, 366, 383, 400, 415–16, 469.
57 A. E. Harrison, 'Joint stock company flotation in the cycle, motor vehicle and related industries, 1882–1914', *Business History*, xxiii (1981), pp. 174–7, 187; Richardson, *British motor industry*, p. 20; Saul, 'Motor industry in Britain', p. 27; *The Times*, 18 May 1921.
58 C. S. Rolls, 'The caprices of the petrol motor', in Northcliffe, *Motors and motor driving*, pp. 168–86.
59 I. Lloyd, *Rolls-Royce: The growth of a firm*, London, 1978, pp. 8–14, 22–36.
60 Richardson, *British motor industry*, pp. 29–35.
61 Earl of Cottenham, *Motoring today and tomorrow*, London, 1928, pp. 116–17.
62 D. G. Rhys, 'Concentration in the inter-war motor industry', *Journal of Transport History*, new ser., iii (1976), pp. 241–64.
63 Andrews and Brunner, *Lord Nuffield*, p. 90; *The Times*, 19 June 1944; I. Lloyd, *Rolls-Royce: the years of endeavour*, London, 1978, pp. 147, 160–6.
64 Montagu of Beaulieu, *The motoring Montagus*, pp. 43–8; Troubridge and Marshall, *John Lord Montagu*, pp. 245–50; Tritton, *John Montagu of Beaulieu*, pp. 237–45.
65 *The Times*, 21 July 1943.
66 Lord Howe (ed.), *Motor racing* [Lonsdale Library, vol. xxvii], 1938; *The Times*, 27 July 1964.
67 *Daily Telegraph*, 23 May 1990.
68 Hon. Mrs Victor Bruce, *Nine thousand miles in eight weeks*, London, 1927, *passim*; Hon. Mrs Victor Bruce, *Nine lives plus*, London, 1977, pp. 13, 24–33, 36–41, 57–8, 81–94.
69 Brabazon of Tara, *The Brabazon story*, pp. 40, 48.
70 P. King, *Knights of the air*, London, 1989, pp. 75–6.
71 Brabazon of Tara, *The Brabazon story*, pp. 1–21, 29–31, 43–6, 50–8, 66.
72 R. Dallas Brett, *History of British aviation, 1908–1914* (2 vols), Surbiton, Surrey, 1988 edn, ii, pp. 174–92; 'L'Ancien', 'Brooklands as an aerodrome', in Gardner, *Fifty years at Brooklands*, pp. 63–84.
73 Tritton, *John Montagu of Beaulieu*, pp. 154–61, 203–15.
74 P. Fearon, 'The formative years of the British aircraft industry, 1913–24', *Business History Review*, xliii (1969), pp. 476–95.
75 King, *Knights of the air*, pp. 39–40; M. Howard de Walden, *Pages from my life*, London, 1963, p. 82.

76 Brabazon of Tara, *The Brabazon story*, pp. 86–98; Rose, *Later Cecils*, pp. 254–8; *The Times*, 27 August 1929; R. Skidelsky, *Oswald Mosley*, London, 1975, pp. 62–4.
77 W. E. Burrows, *Richthofen: a true history of the Red Baron*, London, 1970, pp. 25–8, 111–15, 130, 205.
78 P. Fearon, 'The British airframe industry and the state, 1918–35', *Economic History Review*, 2nd ser., XXVII (1974), pp. 236–51; P. Fearon 'The vicissitudes of a British aircraft company: Handley Page Ltd, between the wars', *Business History*, XX (1978), pp. 63–85.
79 John, Duke of Bedford, *A silver-plated spoon*, London, 1959, pp. 3–5, 23–5, 71–2; C. Seebohm, *The country house in wartime, 1939–45*, London, 1989, pp. 168–9.
80 *Daily Telegraph*, 23 May 1990; Bruce, *Nine lives plus*, pp. 102–49; Hon. Mrs V. Bruce, *The Bluebird's flight*, London, 1931, *passim.*
81 *Dictionary of National Biography, 1961–1970*, pp. 377–9; *The Times*, 31 December 1965.
82 *The Times*, 2 April 1973; P. F. M. Fellowes et al., *First over Everest: the Houston Mount Everest expedition*, New York, 1933; Lord Clydesdale and D. F. McIntyre, *The pilot's book of Everest*, London, 1936.
83 M. Smith, *British air strategy between the wars*, Oxford, 1984, p. 34.
84 J. A. Cross, *Sir Samuel Hoare: a political biography*, London, 1977, pp. 2–4, 10, 83–124.
85 J. A. Cross, *Lord Swinton*, Oxford, 1982, pp. 135–219.
86 Cross, *Hoare*, pp. 86–8.
87 Cannadine, *Decline and fall*, p. 219; Cross, *Swinton*, pp. 202, 213–17; Smith, *Air strategy*, pp. 35–7; Sir Maurice Dean, *The Royal Air Force and two World Wars*, London, 1979, pp. 56, 74, 85.
88 M. Howard, 'Per ardua', *New Statesman*, 26 January 1957, pp. 106–7.
89 Duke of Sutherland, *Looking back*, London, 1957, pp. 108–13; Cross, *Hoare*, pp. 101–7; Viscount Templewood, *Empire of the air: The advent of the air age, 1922–29*, London, 1957, pp. 12, 115–16, 173, 181, 187.
90 Marquess of Londonderry, 'Foreword' to F. Young, *Growing wings* London, 1936, pp. 11–18; Marquess of Londonderry, *Airways of the empire: their history and development*, Nottingham, 1936, *passim*; Marquess of Londonderry, *Wings of destiny*, London, 1943, p. 82.
91 Brabazon of Tara, *The Brabazon story*, pp. 201–6.
92 J. Douglas-Hamilton, *Motive for a mission: the story behind Hess's flight to Britain*, London, 1971, pp. 152–64.
93 Bruce, *Nine lives plus*, pp. 180–6.
94 Dean, *The Royal Air Force*, p. 181; Brabazon of Tara, *The Brabazon story*, pp. 107–10.
95 Lord Douglas of Kirtleside, *Years of combat*, London, 1963, pp. 17–19, 37; Douglas of Kirtleside, *Years of command*, London, 1966, pp. 362–3; R. J. Overy, *The air war, 1939–45*, London, 1980, pp. 138–47; J. R. Colville, *The fringes of power: 10 Downing Street diaries, 1939–55*, London, 1985, p. 278; G. M. Trevelyan, *Illustrated English social history* (4 vols), Harmondsworth, Middlesex, 1964 edn, iv, p. 228.
96 Thompson, 'Nineteenth-century horse sense', p. 62.
97 M. Asquith, *Myself when young: by famous women of today*, London, 1938, p. 232.
98 Lord Dunraven, *Past times and pastimes* (2 vols), London, 1922, i, p. 6.
99 T. R. Gourvish, *British Railways, 1948–73: a business history*, Cambridge, 1986, pp. 144–5, 162–6; W. Whitelaw, *The Whitelaw memoirs*, London, 1989, pp. 1–7, 33–4.
100 Boddy, *History of Brooklands*, p. 232; Montagu of Beaulieu, *The motoring Montagus*, pp. 61–6; Duke of Richmond and Gordon, 'Motor Race Promotion', in S. C. H. Davies (ed.), *Motor Racing* [Lonsdale Library, vol. xxxiii], London, 1957, pp. 302–13.
101 F. M. L. Thompson, 'Britain', in D. Spring (ed.), *European landed élites in the nineteenth century*, Baltimore, Md., 1977, p. 23.

I am most grateful to Professor R. A. Church and Mr R. L. Colley for help with particular references.

The published writings of F. M. L. Thompson

COMPILED BY JENNY WEST

Place of publication is London unless stated otherwise

Books

St Albans School in the Abbey, St Albans: Fraternity of the Friends of St Albans Abbey, 1961, 36pp.
English landed society in the nineteenth century, Routledge & Kegan Paul, 1963, xiii + 374pp.
Chartered surveyors: the growth of a profession, Routledge & Kegan Paul, 1968, xvi + 400pp.
Victorian England: the horse-drawn society, Inaugural Lecture as Professor of Modern History, Bedford College: Bedford College, 1970, 20pp.
Hampstead: building a borough, 1650–1964, Routledge & Kegan Paul, 1974, xi + 459pp.
Ed., *The rise of suburbia*, Leicester University Press, 1982, xii + 274pp.
Ed., *Horses in European economic history: a preliminary canter*, British Agricultural History Society, Reading, 1983, 206pp.
The rise of respectable society: a social history of Victorian Britain, 1830–1900, Fontana, 1988, 382pp.
Ed., *The University of London and the world of learning, 1836–1986*, Hambledon Press, 1990, xxviii + 260pp.
Ed., *The Cambridge social history of Britain, 1750–1950*, Cambridge University Press, 1990; 1: *Regions and communities*, xv + 588pp; 2: *People and their environment*, xv + 373pp; 3: *Social agencies and institutions*, xiii + 492pp.
Ed., *Landowners, capitalists, and entrepreneurs: essays for Sir John Habakkuk*, Oxford University Press, 1994, xiii + 312pp.

Articles

'The end of a great estate', *Economic History Review*, 2nd ser. 8 (1955), pp. 36–52.
'The land market in the nineteenth century', *Oxford Economic Papers*, new ser. 9 (1957), pp. 285–308.
'English landownership: The Ailesbury Trust, 1832–56', *Economic History Review*, 2nd ser. 11 (1958), pp. 121–32.

'Agriculture since 1870' in Elizabeth Crittall (ed.), *Victoria County History, Wiltshire*, 4 (1959), pp. 92–114.

'Whigs and Liberals in the West Riding, 1830–1860', *English Historical Review*, 74 (1959), pp. 214–39.

'English great estates in the nineteenth century, 1790–1914', *First International Conference of Economic History, Contributions, Stockholm*, (Paris, 1960), pp. 385–97.

'Agricultural history', *History*, 48 (1963), pp. 28–33.

'Land and politics in England in the nineteenth century', *Transactions of the Royal Historical Society*, 5th ser. 15 (1965), pp. 23–44.

'Landlords, farmers and commercialisation of English agriculture, 1815–1914', *Voprosi Istorii*, No. 3 (Moscow, 1967), pp. 169–77.

'The social distribution of landed property in England since the sixteenth century', *Economic History Review*, 2nd ser. 19 (1966), pp. 505–17, and in *Proceedings of the Third International Conference of Economic History, Munich, 1965* (Paris, 1968), pp. 471–86.

'The second Agricultural Revolution, 1815–1880', *Economic History Review*, 2nd ser. 21 (1968), pp. 62–77.

'Landownership and economic growth in England in the eighteenth century', in E. L. Jones and S. J. Woolf (eds), *Agrarian change and economic development: the historical problems* (1969), pp. 41–60.

'National and international factors in the surveying profession', *Bulletin of the International Federation of Surveyors*, No. 5 (1969), pp. 16–20.

'Countrysides in the revolution in world agriculture', in Asa Briggs (ed.), *The nineteenth century: the contradictions of progress* (1970), pp. 131–60.

'The end of the Grand Tour', *History of the Twentieth Century*, 7 (1970), pp. 495–99.

Introduction, with D. Tierney, to *General Report on the Gosford Estates in County Armagh 1821* by William Grieg (HMSO Belfast, 1976), pp. 1–36.

'Nineteenth-century horse sense', *Economic History Review*, 2nd ser. 29 (1976), pp. 60–81.

'A terminological confusion confounded', *Economic History Review*, 2nd ser. 29 (1976), pp. 311–13.

'Britain' in David Spring (ed.), *European landed élites in the nineteenth century* (Baltimore, 1977), pp. 22–44.

'Hampstead, 1830–1914', in M. A. Simpson and T. H. Lloyd (eds), *Middle class housing in Britain* (Newton Abbot, 1977), pp. 86–113.

'Introduction' to new edition of Edwin Grey, *Cottage life in a Hertfordshire village* (Harpenden and District Local History Society, 1977).

'Historical background to current trends in agricultural land acquisition and occupancy' in *Report of the Committee of Inquiry into the Acquisition and Occupancy of Agricultural Land* (Northfield Committee) (HMSO 1979), pp. 28–9.

'Landowners and farmers', in Alan Bullock (ed.), *The faces of Europe* (Oxford, 1980), pp. 29–56.

'Free trade and the land', and 'Landowners and the rural community', in G. E. Mingay (ed.), *The Victorian countryside*, 1, 2, (1981), pp. 103–17, 457–74.

'Agrarian change, 1850–1980', in Malcolm Falkus and John Gillingham (eds), *Historical Atlas of Britain* (1981), pp. 186–7.

'Social control in Victorian Britain', *Economic History Review*, 2nd ser. 34 (1981), pp. 189–208.

'Introduction: the rise of suburbia' in F. M. L. Thompson (ed.), *The rise of suburbia*, (1982), pp. 2–25.

'Introduction', pp. 1–3, and 'Horses and hay in Britain, 1830–1918', pp. 50–72 in F. M. L. Thompson (ed.), *Horses in European economic history: a preliminary canter* (1983).

'Dyos and the urban past', *London Journal*, 9 (1983), pp. 67–70.

'John Clutton', in David J. Jeremy (ed.), *Dictionary of Business Biography*, 1, (1984), pp. 701–4.

'English landed society in the nineteenth century' in Pat Thane, Geoffrey Crossick and Roderick Floud (eds), *The power of the past: essays for Eric Hobsbawm* (Cambridge, 1984), pp. 195–214.

'Towns, industry, and the Victorian landscape', in S. R. J. Woodell (ed.), *The English landscape: past, present and future*, (Oxford, 1985), pp. 168–87.

'The Institute of Historical Research', *Historian*, 8 (1985), pp. 3–8.

'Upper class culture in nineteenth-century England and the aristocratic legacy', in *XVI Congrès International des Sciences Historiques, Rapports*, 2 (Stuttgart, 1985), pp. 505–8.

'The British approach to social history', *Storia della Storiografia*, 10 (Milan 1986), pp. 64–6.

'Tot Recuperent la Crisi Agraria de Finale del Segle XIX', *L'Avenc*, 98 (Barcelona 1986), pp. 329–51.

'Private property and public policy', in Robert Blake and Hugh Cecil (eds), *Salisbury: the man and his policies* (1987), pp. 252–89.

'The landed aristocracy and business élites in Victorian Britain', in G. Delille (ed.), *Les Noblesses Européenes au XIX siècle*, (Rome and Milan, 1988), pp. 267–79.

'Los Efectos de la Depresion Agraria en Gran Bretana, 1870–1914', in R. Garrabou (ed.), *La Crisis Agraria de Fines del Siglo XIX* (Barcelona, 1988), pp. 329–51.

'Aristocracy, gentry, and the middle classes in Britain, 1750–1850' in Adolf M. Birke and Lothar Kettenacker (eds), *Bürgertum, Adel und Monarchie* (Munich, 1989), pp. 15–35.

'Rural society and agricultural change in nineteenth-century Britain', in George Grantham and Carol S. Leonard (eds), *Agrarian organisation in the century of industrialisation: Europe, Russia, and North America* (Greenwich, Connecticut, 1989), pp. 187–202.

'Life after death: how successful nineteenth-century businessmen disposed of their fortunes', *Economic History Review*, 2nd ser. 43 (1990), pp. 40–61.

'English landed society in the twentieth century, 1, Property: collapse and survival', (Presidential address), *Transactions of the Royal Historical Society*, 5th ser. 40 (1990), pp. 1–24.

'Introduction', pp. ix-xxiii, and 'The humanities', pp. 57–79 in F. M. L. Thompson (ed.), *The University of London and the world of learning, 1836–1986*, (1990).

'Town and city' in F. M. L. Thompson (ed.), *The Cambridge social history of Britain*, 1, *Regions and communities* (1990), pp. 1–86.

'Desirable properties: the town and country connection in British society since the late eighteenth century', *Historical Research*, 64 (1991), pp. 156–71.

'An anatomy of English agriculture, 1870–1914', in B. A. Holderness and Michael E. Turner (eds), *Land, labour and agriculture, 1700–1920: essays for Gordon Mingay* (1991), pp. 211–40.

'English landed society in the twentieth century, 2, New poor and new rich' *Transactions of the Royal Historical Society*, 6th ser. 1 (1991), pp. 1–20.

'Stitching it together again' (Reply to W. D. Rubinstein), *Economic History Review*, 2nd ser. 45 (1992), pp. 362–75.

'English landed society in the twentieth century, 3, Self help and outdoor relief', *Transactions of the Royal Historical Society*, 6th ser. 2 (1992), pp. 1–23.

'English landed society in the twentieth century, 4, Prestige without power?', *Transactions of the Royal Historical Society*, 6th ser. 3 (1993), pp. 1–22.

Comparative studies on Governments and non-dominant ethnic groups in Europe (1850–1940), *Report of the Steering Committee, European Science Foundation Annual Report 1993*, (Strasbourg, 1994), pp. 49–55.

Editorial contributions

Joint compiler of 'List of publications on the economic history of Great Britain and Ireland', 1960–64, in *Economic History Review* (1962–66), with Joan Thirsk for 1961–63 and Audrey Beecham for 1964.

Joint reviewer of 'Periodical literature of Great Britain', *Economic History Review*, 1962–71.

Joint editor of the *Economic History Review*, 1969–79, with D. C. Coleman in 1969–72 and B. E. Supple in 1973–79.

Editor, *Studies in Economic History* series, Routledge & Kegan Paul, 1976–78.

Editor, *Historical Research* (*Bulletin of the Institute of Historical Research* until 1986) (1977–91).

Joint editor of the *Historical Handbooks* series (with Avner Offer), Faber and Faber, 1986–91.

A selection of review articles and book reviews

François Crouzet, *L'Économie Britannique et le Blocus Continental (1806–1813)*, 2 vols, in *History*, 45 (1960), pp. 272–5.

Joan Thirsk and Jean Imray (eds), *Suffolk farming in the nineteenth century*, in *History*, 45 (1960), pp. 76–7.

Henry Pelling, *Modern Britain, 1895–1955*, in *History*, 46 (1961), p. 166.

Alan Harris, *The landscape of the East Riding of Yorkshire, 1700–1850*; C. Stella Jones, *The agricultural history of Cheshire, 1750–1850*; C. M. L. Bouch and G. P. Jones, *The Lake Counties, 1500–1830*; Rosalind Mitchison, *Agricultural Sir John*; E. W. Bovill, *English country life, 1780–1830*; Lord Ernle, *English farming past and present*, in *History*, 48 (1963), pp. 28–33.

Alan T. Peacock and Jack Wiseman, *The growth of public expenditure in the United Kingdom*, in *History*, 48 (1963), pp. 238–9.

David Spring, *The landed estate in the nineteenth century*, in *History*, 49 (1964), pp. 383–4.

S. Pollard, *The development of the British economy, 1914–1950*, in *History*, 50 (1965), p. 115.

T. H. Hollingsworth, *The demography of the British Peerage*, in *History*, 51 (1966), p. 400.

David Grigg, *The Agricultural Revolution in South Lincolnshire*, in *History*, 52 (1967), p. 346–8.

Viscount Chilston, *W. H. Smith*, in *History*, 52 (1967), pp. 359–61.

J. D. Chambers and G. E. Mingay, *The Agricultural Revolution, 1750–1880* in *Agricultural History Review*, 15 (1967), pp. 54–6.

Ann Saunders, *Regent's Park*, in *Economic History Review*, 2, 23 (1970), pp. 592–3.

E. L. Jones and G. E. Mingay (eds), *Land, labour and population in the Industrial Revolution, essays presented to J. D. Chambers*; R. M. Hartwell (ed.), *The causes of the Industrial Revolution in England*; E. L. Jones (ed.), *Agriculture and economic growth in England, 1650–1815*; J. D. Marshall, *The old Poor Law, 1795–1834*; E. L. Jones, *The development of English agriculture, 1815–1873*; G. E. Mingay, *Enclosure and the small farmer in the age of Industrial Revolution* in *History*, 55 (1970).

Paul Smith, *Disraelian Conservatism and social reform*, in *History*, 55 (1970).

Sidney Pollard and David W. Crossley, *The wealth of Britain, 1085–1966*, in *History*, 57 (1972), pp. 105–6.

Harold Perkin, *The Age of the Railway*, in *History*, 58 (1973), pp. 116–17.

E. Gauldie, *Cruel habitations*; John Nelson Tarn, *Five per cent philanthropy*, in *Times Literary Supplement* (2 August 1974), p. 823.

Simon Jenkins, *Landlords to London*, in *Times Literary Supplement* (5 September 1975), p. 988.

C. W. Chalklin, *The provincial towns of Georgian England*, in *Times Literary Supplement* (24 January 1975), p. 72.

R. J. Adam (ed.), *Papers on Sutherland estate management, 1802–1816*; Eric Richards, *The Leviathan of Wealth*, in *Economic History Review*, 2, 28 (1975), pp. 331–5.

E. L. Jones, *Agriculture in the Industrial Revolution*, in *History*, 61 (1976), p. 303.

G. E. Mingay, *The gentry*, in *Times Literary Supplement* (11 February 1977), p. 163.

Edith H. Whetham (ed.), *The agrarian history of England and Wales, 1914–1939*, 8 in *Agricultural History*, 54, 2 (April 1980).

Peter Roebuck, *Families, estates and fortunes*, in *Times Literary Supplement* (5 September 1980), p. 967.

W. S. Reader, *Macadam*, in *Times Literary Supplement* (7 November 1980), p. 1269.

David Cannadine, *Lords and landlords*; Dennis R. Mills, *Lord and peasant in nineteenth century Britain*, in *Times Literary Supplement* (20 February 1981), p. 211.

P. B. Munsche, *Gentlemen and poachers*, in *Agricultural History Review*, 30 (1982), pp. 162–3.

Ken Young and Patricia L. Garside, *Metropolitan London*, in *Times Literary Supplement* (3 December 1982), p. 1343.

David Goodway, *London Chartism 1838–1848*, in *Times Literary Supplement* (21 January 1983), p. 65.

David Englander, *Landlord and tenant in urban Britain 1838–1918*, in *Times Literary Supplement* (22 July 1983), p. 785.

T. M. Devine and David Dickson (eds), *Ireland and Scotland 1600–1850*, in *Times Literary Supplement* (26 August 1983), p. 910.

Asa Briggs, *A social history of England*, in *Times Literary Supplement* (23 September 1983), p. 1013.

Derek Fraser and Anthony Sutcliffe (eds), *The pursuit of urban history*, in *History Today*, 34 (February 1984), pp. 46, 48.

John Pearson, *Stags and serpents*, in *Times Literary Supplement* (16 March 1984), p. 283.

Lawrence Stone and Jeanne C. Fawtier Stone, *An open élite? England 1540–1880*, in *Times Literary Supplement* (7 September 1984), p. 990.

Peter Clark (ed.), *The transformation of English provincial towns, 1600–1800*, in *Times Literary Supplement* (15 March 1985), p. 297.

Bernard Rudden, *The New River*, in *Times Literary Supplement* (24 January 1986), p. 94.

Harvey J. Kaye, *The British Marxist Historians*, in *Times Literary Supplement* (23 May 1986), p. 572.

Roger J. P. Kain and Hugh C. Prince, *The tithe surveys of England and Wales*, in *Agricultural History Review*, 35 (1987), pp. 113–15.

George Watt, *The fallen woman in the nineteenth-century English novel*; Elizabeth K. Helsinger, Robin Lauterbach and William Veeder, *The woman question*, 3 vols, in *Literature and History*, 13, 1 (1987), pp. 132–4.

J. V. Beckett, *The aristocracy in England, 1660–1914*, in *London Review of Books*, 9 (19 February 1987), pp. 6–7.

Howard Newby, *Country Life*, in *Agricultural History*, 62, 2 (1988), pp. 330–2.

K. D. M. Snell, *Annals of the labouring poor*, in *Economic History Review*, 2, 41 (1988), pp. 147–51.

E. J. Hobsbawm, *The age of empire*, in *London Review of Books*, 10 (7 July 1988), pp. 12–13.

W. D. Rubinstein, *Elites and the wealthy in modern history*, in *Times Literary Supplement*, (4–10 November 1988), p. 1225.

Charles H. Feinstein and Sydney Pollard (eds), *Studies in capital formation in the United Kingdom, 1750–1920*, in *Agricultural History Review*, 37 (1989), pp. 104–5.

Ruth Glass, *Clichés of urban doom*; Peter Hall, *Cities of tomorrow; London 2001*; Peter Brimblecombe, *The Big Smoke*; (Peter Salins ed.), *New York unbound*; Joseph Rykwert, *The idea of a town*, in *London Review of Books*, 11 (31 August 1989), p. 12.

Harold Perkin, *The rise of professional society*, in *Albion*, 22 (1990), pp. 534–8.

G. E. Mingay (ed.), *The agrarian history of England and Wales*, VI, *1750–1850*, in *Economic History Review*, 43 (1990), pp. 489–93.

T. C. Barker, *Moving millions*; Michael Hunter and Robert Thorne (eds), *Change at King's Cross*, in *History Today*, 41 (August 1991), pp. 50–1.

Patrick Joyce, *Visions of the people*, in *Times Literary Supplement* (16 August 1991), p. 7.

Ciaran Brady (ed.), *Ideology and the historians*; Peter Burke (ed.), *New perspectives on historical writing*; G. R. Elton, *Return to essentials*; Harvey J. Kaye, *The powers of the past*; Donald R. Kelley, *Versions of history from antiquity to the enlightenment*; Brook Thomas, *The new historicism and other old-fashioned topics*, in *Times Higher Education Supplement* (6 March 1992), pp. 21, 24

Patrick Scott and Pauline Fletcher (eds), *Culture and education in Victorian England*; W. Gareth Evans, *Education and female emancipation*; W. E. Marsden, *Educating the respectable*, in *Victorian Studies*, 35, 2 (1992), pp. 449–51.

Jose Harris, *Private lives, public spirit*; John Lowerson, *Sport and the English middle classes 1870–1914, in Times Literary Supplement* (1 October 1993), p. 25.

Charles Townsend, *Making the peace*, in *Times Literary Supplement* (29 April 1994), p. 23.

Index